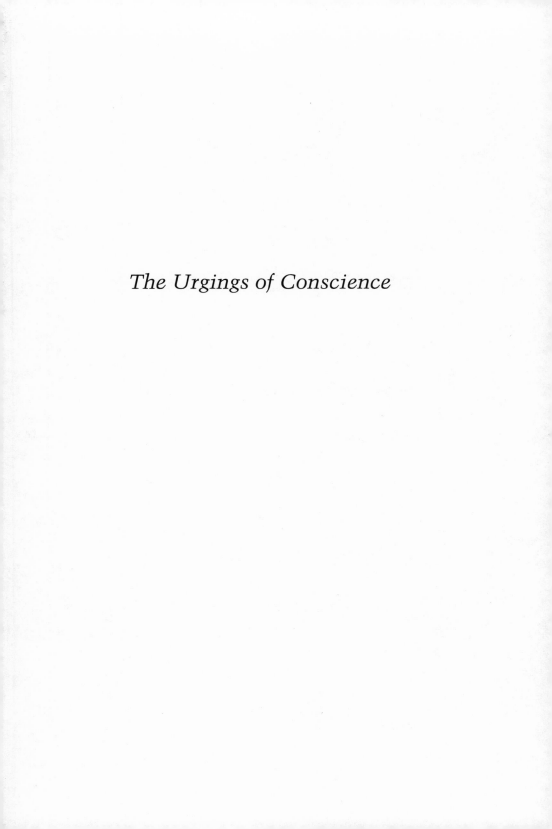

The Urgings of Conscience

The Urgings

OF CONSCIENCE

A Theory of Punishment

━━━

JACOB ADLER

TEMPLE UNIVERSITY PRESS • *Philadelphia*

Temple University Press, Philadelphia 19122
Copyright © 1991 by Temple University.
All rights reserved
Published 1992
Printed in the United States of America

The paper used in this publication meets the minimum
requirements of American National Standard for Information
Sciences—Permanence of Paper for Printed Library Materials,
ANSI Z39.48-1984 ∞

Library of Congress Cataloging-in-Publication Data
Adler, Jacob, 1953–
    The urgings of conscience : a theory of punishment / Jacob Adler.
    p.   cm.
    Includes bibliographical references and index.
    ISBN 0-87722-826-4 (alk. paper)
    1. Punishment—Philosophy.   I. Title.
HV8675.A35   1991   90-24041
364.6—dc20   CIP

CONTENTS

PART TWO: A Theory of Punishment

ACKNOWLEDGMENTS

THE COMPLETION of this work places me under the very pleasant obligation of remembering with gratitude those who have given me intellectual, moral, and financial help.

The present work is an outgrowth of my dissertation; my first thanks therefore go to the members of my committee, Professors Roderick Firth and John Rawls. To Professor Firth, my advisor, I owe especial thanks for his patient and thorough reading of a mass of material. To Professor Rawls, I owe especial thanks for his *Theory of Justice*, which forms the basis of Chapter 7.

My thanks also to Hugo Bedau, the proximate efficient cause of this book. His article on "The New Retributivism" was my direct inspiration for writing on the topic of punishment.

Parts of the work have been read, in one form or another, at meetings of the American Philosophical Association (Central and Pacific Divisions), the Canadian Philosophical Association, the Third International Social Philosophy Conference, the Southern Society for Philosophy and Psychology, the Southwestern Philosophical Society, the Arkansas Philosophical Association, and the Fayetteville (Arkansas) Unitarian Fellowship; and to philosophy departments at Harvard University, Tufts University, the University of Wisconsin, the University of Arkansas, and Louisiana State University. Their acute comments and suggestions resulted in substantial improvements in form and content.

I received invaluable assistance in ways too numerous to mention from my research assistant, Lisa Bivens.

My thanks likewise to Beverly Bader, Nick Pappas, A Clark-Heider, and Christopher Morris, as well as anonymous referees at Temple University Press and elsewhere, who read and commented on the draft. I also benefited from discussions with many people, including Jules Coleman, William Hay, John Kleinig, James Spellman, and James Sterba.

Debra Cochran, Jennifer Hammer, and the staff of the Mullins Library Interlibrary Loan Department at the University of Arkansas enabled me to gain access to a host of books and articles. Without these materials my work would have come to a standstill. No request was too arcane or obscure for them to track down. (The reader will find references in the notes to but a small sample of the esoterica that the Interlibrary Loan staff has put into my hands.) I am pleased to have this opportunity to acknowledge publicly what I have already told privately, that the Interlibrary Loan Department is, to my knowledge, the most efficient department in the university, my own not excepted.

Special thanks are due to my colleagues and friends at the University of Arkansas Philosophy Department. These few words cannot adequately acknowledge their helpful ideas and their support.

My most heartfelt thanks go to those who lent moral support during the work on this project. The first lines were written some ten years ago, and I could not have persisted without their faith and encouragement. Foremost among these have been Steve Adelman, Albert Adler, Aristotle Adler, Robert Avakian, Beverly Bader, Barbara Brown, Patrice Cavanaugh, A Clark-Heider, Cynthia Clark-Heider, Paul Deutsch, Carol DiPietro, Derith Glover, David Helman, Christopher Hill, Richard and Pamela Magahiz, Kathryn Merry-Ship, Timothy Merry-Ship, Herbert Nolan, Thomas Pogge, Hilary Putnam, Celia Shneider, John Sousa, and my former colleagues at the Dana Greenhouse, Arnold Arboretum, Harvard University. A Clark-Heider, Derith Glover, Richard Magahiz, and Celia Shneider receive a double measure of thanks in view of their technical support services. For such services I also owe thanks to Kayla Campbell, Sophia Campbell, Tamara Campbell, Julia Elliott, Leonard Schulte, Ann Lynnworth, L. S. Perry, Vola Shulkin, and Clarke Buehling. As a token of thanks, I have used some of their names in the hypothetical examples here and there in the book.

Parts of the manuscript were typed by James Breedlove, Barbara Croken, and Vola Shulkin; I will not be surprised to hear someday that they have deciphered the Etruscan language. Mrs. Shulkin typed by far the largest portion, and I thank her in particular for her extraordinary patience and persistence. Akbar Golmirzaie and Mark Franklin of the University of Arkansas Department of Computer User Services gave indispensable assistance in preparing the manuscript on the computer.

Work on this book was supported in part by a fellowship from the Charlotte W. Newcombe Foundation and by a research incentive grant from Fulbright College, University of Arkansas; I gratefully acknowledge the help I received from both these sources.

Parts of Chapter 5 have appeared in a different form in the *Pacific Philosophical Quarterly*. I thank the *Quarterly* and its publisher, Basil Blackwell, for kind permission to reprint that material.

My next-to-last acknowledgment goes, in gratitude, to those responsible for transforming manuscript into book. Jane Cullen and Mary Capouya at Temple University Press possess all the editorial virtues. Surely it is the wish of all writers to have their manuscripts fall into such hands as these. Barbara Reitt edited the manuscript with exemplary thoroughness and good judgment. The acute reader will perhaps recognize by some occasional quirky writing those few places where I have chosen not to adopt her recommendations.

Finally, I cannot find words adequate to thank my family, and, above all, my parents, Irving and Eleanor Adler, for their encouragement and financial assistance. This work is dedicated to them.

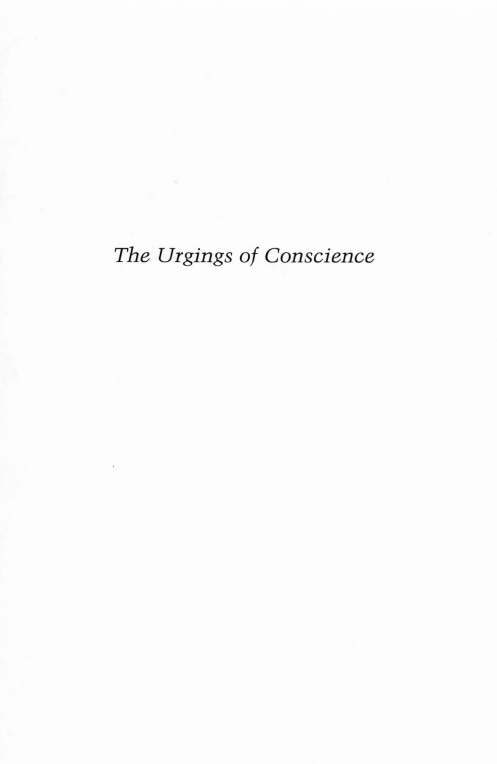

The Urgings of Conscience

INTRODUCTION

MOST PHILOSOPHERS who write about punishment ask, "Why may we punish the guilty?" I want to ask, "Why should the guilty put up with it?" or, more specifically, "To what extent does a guilty person have a duty to submit to punishment?"

This question forms the topic of the present work.

I devote most of this introduction to an overview of what is to follow, turning from this task toward the end to explain two features of my approach to the topics at hand and some special terms.

The book is divided into two parts, of four chapters each. The first part is devoted to more or less conceptual issues, the second to normative ones.

Chapter 1 deals with two issues. First, I set forth some of what I conceive to be the desiderata in a theory of punishment. My primary claim is that an ideal justification of punishment would be twofold: It should establish that punishment is morally permissible and that it is good. These dimensions of justification I refer to respectively as the *legitimation* and the *rationale*. Some theorists writing about punishment (as I point out) fail to distinguish these clearly; a certain confusion results, sometimes even among writers who are otherwise quite astute.

The second, and more substantial, part of Chapter 1 deals with the question of submission to punishment—the question posed at the beginning of this introduction. If we are to justify our system of punishment, or any legitimate system of punishment by the state, I claim that we must explain why persons guilty of an offense are morally bound to submit to punitive treatment, or, indeed, to undertake it on their own. Our own legal system places on convicts a legal duty to submit to their assigned punishment; to evade it is a further breach of legal duty. This duty to submit must be shown to be a moral

1

duty as well as a legal one. Moreover, among the defining features of legitimate government is the requirement that the commands of the government are morally binding on the citizens. (For example, a legitimately imposed tax is one that citizens have a moral duty to pay.) If, then, a legitimate government wishes to punish its citizens for offenses, the government must be able to establish the fact that those who are convicted have a moral duty to submit to the proposed penalty.

We must, then, view punishment from two points of view: that of the punisher and that of the punishee. These two points of view generate two corresponding paradigms of punishment, which form the topic of Chapter 2. I call them the Paradigm of Legal Punishment, and the Paradigm of the Conscientious Punishee. As conceived under the legal paradigm, punishment is something unpleasant imposed upon a passive, unwilling, and unrepentant punishee. As conceived under the conscientious paradigm, punishment is something not necessarily unpleasant, actively undertaken by a repentant wrongdoer because he or she feels it to be morally incumbent.

The conscientious paradigm must, I argue, play a central role in the theory of punishment. For if we can justify conscientious submission to punishment, we can also justify the infliction of punishment on the unwilling; but not vice versa. Moreover, conscientious and willing performance of the duty to submit to punishment is the ideal and the central case, as compared with the less desirable case in which someone performs a duty only under compulsion.

Given this central role of conscientious submission to punishment, the traditional retributive and teleological theories of punishment must be changed or abandoned, for, I claim, they will not (in their traditional forms) justify submission to punishment. Retribution, undertaken by the guilty persons themselves, is either conceptually incoherent or impossible to carry out. Nor can the goals put forward by teleologists be fruitfully pursued by means of a system of submission to punishment. I discuss some novel theories that might succeed in providing the desired justification. Thus ends Chapter 2.

I concentrate in Chapter 3 on one feature of the Paradigm of the Conscientious Punishee: I claim, more specifically, that punishment need not involve pain, suffering, or any other sort of disvalue on the part of the punishee. This claim contradicts nearly all modern conceptions of punishment, which make some sort of disvalue a defining feature of punishment. Indeed, I claim, there are not only odd cases, but standard and central cases of punishment that involve no disvalue to the punishee. As my prime examples of such punishment I consider community-service sanctions (as imposed by some governments) and penances for sin (as required by some religions). If we accept the claim of this chapter, we must take a new view of the task of a theory of punishment. Traditionally, theorists have thought it was the painfulness of punishment that called for justification; but, if there are central cases involving no pain, this cannot be so.

The conclusions of Chapter 3 might leave the reader in some doubt as to what I mean by *punishment*. Chapter 4 therefore attempts to remove this doubt by putting forward a definition of this concept. Punishment, I argue, is defined by its justificatory connection with wrongdoing: Punishment is (by definition) that which is justified by the prior commission of an offense and generally not justified without the prior commission of an offense.

In Part Two I put forward a theory of punishment designed to satisfy the criteria established in Part One. Part Two begins with Chapter 5, where I present what I call the *rectification* theory of punishment.[1] The kernel of the theory is as follows: Consider a society whose members enjoy equal, basic, inalienable rights. (The rights established by the U.S. Bill of Rights will serve as an example.) Such rights guarantee to each person an inviolable sphere of liberty. Now, someone who commits an offense has expanded her sphere by arrogating excess liberties. In order to maintain the equality, she must then forgo an equivalent body of liberties. This forgoing of liberties constitutes the punishment. A system of punishment thus automatically follows from a system of equal, basic, inalienable rights.

Thus, for example, we in the United States enjoy the basic liberty to move about freely in public places, but this liberty is limited by the requirement that in moving about we must not injure others. Suppose Smith is walking down the street and suddenly, without provocation, punches Jones in the nose. Smith has thereby arrogated to herself an excessive share of liberty; she has moved about too freely. In order to restore the desired equality, Smith must give up a comparable liberty. Since she acted in neglect of the physical well-being of others, forgoing an equivalent liberty would require her to act so as to promote the physical well-being of others. She might, for example, work without pay in a hospital.

Now, the rectification theory does not apply to all offenses, only to those by which one arrogates an excess of basic liberties. So, for example, the theory does not apply to someone who steps on the grass in a public park, where this is forbidden by law. Though this is indeed an offense against the law, basic liberties are not involved.

I also discuss the similarities between the rectification theory of punishment and some related views. The most important related view is that of Herbert Morris. The rectification theory may indeed be seen as a particularization of his theory. But the rectification theory is able to avoid certain objections to which Morris's theory falls prey.

In Chapter 6 I present more specific principles for applying the rectification theory. Perhaps the most important of these principles calls for penalties consisting of community service. This principle follows from the nature of basic rights: If the purpose of such a system of rights is to safeguard important interests, then the rectifying punishment must also serve to safeguard those interests; these interests can be safeguarded not by afflictive punishments, but by active service.

Proceeding to Chapter 7, I here incorporate the rectification theory into a more general theory of legal punishment, one based on John Rawls's *Theory of Justice*. Rawls's contractual process—as many readers will recall—yields two principles of justice. The first grants to each citizen the most extensive system of basic liberty compatible with a like liberty for all. The second principle says that inequalities of income, wealth, and other primary goods are to be arranged so as to benefit the least well-off representative person, subject to fair equality of opportunity for the better positions. Any such theory of punishment based on Rawls's contract must overcome a particular difficulty: The contract is designed for a well-ordered society, a society in which there is little or no crime. Why should such a contract apply to badly ordered societies, where crime is a significant problem? I argue that the contract should, for a number of reasons, apply to a badly ordered society; primary is the fact that, outside the contract, we have no other criterion of justice.

Having established the applicability of the contract, I derive punishment from it in three distinct ways. In order of increasing severity they are: by literal application, by reinterpretation, and by repudiation of the contract.

Literal application is the simplest: The contract contains provisions which, when applied in a straightforward way, call for various penalties. These penalties result from the working of the second principle of justice: We arrange a system of penalties so as to maximize the position of those who are worst off (in other words, we use a *maximin* procedure), considering even those who are subject to the penalties. This method applies to crimes that violate the second principle of justice without violating the equal liberties of the first.

If the equal basic liberties are violated, the contract can no longer be literally applied; we cannot establish the system of liberties called for. The situation parallels cases in actual contract law: When a contractually required performance turns out to be impossible, performance of a similar substitute will often be required. Here the rectification theory comes in. We can reinterpret the contract so as to grant the criminal an equivalent, if not identical, body of basic liberties. We can do so only by requiring him to give up a body of liberties equivalent to those he arrogated by his crime. He does not end up with exactly the same body of liberties as the others, but one as close to it as possible, given the nature of the contract.

The last way of deriving punishment from the contract is by repudiation. A person who commits extreme offenses must be interpreted to have repudiated the contract altogether. (The social contract itself, however, cannot really be repudiated, so at most its operation is suspended.) The offenses must be such as to undermine the very possibility of the social contract, and I find only four such: murder; treason; habitual, serious, persistent crime; and crimes that undermine the victim's capacity to choose. People who commit such crimes may be treated much like invaders. They possess a limited body of basic rights, similar in scope to the rights of children. Provided these are observed, the rest of society may set up a system of penalties for social self-defense to safeguard, first, their own basic liberties and, second, the prosperity of all. But society cannot guarantee to the repudiators any but a minimal level of well-being, for it is only by stark incentives that such wild persons can be controlled.

Readers who are not familiar with *A Theory of Justice* may wish, on a first reading, to look carefully at the first and last sections of Chapter 7, and need not be concerned to absorb every detail of the intervening sections.

Finally, in Chapter 8, I discuss some connections among punishment, the social contract, and the political ideal of fraternity. I argue that the theory of punishment set forth in Chapter 7 requires a particular interpretation of the Rawlsian contract: We must see the contract as establishing a relationship of fraternity among citizens. This fraternal relationship is not merely a pleasant after-effect, but is of the essence of the contract. The social contract is thus not merely an arm's-length transaction, as among businesspersons; it also in some ways resembles a marriage contract, in that it establishes a personal relationship among the parties.

So much for our overview of the book. Before we can go on to the thing itself, there are two aspects of the book that call for some comment. First, the reader will note that many examples of punishment in Chapters 1 through 3 are drawn from the sphere of religion, in particular from penitential practices. I use these examples because it seems to me that certain morally relevant phenomena are exhibited more clearly in the sphere of religious practice than elsewhere. I do not intend that the value of these examples should depend on the truth of all the doctrines of the religions from which they are drawn. Indeed, the examples are taken from various religious traditions whose doctrines are not mutually compatible. Rather, these examples presuppose only the following counterfactual: *If* there should exist a Deity as described by the religion in question, *then* the penitential practices in question are justified.

Second, some comments on my choice of Rawls's theory as a background for working out questions of the justification of punishment. Some such background theory is desirable for obvious reasons: Many questions of the justification of punishment make little sense when discussed in the abstract; in order to answer these questions in more than a hand-waving way, one often needs to show how the answers can be developed in detail in the context of a well-worked-out political theory. Any of a number of political theories might have sufficed for this purpose. I have chosen Rawls's theory in part because it seems to be among the most plausible of such theories; in part because it fits well with certain aspects of my own theory, particularly the rectification theory of punishment (Chapters 5 and 6). I also intend my discussion to remedy what some have perceived as a lack in Rawls's theory of justice by showing that this theory, which by its own terms applies only to an idealized society, can be meaningfully applied to a less-than-ideal society, the kind in which crime occurs and punishment is necessary.

I close with some remarks on terminology. In various places I use W. N. Hohfeld's terminology of rights.[2] A *claim-right*, to Hohfeld, entitles the right-holder to have some specific person(s) do some specified thing: For example, if Pogge owes me five dollars, I have a claim-right that he should pay me the five dollars. A *liberty*, or as I call it here, a *liberty-right*, entitles the right-holder to do some specified thing: In other words, it is permissible for her to do it, and no one has a claim-right that she not do it. For example, in the United States, I have a liberty-right to assemble with others and petition the government. I consistently use the term *liberty-right* here for a right of this sort, reserving the word *liberty* for another use (discussed below). Hohfeld defines two more right-concepts, though I make little use of them here: A *power* or *privilege* is the capacity of changing someone's status, in particular of granting or withdrawing rights. For example, the Department of Motor Vehicles has the power of granting or depriving me of the liberty-right to drive a car. Finally, an *immunity* protects the right-holder against having her status changed, and in particular against being deprived of rights: For example, persons who have been tried and acquitted have an immunity against being tried again for the same offense. Hohfeld originally applied these concepts to legal rights, but they work equally well for moral, institutional, and whatever other sorts of rights there are. Readers encountering Hohfeld's terminology of rights for the first time should note that a claim-right is something quite different from a rights-claim. The difference is of the sort one would expect: A claim-right is a kind of right, whereas a rights-claim is a kind of claim. The latter concept is discussed at length in Chapter 5, section 8, and in the Appendix.

I use the term *right* in a normative sense: A right tells people what they must do, and may do. I use the term *liberty* in a descriptive sense to denote the object of a right. For example, if I have the right to vote, then voting officials *ought* to provide me with the opportunity to vote. If I have the liberty to vote, then voting officials *actually do* provide me with the opportunity to vote. Another example: In the pre-*glasnost'* Soviet Union citizens had the right to freedom of religion (it was in the constitution) but not the liberty (just try it). Common usage of these terms is rather inconsistent, paralleling the use of *can* for *may*. My stricter usage on occasion may seem a bit stilted. Where ambiguity does not threaten, I occasionally avail myself of the more common latitude.

The words *government* and *state* I have used interchangeably. They are admittedly not strict synonyms, but nothing here turns on the difference. Likewise, I make no distinction between *duty* and *obligation*, employing them indifferently to refer to any sort of moral or legal requirement. Some people distinguish the two, in various ways; again, nothing here turns on the difference.

PART ONE

*A Metatheory of
Punishment*

CHAPTER 1

Why Submit to Punishment?

MANY have asked, "What gives us the right to punish the guilty?" But I want to ask, "Why should the guilty put up with it?" Or, to frame the question more precisely, "Why should a person guilty of an offense submit to an appropriate punishment?" Let us call this the *question of submission*. The purpose of this chapter is not to answer the question of submission, but to argue for its importance and discuss its significance.

Before anything else, we must be clear about the meaning of the key phrase of this chapter. By *submitting to punishment* I refer to any one or more of the following three things:

not resisting punishment;

performing any actions that may be required as part of one's punishment (for example, hard labor);

taking positive steps to facilitate one's own punishment, or, in the extreme case, punishing oneself.

It is important to note—and I discuss this at length—that I wish to avoid the passive connotations that some may attach to the phrase *submission to punishment*. People who punish themselves are not passive at all, and people who facilitate their own punishment may be justly regarded as punishing themselves with the assistance of others.

I begin with a brief general discussion of the things to be desired in a justification of punishment. After that, the main points of the discussion are as follows:

Most modern philosophical writers on punishment have overlooked the theoretical importance of submission to punishment. (section 2)

11

Any adequate justification of punishment must provide an answer to the question "Why submit to punishment?" (section 3)

The punishment of civil disobedients shows especially clearly the need to answer this question. (section 4)

1. How to Justify Punishment

People generally agree that punishment calls for justification. But what would constitute a satisfactory justification? On the answer to this question there is less agreement and, unfortunately, often much unspoken disagreement. Of course, it is impossible to make all presuppositions explicit, but here it seems especially important to make our task clear to ourselves before we begin it. For, as I will suggest, some of the fruitless disputation about punishment comes from a silent dispute as to what sort of justification is needed.

GENERAL RULES OR PARTICULAR ACTS?

John Rawls has warned us to be careful when we consider the justification of practices, including the practice of punishment.[1] He says we need to distinguish the two tasks of justifying a general rule and of justifying particular applications of that rule to individual cases. Although this distinction is important, it can be finessed for present purposes. For an adequate justification of any practice or rule must encompass the acts to be carried out under the auspices of the practice or rule. To justify a rule in general, without trying to foresee its applications to cases, can result in the most extreme forms of cruelty or inanity; indeed, Wittgensteinians and others would contend that it cannot even be conceived. And, on the other hand, if an individual act is carried out according to some general rule or practice, then a complete justification of the act will include a justification of the general rule or practice; otherwise, we could not even specify which particular act we were dealing with.

But I will not completely avoid answering the question: Whenever one is speaking of punishment in general, as opposed to some individual case, one is always dealing with general rules. Even if an actual, individual case is discussed in the present context, it serves only to illustrate a general rule, though perhaps a very detailed and specific one.

TWO DIMENSIONS OF JUSTIFICATION

Having decided that we are to justify penal *practices* or *rules,* what do we look for in a justification? Here I follow Joel Feinberg: "A basic distinction . . . is that between [penal measures] that are *legitimized* by valid moral principles and those that are *justified* on balance as being both legitimate *and* useful, wise, economical, popular, etc."[2] To justify a practice, then, we must show two things: that it is morally legitimate, and that it has a sufficiently compelling rationale. In other words, in justifying a practice, we must look to the categories of the Right and the Good, and we must be satisfied that it violates no principles of Right, and that it accomplishes some Good. These two parts or dimensions of justification I will call, respectively, a *legitimation* and a *rationale.*

Now, Feinberg declines to give an analysis of these notions of legitimation and rationale, and I will for the most part join him in declining. One thing, however, needs to be pointed out. A legitimation for a particular penal (or other) practice and the rationale for that practice will usually be interrelated, so that the complete legitimation will refer to the rationale, or vice versa. In particular, it will often be found that a certain type of penalty is legitimate *provided* an adequate rationale can be found. For example, if the death penalty is in general a legitimate sort of penalty, it will still take a compelling rationale for the state to be justified in using it. The rationale one often hears is that it deters crime. But someone might argue that the death penalty, though a legitimate kind of penalty, does not in fact deter (nor is there any other compelling rationale), and conclude that capital punishment is therefore unjustified.

It will be found that these concepts of legitimation and rationale, as I am using them, coincide closely with the two elements that courts use in applying the Equal Protection Clause of the Fourteenth Amendment to the United States Constitution. For example, under this clause, if a statute does not use suspect classifications, it is legitimate, provided the classifications that it does use are rationally related to some governmental purpose.[3]

We may thus forestall a possible objection. "If a proposed practice is legitimate," our objector might say, "why is anything further needed to make it justified?" As we have seen, a legitimation may, on its own terms, require a rationale.

Now, this two-dimensional conception of justification is nothing especially profound or novel, yet it has been ignored by some. H. L. A.

Hart, for example, proposes that a particular system or measure of punishment can be justified by identifying a general justifying aim, that is, a rationale; but he does not consider whether the punishments in question are *legitimate* in light of the rationale.[4]

Of course, for consequentialists—who hold that justified acts are those with good consequences (or the best consequences)—justification has only one dimension. Consequentialists can dispense with the category of legitimation and ask merely whether a given system of punishments is optimific, or forms part of an optimific system—that is, whether the system maximally promotes its rationale. But in the present work I do not consider such views. It may be that consequentialism is true, but if so, I assume that it operates at such a deep level that when we think about the justification of punishment, our deliberations will not be explicitly consequentialist. Of course, in rejecting consequentialism, I am not asserting that consequences should *never* be considered. Consequences enter into the justification of punishment by forming (part of) the rationale; I do, however, proceed on the assumption that the expectation of good consequences is, without further explanation, not enough to justify a measure of punishment.

2. Submission to Punishment: A Brief History

We are concerned, then, with the question of submission to punishment. In the present section I present a brief history of answers to this question. In ancient and medieval times, as we will see, philosophers and others took the question seriously, giving various answers to it, but modern philosophers ignore or ridicule it.

We turn first to the ancients. Plato and Aristotle, the most illustrious of these, hold that punishment is at least sometimes a cure for a disease of the soul.[5] Their answer to the punishee's question is: "You should put up with it because it's good for you. What's more, you should obtain it for yourself if it's not thrust upon you." Or, in Plato's words:

> Our recent admissions show, do they not, that a man must take every precaution not to do wrong, since he would thereby suffer great harm?
> . . . But if he or anyone of those for whom he cares has done wrong, he ought to go of his own accord where he will most speedily be punished, to the judge as though to a doctor, in his eagerness to prevent the distemper of evil from becoming ingrained and producing a festering and incurable ulcer in his soul.[6]

In the early years of the Christian era and onward through the Middle Ages, writers continue to address the question of submission. Among these writers we find two groups: religious thinkers, who write of Divine punishment and penance, and political thinkers, who write of submission to punishment.

To begin with the religious thinkers, we find that very many of them persist in the medical metaphor that is found in Plato and Aristotle, and they apply this metaphor both to punishment inflicted by God and to penance undertaken by men and women.[7] This metaphor provides one rationale, at least, for the contrite offender to accept and even seek out punishment.

With particular regard to Divine punishments, one might think that the question of submission is moot: How could one hope to escape? Yet even here at least one writer points out that an offender ought willingly to accept the punishments that God inflicts; though there is no question of evading the punishment, it is still important to accept it in the proper spirit.[8] It is in regard to penance, however, that the question of submission comes to the fore. The writers we are considering classify acts of penance (or of "satisfaction," as it is often termed) as a form of punishment.[9] These penances almost always involve actions undertaken by the penitent, such as prayer, fasting, visiting the sick and imprisoned (and in general helping the unfortunate), giving to charity, and so on. Thus the theory of penance must by the nature of things consider the question of submission: A member of the clergy may *assign* a penance, but it is up to the penitent to carry it out.

Within the theory of penance we find authors considering as well a variety of subsidiary questions that are raised by the question of submission. Some consider penance to be optional, holding that sincere inner repentance is sufficient.[10] Others, especially after A.D. 950, hold that penance is mandatory. Controversy on this question came to a head in the twelfth century, until it was finally resolved by the Fourth Lateran Council's (A.D. 1215) decree that penance is mandatory for Roman Catholics.[11] Some claim that an offender may act as his or her own judge, assigning and then carrying out a penance.[12] Our authors discuss as well the proper motive for penance. Some hold that it is proper to do penance even if one's sole motive is to avoid a worse punishment.[13] Others insist that penance must be done out of sincere repentance, or indeed from the love of God.[14] Aquinas goes so far as to claim that the obligation to do penance is a principle of the *natural* law, and not merely of the revealed, and thus binding on Christians and non-Christians alike.[15]

Turning next to political theory in the West during the same period—that is, the early Christian era and the Middle Ages—we find much the same teaching with regard to punishment by the state. It is true that these political theorists do not so much mention submission to punishment as such; rather, they speak extensively of submission to the state in all matters, including punishment.

These political theorists fall into two groups. Both agree on this: Men and women, in their imperfect state, often stray far from justice in their treatment of each other; to remedy this, an earthly ruler with the power to punish is needed.[16] But regarding the authority of the ruler, the two groups of theorists differ. The first group—we might call them divine-right extremists—hold that the ruler's authority is sacred: Whether good or wicked, the ruler's power comes from God, and to resist the ruler is to defy God.[17] This view is found in perhaps its most extreme form in the works of Saint Gregory the Great.[18] This view, of course, is based on biblical passages such as that found in Romans: "Let every person be subject to the governing authorities. For there is no authority except from God, and those that exist have been instituted by God. Therefore he who resists the authorities resists what God has appointed, and those who resist will incur judgment" (Rom. 13:1–2, RSV). Writers of this first group tend to hold that wicked rulers are sent by God to punish wicked nations.[19] Hence the divine-right extremists hold that subjects should submit to all punishments inflicted by earthly rulers, whether inflicted with justice or injustice.

The second group of political theorists are the divine-right moderates. They also hold that the ruler has divine sanction, but only when he acts within his authority. Hence, a subject's obligation to obey such a ruler is limited, and perhaps in some cases negated.[20] In some cases this second group of theorists would allow for civil disobedience. Yet they, like the first group, concede that punishment is a legitimate function of government and lies within the ruler's authority (at any rate, when the ruler punishes proportionately). So this second group of theorists also hold that there is an obligation to submit to punishments inflicted by the state, at any rate when these punishments are justly inflicted.[21]

Both groups, it should be recalled, have a powerful rationale for their view that one should submit to punishment by the state. They generally hold to the Judeo-Christian doctrine that all afflictions that a person suffers in this life are God's punishment for sins, and one should bear them willingly.[22]

By modern times, things have changed drastically. Although religious writers continue to consider the conscientious penitent—one who does penance willingly—the majority of writers on political subjects hold least one of the following interrelated views:

> No one (or hardly anyone) ever willingly submits to punishment.
>
> If someone willingly submits to a certain kind of treatment, then that treatment is not punishment.
>
> If someone willingly submits to a certain kind of treatment, then that treatment, even if it counts as punishment, is an odd or inappropriate case of punishment.

The general idea is that willing submission to punishment is either pointless or (logically or psychologically) impossible. Someone who holds such a view would have little need to consider the question of submission.

A number of distinct lines of thought converge on this conclusion about punishment. First, we have the closely related doctrines of psychological egoism and psychological hedonism. Psychological egoism is the view that everything that a person does, she does from selfish motives. Psychological hedonism holds that the only motive for action is desire for one's own pleasure.[23] The idea is not that people are selfish for the most part, but that they are always and necessarily selfish. These views have been enormously influential. Among their supporters we find Hobbes,[24] Locke (in his later years), Bentham, and, in a way, Freud. Behaviorist psychologists often hold what is in effect a disguised version of psychological hedonism, with the concept of reinforcement replacing the concept of pleasure.[25] Another variation is found among advocates of the Law and Economics school: For them, punishment is a kind of cost, which naturally almost everyone (at least everyone who is economically rational) wants to avoid.[26] Now, to a supporter of these views it is fairly obvious that practically no one willingly submits to punishment. For (as they think) punishments are painful, nor does it serve any selfish purpose if a man or woman submits to punishment. Therefore, no one will. Thus Locke states quite baldly:

> If anyone presume to violate the laws of public justice and equity, . . . his presumption is to be checked by the fear of punishment consisting of the deprivation or diminution of those civil interests or goods which otherwise he might and ought to enjoy. . . . [N]o man does willingly suffer himself to be punished by the deprivation of any part of his goods, and much less of his liberty or life.[27]

We find similar statements in Hobbes, Bentham, and Freud.[28]

A second line of thought is based on the moral purity of the punisher. Punishment, a moral act, can be imposed only by someone who is morally good. The offender, however, is morally bad. Therefore, the offender lacks the status to punish herself. Kant, par excellence, represents this view:

> No one suffers punishment because he has willed the punishment, but because he has willed a punishable action. If what happens to someone is also willed by him, it cannot be a punishment. Accordingly, it is impossible to will to be punished. . . . In my role as colegislator making the penal law, I cannot be the same person who, as subject, is punished by the law; for, as a subject who is also a criminal, I cannot have a voice in legislation. (The legislator is holy.)[29]

How can we understand this view? A suggestion: If an action is mine, I must see the action as good. If I am to punish someone for an action, I must see her action as bad. In order to punish myself for something I have done, I must therefore see my action as both good and bad—obviously impossible.[30]

A third line of reasoning focuses on the rationale of punishment. The reasons for punishing, according to this view, are deterrence, reform, and perhaps retribution. If these rationales are to do their work, the punishment must not be something that the offender is willing to undertake. A potential offender cannot be deterred by something that he would willingly accept. As for reform, the person who needs reform is precisely the one who sees no need for it and therefore rejects it. If someone welcomes efforts to reform him, then he has already reformed; and if further reformation is needed, he can do this by himself. Finally, no seeker of retribution will be satisfied if the offender gladly receives the treatment that was intended to be retributive; it would be like throwing Br'er Rabbit into the briar patch.[31] (On this topic, see further Chapter 2, section 3.) According to this last view, it is possible that someone might willingly submit to punishment, but in that case the punishment is unnecessary or even counterproductive.[32]

Hegel and his followers would appear to constitute an exception to this trend, but it is only an apparent exception. Hegel is, for example, noted for having said that the criminal has willed his own punishment and that "punishment is regarded as containing the criminal's right and hence by being punished he is honoured as a rational being."[33] But such selected passages are misleading. When Hegel says that the criminal has willed his own punishment, he is speaking of what he calls the universal, implicit will, a will that is not peculiar to the criminal or any other single person; indeed, the crime consists in the criminal's setting his own single, explicit will in opposition to the universal.[34] And as to Hegel's statements that punishment is the criminal's right, he does not mean that the criminal has the right to accept or reject the punishment, but that in punishing the criminal we are acting in accordance with the criminal's own *principle of right*—that is, the principle that is implicit in the criminal act.[35] In the final analysis, we must put Hegel in the same camp as the rest, for he states that "retribution is *inflicted* on the criminal and so it has the look of an alien destiny, not intrinsically his own."[36]

More recent writers are less dogmatic than Kant and Bentham but fall into the same line. Criminological writers, concerned as they are with the typical criminal that police and judges must deal with, naturally say little about the case of willing submission. Among philosophical writers, some ridicule the idea that a person might willingly accept punishment. Others admit that it might happen but suggest that such cases are odd or rare. Thus S. I. Benn writes that the criminal's "efforts to elude the police are evidence that he does not will his own punishment in any ordinary sense."[37] And Sir David Ross remarks: "It is said that [the criminal] has a right to be punished, and that not to punish him is not to treat him with due respect as a moral agent. . . . This is, however, not a point of view likely to be adopted by a criminal who escapes punishment, and seems to be a somewhat artificial way of looking at the matter."[38] Regarding this same alleged right, Anthony Quinton makes the observation: "It is an odd sort of right whose holders would strenuously resist its recognition." Ted Honderich, echoing Quinton, speculates that this "odd sort of right" is probably "a projection of . . . feelings of guilt" on the part of those who argue for it.[39]

In recent years some writers have come closer to a serious consideration of the question of submission. C. S. Nino puts forward a justification of punishment based on the offender's consent. Sir Walter Moberly and Jean Hampton go further, and argue that the offender must not only consent to, but must appreciate the justice of the punishment imposed on him; only then can punishment serve the morally educative function that makes it justified.[40] These views represent an important step toward the question of submission, but they do not go all the way. For still the punishee might say, "Well, *you* are certainly justified in punishing me, but *I* would be a fool if I didn't try to avoid it." Justice in infliction may contribute to an answer to the question of submission, but justice in infliction is not in itself an answer.

One of the few recent philosophers to face the question of submis-

sion squarely is Herbert Morris, who writes seriously about a right
to be punished, a right that some might actually choose to exercise.[41]
But even Morris seems to flinch a bit at the question of submission:
The right to be punished, as Morris conceives it, is a right *not* to
be subjected to mandatory therapy—a right that could apparently be
honored if we merely left convicts alone, without imposing either
therapy or punishment.[42] Consequently, Morris does not address the
most basic form of the question of submission: Why should an offender submit to punishment when she could avoid punishment or
other mandatory treatment altogether?

Aside from Morris's, we find a small number of recent philosophical discussions of the question of submission. But these are infre-
quent and often consist of remarks in passing. For example, A. R.
Manser writes, "The neurotically guilty person's desire for suffering
is a desire to be purged of some burden of guilt. (Of course, it would
also seem to follow that a genuinely guilty person might feel the
same thing.)"[43] On the whole, one encounters very little sustained
discussion of the question.

What accounts for this change between medieval and modern
thought? How did we get from Abelard, who tells us to do penance
out of love of God, to Locke, who tells us that no one ever willingly
does the very sorts of things that Abelard recommends that we do?
The change, evidently, came about as part of the rise of liberalism—
in particular, the growth of a separation between church and state.
Let us grant Abelard his claim that it is possible to do penance out
of love of God—for the goodness of God, as His saints describe Him,
is great enough to inspire such efforts. If men and women will go to
great lengths for the sake of their earthly lovers, how much further
for the love of heaven. In medieval times, the state was viewed as
a part of the Divine government, and the law of the state a part of
the law of God. So the state was infused with some of the Divine
goodness, and submission to the state's penalties seemed possible
as an indirect submission to God. Indeed, there appeared to be one
great system of criminal jurisprudence, encompassing punishments
inflicted by God, punishments inflicted by the state, and penances
undertaken by the penitent. A vivid example can be found in Jewish
law, which holds that a sinner deserving death at the hands of God
should instead be flogged by the earthly court:

> Scripture says: *Thou shalt not take the name of the Lord thy God in
> vain; for the Lord will not hold him guiltless* [Exod. 20:7]—the Upper
> [Divine] Court will not render him guiltless, but the lower [human]
> court inflict stripes and render him guiltless.[44]

Since the Upper Court recognizes the jurisdiction of the lower court, it regards the flogging as a punishment for the offense. The principle of double jeopardy then prevents the Upper Court from retrying the offender and imposing the death penalty. Similarly, even if there is no earthly court to administer a flogging, the offender can still stay the Divine death sentence by means of a self-imposed penance: "A man commits a sin and is liable to death before the Almighty, what shall he do and live? If he was accustomed to studying one page, he shall study two, to studying one chapter, he shall study two chapters."[45] With this view of human and Divine government, we can at least conceive of the motive of someone who submits willingly to punishment by the state.

Things change profoundly with the advent of liberalism (in the classical sense), and in particular of the separation of church and state. It is no coincidence that the quotation from Locke seen above— asserting that no one ever willingly submits to punishment—is taken from the same work in which he argues for church–state separation. We can view the change from two perspectives. First, there is the earthly ruler's demotion in status—desanctification, we might say. Before the change, he[46] was God's vicar on earth. Now his status is reduced: He is either a party to a contract (or perhaps a contractual agent), or else a utilitarian calculator, a bureaucrat. Out of love of God we might be willing to submit to His vicar, but who loves a bureaucrat? And as for the contractual parties or agents, all we want from them is that they do their job; love does not enter into it. The very same act of submitting, say, to a flogging now loses the context that once gave it meaning. The judge now orders me to be flogged because that is part of her job; those who hired or appointed her ordered such floggings as a general policy for reasons having nothing to do with me. It is indeed hard to see why someone would put up with such a thing.

The other side of the coin is freedom of conscience. The new state does not try to probe the conscience of its subjects, but merely tries to induce them to avoid violating the rights of others.[47] Kant makes the same point in terms of his distinction between ethics (*Ethik, Tugendlehre*) and justice or jurisprudence (*Recht, Rechtslehre*). Ethics, for Kant, is concerned with duty done for duty's sake, whereas jurisprudence—and consequently, the state—is concerned with actions that one can promote by the carrot and stick (mainly the stick).[48] The liberal state, as part of its grant of freedom of conscience, does not even try to determine if a person is accepting punishment for reasons of conscience.

Later formulations of liberalism generalize this idea of freedom of religion to include all personal values. It is thus often considered to be a defining feature of liberalism that the state should not endorse or promote any one set of personal values, any one preferred mode of life. But it would seem that submission to punishment makes sense only if the person has some particular values that make sense of the motive for it. Hence, apparently, liberalism puts the question of submission to punishment beyond the pale of political theory.

Under a liberal regime the cure of souls is a purely private matter. If there is any institution that takes charge of such affairs, it will be a voluntary institution. Such an institution—most typically, a religious organization—will likely be the only venue of a system of penalties that are undertaken willingly, for reasons of conscience. The result: punishment inflicted by the state on the one hand, and voluntary penance in church on the other, with no connection—indeed, a veritable wall of separation—between them.

3. The Need to Address the Question of Submission

We have seen that the question of submission is mostly ignored in modern political theory. Yet we must answer the question of submission if we are to justify a system of punishments imposed by the state, as I next attempt to show.

The essence of the argument can be presented quite briefly. We begin by asking, "What is a legitimate state? What is the difference between a legitimate state and the regime of a gangster chief, someone like Al Capone?" Both Capone and the legitimate state issue directives backed by threats of coercion. One might be tempted to answer: "The legitimate state is one that engages in justified or benevolent coercion, whereas Capone's use of coercion is malevolent and unjustifiable." Although that is certainly so, it is not a good enough answer. For a benevolent dictator might be justified or benevolent in her use of coercion, but that does not make her regime count as legitimate. A legitimate state, I shall say, is one that commands the *moral* allegiance of its subjects: When it binds them, they are morally bound—or, in plainer terms, such a state has a moral status that enables it to issue directives that constitute true moral obligations for its citizens.[49] If such a state resorts to coercion, as it sometimes must, it is only coercing people to do what in any case they are morally obligated to do.

On this view, a legitimate prohibition—say, an antipollution statute—does not merely authorize the sheriff to stop polluters; it means that henceforth people *should not* pollute—and conscientious people then will not pollute, even if they know they can get away with it. A legitimate tax is not merely a justifiable extraction of money; it is a tax that a conscientious citizen pays willingly (if perhaps grudgingly). In general: A legitimate state does not say "You will do this" unless it can first say "You must do this."[50]

If this is our view of legitimacy, and if we apply it consistently to criminal punishment, the conclusion follows obviously: A legitimate punishment is not merely one that courts are authorized to inflict upon criminals; it is one that the criminal is morally obligated to submit to. And a legitimate criminal court does not inflict punishment unless it can morally obligate the convict to submit to that punishment.

Now, few criminals in fact submit willingly—one would be deluded to deny it—but that fact is irrelevant to the issue at hand. Taxes, too, require a lot of enforcement. Indeed, there is scarcely a law on the books that does not require enforcement to some degree. The point is that this enforcement is (or ought to be) the enforcement of a duty, not the application of brute force for a justifiable end.

Many people, it seems, accept this general conception of legitimacy but balk when asked to apply it to punishment. This idea of legitimacy requires seeing our fellow citizen as a moral subject, and there is a tendency to see the criminal only as a moral object.[51] To put it another way, legitimacy requires us to ask, "How should we behave toward our fellow citizens, and how should they behave toward us?", but when it comes to dealing with criminals, we often are tempted to drop the second half of the question. We ask only, "What can we do with them?" or ". . . to them?" as if they were things to be manipulated. This way of viewing criminals is natural and even—in a certain sense—justified. For serious criminals seem to have proved by their actions that they give little thought to their moral obligations toward others, or, perhaps more often, they think about these obligations in such a distorted way that they come to grossly immoral conclusions.[52] These moral deficiencies of criminals, however, do not absolve the rest of us from thinking about the moral obligations of those who have comitted offenses. If criminals do incur moral obligations, then we owe it to the small number of repentant criminals to enable them to carry out those obligations; and, for the large number of unrepentant criminals, we cannot know how we ought to deal with them unless we have some idea of how they ought to deal with us.

Of course, there are few people who come out and say that the state may impose penalties on offenders even when the offenders have a right to resist the penalty. Mostly there is simply a lack of attention to the question of submission. Sometimes one gets a feeling that the infliction of punishments is such an unavoidable necessity that we cannot seriously consider abandoning the practice, even though there may be some morally questionable aspects to it.[53] Some theorists make the infliction of punishment a defining feature of a legal system. For them, it remains only to ask how and when and upon whom these penalties should be inflicted.[54] Others simply abandon the present conception of legitimacy.[55]

This conception of punishment and the legitimate state needs a more careful view; that will be the task of the present section. I propose to establish the following claim: *If a state that aspires to legitimacy proposes to punish persons who have been convicted of crimes, it must first establish that they have a moral obligation to submit to the proposed penalties; this obligation, furthermore, cannot be taken for granted as part of a subject's ordinary duty of obedience to a legitimate state, but must be established by additional considerations.* I pursue the following plan. First, I discuss the general conception of legitimacy that is in play here and, after that, the specific political presuppositions for the argument to follow. I then present two arguments for the main claim. The first is based on a demanding conception of legitimacy, the second on a less demanding one that I call *minimal legitimacy*. Finally, I discuss the possible rationale for submitting to punishment by the state.

Before I can proceed with this plan, there are some details to be filled in and a possible misinterpretation to be forestalled. First, when I say that an obligation to submit must be established, just what obligation do I have in mind? Presumably, if I have been convicted in a fair trial, I must not resist the officials who come to punish me. But must I also help them? Must I go so far as to punish myself? The answer is clear: The state is proposing to make me undergo and do certain things. It must then establish that I have a duty not to resist what they are trying to make me undergo; and that if the punishment calls for me to do certain things, such as hard labor, that I have an obligation to do them.

Second, there are questions of the extent of this proposed moral obligation. Does it apply only to those who have been convicted? Does it include those who have been mistakenly convicted? Or actual criminals who have been acquitted? Must a criminal go so far as to confess his offense so as to be punished, or punish himself if no one else will do it? These questions are important, but for the most part we must pass over them in silence: They are to be answered by a normative theory of punishment; I am not now offering any such theory, but rather a metatheory. But we may give a preliminary answer: We are concerned with governments that propose to punish persons who have committed offenses and have been convicted of the same; such governments must therefore show that these persons have a moral obligation to submit—in the sense mentioned in the previous paragraph—to the proposed punishments. Whether there exists any duty to submit beyond this minimal one will be left open.

Third, we must show that the offender has a moral obligation to submit to punishment, but it should not be supposed that one must convince the offender herself that she has such an obligation. It would be nice if we could do that, but in the case of most criminals that would be impossible. What we want to do is establish this obligation on the grounds of moral theory.

With this, we turn to the political presuppositions.

POLITICAL PRESUPPOSITIONS

We consider here first the general conception of legitimacy that underlies the argument of the present section, and then some of its specifics.

First of all, I consider the problem of political obligation to be primarily a moral problem. Its chief question is "What moral obligation does a subject have to support the state and obey its directives?" There are those, of course, who hold that this is the wrong sort of question; that the inquiry should be sociological, or linguistic, or logical, or something other than moral.[56] But I will ignore such views here. In particular, I am not using the sociological concept of legitimacy, which sees a state as legitimate if its subjects accept its directives—if, in H. L. A. Hart's term, they take the internal point of view toward the directives. (In terms of legal theory, we are dealing with a question of critical morality, not positive morality.) Aside from my mere fiat, there are some important reasons behind this approach (though this is hardly the point for the depth of discussion the question requires). One wishes to be able to raise the question "Is our state legitimate, as now constituted?" And it is not enough to answer, "Well, *we* all like it. You are the single exception. Therefore, by definition, it is legitimate." In particular, we should be able at least to raise the possibility that a group of people might be unjustly oppressed to such a degree that they accept the propaganda of the oppressors and consider the oppression appropriate.

With this moral view of political obligation, we can then define a legitimate state as one in which the state has a (no doubt limited) moral right to issue directives, and the subjects have a correlative moral obligation to obey.[57] The limited sphere in which the state has a right to command may be called its *competence*. Ideally, a state's competence is defined by a publicly known constitution, so that all may know what sorts of commands are morally binding. When a legitimate state issues a command that is within its competence, the subjects automatically have a morally sufficient reason for obeying the command: the state does not have to adduce any further reasons or justifications, beyond the fact that it is a legitimate state acting within its competence.[58] On the other hand, if the state issues a directive exceeding its competence, I assume the command to have no automatic moral effect: The subjects may perhaps have a moral obligation to obey, but this obligation rests on other grounds; it does not fall within the subject's general moral obligation to obey the law. For example, Aquinas holds that even illegitimate commands of a sovereign should be obeyed, if such obedience is the only way to avoid scandal or chaos.[59] If the state wants the subjects to comply with such extraordinary commands, it must give a special justification, explaining why the commands are morally obligatory. (Some of Lincoln's extraordinary Civil War directives serve arguably as examples of this category.)

Now, it may seem to some that this view ascribes too great a moral power to the legitimate state; but recall that we have not determined the extent of the state's competence or the stringency of the subject's moral obligation to obey even a legitimate state. Depending on one's view, this obligation may be absolute and unconditional, or prima facie and conditional. According to the latter view, the state has a more modest moral power.

Second, I assume that this chief question of political theory can be answered in a positive way. That is, a government meeting certain requirements—roughly, those defining a liberal democracy—will in fact be legitimate. Its subjects will have a prima facie moral obligation to obey its directives (at any rate, when the government is acting within its competence). Again, there are those who differ: Some authors agree that the problem of political obligation is a moral one but answer the chief question negatively. They find that subjects have no general moral obligation to obey the directives even of an ideal state. Again, I will for the most part ignore such views.[60] Even if we were to concede that subjects have no general obligation to obey the law as such, still one might hold that they have various other moral obligations that in fact require them, for the most part, to obey the law. A *legitimate state* could then be redefined as one that systematically seeks to issue only directives that are, on whatever ground, morally obligatory upon its subjects. Even this attenuated definition would suffice for present purposes.

Now, legitimacy, as I have defined it, is a strong concept. My second argument is therefore based on a weaker concept, which I call *minimal legitimacy*. A *minimally legitimate state* may be defined as one that ought not be subverted. In other words, the subjects of a minimally legitimate state are morally obligated not to subvert it, either by active rebellion or by large-scale passive resistance that prevents the government from effective operation. According to present definitions, then, any legitimate government will be minimally legitimate, but not vice versa.

Such are our definitions of *legitimacy*. A central part of this conception is a moral requirement: A state that aspires to legitimacy must strive to issue only commands that will also be morally obligatory upon its subjects. Why is this so, and why so important? What would be the harm if the state issued some commands that the subjects were morally at liberty to ignore? To answer these questions we must go into the general political views that underlie the present conception of legitimacy. I will consider two lines of reasoning that lead up to this conception. The first concerns the state's role as resolver of disputes; the second concerns the concept of autonomy.

To begin with our first line of reasoning, one of the prime desiderata in a state is that it should obviate the appeal to force or the threat of force as a means of settling disputes between persons. The state does this most obviously by means of judicial proceedings, but the whole apparatus of laws, regulations, and other commands is also involved. Now, a state must have force at its disposal as a means of enforcing its settlements; but, as Locke argues, if a state merely appeals to its superior force, it is no better than an individual or group that is powerful enough to impose its will. The dispute is not really settled, but only suppressed. If a state operates in such a way, according to Locke, "*War is made* upon the Sufferers," who have no remedy except an "appeal to Heaven,"[61] that is to say, an appeal to force in which the sufferers hope that heaven will help them. Prudential reasons may lead a person not to avail herself of an appeal to force, but a determined and conscientious person may be willing to do this, even with little hope of success, rather than accept a solution that is imposed merely by force. True settlement of disputes requires that a reason be given why a dissatisfied party should accept the proposed settlement. Since we are taking the question of legitimacy to be a moral question, this reason must be a *sufficient moral reason*. And this morally sufficient reason must apply not only to the decreed settlement of particular disputes, but (as I have said) to the whole system of laws and regulations that form the background for settling disputes, and that indeed prevent disputes from arising. A government that aspires to legitimacy must then seek to issue commands and laws only if it can give a sufficient moral reason why they should be obeyed; that is, it should seek to issue none but morally binding commands and laws.

Some qualifications are obviously necessary here. Clearly (first of all) not every person could actually be convinced of the moral obligatoriness of the laws; to require that would be to impose an impossible task. What is required is that the laws be shown to be morally binding according to some background theory, and that challenges be taken seriously. Second, even if we judge by the standard of the background theory, there may be laws which, considered in isolation, would not seem to be obligatory; still, in context, one probably is morally bound to obey them unless they are egregiously unjust; otherwise, the clash of individual judgments would tend to defeat the dispute-resolutive function of the state. Third, a state that aspires to legitimacy ought nonetheless systematically try to eliminate any such laws, since they tend to undermine the state's effectiveness and moral authority as resolver of disputes.

The second line of reasoning for the present conception of legitimacy turns on the concept of *autonomy*. On this view, a state that aspires to legitimacy must respect its competent, adult subjects as autonomous moral persons. Here we play on themes from Kant and J. S. Mill, though no deep commitment to either is needed to make the point. Simply put, competent adults are to be allowed to run their lives, as much as possible, according to their own choice. Sometimes their autonomous self-control must be limited, since the unlimited autonomy of any one person will conflict with that of others. When it is necessary to limit subjects' autonomy, the state should control them not by coercion or threat, but by reasons that appeal to them as autonomous beings; that is, by showing them that a certain kind of behavior is morally obligatory.[62] Thus, if a state that aspires to legitimacy wishes to impose a legal obligation on its subjects, it must show that the proposed legal obligation, when duly enacted, will be morally obligatory.

Of course, real people approach autonomy only as an ideal, so coercion will be necessary to enforce the laws; but coercion itself does not make the laws legitimate.

So much for our general conception of legitimacy. As to specifics, I assume that a state must meet certain substantive and procedural requirements if it is to be legitimate, or even minimally legitimate. Among these requirements:

1. The state must treat its subjects with equal concern and respect.[63]
2. The state must grant its subjects a set of important basic rights, including:
   a. the right to bodily integrity and physical liberty;
   b. the rights encompassed by the concept of the rule of law; and
   c. the right to choose one's own plan of life and, within broad limits, to pursue it.

These requirements constitute limitations on the state's competence; it may exceed these limitations on its authority only by presenting a special justification, explaining the basis for the extension of its authority. I likewise assume that persons generally have a moral right to self-defense; that is, they may defend themselves against (some kinds of) imminent harm by the use of force proportional to the threatened harm. Clearly, some theory of self-defense is needed to tell us what kinds of harm justify the use of force, and what degree of force is proportional to a given harm. But at the very minimum a threatened violation of one's basic rights justifies the use of force in self-defense, especially if the threatened harm is irreversible. This right holds not only against legitimate governments but against all persons.

OBLIGATION TO SUBMIT MUST BE ESTABLISHED: FIRST ARGUMENT

We now have hung the backdrop for the arguments of this section, and so we turn to the first one. The argument, it will be recalled, is to support the following claim: *If a state that aspires to legitimacy proposes to punish persons who have been convicted of crimes, it must first establish that they have a moral obligation to submit to the proposed penalties; this obligation, furthermore, cannot be taken for granted as part of a subject's ordinary duty of obedience to a legitimate state, but must be established by additional considerations.*

I begin by observing that if a legitimate state seeks to punish criminals, it must first place them under a legal obligation to submit to the proposed punishments. (As yet I say nothing about a moral obligation.) Why is this so? It follows from the concept of the rule of law. This heading covers a number of specific requirements about which there are some differences, but we may safely include the following: A legitimate state must rule not by force, but by law: If the state is to require its subjects to do this or that, it may not simply coerce or threaten them, but must establish a legal requirement that they do the required thing.[64] So if the state wants certain persons to pay fines, or go to prison, or be put to death, it must not merely apply brute force; it must first establish that the persons have a legal duty to pay the fine, or go to prison, or to die at the hands of the executioner.

The previous paragraph seems sufficient on this point. But if one still has doubts, consider the alternative. This alternative would be for the state to impose punishment on persons without placing them under a legal requirement to submit to the proposed treatment. These punishments could still be administered after a fair trial and in accordance with established, public rules. All that would be missing is the convict's legal duty to submit.

When we examine the consequences of this alternative, it can be seen to be incompatible with the rule of law. For if convicts are under no legal duty to submit to punishment, then, by definition, they are legally at liberty to resist. This liberty-right gives rise to a competitive situation: The state may (legally) impose the punishment, if it can, and the convict is legally at liberty to evade it, if she can. The convict's legal liberty to evade punishment (if she can) gives rise to two consequences which, taken together, are strikingly odd. First, evasion of punishment, or the attempt to evade punishment, cannot be considered a crime, nor, therefore, can it be punished. Why so? To say that evasion cannot be considered a crime is merely to restate the premise that the convict enjoys a liberty to evade punishment. And the rule of law, if it requires anything, forbids the state from punishing persons for behavior that is not legally forbidden. The state may, of course, impose the original punishment on the convict, but it may not impose any further punishment for evading it, or attempting to evade it. Second, this legal liberty to evade punishment must include the liberty to take measures that are reasonably necessary for the end in question. To permit the end but deny the means would make a sham out of the liberty to evade punishment; it would say, "You may evade this punishment, but you may not do the things that might enable you to evade punishment"—an absurd proposal. But what are these means of evading punishment? Quite clearly, one who wishes to evade punishment must usually use force to prevent the punishment from being imposed, or to escape from it: Depending on the case, one would have to attack officers of the law, using

physical force to abduct, confine, injure, or even kill them, as necessary; persons already confined in prison would often need to destroy
parts of the prison structure, thereby endangering both inmates and
guards. (The permissible level of violence would no doubt depend on
the intensity of the law officers' efforts to impose the punishment.)

Combining these two consequences, we get this result: Convicts
would be legally at liberty to use violence to evade punishment, and
their use of such violence could not be considered a crime or be made
punishable. What we would have, then, is essentially a trial by com-
bat—if one has the strength to ensure a desirable outcome, then one
is legally protected in obtaining it. Whatever the ideal or the rule
of law may include, it cannot include this, for in such a case the
law would sanction its own effective annulment by those who are
physically able to annul it.[65] We may conclude, then, that the first observation is true: If the state seeks to punish criminals, it must place
them under a legal obligation to submit to the proposed punishment.

This state of affairs in fact prevails in most liberal democracies:
Certain types of behavior are made criminal offenses, with punishments attached; persons suspected of these offenses are tried and, if
they are found guilty, they incur a legal duty to submit to the required punishment. The existence of this duty is shown by the fact
that evading punishment is in most cases an offense in itself, a breach
of the convict's legal duty, for which an additional penalty may be
imposed.[66]

Thus, a state that wishes to punish persons must first put them
under a legal obligation to submit to the proposed punishments. But,
clearly, this legal obligation must also be established as a moral obligation, for we have premised that a legitimate government must impose upon its subjects no legal obligations other than those that also
constitute moral obligations.

We now turn to the second part of the claim. The argument here is
a bit more involved. We are concerned to show that the moral obligation to submit to punishment is not normally included within a subject's moral obligation to obey the law; or, in other words, the right
to punish is not within the state's inherent competence. If the state
is to punish convicts, it must present a special argument establishing their obligation to submit. A state that punished persons without
presenting any such argument would thereby become illegitimate.

One might at first think that our point here could be established
quite easily. We could (one might think) establish that the state has
a right to punish the guilty: This right might be established without
even considering whether the guilty have an obligation to submit.

This obligation (one might suppose) would then follow easily by reason of the logical correlativity of rights and duties: If there is a right to punish, there must be a duty to submit. But it is not so easy. A football tackle has the right (according to the rules of the game) to tackle his opponent—but no one would claim that the opponent has a correlative duty to fall down. So even if we were to concede that the state has a right (in the weak sense of its being morally permissible) to punish the guilty, we could not automatically conclude that the guilty have a duty to submit. What we need to show is that imposing punishment lies within the state's competence—that is, that it is morally permissible for the state to punish *and* morally obligatory for the punishee to submit. This *could* be called establishing the state's "right to punish," but in this case it is a claim-right, which does not follow automatically from the weaker right mentioned above.[67] If hereafter I speak of the state's right to punish, it is to be understood in this weaker sense.

Nor would we do any better even if we were to concede that the punishee has *consented* to a particular punishment, or to a system of punishments.[68] For, when I consent to a certain kind of treatment at your hands, what I am doing is agreeing to hold you harmless if you treat me that way. I do not thereby also promise to cooperate with you in imposing the treatment in question. Our football example makes this clear: If a person, knowing the rules of football and the nature of the game, freely enters into a game of football, she may be taken to have consented to the sort of treatment that football players undergo, and this includes being tackled. But she has not agreed— it would indeed be ridiculous to suppose—that she must fall down when an opponent tries to tackle her. So, similarly, even if a person has given his consent to punishment on the part of the state, it does not follow that he has also obligated himself to submit.

These quick and easy arguments having been shown inadequate, one might, upon a little more thought, suppose that the right to punish (including the correlative duty to submit) falls obviously within the limits of the legitimate state's competence. A state, if it is to be a state, must have a broad competence to command its subjects, and this competence (one might suppose) includes the claim-right to impose punishments. But in most cases it is not so. For we have taken it as a premise that a legitimate state's actions must be limited by certain requirements (listed above); most sorts of punishment, however, turn out to violate one or another of those requirements. Let us consider the relevant requirements one by one.

First, the state must grant its subjects the right to bodily integrity and physical liberty. But imprisonment and capital punishment are violations of physical liberty and integrity. (Corporal punishment, too, falls into this category, as do some more arcane penalties.)

Second, the state must grant its subjects the right to choose their own plans of life and, within broad limits, to act on them. Of course, virtually any governmental action limits to some degree a subject's opportunity to act on a self-chosen plan of life. We cannot apply this right indiscriminately as a veto on government action. But some punishments—in particular, lengthy terms of imprisonment—limit a person's opportunity so severely that they must constitute infringements of this right.

Third, the government must treat its subjects with equal concern and respect. In particular, it must not deliberately make any of its subjects objects of scorn or contempt. But one of the intrinsic functions of punishment is to express the punisher's condemnation of the punishee. Indeed, some would make this expressive function part of the very definition of *punishment*.[69]

The requirement that a government treat its subjects with equal concern and respect is thus the most sweeping with regards to punishment. The previous two requirements would place no bar in the way of some lesser punishments (such as fines), but the present requirement stands in the way of virtually all punishments that the state might propose. The only exceptions are inflictions so mild and insignificant that their reprobative value is nil: These are what Feinberg terms *penalties*, as opposed to punishment proper.[70] A parking ticket might serve as a good example of a mere penalty, since receiving a ticket does not make the unlawful parker into an object of scorn. It may be hard to draw the line between these two categories of penalty and true punishment, but we do not need to: It is enough to say that any punishment that expresses contempt for the punishee lies outside the limits of the state's intrinsic competence.

Thus (with the exception of mere penalties), it is not within the inherent competence of the state to obligate a subject to submit to punishment. If a legitimate state is to impose punishments upon its subjects, it must then present some special considerations showing that the subjects have a moral duty to submit. This establishes the second part of the claim, completing the first argument.

THE SECOND ARGUMENT

The first argument is based, as I have said, on a very strong conception of legitimacy. Some may think that it makes too great a demand on a state. I therefore present this second argument, based on the weaker conception that I have called minimal legitimacy. A minimally legitimate state need not issue only morally obligatory commands, but it must be worthy enough so that one ought not subvert or overthrow it. The claim I seek to prove here varies in only one detail from the claim of the first argument: *If a state that aspires even to minimal legitimacy proposes to punish persons who have been convicted of crimes, it must first establish that they have a moral obligation to submit to the proposed penalties; this obligation, furthermore, cannot be taken for granted as part of a subject's ordinary duty of obedience to a legitimate state, but must be established by additional considerations.*

Let us consider the first part of this claim first. We need to show that our aspiring minimally legitimate state must show that its subjects have an obligation to submit to its punishments. To say the same thing another way: If a state punishes persons who do not have a moral obligation to submit to their punishments, the state thereby loses even minimal legitimacy. This claim certainly holds good with regard to imprisonment, capital punishment, and severe corporal punishment. Indeed, if we remove the honorific designations, we see that "imprisonment" refers to something much akin to kidnapping; "capital punishment" seems to be a form of juridical murder; and "corporal punishment" bears a curious resemblance to assault and battery. Now, if a group of people approach me with the avowed intent and apparent ability to kidnap, murder, or assault me, certainly I may exercise my right to self-defense. This is indeed the paradigm case for the exercise of this right. And the imminent harm is so great that I would be justified in using a considerable degree of force to incapacitate the attackers. Moreover, bystanders may join me in repulsing the attackers and are indeed to be commended if they do so. What difference does it make that the attackers wear uniforms and call themselves sheriffs or police officers? By itself, none. The right to self-defense is not automatically suspended by the mere fact that the attacker is a police officer. Thus, unless we can produce reasons to the contrary, if a government tries to imprison, execute, or corporally punish any of its subjects, the subjects generally may join those under attack in resisting the government by force.

Now one might object: A person can resist punishment without subverting the government. Indeed, in single cases, it is so. It is otherwise if the government *systematically* tries to impose such punishments. If an attempt were made to prevent each such punishment, the enforcement of law would in effect be prevented—that is, the government would be subverted. Moreover, it would be permissible as a matter of self-defense to go straight to the root and disable the whole penal mechanism of such a state. If it were only a matter of an occasional imprisonment or execution now and then, perhaps self-defense and defense of others would entitle us only to resist each punishment as it occurred. But when there exists a conspiracy that systematically imposes such unacceptable treatment on people, self-defense and defense of others entitle us to break up the whole conspiracy. The fact that this conspiracy is called a government in no way alters the case.

A persistent questioner might press this objection further: Couldn't we disable the prison system without disrupting the rest of the government? Well, this is possible, but just barely. In practice, it is hard to make such a clean separation: One would want to withhold taxes that support the penal system but not those that support other government functions. One would want to boycott court proceedings that could lead to imprisonment or execution, but respect other proceedings. And even if the separation can be made, the part that remains in existence would have no coercive powers, and so would no longer be a government at all. Even in this rump of the state, the resisters could apply the threat of force until the rump government explicitly renounces the sort of afflictive penalties that had been in use. In sum, a state imposing such penalties without establishing the punishee's moral obligation to submit is not minimally legitimate.

The essentials of the foregoing argument can be found in Hobbes (though he draws quite a different conclusion). His words are so striking as to be worth quoting at length:

> There be some Rights, which no man can be understood by any words, or other signes, to have abandoned, or transferred. As first a man cannot lay down the right of resisting them, that assault him by force, to take away his life. . . . The same may be sayd of Wounds, and Chayns, and Imprisonment.[71]

> But in case a great many men together, have already resisted the Soveraign Power unjustly, or committed some Capitall crime, for which every one of them expecteth death, whether have they not the Liberty then to joyn together, and assist, and defend one another? Certainly they have: For they but defend their lives, which the Guilty may as well do, as the Innocent. Their bearing of Arms . . . if it be onely to defend their persons . . . is not unjust at all.[72]

Hobbes would thus justify a revolt on the part of those condemned to severe punishments. It seems that his conclusion would indeed be right, if there were no moral duty on the part of criminals to submit to their assigned punishments.

(Hobbes would say that *only* the condemned are justified in revolting; bystanders may not assist them, as I have suggested they can. But this does not effect my argument: The only result would be a smaller revolutionary force. In any case, Hobbes's restriction on the participation of bystanders is based on one of the less plausible aspects of his theory.)[73]

If, then, a government aspiring to minimal legitimacy wants to impose the punishments of imprisonment, execution, or corporal punishment upon any of its subjects, it must show that their moral right to self-defense does not apply, or, in other words, that the affected subjects have a moral duty not to resist the proposed punishment.

One might object here that before resorting to revolution, subjects ought first petition the legislature, or other authorities, for an end to the unacceptable practice; one might claim, hence, that a government retains minimal legitimacy so long as there seems to be a reasonable chance of peacefully persuading the government to abandon its course of action. Yet in this case irreversible harm is threatened: One's life's work may be ruined by a term in prison; one may fail to recover from the physical injuries of corporal punishment; and those who are executed cannot be made whole. Thus the resort to force seems justified: At any rate, subjects would be justified in subverting such a government by passive resistance, *unless* the government can show that those whom it condemns to punishment have a moral obligation not to resist (that is, to submit).

The argument so far holds only for afflictive punishments—imprisonment, execution, corporal punishment, and the like. We can broaden it, however, by once again using the concept of equal respect. Now, if a person is treated disrespectfully, she would not usually be justified in using force against her detractor. Nor would contemptuous treatment by the state seem to justify violent revolution. It may indeed be so in single instances, but if a government systematically holds up a class of subjects as objects of contempt, it would not be morally wrong for its subjects to engage in large-scale passive resistance—and even those who are not the objects of the state's contempt might justifiably join the victims in resisting. This may seem like an extreme claim, but one must consider what is at stake: The person's moral personality is being attacked. If a single unjust law were passed in an otherwise just state, the citizen might disobey only that law, without trying to undermine the state as a whole; but if the state declares a class of subjects to be fit objects of contempt, not worthy of their fellow citizens' equal concern, it is another matter. Consideration of actual cases may here prove persuasive: South Africa treats its black subjects this way;[74] Nazi Germany, even before the Holocaust, adopted policies aimed at subjecting the Jews to scorn and contempt; and one could extend the list to unfortunate lengths. Certainly such policies would justify large-scale passive resistance sufficient to prevent the government from functioning. If the claim is granted, then a government that systematically holds up a class of subjects as objects of contempt is not even minimally legitimate. But, as noted before, punishment holds up the punishee as an object of contempt. A state, then, that systematically punishes some subjects would fail to be even minimally legitimate, *unless* it can show that those subject to punishment have a moral obligation not to resist.

In thus broadening the argument to cover almost all punishments, we have, I recognize, deprived it of some force. One might well object: The government of the United States once subjected its black population to contemptuous treatment in a systematic way; yet it would have been wrong, even in the days of slavery, to subvert the United States government. It seems that this objection must be conceded: Yet one could hardly blame the slaves if *they* did what they could to subvert the government that enslaved them or at the very least to subvert its ability to govern *them*. In that case, the United States government, though in some ways legitimate, lacked even minimal legitimacy with regard to the enslaved population. And this is sufficient for present purposes: If the government systematically punishes those who have been convicted of crimes, it holds them up to contempt. They may resist the government with the aim of subverting its ability to govern them, for (from their point of view) it is not even minimally legitimate, *unless* some special argument is presented to show that they have a moral obligation to submit to the proposed punishments.

Thus, if a government aspiring to minimal legitimacy proposes to make systematic use of any but the most innocuous punishments, it must show that those subjected to the punishments have a moral obligation not to resist them. This completes the first half of our argument.

It remains to be shown that this moral obligation is not included within the subject's general obligation to obey the law. But this is easy: The punishments in question impinge on the basic rights of those who are punished. Surely their political obligation cannot require them simply to forfeit the basic rights of self-defense and equal respect. One might say that a person should endure such things for the sake of peace and stability. This is quite evident from real-world cases: No one, surely, would think that a mistaken conviction gives the innocent convict a right to overthrow the government. But we are not dealing with an occasional unintentional infliction, but a calculated, systematic deprivation of basic rights. Our ordinary obligation to obey the law cannot include the obligation to accept such treatment.

This completes the second part of our argument: If a state that aspires to minimal legitimacy proposes to make systematic use of any but the most innocuous punishments, it must show that those subjected to the punishments have a moral obligation to submit to them; and this obligation cannot be part of the subject's usual moral obligation to obey the law.

AN OBJECTION

Despite the foregoing arguments, one might still doubt the conclusion. For (as an objector might argue) some punishments, such as death or long-term imprisonment, seem so harsh that no one could ever be expected voluntarily to accept them. Picture a conscientious person—as conscientious as could be desired. Suppose that she has been justly convicted of a serious crime, for which she is now remorseful. Still, if she faces the death penalty, or fifty years in prison, we could scarcely think ill of her if she took advantage of a chance to evade her sentence; not everyone can be a Socrates. Nor can we expect a state to forgo the use of harsh punishments, at least not under commonly prevailing conditions. There must, of course, be safeguards. These harsh punishments should not be imposed arbitrarily or capriciously, but only in accordance with the rule of law: The crime and its penalty must be announced in advance, the criminalized behavior must be such as a reasonable person could be expected to avoid, the accused must be afforded a fair trial with access to counsel, and so on. Let us use the phrase *extremely harsh punishment* to refer to punishments so severe that no one is morally obligated to submit to them. The existence of extremely harsh punishments indeed enables law-abiding persons to live in peace; they therefore have a moral obligation to the state not to interfere in the administration of such sanctions and, when called on, to assist in imposing them on convicts. In other words (according to this objection), a state might be legitimate, even though it imposes punishments on some convicts to which the convicts have no moral obligation to submit.

The supporter of my view is hence put into a dilemma: Either the state must forswear the use of extremely harsh penalties, or else it must fall short of legitimacy. This dilemma, I maintain—when properly explained—expresses the true state of things. Yet the state is not as helpless as the dilemma might make it seem, as I shall contend.

Let us first look at the first horn of the dilemma. Human nature being what it is, could a state function without extremely harsh penalties? Perhaps. The main claim of this section says that the state may not simply impose extremely harsh punishments on anyone. It may, however, use extremely harsh punishments as a means of enforcing more reasonable penalties. In particular, if after conviction the offender has an opportunity to undergo a moderate punishment, it is permissible to impose an extremely harsh punishment on those who refuse. I argue below, for example, that community-service sanctions should form a significant part of the legal penalties for crime. (See Chapter 6, section 4.) Such penalties are not beyond what one might expect a conscientious person to undertake. Indeed, a conscientious person who had been convicted (perhaps of a crime committed in a moment of passion) would undertake her community service with minimal supervision. But if a convict gives reason to think she will not comply with such a penalty, the state may impose custodial measures—including imprisonment, if necessary—as a means of enforcement, to make sure that she does comply. Thus a recalcitrant convict might find herself subjected to a long term of imprisonment, not as a punishment for crime, but as a means of preventing her from evading her punishment. In other words, a state may under this scheme use extremely harsh measures, yet it must give all convicts an opportunity to avoid such measures.

It may be that such extremely harsh measures, used in this way, are enough to ensure social order. Yet the remorseful and conscientious convict need never be subject to penalties or enforcement measures that go beyond what one might expect a reasonable person to accept. And even vicious convicts under this scheme still enjoy the rights assured to them by our conception of legitimacy, although a condition is placed on their exercise: That is to say, they enjoy these rights only if they submit to the lesser penalty. If this scheme offers a reasonable option, why should a state ever impose such harsh measures on remorseful and conscientious convicts? To do so would gratuitously violate the rights that a legitimate state must accord to its subjects. A state thus calls its legitimacy into question if it does not at least give its convicts an opportunity to avoid extremely harsh measures.

Yet—to turn to the second horn of the dilemma—in extreme circumstances a state may be justified in imposing extremely harsh penalties on its convicts, without giving them an opportunity to undertake a less harsh punishment. I argue below that this is the case when we must deal with the most vicious crimes and recalcitrant criminals. (See Chapter 7, section 5.) But though such penalties may be justified (under certain circumstances), a state that uses them falls short of the ideal of legitimacy.

This point can be seen more clearly in relation to the two lines of thought that underlie the present conception of legitimacy. First, there is the idea that a legitimate state has the moral authority to resolve disputes. This authority must encompass disputes between the state itself and one or more of its subjects. A legitimate state, acting as resolver of disputes, must present to the dissatisfied party a morally sufficient reason why he should accept the proposed solution. (As we have said, the dissatisfied party may not find the proffered reason acceptable, but still a reason must be given that takes his claims seriously.) Now, if the state proposes to punish someone, we usually have a dispute between the state and the person it proposes to punish, for she typically wishes to avoid being punished. The state in its dispute-resolutive capacity must resolve this dispute, giving a morally sufficient reason to the dissatisfied party. But if the state imposes punishments that the victim is not morally obligated to accept, it must admit that it has failed in its function as resolver of disputes. It has merely had recourse to force to impose the solution on the unwilling punishee. It may, of course, be necessary for the state to resort to such use of force. But the state that takes such measures falls short of this aspect of the ideal of legitimacy.

Alternatively, our second line of thought conceives of a legitimate state as one that respects the autonomy of its competent adult subjects. If it wishes to control them, it must do so in ways that respect their status as autonomous moral persons; in other words, it must control their behavior, in the first instance, by giving morally sufficient reasons why they should do what the state wants them to do. But in imposing extremely harsh punishments, the state admits that it can give no such reason.

It may be suggested that criminals are ipso facto not autonomous persons. That is true, but then in the strict sense, no one is. A criminal's departure from the ideal of autonomy does not in itself justify extremely harsh measures any more than does a similar departure on the part of any of the rest of us.

As before, the state may on occasion be justified in imposing extremely harsh punishments on convicts, that is (as defined above), punishments to which no one is morally obligated to submit. Still, in justifiably imposing such punishments, the state has departed from the ideal of legitimacy.

A state that imposes extremely harsh penalties upon some of its subjects is, as Locke might say, making war upon them. What it does to them is akin to what it does to enemy forces in war. If the war is just, we cannot blame the state for undertaking it; but neither can we claim that making war on enemy forces is a way of exercising legitimate authority over them. The war on crime is carried out by imposing on convicts penalties they have no obligation to accept—penalties that they might justifiably resist, if they can; penalties that apparently violate their basic rights. This may be a just "war," but it is no part of the practice of legitimate government.[75]

It must be conceded that a state does not lose legitimacy at a single stroke. If a state occasionally penalizes convicts with measures that the convicts have no moral obligation to accept, the state is not instantly turned from legitimate to illegitimate. But if the practice becomes more common, the state's legitimacy is called more seriously into question.

And what if no argument at all can be found to establish a moral obligation to submit to punishment? I consider this unlikely. Indeed, I offer one such argument in Part Two. But if in fact no such argument could be found, should governments stop punishing lawbreakers? No, that would hardly be conceivable. But in punishing lawbreakers who have no obligation to submit, the government would be conceding that it cannot achieve the ideal of legitimacy.

It seems clear, then, that an adequate theory of punishment must establish a duty to submit to just punishments. But at this point it is still not clear how far this duty extends. If we are dealing with a criminal, must she merely submit to punishment imposed upon her, or must she, like the penitent, seek out punishment whenever it is deserved? Must she plead guilty in order to secure such a punishment, or may she try to escape conviction in court? If so, ought she perhaps punish herself outside the legal system? Some of these we will answer as we go along; others we will leave for future inquiry.

THE RATIONALE FOR SUBMITTING TO PUNISHMENT

I have just argued that any state that aspires to legitimacy must establish that its subjects have a moral *obligation* for submitting to the punishments that it proposes to inflict upon (some of) them. I now argue that the state must also show that the subjects have a *rationale* for submitting to these punishments.

Indeed, given our present conception of justification (see section 1), a rationale must be given as an integral part of a justification of punishment, or of anything. The state here claims to impose upon some citizens a moral obligation to submit to punishment. This claim must be justified. The state may show that requiring submission to punishment is indeed within the state's competence, yet this is not enough: even when acting within its competence, the state must have some respectable purpose that will be accomplished by the convict's submission to punishment.

This requirement is particularly connected with the fact that the state bears a heavy responsibility to the public. A private citizen, by contrast with the state, may act arbitrarily and capriciously, so long as she does not violate the rights of others. If it strikes her fancy, she may stand on her head and whistle "Dixie," and it does not matter whether she can give a good reason, or any reason, for doing so. But the state must avoid such arbitrary and capricious action (as, in general, anyone bearing responsibility toward others must avoid arbitrary and capricious action). And one refutes a charge of capriciousness by showing that one's actions have a respectable rationale. So, even if we concede that the state has the moral capacity to obligate subjects to submit to punishment, it would be arbitrary and capricious (and therefore irresponsible and forbidden) for the state to exercise this capacity unless it could show that there is some rationale for convicts to submit. One must show, indeed, that the *punishee* has a rationale: The state's rationale for imposing the punishment may not ipso facto provide one for the convict.

And in fact, our system of penal law reflects this supposition that there is—or must be—some rationale for convicts to submit to punishment. For within our system, submission to punishment is considered a praiseworthy act, particularly if the convict submits wholeheartedly and conscientiously, going beyond a minimal fulfillment of her legal obligation. Such a convict is called "model prisoner," and this designation has legal consequences, such as an early parole. But nothing could be considered praiseworthy if it were thought to be pointless. Our system of penal law, therefore, operates on the supposition that submitting to punishment is not pointless or, in other words, that there is a rationale for it.

4. Civil Disobedience

Civil disobedience stands as an exception to the trends I have just noted in philosophical discussions of punishment. For (as I have already remarked) writers on civil disobedience usually hold that those who break the law for this purpose ought to submit to punishment, and, moreover, these writers seem to expect that civil disobedients, unlike common criminals, will often be willing to fulfill this duty of submission.

I claim that these facts argue further for a general duty to submit to a just punishment. The only alternative is that the civil disobedient has some special duty that does not apply to other lawbreakers. But what sort of duty could this be? If I am justified in violating Statute XYZ—say, the act levying taxes for the Mexican War—as an act of civil disobedience, the very considerations that justify nonpayment would also appear to justify violation of the statute that would have me punished for nonpayment. (After all, these two statutes are probably just two clauses of the same statute.) Indeed, if I submit to punishment, am I not symbolically admitting that what I did was wrong after all? Wouldn't this negate the act of civil disobedience? If civil disobedients feel that it is important for them to submit to punishment, it can only be because they believe that convicts in general should submit to punishment. This point can be seen more clearly if we contrast civil disobedience with other justifiable violations of law. Suppose I steal a boat to save a drowning person, or I privately practice my religion in violation of a law that unjustly forbids it. No one suggests that I should give myself up for punishment in either of these cases. Why in the case of civil disobedience?

The usual answer involves the fact that civil disobedience is a public, symbolic act. In committing this act, the civil disobedient says, "You, my fellow citizens, are committing an extreme injustice. You are violating the basic principles of justice which we hold in common, and on which our system of justice rests. I call upon you, with all the means at my disposal, to cease." The civil disobedient must then submit to punishment in order to reaffirm her loyalty to the existing legal system, in spite of her disobedient act. If this loyalty were in doubt, she would not have the right or the status to appeal as one citizen to another, nor to invoke shared basic principles. If she were to evade or resist punishment, she would look like an ordinary lawbreaker, or perhaps a revolutionary; her act of civil disobedience would no longer serve the end that justified it.

But this usual answer itself presupposes a general obligation to submit to punishment. In the absence of such an obligation, the usual answer does not build a very strong case for submitting to punishment after civil disobedience. The civil disobedient, after all, has already shown her loyalty to the legal system by consistently obeying the law up to the time of her act of disobedience. (If not, she should not be committing civil disobedience: People will only say, "She's just breaking the law again.") The civilly disobedient act may itself involve several distinct violations of the law. One more need not make a great difference in the act's symbolic message. The decision whether to submit to punishment would then rest on the same grounds as the original decision to disobey the law. In some cases, evading punishment might make a more effective symbolic statement; in other cases, submission might have a better effect. One might, for example, refuse to cooperate in one's own trial, rather than pleading guilty in the manner of the classical civil disobedient, in order to show one's contempt for a contemptible part of the law. This is how things are, at least, if there is no general duty to submit to punishment. But we do think that those who commit civil disobedience ought to forthrightly accept their punishment. We must therefore assume that there is a duty to submit to a legitimate punishment. The civil disobedient says, "Although I am willing to violate this one statute, I am also willing to undertake the obligation that is incurred by those who disobey the law, namely, the obligation to submit to punishment."

Our observations on civil disobedience underscore the main point of this chapter: Any adequate theory of punishment must establish that the punishee ought to submit to the penalties it proposes for him. If it does not say why he should put up with it, he probably should not.

CHAPTER 2

━━━━━━

Two Paradigms of Punishment

CHAPTER 1 has established that in a legitimate state a person being punished has a moral duty to submit to the proposed punishment. The punishee, of course, may or may not take this duty seriously. Corresponding to these two possibilities, there are two paradigms of punishment. In one paradigm the punisher is active and the punishee passive, or even resistant; in the other the punishee, recognizing her duty to submit, is the active party. I will refer to these, respectively, as the *Paradigm of Legal Punishment* and the *Paradigm of the Conscientious Punishee*, or, for short, the legal paradigm and the conscientious paradigm. I intend the name "Paradigm of Legal Punishment" to be not so much descriptive as diagnostic; it tells what I take to be the origin of the paradigm. A more descriptive name would be "The Paradigm of the Forced Punishment of the Unrepentant Punishee," which the reader should keep in mind to prevent misunderstanding. But I think the phrase *legal punishment* is, if anything, more evocative of the features that I include under the corresponding paradigm. In this chapter I explore these two paradigms, especially the conscientious paradigm. Sections 1 and 2 consider the nature and history of the two paradigms and document in particular the fact that the conscientious paradigm has been relatively neglected in modern times. It is, nonetheless, more important than the legal paradigm for the theory of punishment, as I argue in section 3. Finally, in section 4, I consider what kinds of theory could and could not provide a justification for punishment along the lines of the conscientious paradigm. Now, few will doubt that the discussion has been dominated by the legal paradigm, but many may deny that this amounts to a distortion. Indeed, I expect that some readers will deny that what I describe under the heading of the "Paradigm of the Conscientious Punishee" is punishment at all. So the most important part of the argument of this chapter aims at explaining why the conscientious paradigm is in fact a paradigm and ought to be taken as such by philosophers who discuss punishment.

1. The Two Paradigms

First of all, what do I mean by *paradigm*? Let us take as an example some class or group of things—say, automobiles. A paradigmatic automobile must, first of all, be a sort of automobile that one would expect most people who are familiar with cars to know about: for example, a Model-T Ford, not a Marmon. Second, a paradigmatic automobile must typify automobiles in one or more of three ways: (1) Our paradigmatic automobile may closely resemble a large proportion of existing automobiles. I call this a *standard* case. The Model-T is an example of this, as opposed to, say, a Stanley Steamer. Note that this part of the definition allows for a concept to have more than one standard case. For example, coins and bills are standard cases of currency, as opposed to cigarettes, glass beads, and other things that have been similarly used. (2) Our paradigmatic automobile may be a very good one; I call this an *ideal* case. Most readers can probably supply their own example of an ideal automobile, or the opposite. Finally, (3) a paradigmatic automobile may conform closely to the laws and regularities that apply to automobiles: We may call this a *regular* case. A car getting 120 miles on a gallon of fuel (approximately 50 kilometers per liter) would be highly irregular, though perhaps ideal. A regular automobile would be the kind one would want as a demonstrator for a class of aspiring car mechanics. A paradigm of the concept *car* is, then, a description of a paradigmatic case.[1] This concept of paradigm is close to the concept of a *stereotype* as introduced by Hilary Putnam in "The Meaning of 'Meaning.'" If we think of a paradigm as a stereotype, then knowing the paradigm is part of knowing the meaning of the associated word.[2]

DEFINING FEATURES OF THE TWO PARADIGMS

Under the Paradigm of Legal Punishment I want to include cases like the following: Green commits a crime (say, robs a bank) and tries to make good his escape with the money; but he is caught by the police, tried, convicted, sentenced to a term of years in prison, and taken there quite against his will. He would escape if he thought it possible. Under the Paradigm of the Conscientious Punishee I include cases like this one: Hampshire commits what he takes to be a sin and, out of remorse, does penance as prescribed by his religion, which consists of saying certain prayers and doing charitable work. (Perhaps Hampshire visits the sick and lonely.) The conscientious paradigm also includes secular cases: Ives, for example, commits a nonviolent crime (say, embezzlement) for which the prescribed penalty is public-service work. She has cooked the books so well that the money has not even been missed, and she feels sure that she has gotten away with the crime. Still, she finds herself feeling remorseful; she turns herself in, is tried and convicted. She expresses a desire to serve her sentence by working without pay in a hospital that serves poor patients. The judge so decrees, and thereafter Ives appears regularly to perform the allotted service. No enforcement mechanism needs to be invoked in her case. (Perhaps she even finds this work so satisfying that she continues as a volunteer after her term is finished.)[3] These two paradigms were noted and distinguished already by Thomas Aquinas, who uses the terms *poena simpliciter* ("punishment pure and simple") for the legal paradigm and *poena satisfactoria* ("expiatory punishment") for the conscientious paradigm.[4]

The legal paradigm is quite familiar to most students of punishment or criminology, the conscientious paradigm less so. I therefore devote a few words to the latter.

The conscientious paradigm is meant to be a generalization of the notion of penance, broadened to include secular as well as religious cases. Of course, not all cases of religious penance will serve equally well as examples, so we must look a little more closely at the varieties of penance. One important distinction can be made by applying Lawrence Kohlberg's three levels of moral development. (Kohlberg actually divides each level into two stages, yielding the widely known six stages; but we do not need such fine distinctions here.)[5] The first level—first in time, and also conceptually simplest—is the *preconventional*. The idea here is merely to appease God: The penitent does whatever it takes to assuage God's anger, or to make Him refrain from punishing. Preconventional penance is thus a sort of cosmic boot licking or apple polishing—not the sort of thing to be made part of the paradigm. The second level is *conventional*. At this stage God is conceived of as having laid down principles of behavior by which God Himself is bound, along with human beings. These principles, however, are not (or not completely) internalized by human beings. At this level, believers accept principles that declare how sinners can conciliate God. They ascribe to these principles not merely an instrumental value (as at Level 1) but also intrinsic value: They are thought of as correct principles. Typical here are lists of possible sins, together with the penance for each type of sin that will appease God and turn aside the punishment. No longer must the sinner grovel, as at the first level, but, having done the appropriate penance, she knows that she is entitled to forgiveness. Since the basis here is conventional, no particular motivation is required: Even an unrepentant sinner, desiring merely to avoid punishment, can succeed according to this view. We find many Jewish and Catholic authorities at this level.[6] It is precisely this commercial aspect of penance at this level that led many religious thinkers—most notably those of the Reformation—to object to this conception, Protestants largely abandoning the concept altogether.

Many Jews and Catholics, however, went beyond this to work out a third level of penance, the *postconventional and principled level*. To do penance on this level, mere desire to avoid punishment is not enough; the penitent must act from a feeling of remorse, the awareness that he has done wrong. Catholics distinguish this feeling as *contrition*, as opposed to the more selfish motivations for penance that are called *attrition*.[7] A striking example of this view can be seen in an observation attributed to Jacob Isaac, the "Seer" of Lublin:

> Said the Lubliner: "The Talmud declares that Rabbi Elisha ben Abuya became an unbeliever. A former disciple sought to persuade him to repent, and Rabbi Elisha answered, 'I heard a Voice from Heaven calling: "Repent, ye transgressors,—except Elisha." ' "
>
> The Lubliner made the comment: "If Elisha had been but wise, this was his opportunity to become the greatest of all men. Believing that his repentance was unacceptable, and therefore expecting no reward from it, had he returned to the service of the Lord despite this, his service would have been most pleasing in the eyes of the Lord."[8]

The Seer's counsel is admittedly rather extreme; in reality, remorse as well as fear of punishment will typically be combined in a sincere penitent on this level. As to the penance itself, on this level it is selected not at God's pleasure, nor just by convention, but in order to uphold some divine principle that has been violated by the sin. Very typical is the idea that sin has upset the order of the universe, and one does as penance whatever is necessary to restore it. Here we have, for example, the Roman Catholic notion of penance as restoration of *ordo debitus,* and the Jewish mystical idea of *tikkun olam* (rectification of the world).[9] It is this highest level of penance that I am taking as a paradigmatic case of punishment.

Returning from this excursion into religious doctrine, we should recall that it was a voyage for study—anthropology, one might say— not a pilgrimage. We find, among the adherents of some religions, morally significant practices that are not essentially theological and that can have important secular applications (as will be seen). Can the notion of penance survive its separation from theology? Certainly, it can. Just the Seer of Lublin's rather subversive remark by itself makes this clear. In a more prosaic way, however, the notion of the restoration of order, or rectification of the world, is what allows us to make sense of penance as a secularized concept: If religious penance is the restoration of the sacred order, we can equally well conceive of civic penance as restoration of the civic order (if only we can say what the civic order is).

In particular, the validity of these observations is not meant to hinge—and I do not think that it does hinge—on the existence of a Deity.

Indeed, not only is it possible to apply the concept of penance to secular purposes, but I would claim that it actually has been so applied. I argue (Chapter 5) that criminal sanctions consisting of community service are best understood as acts of restoring the civic order, and hence as secular penances.

The Paradigm of the Conscientious Punishee has also anti-theistic antecedents, for it can be thought of as a model of unalienated punishment—unalienated in the same sense that the young Marx uses when he speaks of alienated and unalienated labor.[10] As with Marx, we can see in this conception the negation of Hegel, who says (as we have already seen) that "retribution is *inflicted* on the criminal, and so it has the look of an alien destiny, not intrinsically his own."[11] Under the conscientious paradigm, on the other hand, the offender sees the punishment as intrinsically his own, not inflicted but undertaken. If anyone is to see punishment as something other than pointless suffering, it will be by appropriating the punishment and making it a meaningful part of one's own life. I hasten to add— not of one's ideal life, but of the best life that a person can think of, given that she has gotten herself into a bad situation.

From these cases and considerations I discern the following seven pairs of features, which define the two paradigms of punishment:

Paradigm of Legal Punishment	Paradigm of the Conscientious Punishee
(1) Punishment consists of treatment that people typically wish to avoid (e.g., it is unpleasant, bad, painful, etc.).	Punishment consists of things that people often willingly accept or choose for themselves, and it is not particularly unpleasant, bad, painful, etc.
(2) It is undertaken at the *initiative of someone other* than the punishee, who is	It is *undertaken by the punishee himself or herself*, who is
(3) *unrepentant*, and	*repentant* and *motivated by reasons of conscience*
(4) *wishes to avoid* the punishment	to *accept* the punishment
(5) and is *passive* with respect to the things that constitute the punishment (i.e., the punishment is inflicted upon the punishee).	and is *active* with respect to the things that constitute the punishment.
(6) The *rationale* for punishment is *retribution* or *deterrence*, or perhaps reform.	The *rationale* for punishment is *expiation* or *reconciliation*.
(7) The *typical* punishment is *legal* punishment.	The *typical* punishment is *religious*.

The features are united within each paradigm by the fact (already mentioned) that in one case the punisher, in the other case the punishee, takes the active role.

I do not mean to suggest that all cases of punishment, or even a majority, fall exactly under one of these paradigms. On the contrary, many cases partake somewhat of both. (For example, a religious person may say penitential prayers at the instigation of a priest and may be motivated not only by a desire for reconciliation with God but also by a suspicion that an unreconciled God will send him to hell.) I put forward the paradigms as important conceptions for understanding punishment, and as such they apply to nearly all cases.

Some of these features call for comment.

(1) Imprisonment and confiscation of money—typical legal punishments—are things that most people generally try to avoid. On the other hand, many people willingly do charitable work, say prayers, and engage in public service. These are, moreover, not particularly unpleasant, bad, or painful things to do. In the next chapter I argue

that they are often not disvaluable at all; but even if, for now, I were to concede that charitable work, prayer, public service, and other penitential activities are always or usually unpleasant (or bad or painful), still it is not for the sake of the unpleasantness that we engage in them. (I discuss this further within a few pages.)

(2) This pair is clear enough, so we go on.

(3) By "reasons of conscience" I refer to whatever sort of moral motivation one takes to be proper. This might be the Kantian notion of acting out of duty, but it might equally well be the Thomistic notion of acting out of friendship toward God, or yet again the notion of acting out of sympathy with one's fellow humans, or whatever. The corresponding proviso with regard to legal punishment (not indicated in the table) is that the punisher should act from reasons of conscience.

(4) This item is fairly obvious.

(5) We might restate the active–passive distinction thus: According to the legal paradigm, punishment is something *done to* the punishee; according to the conscientious paradigm, it is something *done by* the punishee. For example, a typical criminal is taken to prison; or, in former days (and, unfortunately, sometimes even now), a prisoner may be whipped. Compare these with the sanctions mentioned under the conscientious paradigm.

It is important to distinguish the distinction made here from that made under item 2. There we were concerned with how it comes about that someone is punished. What we are concerned with here (in feature 5) is the nature of the sanction itself.

(6) I include retribution here despite some uncertainty as to what it is.[12] Expiation and reconciliation are discussed further momentarily.

(7) Finally, the reader should note the qualifier *typical* inserted in the two final features of the paradigms. As I have already mentioned, there are examples of nonreligious punishment that fall under the conscientious paradigm, as well as examples of nonlegal punishment that fall under the legal paradigm (for instance, the punishment of children). But the spheres of law and religion provide the standard examples for the two paradigms and are, in a sense, their home turf.

INTERCONNECTIONS AMONG THE DEFINING FEATURES

As I have said, the keynote of the paradigms is the passivity or activity of the punishee. These concepts hold each paradigm together. Activity is expressed directly in the fact that punishment under the conscientious paradigm is undertaken by the punishee herself (feature 2) and involves actively doing things, rather than passively undergoing them. Moreover, when the punishee is active, I have assumed (in the paradigm case) that he or she is properly motivated: motivated, that is, by reasons of conscience, and not, for example, by a mere desire to look good, or a fondness for prison life.

Passivity is connected with the legal sphere (feature 7) because the law is the primary coercive institution in contemporary society— that is, the institution most likely to impose punishment on people who do not actively seek it out for themselves. As, indeed, it must be: One of the functions of government is the maintenance of order among people with disorderly tendencies. We may be concerned with *social* or *moral* order. It would scarcely be possible to maintain social order without recourse to the threat of punishment imposed upon people who have not asked for it. (Brainwashing might also work, but it is less desirable.) And if government is to maintain the moral order, it must make sure that citizens flourish in accord with their deserts (or lack of them). This requirement means that many undeserving persons must make sacrifices if they are flourishing beyond what they deserve. Will they make these sacrifices voluntarily? Not likely. Most of them will need to be coerced by the government, or at least prodded. Hence, in most cases a person undergoing legal punishment will be passive.

The case is different if we consider religious penalties, simply because in contemporary Western societies religious authorities have no coercive power. This is of course not a defining feature of religion; in other times and places religious authorities have had tremendous coercive power. But here and now religious institutions are organized on a voluntary basis. Hence, if punishment is to take place under religious auspices, it must be undertaken by the punishee, who is thus active. (In line with the highest conception of penance, I omit the possibility that God punishes those sinners who do not punish themselves; to the extent that religionists believe this to be true, they are not actively punishing themselves, but are being coerced into it.) Religion is, in fact, the most important contemporary institution under which people actively seek out self-punishment. (Other voluntary associations sometimes have systems of penalties, but such associations are less important, and the penalties are more often inflicted by some official, such as a baseball umpire.) The only thing that might compare would be a purely moral self-punishment. This would, indeed, be a better example of actively undertaken punishment, if we had any examples fitting unambiguously into the category. But we do not.

This distinction enables us now easily to connect the fact that the conscientious punishee wishes to accept the punishment whereas the legal punishee typically wants to avoid it. Obviously, legal punishment could not serve its deterrent function unless most criminals wished to avoid it. And if criminals were generally willing to accept their own punishment, we would not even need a coercive legal order to impose it upon them. On the other hand, punishment in a noncoercive context would not take place unless the punishee was willing to accept it.

Perhaps the most important connection is that between the rationale for punishment and the badness of punishment. The rationales listed in feature 6 for the legal paradigm require the punishment, according to this paradigm, to be unpleasant, bad, painful, or otherwise disvaluable, whereas the rationales for the punishment of the conscientious punishee call for, if anything, a nonpainful punishment.

This connection is easy to see for the rationales of retribution and deterrence. Retribution, by definition, involves some kind of loss to the person from whom it is exacted. One might suspect that deterrence could be accomplished without pain, but I am using *deter* and its cognates in their usual, etymological sense—that is, to deter is to *frighten someone away* from a contemplated course of action, which can be done only by the threat of consequences that the person would rather avoid.[13]

It might be thought odd that I associate reform with unpleasantness. Reformatory legal punishment is needed in order to reform those who do not choose to reform of their own accord. They, indeed, usually think they are just fine the way they are and need only to refine their criminal skills so as to avoid detection in the future. So this reform is imposed upon them against their wills, and it is therefore bound to be unpleasant.

On the other hand, why is there no connection between pain and expiation or reconciliation? To some people the word *expiation* may call to mind religious sects of flagellants who expiate their sins by whipping themselves or, at any rate, by milder but still unpleasant undertakings. This certainly is one way of expiating. But I would argue that it is far from the only way, and not the best way, of expiating one's wrongdoings or of achieving reconciliation.

First, expiation. *Expiation* suggests purging oneself of guilt or evil, propitiating the higher authorities, or both. To say how one might best purify oneself of guilt or evil requires more moral psychology than I can go into here. But there would certainly seem to be better ways than the self-administration of pain or harm. The idea behind this sort of expiation is, apparently, a desire to destroy or harm the

evil part of oneself; or perhaps the guilty party is applying to himself the same sort of behavioral conditioning by which people train
dogs to avoid unwanted behavior. In either case, it would seem better
to examine oneself and one's motives in having acted badly, and to
engage in spiritual exercises that might change these motives. If this
self-examination succeeds, the evil inclination is eliminated or reduced, and one's outward behavior is improved. A remorseful robber
might, for example, go out and see the misery caused by robbery. He
might analyze himself to see if his robbery was serving any neurotic
function. He might spend time aiding victims of robberies, knowing
that this would give him a vested interest in maintaining the security of property, a project that he would then be less likely to undo
by going out and robbing people. All these things would, we hope,
make the robber take less delight in robbery and would make him
less likely to rob in the future. They may be strenuous or difficult to
carry out, and this strenuousness is important. But pain plays no role.

The other part of expiation is propitiation. The expiator hopes to
make the higher authorities look upon her more favorably and abandon any plans to punish or harm her. The sight of someone flogging
herself might, indeed, accomplish this. But this approach is rather
simple-minded. "I'll flog myself, O Great One, so as to spare you the
necessity of doing it!" It is hard to believe that an enlightened or
admirable ruler would prefer this sort of propitiation. Better for the
propitiator to make strenuous and extraordinary efforts to promote
the goals of the authorities. If the authorities are venal, bribes are
in order. (In the religious sphere, these are called sacrifices.) But in
the ideal case, which is most important for our consideration, these
goals are of a higher order. This ideal is best expressed by the prophet
Isaiah, who speaks of a fast that will propitiate God:

> Why have we fasted, and thou seest it not?
> Why have we humbled ourselves, and thou takest no knowledge
>   of it? . . .
> Is such the fast that I choose, a day for a man to humble himself?
> Is it to bow down his head like a rush, and to spread sackcloth and
>   ashes under him? . . .
> Is not this the fast that I choose: to loose the bonds of wickedness, to
>   undo the throngs of the yoke, to let the oppressed go free, and to
>   break every yoke?
> Is it not to share your bread with the hungry, and bring the homeless
>   poor into your house;
> when you see the naked, to cover him, and not to hide yourself from
>   your own flesh? (Isaiah 58:3–7, RSV)

An earthly ruler might be propitiated by extraordinary devotion to the goals of the community; the principle is the same. Under this heading comes the idea that the offender must restore an order—cosmic or social—that she has disturbed by doing wrong. Propitiation then becomes less personal and more principled. In the end, the concept of propitiation can even be divorced from the idea of appeasement, as we have seen above in the case of the heretic Elisha ben Abuya.

So much for expiation. As for reconciliation, this may be reconciliation of a person with superiors, or reconciliation of a person with peers. The former is what I have called propitiation. What of the latter? The sight of someone hurting or harming herself might evoke pity in her coequals. But pity is hardly the sort of relationship we desire in most circumstances. Again, strenuous work to promote common goals would serve better to restore a proper relationship with one's peers and thus bring about reconciliation.

In all these cases we see that the goals of expiation and reconciliation are not served especially well by pain, suffering, or loss. I have therefore omitted from the paradigm of the conscientious punishee any particular requirement for pain, suffering, or loss. It has, indeed, often been held that pain or suffering is an essential feature of expiation,[14] and the conscientious paradigm does not go so far as to exclude it. In Chapter 3, however, I argue that there actually are important cases of punishment under the conscientious paradigm that involve no pain, suffering, or other disvalue for the punishee. For now, it is enough to say that pain and suffering are not essential to punishment under the conscientious paradigm.

So far, we have discussed the punishment of a single person. We can also extend these paradigms and consider a society in which the large majority of cases of punishment correspond to one or the other. If we consider punishment by the state, our society of course follows the legal paradigm. Could there be a society run along the lines of the conscientious paradigm? What would it be like? It would be a society in which criminal justice was administered on the honor system. There would probably continue to be police and courts; the police would continue to apprehend suspected criminals, and courts would continue to try them and convict some, sentencing them to various punishments. But the penalty would be selected in consultation with the offender, and once the sentence had been issued, it would be left up to the offender to carry out. There would be no one to force her. And, in such a society, most people would in fact carry out their assigned punishments.

One might call this idea unrealistic. Well, yes: unrealistic, but not far-fetched. We are no doubt safe in predicting that no industrialized society could administer criminal justice on the honor system. But it is not uncommon for other burdensome social duties to be administered this way. Until recently, the United States income tax showed a high degree of voluntary compliance, even though its requirements are burdensome and relatively easy to avoid. Yet the concept of a society run on the conscientious paradigm is important mostly as a theoretical concept, much like the concept of a social contract. Although very few societies are formed by an actual contract, the concept of a social contract has been extremely fruitful in political theory. Similarly, by imagining a society in which all convicts voluntarily submit to punishment, by considering what things would be like, we can gain a greater insight into the problems of punishment in our own, very different, society.

2. The Status of the Two Paradigms

WHY ARE THEY PARADIGMS?

Now that these paradigms are spread out before us, we must consider two questions: What makes them paradigms? And what makes them both paradigms of *punishment*?

I anticipate few objections to the claim that the Paradigm of Legal Punishment is a paradigm of punishment. But some people may object to my second purported paradigm. My response: The Paradigm of the Conscientious Punishee describes cases of punishment that are *ideal*, *standard*, and *regular*, as I have defined those terms, and hence is indeed a paradigm.

The conscientious paradigm is *ideal* in a number of ways. The first and most important of these involves the duty to submit to punishment, established in Chapter 1. As with any duty whatsoever, the ideal case is that in which a person does his duty willingly and conscientiously. If the duty calls for action, then in the ideal case the person who does his duty is active. And if someone does his duty unwillingly, and only under constraint, it is an anti-ideal, a bad example of doing one's duty. If there is, for example, a duty to contribute to charity, surely the ideal case is that in which a person gives freely, out of concern for the needy or out of a sense of duty, rather than the case in which, say, her employer coerces her. If there is a duty of honesty, then surely the ideal case of honesty is that in which a person avoids lies and deception because she feels they are wrong—not because she fears a perjury conviction. If there is a duty to save lives when the cost is small, then surely the ideal case is that in which a person saves lives because she feels that lives are precious—not because she hopes to get a medal. It would be odd indeed if we took as our paradigm cases those in which a person does her duty from motives of coercion, vanity, or greed. It is no less odd to take as our sole paradigm of punishment the case in which punishment is forced upon an unwilling and unrepentant punishee.

Second, even if we do not suppose a duty to submit, submission is still a praiseworthy act in many cases. But it is praiseworthy only to the extent that it is done willingly and conscientiously. This point is, in a way, more forceful than the similar one about duty of the previous paragraph. For those who do their duty under duress still have done their duty, but a praiseworthy act is no longer praiseworthy if done only under duress.

Third, punishment conforming to the conscientious paradigm is ideal in that it avoids the morally problematic issue of inflicting suffering or evil on an unwilling victim; for here the victim is willing, and the punishment may not even involve suffering or evil. Similarly, with such punishment there is no problem of treating the punishee merely as a means. For the punishee acts autonomously in choosing punishment for herself. Indeed, it is the punish*er*, if anyone, who is used as a means, for the punishee may require help in securing for herself a just punishment.

More generally, punishment under the conscientious paradigm conforms to our conception of the legitimate state, for it recognizes the autonomy of those who are punished.

One can argue in a fourth way that such punishment is ideal. Many people find that their moral intuition approves of such punishments—community service, as well as penance for sin—as just responses to wrongdoing. Such penalties, moreover, often seem superior precisely because the punishee can take the active role. Anyone who shares these intuitions has an additional reason for calling the conscientious paradigm a paradigm.

The punishment of the conscientious punishee is also a *standard* case—that is, we see many actual incidents conforming closely to it. Perhaps few convicts go willingly to jail, and perhaps few contribute willingly to community-service programs. But nearly all penitents do penance willingly. No one drags them off to the house of prayer; no one garnishes their wages to put in the poor box; there is no knock at the door in the middle of the night should they fail to do charitable

work. Some, indeed, may act from other motives along with conscientiousness, but this does not generally spoil the conscientious
nature of the act. Now, these penitents are not a small number of
people. No doubt, the number of Roman Catholic penitents is vast,
though they are hard to count, since they repent in private. But one
can perhaps extrapolate on the basis of the large number of Jews
who fill synagogues to pray and fast on the Day of Atonement—a
number all the more impressive when one recalls that their religion
does not vividly dangle the hope of eternal bliss as an inducement to
this performance.[15]

Finally, the punishment of the conscientious punishee is regular.
Remorse is a well-attested feature of the human personality, and it
moves us to seek out and accept punishment.[16]

The conscientious punishee is, then, a paradigm. "But not of punishment. What you describe is penance." In part, the objection must
be conceded. English usage is divided on whether to apply the word
punishment to instances of penance, expiation, and the like; a similar uncertainty is found in medieval Latin, and no doubt in other
languages as well. The uncertainty over this point is concisely illustrated by one author, who writes that the "[Asian] Indian theory of
punishment consists of both punishment and expiation."[17] Aquinas
presents the locus classicus: "Expiatory punishment is punishment
in a somewhat diminished sense. Part of the proper meaning of punishment is that it goes against the will; although an expiatory punishment when considered in the abstract would be against one's will,
in the actual instance and as expiation it is voluntary."[18] Likewise,
Saint Anselm refers to penance sometimes as a punishment, sometimes as a substitute for punishment.[19] Competent speakers, then, are
in good company whether or not they are willing to apply the word
punishment to cases corresponding to the conscientious paradigm.
If we want to be more precise than common usage, any suggestion
within this range is in order.

My suggestion, not surprisingly, is that the conscientious paradigm is a paradigm of punishment. Consider the alternative. If penance is not punishment, we have an odd situation: No one could then
carry out the duty to submit to a just punishment, since it would
then take on the nature of penance, and it would no longer be a
punishment at all. (One is reminded of the employee's retort: "You
can't fire me—I quit!") The case is stronger if we consider the situation in which voluntary submission to punishment is the general
practice: If only a few people submit willingly, we can easily call
their fate punishment because it is the same fate as those who must

be coerced. But if nearly everyone submits willingly, enforcement is hardly necessary, and what the offenders are doing takes on the appearance of a penance; yet, what they are doing is trying to carry out their duty to submit to punishment. It seems odd to say that the duty loses its nature when many people decide to take it seriously.

Those who still balk at my suggested usage may find it more acceptable if they consider the verb in place of the noun: If a person is doing penance, it is quite natural to describe her as *punishing herself* for her sins or misdeeds.

There is, of course, a point in making a distinction between punishments that are inflicted and punishments that are undertaken, and there is a certain tendency to restrict the word *punishment* to the former (as Aquinas notes). But this narrow usage does not preempt the wider one.

In the end the question is not really linguistic. If someone were to insist that the word *punishment* in English cannot possibly bear the meaning I am trying to give it—even then, the answer is simple: We simply speak of two paradigms of retributive justice, or of criminal justice, or of sanctions for wrongdoing. The word *punishment* could then be restricted to the legal paradigm and cases resembling it. But the theoretical unity of penance and punishment—in part seen above, in part to be seen below—pulls toward the more unitary concept. The only essential difference between penance and (other kinds of) punishment is in the need for enforcement, which does not seem decisive.

THE PREVALENCE OF THE LEGAL PARADIGM

Despite the paradigmatic nature of conscientious submission, most modern writers on punishment adhere to the legal paradigm to the exclusion of the other. One has to search hard for a counterexample.

We have already seen how most modern writers on punishment hold that willing submission to punishment is impossible or rare or pointless. This contention lays the foundation of the legal paradigm, since it means that the punishee is usually the passive recipient of something that is inflicted upon him or her. Four features follow rather directly from this view: That is, punishment is (feature 2) undertaken at the initiative of someone other than the punishee (feature 3), who is unrepentant and (feature 4) wishes to avoid the punishment and is (feature 5) passive with respect to the things that constitute the punishment.

Feature 1, which states that punishment consists of treatment that people typically wish to avoid, is documented in the next chapter.

Feature 6—requiring a retributive, reformatory, or deterrent rationale—should be familiar enough. One or more of these rationales is, in fact, included by some authors in their very definition of punishment. Hobbes, for example, stipulates by definition that punishment is reformatory or preventive: He states in his definition that punishment is inflicted "to the end that the will of men may thereby the better be disposed to obedience."[20] Even when these rationales are not included in a definition of punishment, they still dominate the literature. Nearly any contemporary general treatment of punishment runs through the standard retributivist and utilitarian theories, with deterrence and reform being the versions of the utilitarian view. (Sometimes prevention and rehabilitation are included here, too, but the difference is not substantial.)

We go back once more to Hobbes to find the apparent beginning of the concentration on legal punishment specified by feature 7. Before Hobbes, and sometimes after, writers tend to include religious punishments, or punishments carried out under the law of nature. But Hobbes is clearly different: "A punishment, is an Evill inflicted by publique Authority, on him that hath done, or omitted that which is Judged by the same Authority to be a Transgression of the Law; to the end that the will of men may thereby the better be disposed to obedience."[21] It is true that, for Hobbes, God is included among "publique authorities," and His laws among the laws that bring punishment on their transgressors.[22] But the difference is not great: Hobbes holds that God is literally a monarch, not merely one by analogy,[23] and the same principles—including principles of punishment—apply to Him as to any earthly monarch.[24] Rawls and Hart also include in their definitions a reference to legal institutions.[25] More typically, this feature of the legal paradigm is not explicitly stated but is manifested in the fact that most writers use examples of punishment drawn only, or mostly, from the legal sphere. A particularly revealing case is found in an essay of S. I. Benn: His definition of punishment includes, as one of its criteria, the following: "It must be imposed by authority . . . , conferred by the system of rules (hereafter referred to as 'law') against which the offense has been committed."[26] Soon we see him referring to "crime" and "the criminal." He thus makes an easy transition from a system of rules of any sort to the system of legal rules of the state. A strong statement of the legal paradigm can likewise be found in the introduction to a recent book by Igor Primoratz.[27]

The Paradigm of Legal Punishment receives its best expression in the definition given by H. L. A. Hart, which is also the most influential contemporary definition.[28] It is therefore worth quoting in full:

> I shall define the standard or central case of 'punishment' in terms of five elements:
>
> (i) It must involve pain or other consequences normally considered unpleasant.
>
> (ii) It must be for an offense against legal rules.
>
> (iii) It must be of an actual or supposed offender for his offense.
>
> (iv) It must be intentionally administered by an authority constituted by a legal system against which the offense is committed.
>
> In calling this the standard or central case of punishment I shall relegate to the position of sub-standard or secondary cases the following among many other possibilities:
>
> (a) Punishments for breaches of legal rules imposed or administered otherwise than by officials (decentralized sanctions).
>
> (b) Punishments for breaches of non-legal rules or orders (punishments in a family or school).
>
> (c) Vicarious or collective punishment. . . .
>
> (d) Punishment of persons (otherwise than under (c)) who neither are in fact nor are supposed to be offenders.[29]

Until very recently the only influential apparent divergence from this paradigm in modern times has been that found in the theories of Hegel, Bernard Bosanquet, and their successors, who say that punishment is the offender's right, an expression of the offender's own will, a way of doing honor to the offender.[30] But, as I have claimed above (Chapter 1, section 2), this kind of talk is misleading. So the Hegelian theory does not really diverge from the legal paradigm.

Recently some writers have taken issue with one or another of the seven features defining the legal paradigm, as we have seen in Chapter 1. Large parts of the conscientious paradigm are espoused by Unto Tähtinen,[31] who presents this avowedly normative definition:

> Punishment is a non-injurious measure applied on a responsible offender for breaking a morally justified rule.[32]

Here the punishment is not an evil—perhaps it is actually a good; yet the punishee is still pictured as a passive being on whom the punishment is applied. Though Tähtinen elsewhere mentions a case of punishment that is actively undertaken by the punishee,[33] he never appears to unite these elements. James Doyle comes close, defining punishment as ". . . the satisfaction of all the just claims invoked by the commission of criminal offenses,"—a definition that, taken by itself, is compatible with either paradigm; yet he expects that these claims can be filled only by "deprivation or coercion."[34] Apparently, the only philosopher to come out clearly with something like a statement of the conscientious paradigm has been Richard Swinburne.[35]

3. The Priority of the Conscientious Paradigm

So far we have argued that a theory of punishment must consider both the question of infliction and the question of submission; and we have developed a paradigm corresponding to each of these cases. From what has been said, the two paradigms may seem equally important, but it goes beyond that: The Paradigm of the Conscientious Punishee is more important. The central question of a theory of punishment is, I claim, the question of submission, conceived in terms of the conscientious paradigm, namely: Why should an offender submit to punishment, and what sort of punishment should she submit to?

Here, again, we see a parallel with social contract theory. Social contract theory justifies the coercive powers of government (to which no one consents) in terms of an ideal case, in which all citizens give their consent to a government by means of a social contract. This concept of a social contract is useful in spite of the fact that few, if any, governments rule by the contractual consent of the governed. Similarly, few people who undergo legal punishment do so by their own consent. (Though more people consent to punishment than to government.) But we can understand the actual situation better if we first consider the notional situation in which all people willingly submit to punishment. In both cases the gritty, real-world situation is understood by reference to an immaculate, idealized situation. The real is an imperfect copy of the ideal.

A THEORY OF SUBMISSION YIELDS A THEORY OF INFLICTION

Of course, this use of an idealized concept makes sense only if it does in fact help us deal with the real world. Not only that: It must help us deal with the real world better than the unaided real world deals with itself. And indeed it is so, as we shall next see. For even the real world by itself needs an answer to both questions of punishment: Conscientious convicts—however few in number—need an answer to the question of submission, just as unrepentant convicts require an answer to the question of infliction. Now, if there is just one of these two questions which, when answered, yields an answer to the other, then that one question is in an important way the central question of the theory of punishment. It turns out in fact that there is such a question: It is the question of submission.

We shall first see why an answer to the question of submission yields an answer to the question of infliction. We have already shown that, in a legitimate state, persons who have been convicted of an offense have a duty to submit to punishment. (I assume that the proposed penalty meets all other applicable principles of justice.) I require one further premise: When a person's wrongful failure to act creates a situation of injustice, it is within the competence of the state to force the person to act. Let us call this the *principle of perfect duty*.[36] An example—uncontroversial, I hope: Suppose Smythe has borrowed $5,000 from Orloff. The time to repay has come and gone, and Smythe has enough money, but he simply prefers not to pay. Surely this is one of the occasions when we expect the state to step in and force repayment, or even confiscate some of Smythe's property and sell it off to pay the debt. Now, if the duty to submit to punishment is a perfect duty, it may be enforced against the punishee should she fail to perform on her own. Is the duty to submit a perfect duty? Would neglect of it create injustice? The answers must be drawn from a more detailed normative theory of punishment, but we may confidently anticipate that they will be in the affirmative. The fact that punishment falls under the heading of retributive *justice* may itself be sufficient guarantee for now. But we may in addition note: First, if the penalty is in the form of a fine, then unexcused failure to pay creates no less injustice than Smythe's failure to repay his loan. Second, comparative justice gives the same answer for a broader set of cases: If some persons are justly convicted, sentenced, and punished, an injustice results if others are convicted of the same crime and sentenced to a similar punishment only to evade the penalty. In particular, if some people submit willingly, a comparative injustice results if others evade their punishments in like circumstances. This injustice is to be corrected by enforcing the punishment on those who do not willingly undertake it.

Indeed, authors who recommend penance for wrongdoing often justify the infliction of punishment in just this way. For example, Saint Anselm first establishes a duty to make satisfaction for sins and then argues that God may, indeed must, extract this satisfaction if the sinner does not render it voluntarily.[37]

A THEORY OF INFLICTION DOES NOT YIELD A THEORY OF SUBMISSION

On the other hand, it seems hard to establish a duty to submit on the basis of a theory of infliction. I cannot, of course, refute every conceivable argument, but the ones that come most readily to mind fail of their goal.

As I have already noted, we cannot argue directly from the liberty-right of the state to punish to the duty of a guilty person to submit, any more than we can argue from the liberty-right of a football tackle to tackle to the duty of the ballcarrier to fall down. But there might be a less direct argument. I will consider three such.

The Argument from Political Obligation.   First, one might argue as follows: As part of their political obligation, all subjects have a general duty to obey the legitimate laws and directives of the state. Since the state may legitimately order the punishment of guilty criminals, the criminals themselves have a duty to obey—that is, to submit to the proposed punishment.

But there is a confusion here: The supporter of this argument equivocates when she says that the state may legitimately order the punishment of guilty criminals. The state may indeed legitimately order bailiffs, prison guards, and other officials to impose punishments upon convicted criminals; but we have not supposed that the state may legitimately order criminals to submit to such efforts.

"But the state may, in effect, make the convicted criminal a special deputy sheriff and then order her to inflict punishment on a particular criminal, namely, herself."

This refinement strengthens the argument—indeed, strengthens it too much. For we could turn the argument around and apply it to noncriminals as well. If it establishes a convict's duty to put himself in prison, say, for a period of twenty years, then it would also establish a similar duty for an innocent person to devote twenty years of his life to (unpaid) criminal-justice work. This is excessive. We do expect citizens generally to contribute to the administration of criminal justice, but only in relatively minor ways. Liberalism forbids an act that would force people so drastically to curtail their life plans in order to ensure that criminals are punished.

The Argument from Justice.   The second argument depends on the duty to promote justice. Such a duty has been suggested by

Rawls[38] and seems to me quite reasonable. According to this duty, everyone must act in ways that promote justice. Since punishment is a form of justice, convicts have a duty to promote justice by bringing about their own punishment.

This argument may indeed establish a duty to submit to minor punishments, but not a general duty to submit. We would not expect someone to bear such a heavy cost. For the duty of justice (as Rawls reasonably defines it in the place just mentioned) involves two requirements: "This duty requires us to support and to comply with just institutions that exist and apply to us. It also constrains us to further just arrangements not yet established, at least when this can be done without too much cost to ourselves." Now, the duty to submit could not come under the first clause, for we are assuming that there is as yet no existing, just institution that applies to criminals and requires them to submit to punishment. (What we are trying to prove is that there *should* exist such an institution.) The supposed duty to submit must, then, be established under the second clause. But it cannot be, since the cost would be too great. As before, we cannot expect someone to give up twenty years of his life in order to promote justice by ensuring that a convicted kidnapper should spend his just term of twenty years in prison. It makes no difference here that the promoter of justice and the convicted kidnapper might turn out to be the same person. For the duty to further just arrangements applies equally to everyone. If it could establish the duty of this kidnapper to submit, it would equally require the average law-abiding citizen to spend twenty years in a ceaseless effort to bring kidnappers to justice—which no one would suppose.

The Argument from Fear of Anarchy. The third argument is based on the fear of anarchy. If many criminals go unpunished, potential criminals will have a low estimate of the probability of their being punished; deterrence will be less effective, and social order will break down. To prevent this very serious consequence, criminals have a duty to submit to punishment.[39]

As with the second argument, this third argument would, I think, establish a duty to submit to punishment in certain cases, but these cases are very few. Deterrence works in general because criminals fear that they will be punished despite their attempts to get away with their crimes. They do not usually fear that they will suddenly repent and accept the punishment that they deserve. Hence, voluntary submission by the conscientious has little deterrent effect, for it does not affect the probability that unrepentant criminals can escape being punished. (Actually, it might have a slight counterproductive effect: If prisons contain a lot of trusties, security need not be very tight, so vicious criminals will find it easier to escape.) There would, perhaps, be some deterrent effect on civil disobedients and others who break the law for reasons of conscience: They might feel constrained to follow the example of other conscientious punishees and might therefore refrain from crime rather than incur the moral duty to submit to punishment. But the conscientious punishee does not usually present an immense threat to civil order.

Moreover, this argument, like the last one, applies to the wicked and the good alike. If it obligates a criminal to serve twenty years in prison for the prevention of anarchy, it equally obligates the innocent to spend a like term in prison if by that means anarchy could be prevented. But what we want is a special duty of the guilty to submit to punishment.

In the end, it seems unlikely that the duty to submit can be derived from the liberty-right to inflict punishment. Any attempt at such a derivation will probably fail for reasons that should by now be clear. Without a special duty requiring guilty persons to submit to punishment, any attempted derivation will almost certainly support unacceptably burdensome duties for the innocent.

An answer to the question of submission thus provides an answer to the question of infliction, but not vice versa. This conclusion confirms the priority of the conscientious paradigm.

It must be admitted that two other possibilities remain: The question of infliction and the question of submission might be answered independently, or both answers might be derived from a single more basic principle. These two ways of answering the questions treat them symmetrically and hence accord no priority to one or the other. But even if the questions could be answered this way, it would not undermine the priority of the conscientious paradigm, for it would not negate the conclusion just proved.

THE MORAL PRIORITY OF THE CONSCIENTIOUS PARADIGM

In addition to this logical priority, the conscientious paradigm also has a moral priority over the legal paradigm. For the conscientious paradigm agrees with a conception of the liberal state, as the legal paradigm does not. The latter involves a severe violation of autonomy, whereas the former respects it. Then, too, given that there is a duty to submit, the ideal case—the case with moral priority— is that in which this duty is conscientiously undertaken. One might say, "What about the sheriff's duty to inflict? This can be undertaken only if people resist. Hence neither paradigm has priority on this score." But the sheriff's duty is to ensure that people get the punishment they are sentenced to. She can carry out this duty in either case. If the convict is vicious, she inflicts punishment. If the convict is conscientious, the sheriff assists and observes. Thus the conscientious paradigm allows both parties conscientiously to fulfill their duty, whereas the legal paradigm presupposes that one of them does not.

When punishment must be inflicted, it is, then, a less satisfactory version of what is done when punishment is conscientiously undertaken, just as charity given under duress is a less satisfactory version of charity given out of a spirit of charity. The result is a method for the theory of punishment paralleling Rawls's method for political philosophy in general. In his *Theory of Justice* he argues that ideal theory—which assumes full compliance with principles of justice— takes priority over nonideal theory and serves as its basis.[40] Similarly, when we turn to nonideal theory (which includes the theory of punishment), we begin with the most nearly ideal part of nonideal theory. And the most nearly ideal part of the theory of punishment is the theory of the conscientious punishee.

4. Submission to Punishment and the Traditional Theories

The central task of a theory of punishment is, then, to answer the question of submission. The first thing that comes to mind is that the traditional theories of punishment—utilitarian and retributive— might be equal to this task. In this section I show that they are not.

Our present view says that any adequate theory of punishment by the state must provide arguments that establish that all those who are to be punished have a moral obligation to submit to the proposed punishments. If a theory proposes inflicting some punishments without establishing an obligation to submit to them, it is to that extent inadequate.

By this criterion, the traditional theories in their usual forms are found wanting: They either fail totally to support a moral obligation to submit to punishment or else justify the infliction of many punishments without supporting a moral obligation to submit to those same punishments. Either situation is unacceptable. I will first look at utilitarian theories, then retributive.

Please recall that submission to punishment must be justified in its own right; as I have argued above, we cannot first justify infliction and then, on that basis, establish a duty to submit. In the present section I therefore consider only *direct* justifications of submission to punishment, those that do not depend on a prior justification of inflicted punishment.

Throughout this section we will be considering the conscientious punishee, the kind of person likely to submit willingly to punishment. But how could it ever come about that such a person should have committed an offense in the first place? One might expect such a person to be innocent of such wrongs. Still, it does happen occasionally. I discern two main possibilities, with several subcases: (1) A person of bad character may do wrong, and then undergo a change of character and become conscientious. (2) A person of generally good character may occasionally lapse, and do wrong (*a*) through impulse or (*b*) in the face of powerful temptation or (*c*) in a state of confusion, or (*d*) he may simply be subject to wicked moods. I will sometimes need to distinguish these cases, but where I do not mention them, what I say may be taken to apply to all.

THE INADEQUACY OF UTILITARIAN THEORIES

Let us turn to utilitarian theories of punishment. It should be noted that I am not taking utilitarianism here as a general normative theory. I am considering only utilitarian justifications of punishment (which even a deontologist can in principle accept). A utilitarian theory of punishment, then, need not (though it may) claim that a certain type of penal system is a necessary means for maximizing happiness. A utilitarian theory might rather simply claim that a penal system will promote (not maximize) some worthy goal, such as deterrence, restraint, or reform. Of course, any reasonable utilitarian theory of punishment will weigh these goals against other important ends, the weighting to be specified by the theory itself. So if a penal system of a particular sort is too detrimental to these other ends, it is unjustified. Similarly, a proposed penal system is unjustified if some other feasible system is far better at promoting the specified goals.

The three goals just mentioned—deterrence, restraint, and reform–rehabilitation—are the ones most often proposed by utilitarian theories of punishment. Advocates of the first goal hope to *deter* people from the commission of offenses by the threat of punishment; advocates of the second hope to *restrain* the offender from the commission of offenses during the period of punishment; and advocates of the third hope to *reform* or *rehabilitate* the offender. (These goals

may be taken to be ends in themselves, or means to some other end.)
We thus get three versions of utilitarian penal theory. None of the
three, I claim, gives us a satisfactory argument for an obligation to
submit to punishment.

The basic problem is obvious: Not much is to be gained on any
of these three accounts by the punishment of conscientious people.
Suppose Pereira is conscientious enough to submit to punishment—
a term in prison—even though he knows he could avoid it. Who will
be deterred if Pereira walks into jail? The criminal classes would
only snicker at such a sucker. Will Pereira be restrained from further
crimes? That's possible, but not likely: If he's good enough to turn
himself in, then most likely he's good enough to be good on the outside as well. Will Pereira be reformed? Maybe. But he hardly needs it,
and the inconvenience of going to prison surely outweighs the slight
benefit to society of a marginally improved Pereira.

But let us look at this in a little more detail. I will consider restraint and reform together—since reform is an internal restraint—
and then deterrence separately. We want to know whether a duty to
submit can be founded on grounds of good consequences. To do this,
we will compare two conceivable sorts of penal system: In the first
there is no duty to submit to punishment; in the second there is
such a duty. (This duty, of course, is an institutional duty, one that
is prescribed by a rule of the system. Whether it is also a *moral* duty
remains to be shown.) In the first sort of penal system, when a lawbreaker is convicted, she is punished; but there is no rule requiring
lawbreakers to submit to punishment. They in fact do not generally
submit willingly, nor are they expected to. They submit only under
coercion, or to avoid some less favored consequences. Under this first
system it is not considered a crime to evade or resist one's assigned
punishment. Under the second sort of system punishments are also
imposed on lawbreakers, but here they are expected to submit willingly (that is, even without coercion). Those who are conscientious
actually do submit willingly, without having to be forced, and those
who evade or resist punishment are deemed guilty of a further offense
beyond their original crime. If the second sort of system is clearly
superior in achieving the desired consequences, then a moral obligation to submit to punishment has been established. If the first sort
excels, then no such obligation has been established.

To simplify things, I will ignore the varying degrees of vice and
virtue, and simply divide convicts into two groups: the conscientious
and the depraved. Now, practically speaking, what is the difference
between our two types of penal system? For the depraved, there is

no difference. They do not care about any duty to submit. They only care about whether they can evade the bailiff, who we presume is equally diligent in either system. The only difference is for the conscientious. In the first sort of system there is no duty to submit, so they will join their depraved brothers and sisters in evading the punishment, if possible. The conscientious might stop short of using some of the extreme means favored by the depraved, but if Pereira, our conscientious criminal, can make it over the border and avoid extradition, he will gladly do so. It is different in the second sort of system. Here, when the rule says "Submit," the conscientious will listen. The net result: under the second sort of system, a slightly higher rate of punishment among conscientious convicts.

Of course, officials will have thought these very thoughts (or, more likely, their assistants will have thought these thoughts for them) and might respond, "Well, let's just make conscientious persons exempt from punishment." And this would be a fine plan, if one could carry it out. It is, however, too hard to distinguish the conscientious from the depraved. It is hard enough ordinarily, but if officials let every reformed criminal off without punishment, there would be an even larger than usual number of vicious persons trying to feign virtue for the state examiner.

In any case, the number of reformed offenders is likely to be much smaller than the number of the obdurate. For every reformed offender mistakenly punished, there are likely to be several unreformed offenders mistakenly unpunished. The harm caused by not punishing these vicious persons, added to the cost of trying to distinguish them, certainly outweighs the benefit of not punishing the reformed characters. The state, then, cannot make reformed convicts exempt from punishment but must punish all.

We turn, then, to *reform* and *restraint*. The penal authority, on grounds of utility, is justified in restraining all convicts, or trying to reform all of them, whether they are now virtuous or vicious. But, as we have seen, it is a waste of effort for the state to try to reform or restrain conscientious persons. The first sort of penal system now has the virtue of punishing somewhat fewer of these persons than the second sort of system. The first sort—that is, the kind with no duty to submit—is therefore preferable.

And what about *deterrence*? The problem here is that potential criminals are mostly deterred by the fear that they will be punished against their will. They are not deterred by the fear that they will suddenly repent and turn themselves in. But let us consider it formally. The punishing authority, as before, will produce the best results if it seeks to punish all convicts, conscientious or depraved. But which sort of system is better, the first or the second? The difference, once again, is seen only in the conscientious. In a system of the first sort the conscientious will evade punishment if they can do it without too much difficulty. In a system of the second sort they will accept the punishment assigned to them, even without coercion. Now, a system of the second sort will have *some* additional deterrent effect upon the conscientious: A conscientious person may well be deterred from doing wrong if she knows that by so doing she will incur an obligation to submit to punishment. For example, I am a fairly conscientious person. I acknowledge an obligation to pay parking tickets, and in fact I do pay them, even if they come from other states and cannot be enforced against me. This deters me (to a certain extent) from illegal parking. How great is this deterrent effect? Is it sufficient to justify a system of the second sort, with an obligation to submit? Probably not. Recall the kinds of situations in which a conscientious person is likely to do wrong. If he acts impulsively, he takes little consideration of consequences. If he acts in the face of powerful temptation, he discounts the consequences. If he is in a state of confusion, he is likely to miscalculate the consequences. A person in any one of these states will not be effectively deterred except by an extremely severe punishment, one that will cut through the fog. But such punishments probably cause more harm than they prevent and so in most cases are unjustified on utilitarian grounds. A system requiring submission to such punishments is likely to produce more harm than good. A system of the first sort—with no duty to submit—will yield better results.

Hence a deterrent theory of punishment—the last of the three utilitarian varieties—cannot ground a moral obligation to submit to punishment. Perhaps some untraditional kind of utilitarian penal theory can do the job, but I leave the task of devising one to others.

We turn, then, to retributivism.

THE INADEQUACY OF RETRIBUTIVE THEORIES

I myself find the word *retributivism* too vague to be of much use.[41] Nonetheless, we can distinguish and consider two most prominent conceptions of retributivism. The first conception centers on the concept of desert; on this view, punishment of offenders is justified because it is deserved, without reference to the consequences of punishment. The second conception centers on the metaphor of repayment.

I consider the first view first. Desert does indeed ground an obligation to submit to punishment under certain circumstances. If I deserve punishment, then I ought to see to it that I get the punishment that I deserve, or at least I should refrain from resisting those who attempt to punish me as I deserve. But I shall argue that a desert-based theory of punishment can justify submission only at the cost of becoming very implausible on other grounds.

If a desert-based theory is to ground an argument for an obligation to submit to punishment, it must satisfy two conditions. First of all, to use Feinberg's terminology, the theory must use a concept of desert proper, rather than desert as qualification.[42] We can illustrate the distinction as follows: In the first sense of *desert* we may decide to set up a system of punishing people because we think they deserve it; in the second sense we can say that persons deserve punishment only *after* we have set up a system of punishment that assigns them sanctions on some other grounds. The second sort of system may be said to *involve* desert, but it is not *based* on desert. The question of grounding a duty to submit here reverts to the question of justifying a system of punishment that requires submission. And this is the very question that we have just found so intractable. Only a system of punishment *based on* desert *proper* will serve our present needs.

But such systems have a certain drawback. They generally offer little explanation of this sort of desert. They say, "Smith ought to be punished because she deserves it," but this is very unhelpful unless we know what this sort of deservingness amounts to. Usually it amounts to an affirmation such as:

> Smith ought to be punished because Smith has done
> something wrong,

which is a mere restatement of the problem; or else such theories seem to explain desert by saying,

> Smith ought to be punished because Smith is the
> sort of person who ought to be punished,

which still leaves us in the dark. Even if we accepted these affirmations as true, they would still not provide the desired explication of the concept of desert. An exception, of course, is the sort of theory that says that persons should suffer or prosper in proportion to their wickedness or goodness. Notoriously, this justification works well for God but not for humans. We are not in a position to judge a person's wickedness or goodness over her whole life. We are not even in a very good position to make such a judgment about ourselves.

A second thing is required if a desert-based theory is to justify submission to punishment. The theory must not merely permit the punishment of those who deserve it; it must *require* the punishment of everyone, or almost everyone, who deserves it. Otherwise, the guilty person might reason thus: "I am guilty, and I deserve punishment. But I will show mercy to myself and remit the penalty. Moreover, my punishment would involve greater suffering without any counterbalancing good effects. Therefore, considerations of utility also lead me to refrain."

A theory satisfying this second condition has limited appeal. It is attractive only to rigorists *à la* Kant, who never permit themselves to remit or even reduce a punishment for reasons of utility or mercy. And it is impractical as a theory of punishment by the state, since it would apparently require a government to investigate every suspected crime, prosecute every suspect, and punish every convict. Such a policy would be unworkable for any number of reasons.

Perhaps there is some plausible form of desert-based retributivism that can overcome these difficulties. This, in any case, is the most plausible direction in which to look among the traditional theories for one that will ground an obligation to submit to punishment.

The second variety of retributivism is based on the metaphor of *repayment.* This, in turn, has two subvarieties. Sometimes we conceive that society must pay the offender back in her own coin; at other times we conceive that the offender must pay society back, must pay the price for the offense. Both subvarieties try to justify punishment as a transaction between society and the offender. This rules out self-punishment, since self-punishment involves no transaction. Penances, in particular, are unexplained on this view, since they are almost always undertaken by the penitent himself. Writers on penance are aware of this difficulty. Aquinas, for example, tries to get around it by saying that the penitent somehow repays something to God. This tactic merely raises another problem, since everything is in God's power. We cannot give Him anything, nor can we make Him better off. Aquinas—or more precisely, the compiler of the Supplement to the *Summa Theologica*—is aware of this further problem and resorts to handwaving.[43]

This objection has the greatest force against the first variety of the repayment theory. If I want to pay you back for your evil deeds and you upstage me by doing to yourself what I had planned to do to you, then I will feel that retributive justice has been frustrated. Hence we carefully prevent death-row inmates from committing suicide ("foiling the hangman," as they say). The punishment was supposed to be a sort of transaction involving two parties, but self-punishment involves only one. Even if you do not go so far as to punish yourself, I will still feel that justice has been frustrated if you willingly accept the things that I inflict upon you. Here we recall Br'er Rabbit's "punishment" by briars.[44] An interesting parallel can be made with consensual crimes, that is, crimes in which all parties, even the apparent victims, participate by free consent. Just as consensual crime lacks what is usually essential to crime, so too (according to this version of the repayment theory) does consensual punishment lack what is essential to punishment; for we are to pay the criminal back in her own coin, and consensual punishment is merely counterfeit.

If we take the second variety of the repayment theory, we seem better off. Under this conception the offender is conceived as owing a debt; and, certainly, voluntary repayment of a debt is, if anything, better than payment extracted from an unwilling debtor. But if we press this metaphor too much, it begins to collapse. With a real monetary debt, there is a contrast between debits and credits. For example, if I make a $100 overpayment on my credit card account, this overpayment serves to cancel debts that I incur later on. But one cannot acquire a credit balance on one's punishment account by spending time in jail before committing crimes. In the case of real debt, there need not be any intention to repay: If you owe me ten dollars and the wind rises and blows a ten-dollar bill from your hand into mine, your debt is canceled. But a criminal's "debt" of a month's confinement is not canceled by his accidentally locking himself into his kitchen for a month. In the case of a real debt, payment from a third party will cancel the debt. For example, if you are benevolent, you could pay off my credit card balance, and that debt is no more. But if I am sentenced to a term in prison, you could not pay my "debt" by going to prison for me. Indeed, the only operative aspect of the metaphor seems to be this: The offender has an obligation to society (or God or someone else) to serve out his punishment, just as a debtor has an obligation to her creditor. But this is little more than a restatement of the claim that there is an obligation to submit. The only further function served by the debt metaphor is to model the variation in degree and kind of punishment: Just as debts are of various amounts and denominated in various currencies, so offenders are liable to punishments in various amounts and of various sorts.[45] The metaphor supplies no justification for an obligation to submit, nor does it even explain how the "debt" comes to be incurred.

Thus the traditional theories of punishment apparently fail to ground a moral obligation to submit to punishment. It is not impossible that some new form of these old theories might succeed where the traditional forms fail. But I leave this possibility to be explored by others.

5. Nontraditional Theories

If traditional theories cannot ground a moral obligation to submit to punishment, perhaps some other theory can. I next look at some possibilities. Though I do advocate a number of them, for now I am not asserting them as true, but merely putting them forward for examination.

DESERT-BASED THEORIES

As already suggested, a desert-based retributivism, and, in fact, any desert-based theory of punishment, would satisfactorily ground a duty to submit to punishment. Now, desert-based retributivism says that someone who has committed an offense deserves to undergo some sort of disvalue proportionate to the gravity of the offense. But what would constitute a desert-based *non*retributive theory? Well, there are two possibilities: First, such a theory could hold that the deserved disvalue is not proportioned to the offense, but to something else, say, wickedness of character. Second, such a theory could hold that the penalty need not be disvaluable. I discuss this at length in Chapter 3, but for now an example may suffice: A person who has sinned may deserve as his penalty the requirement to say ten Hail Marys. Now, saying Hail Marys is not particularly an evil; the sinner may himself be delighted to say them as a means of reconciliation with God. Hence this sort of penalty is not a recompense of evil for evil, and therefore not retributive.

EQUILIBRIUM THEORIES

An equilibrium theory sees punishment as restoring the balance that is upset by wrongdoing. The balance may be one of well-doing and well-being, of benefits and burdens, or of something else. A desert-based theory is, in fact, one type of equilibrium theory. If such an equilibrium is prescribed by a stringent moral standard, then it is wrong for anyone to create or perpetuate a disequilibrium. Unpunished wrongdoers do precisely this; wrongdoers thus have a duty to secure their own punishment and restore the equilibrium.

Note how this sort of theory avoids the problems that plagued us before. We saw that some theories ground a duty of submission to punishment only at the cost of justifying unacceptably burdensome duties falling on the innocent. Under the present theory there is a duty not to create or perpetuate disequilibrium *by one's own actions or omissions*, and this duty applies to the unpunished offender. But there is not necessarily any duty to rectify a disequilibrium created or perpetuated by others. If there is such a duty, it is probably much less stringent than the primary duty of the offender. Moral autonomy suggests that we are for the most part responsible only for the disequilibria that we ourselves create or perpetuate. (To give a parallel, if I accidentally injure you, I have upset an equilibrium, which I ought to restore by making sure you are cared for. Third parties have *some* duty to make sure that you are cared for, but their duty is much weaker than mine.) In a similar way, the duty of third parties to secure punishment of the guilty is on this view much less stringent than the duty of the guilty to secure their own punishment. The innocent are not burdened with an oppressive duty to bring the guilty to justice.

CONTRACT THEORIES

Societies, families, religious communities, and other social units are often conceived to be based on a fundamental contract—usually, of course, a hypothetical or notional contract. If such a contract provides for punishment of the guilty, then it would in particular justify their submitting to punishment. This contract must contain an explicit or inferred agreement on the part of the guilty to submit. It is not enough if someone else is authorized to inflict the punishment on them. For example, Hobbes's social contract, as he himself notes, does not require submission to punishment; it merely authorizes the sovereign to punish others.

ASSURANCE THEORIES

Under this heading I place a sort of theory that has not, to my knowledge, been explicitly offered before as a general theory of punishment.

Consider this situation: I have been using dynamite on my property, and some of the flying debris has barely missed my neighbor. I have a duty, one would think, not only to stop my unsafe blasting but to provide my neighbors with some assurance that they are no longer in danger. I might take them on a tour of the property, show them that the apparatus has been dismantled or sold, or do anything else to provide the needed assurance. I am not at all certain about the scope or stringency of this duty, but I feel certain that reasonable people would behave in this way. So let us accept it for the moment. In that case, we can tell the following story: Suppose Smith has harmed others in the past and has thereby given people a good reason to fear that they may be his next victims. By the principle just cited, Smith then has a duty to assure these potential victims that he will refrain from doing whatever it was that has made them so edgy. If Smith's harmful actions had been unintentional, it might be enough for him just to say, "Sorry, I won't do it any more." But if Smith had wilfully caused the harm, this avowal will be worth little. Smith would then have to do something more serious, and this might constitute a punishment. Smith might, for example, undergo a course of moral reeducation, or submit to a probation program, or place a sum of money in escrow as surety against future misbehavior.

Indeed, this duty of assurance requires guilty persons to assure not only others but also themselves. Even if they feel remorseful, they do not know that they will refrain from similar evil deeds in the future. Even if they beat their breasts and make good resolutions, they may—we know all too well—repeat the same evil deed at the first opportunity. Remorse, resolutions, and breast-beating are notoriously poor predictors of future behavior, whether one's own or others'. The guilty people must assure themselves that their motivational structure and their surroundings will not make likely a repeat of similar evil deeds.

Three questions must be answered to make an assurance theory work. First, what entitles us to conclude that a certain offender is likely to offend again? We might consult statistical tables concerning recidivism. Or we might psychoanalyze the offender. Or we might just say, "Anyone who behaved like that must consider it permissible to disregard the rights and welfare of others; we are therefore entitled to some assurance that it won't happen again."

Second, we must ask: To what lengths must an offender go to assure us that she will not offend in the future? Obviously, it would assure us more than sufficiently if the offender were to lock herself in jail and throw away the key, or commit hara-kiri, but that would clearly be too severe. We need a limiting principle. At the present I have none to suggest.

Third, how can an offender assure us that she will not offend any more, or at least that she will be less likely to? And how can she do this without exceeding the limiting principle? Considering both factors, one might suspect that the only suitable assurance would consist of five years or so of clean living. This would, at the end of five years, provide the desired assurance but leave us nervous in the meantime.

In any case, close examination of these questions must wait for another occasion.

Finally, with regard to the assurance theory, we may note that the conventional preventive theory of punishment follows from it as a special case. If the nefarious Smith owes us a duty of assurance and fails in this duty, then we arguably have a right to assure ourselves. That is, we may take measures to prevent him from committing crimes.

EXPIATION AND RECONCILIATION THEORIES

Expiation, reconciliation, and atonement all provide the offender with a good reason for submitting to punishment. But do they ground a duty? It would seem not. It would be obnoxious, but not obviously contrary to duty, if a past offender were to obey the moral, religious, or civil law and yet remain unatoned, unreconciled, and stained with guilt. But if we were to hold that fraternity or purity were mandatory, then expiation and reconciliation might ground a duty to submit to punishment. In another place I argue for this; for now I merely suggest it.[46]

MORAL EDUCATION THEORIES

A moral education theory says that punishment is justified in that it teaches the offender a moral lesson: It tells her something about how bad her offense was.[47] If this kind of theory is to work, we must, of course, explain why this lesson must come in the form of a punishment. (Why not just *say* how bad it was? Or why not just make the offender take a written test to show that she has learned, somehow or other, how bad it was?) Of course, the lessons of experience speak louder (as teachers know), and this fact may be enough to support the moral education theory. Now, the interesting thing is that the offender can apply this view to herself: She punishes herself to educate herself, so that she will know the badness of what she did. So, if the moral education theory justifies the punishment of others, it will also justify the punishment of oneself, or submission to punishment at the hands of others.

RESTITUTION THEORIES

Some writers would justify punishment as a form of restitution—that is, compensation for harm done by the criminal.[48] Now, ordinarily, restitution seems quite distinct from punishment: If little Billy slugs a home run through my sunroom window, he is not being punished if he is made to pay for it to be reglazed; indeed, his action is probably not a crime. Yet crime has other costs besides those incurred by the victim. If I engage in, say, burglary, my crime gives rise to costs of detection, apprehension, trial, and incarceration. Private citizens must now install locks and alarms, put bars on the windows, hire security guards, and so forth. What we have traditionally called punishment can well be understood as payment for the criminal's share of these costs.

Now, if I accidentally smash a window, I am morally, as well as legally, obligated to pay. Equally so, if I should commit a crime, I am obligated to pay for its direct and indirect costs.

These, then, are the principal nontraditional theories that might ground a duty of submission to punishment. In Part Two I develop a theory that combines elements of the contract, equilibrium, assurance, and atonement theories.

CHAPTER 3

It Doesn't Have to Hurt: Punishment, Suffering, and Other Evils

PHILOSOPHERS who write about punishment often disagree, but there is one thing on which they are nearly unanimous: Punishment has to hurt. If something is to count as a punishment, it must involve pain, suffering, deprivation, or other unwanted or unpleasant consequences to the punishee; or (to subsume these under one head) these philosophers say that *disvalue*[1] to the punishee is an essential characteristic of punishment. This view is so widespread that I will refer to it as the *Standard View*.

This view is wrong; or, at any rate, so I argue in this chapter. I claim, in fact, that there are not merely borderline cases, but important, central cases of punishment involving no disvalue to the punishee. In accord with the Standard View, such cases have been almost entirely overlooked.

My thesis will seem ridiculous to some and obvious to others. Those who know the suffering that punishment can bring will likely think it ridiculous. And, indeed, it would be a profound insult to suggest that they are not suffering. Most punishments are, in fact, painful—all too often, inhumanly painful—and practically speaking most punishments must involve at least some unpleasantness. But this quality cannot be a defining characteristic of punishment.

I doubt that this thesis will be as obvious to the second group as it is ridiculous to the first. Yet some may think that I expound it in detail far exceeding any need. I apologize to this group for the inconvenience, but the detail really is needed. The practice of defining punishment as an evil is so widespread and so entrenched that we must be patient and thorough if we are to eradicate it. Otherwise, my proposal will strike many people as a mere verbal trick. I will cite more than one case in which someone has thought that he has uprooted this traditional view only to have it spring back like a dandelion.

The Standard View comes in varying degrees of strictness. A strong view holds that disvalue (in some form) is a necessary feature of punishment, and usually one of a set of jointly sufficient conditions. Often this is put forward as a meaning analysis; that is, it is claimed that the sentence "All punishments are disvaluable" is analytic, true by the very meaning of the words. But sometimes not.

A weaker version holds that disvalue characterizes any standard or usual or proper case of punishment, though there may be a few odd cases in which punishment involves no disvalue. Some people who espouse this version say explicitly that they are characterizing the standard or central case.[2] Others present a teleological definition: That is, they define punishment as an action or institution whose aim or purpose is the infliction of disvalue. This allows for the possibility that we may sometimes fail to achieve our aim; or, if we are talking about an institution, there may be some who do not even share the aims of the institution.[3] (Similarly, one might define *can opener* as "a device for opening cans" even though there are some— broken or badly designed ones—that can open no cans, and others are simply put to other uses.) Yet a third way of making this weaker claim involves the mere acknowledgment that borderline cases will occur.

I am concerned to refute both the strict and lenient versions of the Standard View. Consequently, I must show that there are standard or central cases of punishment that involve no pain for the punishee.

It is important to notice the nature of this task. I am not trying to find a set of conditions that will be analytically true (that is, true by virtue of the meaning of the words) of all and only punishments. Nor am I even trying to find such a definition that will apply—analytically or not—to punishment and only punishment. Rather, I am making a claim about which cases of punishment are important or ideal, a claim that rests on moral and sociological facts as well as linguistic ones. In a broad sense, one might call this claim a piece of conceptual analysis. In any case, it follows as a corollary that any conceptual analysis is false if it precludes the existence of such cases of punishment; and any discussion of punishment that ignores such cases is seriously incomplete.

The second part of this corollary is probably the more important one. Nearly all modern discussions of punishment concern themselves primarily with those cases of punishment that the Standard View sees as important. For example, the task of justifying punishment is typically seen as one of justifying the imposition of pain or suffering on an unwilling victim. But if there are central cases of punishment involving no pain or suffering, then such a justification will be at best incomplete, and at worst totally vitiated. (Indeed, I go on to claim that even when punishment involves suffering or other disvalue, it is not the disvalue that demands justification, but other features. See especially section 6.)

Now, one might object: "All you are doing is distinguishing two senses of *punishment*, a narrow one to which suffering or other disvalue is essential, and a wide one to which it is not; and this is a rather jejune linguistic point." To this I reply as in Chapter 2, section 2: One can distinguish two senses, but the phenomena they refer to are so closely intertwined that it makes more sense to put them under one heading, and this heading is *punishment*, in the usual sense of the term. But even if you insist that the two senses cannot be combined in this way, still we are considering an important phenomenon which—if not actually punishment in the narrower sense—is closely related to it and needs to be considered together with it. It is, moreover, crucial to examine the till now little-noted wide sense. My argument might then be construed as establishing that this wider sense is by far the more important one. From this would follow the same important consequences mentioned in the previous paragraph.

This view of my task has another important consequence: I do not care if someone looks at my examples and says, "But that's not punishment! It's not even punishment in your wider sense." The reply, again, is as in Chapter 2: "Perhaps not; but still, my examples show that there are paradigm cases of retributive justice for wrongdoing that involve no disvalue for the wrongdoer." If I can establish this attenuated claim, I consider my point made, though I still think the word *punishment* appropriately subsumes such cases.

The chapter proceeds as follows: In section 1, after documenting the Standard View in the literature, I distinguish three main versions in which it has been held. My strategy is then to show that none of these versions is acceptable, nor is the combination of all three. The main argument against the Standard View is presented in section 2. This argument revolves around two central examples of non-disvaluable punishment. Section 3 sets forth some less central, but still interesting, examples of punishments not conforming to the Standard View. Section 4 is devoted to the psychology of non-disvaluable punishment. In the two final sections (5–6) I discuss some consequences of my Non-Standard View, and concessions to its rival.

1. The History of the Standard View

DOCUMENTATION OF THE STANDARD VIEW

Here I make note—without much comment for now—of some of the historical and recent partisans of the Standard View. Plato and Aristotle espouse the medical view of punishment: They hold that at least some punishments act as medicine for a diseased soul, a bitter medicine that works by its very painfulness.[4] Aristotle gives an allopathic explanation: We cure disease by means of a treatment that causes symptoms opposite to those of the disease. Thus, for fever we give drugs that cause chills, and for excessive indulgence in pleasure we administer pain. Plato also holds that deterrent punishment should be inflicted on the incurably wicked.[5] From Plato's time until the beginning of the twentieth century, the large majority of authors make painfulness an essential property of punishment though some use *pain* (or a word translated as "pain") as a general antonym for *pleasure*, whereas others reserve the word for a particular subclass of unpleasant things.

In the *Summa Theologica* of Aquinas we read that "sorrow or pain belongs to the punishment of sin."[6] In Latin the connection between punishment and pain is reinforced by the fact that *poena* means both "punishment" and *pain* (as well as "satisfaction" for a wrong).[7] To refer unambiguously to punishment, the phrase *poena peccati* (pain of sin) is often used, as in the quotation above. The connection between punishment and pain is reinforced yet further by the doctrine—held by Aquinas and other Jewish and Christian authorities—that all of our sorrows and pains are sent by God as punishment for sins.[8]

Several centuries later Hobbes writes,

A punishment, is an Evill inflicted by publique Authority on him that hath done, or omitted that which is judged by the same Authority to be a Transgression of the Law; to the end that the will of men may thereby the better be disposed to obedience.[9]

And if we turn back a few pages, we find that Hobbes defines *displeasure* as "the apparence, or sense of Evill"—that is, displeasure is the way it feels when an evil is done to us.[10] So Hobbes's definition of *punishment* falls in with the rest. Locke, also equating "pain" and "evil," defines *punishment* indifferently in terms of either one.[11] Bentham also requires pain.[12] Kant differs somewhat by making "physical harm"[13] or "physical evil"[14] an essential property of punishment.

Hegel classifies it as "injury."[15] These two views represent a significant change from what has gone before. If punishment is pain, still it might be good for a person being punished; Plato and Aristotle, indeed, say that punishment often acts as medicine, curing the evil-doer by its very painfulness. On the other hand, the terms *physical harm* and *injury* suggest that the punishee is not helped, but necessarily made worse off by punishment. Of course, this conception of punishment still falls squarely within the Standard View.

Interpreting Hegel, J. Ellis McTaggart returns to a definition of *punishment* in which painfulness is an essential property.[16] Hastings Rashdall also demands painfulness: "Punishment is necessarily painful (positively or negatively), or it ceases to be punishment."[17] Ross likewise characterizes it in terms of pain.[18]

In an influential article Antony Flew carries on the Standard View: "I *propose*, therefore, that we take as parts of the meaning of 'punishment', in the primary sense, at least five elements. *First*, it must be an evil, an unpleasantness, to the victim. By saying 'evil'—following Hobbes—or 'unpleasantness' and not 'pain', the suggestion of floggings or other forms of physical torture is avoided."[19] Of course, Flew's change in terminology is merely a change from the narrower to the wider sense of *pain* noted above. Though (or perhaps because) Flew presents his definition merely as a proposal, it was accepted wholeheartedly by subsequent writers. We find it pretty much intact in J. D. Mabbott, S. I. Benn and R. S. Peters, H. L. A. Hart, H. J. McCloskey, Thomas McPherson, Richard Wasserstrom, George Fletcher, and Richard Burgh, and with only slight changes in Ted Honderich and Igor Primoratz.[20] Mabbott thinks that we should say "disliked" or "deprivation of good" rather than "evil" or "unpleasant." Benn and Peters add to Flew's definition the requirement "that the unpleasantness should be an essential part of what is intended and not merely incidental to some other aim." Hart varies Flew by speaking of "pain or other consequences normally considered unpleasant." Wasserstrom, Fletcher, and Burgh, in turn, cite Hart or Flew with general approval.

Not only is the Flew–Benn–Hart view widely accepted, it is also perceived, both by its supporters and opponents, as representing the consensus of philosophers of punishment. Thus Burgh (who generally agrees with Hart) and Hugo Bedau and Tziporah Kasachkoff (who do not) see Hart's view as the generally accepted philosophical view.[21] Kasachkoff adds that the requirement that punishment be an evil or unpleasantness to the victim is "seemingly the least controversial" and "is regarded by most as the minimal requirement for punishment."

The Standard View is thus both widely accepted, and perceived as such. Its standardness is further demonstrated by the fact that it is often asserted as if it were obvious. Thus McTaggart writes, "That it must be painful . . . will be generally admitted."[22] And Wasserstrom writes: "Punishment, whatever else may be said of it, involves the intentional infliction of unpleasantness or pain upon human beings by other human beings."[23]

As the reader will notice, even among the joiners of the Flew–Benn–Hart consensus, there is a fair amount of variation in the terms they use to define *punishment*, though they all make some sort of disvalue an essential property. Thus we see them define punishment as evil, unpleasantness, something disliked, deprivation of good, or pain, administered under certain conditions. This casting about for just the right word seems to begin in the 1890s with an exchange between Bradley and Rashdall. Rashdall attributes to Bradley the view that punishment consists of "the infliction of pain for pain's sake."[24] Bradley protests:

> Pain, of course, usually does go with the negative side of punishment, just as some pleasure, I presume, attends the positive side. Pain is, in brief, an accident of retribution, but certainly I never made it more, and I am not aware that I made it even an inseparable accident. If a criminal defying the law is shot through the brain, are we, if there is no pain, to hold that there is no retribution?[25]

And Rashdall replies:

> I admit that for 'pain' I ought to have said 'or other evil, loss of something good being treated as an evil.' If it were not thought an evil to be shot through the brain, the shooting would certainly not be a punishment.[26]

If we read through the various twentieth-century philosophical treatments of punishment, we find an ever greater variety of disvalues in various combinations being made defining characteristics of punishment: hardship,[27] suffering or harm,[28] hard treatment,[29] a humbling of the will,[30] pain, suffering or loss,[31] suffering or deprivation,[32] and so on.

Aside from those who explicitly define *punishment* in terms of disvalue, there are those who make it obvious through their writings that they accept such a definition, or at least that they hold that disvalue is a property of all but odd cases of punishment. Often it is said that it is the painfulness of punishment that calls for a justification; such a justification would not be needed if pain were merely an incidental feature of some punishments, for in that case we could inflict only the painless kind and no justification would be needed. Thus Richard Brandt asks, "What justifies anyone in inflicting pain or loss on an individual on account of his past acts?"[33] We find similar thoughts expressed by Wasserstrom[34] and Jonathan Bennett.[35] Similarly, George Schedler sees the problem of punishing the innocent as one of making innocent people suffer.[36]

Others show their acceptance of the Standard View by their answer to the question "How much punishment is deserved for a given crime or wrongdoing?" In many cases the appropriate punishment is described as an amount of suffering or harm. As above, this approach makes sense only on the assumption that suffering or harm characterizes all but perhaps a small number of odd cases of punishment. In this vein Claudia Card says: "The Full Measure [of punishment] consists in a deprivation of rights exposing the offender to a hardship comparable in severity to the worst that anyone could reasonably be expected to suffer from the similar conduct of another if such conduct were to become general in the community— but no greater deprivation than that."[37] Robert Nozick denominates the severity of deserved punishments in units of *disutility*.[38] Andrew Von Hirsch writes straightforwardly, "Severity refers to how unpleasant the punishment is."[39] Alan Wertheimer proceeds similarly.[40] In none of these treatments of the question is there a place for painless punishments.

Thus the view of punishment as disvalue deserves the title of Standard View, which I have given it.

PREVIOUS OBJECTIONS TO THE STANDARD VIEW

Now, I am hardly the first to question the Standard View. As early as the fifth century an anonymous writer (whose works are conventionally attributed to Dionysius Areopagita) writes, "To be punished is not an evil; but it is an evil to be made worthy of punishment."[41] But this statement is not very impressive, for this author maintains that evil is totally nonexistent.[42] (Indeed, it is a surprise that he is willing to admit that deserving punishment is an evil.)

More recent authors question the Standard View in a more meaningful way and offer different conceptions of punishment. But virtually none seems to consider the change very significant. Some fail to notice that it is a change at all. The rest consider it unimportant and often proceed (sometimes intentionally, sometimes accidentally) as if they had made no change. None seems to be aware that this recharacterization of punishment allows for the possibility (as I shall argue) that some punishments may be neither unpleasant, nor unwanted, nor undesirable from the point of view of the punishee.

These authors fall into three groups.

The first group defines punishment as a violation or deprivation of rights. These writers are often motivated by the use of mandatory psychiatric treatment as a criminal sanction, which can be as penal as any other measure, although imposed with benevolent intent. Violation of someone's rights is, of course, a prima facie bad for the person whose rights are being violated. Yet it may be good on the whole for her, and she may even want it to occur and find it pleasant when it does. For example, if I steal a cake belonging to a weak-willed diabetic, I do her a great benefit. She may even secretly have hoped that someone would steal the cake (though she was too weak-willed to ask someone to do so). So if punishment is to be defined as a violation of rights, the possibility is left open that some punishments may not be disvaluable at all.

In this first category we find John Rawls, Claudia Card, and Hugo Bedau.[43] Rawls writes in "Two Concepts of Rules":

> a person is said to suffer punishment whenever he is legally deprived of some of the normal rights of a citizen on the ground that he has violated a rule of law.[44]

(He adds several other conditions to his definition.) Yet in a footnote to this very definition, he equates it with that of Hobbes who (as we have seen) defines punishment in terms of pain or evil. In general, he shows no awareness that a change has been made—at least, he never alludes to the fact. Bedau, on the other hand, explicitly notes the change from "pain" or "suffering" to "deprivation of rights"; in fact, he seems to be the first to do so. Yet he also says that the change he contemplates is "relatively minor." Indeed, one can see that the change he has in mind is, in fact, minor: His example of a nonpainful punishment is the death penalty (painlessly administered).[45] So, in fact, he seems to have made no significant departure from the Standard View. This is confirmed by what he writes elsewhere in the same article. "A punishment . . . always deprives a person of something . . . of value." "Punishment . . . leaves the person punished worse off than before."[46]

The second group of dissenters make small concessions to opponents of the Standard View. Some note that some punishments may involve no pain, suffering, or loss, but they consider such punishments to be odd or inappropriate. In this category we find Kurt Baier, Tziporah Kasachkoff, and Richard Wasserstrom.[47] As I mention above, these people are really just offering the Standard View in a weaker form.

The third group comprises those who straightforwardly categorize punishment as something other than a disvalue. In this group we find A. R. Manser and James Doyle. Manser reacts thus to Flew's definition:

> If we are concerned only with reforming or deterring, then there is no obvious *necessity* to do it by means of unpleasantness; that such means are best would be a matter of empirical investigation. But whatever the result of such research, there is no reason, if retribution is not accepted, to include unpleasantness in the *definition* of punishment. Plato saw this: "When anyone commits any injustice, small or great, the law will admonish and compel him either never at all to do the like again . . . and he must in addition pay for the hurt. Whether the end is to be attained by word or action, with pleasure or pain, by giving or taking away privileges, by means of penalties or gifts, or in whatsoever way the law shall make a man hate injustice, this is the noblest work of the law."[48]

The quotation from Plato makes it unclear whether we are still talking about punishment at all. For Plato seems to be giving us a more general list of crime-preventive measures, only some of which count as punishment. In any case, Manser is an ambivalent retributivist (p. 306) and so is not certain whether he wants to omit unpleasantness from the definition of punishment. Doyle presents us with an apparently robust denial of the Standard View:

> Therefore we should describe justifiable punishment (if there be such) as the satisfaction of all the just claims invoked by the commission of criminal offenses. Punishment interpreted in this way is obviously not an unqualified evil—though neither is it an unqualified good.[49]

He does not mention, but we may remark, that the satisfaction of claims is not, in general, an unpleasant thing. (If I promise to go to the movies with you, then you have a claim against me that I go to the movies with you—hardly an uncomfortable prospect.) Yet, on the next page, we find him saying that punishment may be "interpreted neutrally as some kind of legally imposed deprivation or coercion." So Doyle has not abandoned the Standard View after all—although his definition at least has the merit of not excluding it. His view seems to be that punishments are probably all disvaluable, but that is not what is important about them. The only unambiguous denial I have encountered is in the work of Unto Tähtinen:

> What is most vital, the definition of punishment should not imply violence in the form of inflicting any sort of injury, not even in the sense that an offender is subjected to a measure against his will. His co-operation may be acquired by convincing him of the good intentions of society.[50]

In the penological literature one encounters authors who advocate measures of criminal justice that may not be disvaluable (see Chapter 6, section 4). But these authors almost always place such measures under the heading of *restitution*, rather than *punishment*, since they tend to think that punishment must, by definition, be disvaluable to its victim. A certain conceptual confusion ensues. For in restitution, someone who has (perhaps blamelessly) harmed another compensates the person harmed. Crime or wrongdoing is only one way of becoming liable to make restitution. But these penologists advocate measures that ill fit this description. For example, after some crimes there is no victim to whom restitution can be made. (The crime may be a victimless one, or the victim may be dead or unavailable, or may not want compensation.) In such a case advocates of "restitution" either recommend no sanction, or else call for a "substitute victim" to whom restitution is made.

I would tend to say that these penologists are actually advocating non-disvaluable punishments—that is, they are opposing the Standard View. But the Standard View grips them so firmly that they cannot use the word *punishment* for something that involves no pain or suffering. So they pick another word—*restitution*—with all its inappropriate conceptual baggage. We cannot, then, count them as unequivocal opponents of the Standard View, though their position will serve as evidence against it.

In the end, we find virtually no significant, articulate dissent from the Standard View.

VERSIONS OF THE STANDARD VIEW

Before going on, we must consider the several variants of the Standard View. "Several" is an understatement. As we have seen, in defining punishment, partisans of the Standard View have nearly exhausted the thesaurus heading of *harm*. These differences between one term or another are significant, but unless we manage to cut the list down somewhat, we will never get anywhere. I therefore propose to consolidate them under three headings.

Even before making this trichotomy, we may eliminate *pain* from the list. It is now agreed, even among proponents of the Standard View, that *punishment* is not to be defined as pain.[51] Even some of those who define punishment as pain were no doubt following the common practice of using *pain* as an antonym for *pleasure* in place of the more accurate, but odd, word *unpleasure*.[52]

The remaining words in our list seem to fall under the headings of *unpleasant, unwanted,* and *undesirable*. This is not meant as an absolutely precise classification, but I should note two points. When I call something *unwanted* here, I do not mean that people merely fail to want it, but that they actually want to avoid it. And when I call something *undesirable,* I mean that it is bad for the person who gets it; this person himself may in fact desire the undesirable things that he receives or undergoes. I might equivalently have said that punishment is a *bad* (that is, the opposite of a good) for the punishee; and sometimes I will use this term synonymously. But in this case we must be sure to remember that I mean bad *for the punishee*. That does not mean that it is bad from some impersonal standpoint, nor that it is a bad thing to do (that is, a morally wrong act).

I accordingly categorize our list as follows:

Unpleasant	Unwanted	Undesirable
suffering	unwanted	harsh treatment
hardship	imposition	evil
unpleasant	bending of the will	deprivation

(I do not attach any great importance to precisely this classification, and I will not argue with anyone who disagrees.)

The three headings are usually connected with different concerns. Those who consider the punishee's perception of punishment tend to speak of it as unpleasant. Those who are concerned with deterrence tend to emphasize the unwantedness of punishment, for people are often concerned to avoid things (such as death) that are not strictly speaking unpleasant. We also find terms from this category used by those concerned with the issue of mandatory treatment as a criminal penalty. Still others speak of punishment as a bad (or deprivation of a good) when they notice that it usually consists of treatment considered bad by some social standard, treatment that some individuals may desire and find pleasant. Some retributivists also tend to speak this way when they seek to balance the badness of a crime against the badness of its punishment.

Though these three dimensions of disvalue are distinct, it is not always clear under which heading a given definition should fall, perhaps because some authors are careless, perhaps because the headings themselves are less than perfect, but—most interestingly—because many philosophers have held that some or all of the categories coincide. Psychological hedonism holds that the only thing ultimately desired for its own sake is pleasure, and hence that the only thing we ultimately desire to avoid for its own sake is unpleasure. Ethical hedonism holds that pleasure is the only thing that is intrinsically good and unpleasure the only thing that is intrinsically bad. If we combine these views, as many have, we merge the three categories into one.

These three dimensions of disvalue give us, not three, but many more versions of the Standard View. For one may define punishment in terms of one of these dimensions, or one may use several of them in combination, and the number of combinations is great. Obviously I cannot anticipate everything that the Standard Viewers may claim. Fortunately, I need consider only one of these complex versions; namely, the one that holds that punishment is, by definition, unpleasant *or* unwanted *or* bad. Clearly this is the hardest version to refute; and if I succeed here, all the others are seriously called into question. I therefore stick to the three simple versions, and this one complex one.

2. Refutation of the Standard View: The Main Grounds

TWO IMPORTANT EXAMPLES

I want here to set forth two examples that will be important in our discussion of the Standard View. These two are to exemplify punishment under the conscientious paradigm. One aspect must particularly be kept in mind: We are considering a punishee who *wants* to submit to punishment, who believes that she can achieve reconciliation, atonement, expiation, renewed innocence, greater moral knowledge, or some other good by undergoing the punishment. Of course, if she had not committed any crime or did not think that the punishment would produce any good effect, she would probably not want to undergo it. We must therefore consider our examples in their proper context: We assume that the offender has committed an offense and believes that the punishment in question can promote expiation, reconciliation, or the like.

The first example: community-service work as a criminal sanction. An offender who receives such a sentence is required to work (usually without pay) on some project for the benefit of the community. In Canada, according to Calvert Dodge, such projects have included "working with handicapped people, repairing damage which [the offender] might have done in the community, coaching a sports team, cleaning a park, or helping build a public dock." Dodge notes that "a number of offenders have continued as volunteers in their work order placement after the terms of the order were satisfied."[53] The following points should be noted:

Community-service orders are punishments.

They are used alongside imprisonment, fines, and other usual criminal penalties.

They are just and fair sanctions for at least some offenses.

This I commend to readers on the basis of moral intuition.

Their fairness does not depend on identifiable harm's having been done to identifiable victims.

Community-service sanctions are therefore not a matter of restitution—not in any obvious way. (See fuller discussion, Chapter 6, section 4.) A community-service order could with fairness be imposed on someone found guilty of an attempt, from which no harm eventuated, or a victimless crime.

The second example is penance for sins. I have in mind such things as praying, fasting, donating money to charity, or doing charitable works. The penances imposed by the Roman Catholic church are a particularly good example, since the procedures are formalized and well known, and they are the subject of a considerable body of literature; but I do not mean to exclude other penances. As discussed above (Chapter 2, section 1), *penance* is not an exclusively religious concept, since even a nonreligious person may do penance for wrongdoing, though perhaps the concept of penance is most at home in a religious context.[54]

Again, I invite you to accept several claims:

Penances are punishments.

This point has been discussed in Chapter 2, section 1.

If there is a Deity, penance is at least sometimes a reasonable and just response to sin or wrongdoing.

Indeed, one can go so far as to say that, whether God exists or not, penance is sometimes a just and reasonable response.[55]

Penances are often undertaken willingly by the penitent.

This point we have also discussed in Chapter 2. Of course, if someone does penance only to avoid hell, it is not really done willingly; but I assume that it is sometimes done at least partly for other, conscientious motives.

These two examples—community-service sanctions and penances—fall squarely under the Paradigm of the Conscientious Punishee and are therefore paradigm cases of punishment, and not merely odd or unimportant cases. They may be unusual—at least they are not the most frequent kind of criminal penalties—but still, they are paradigms. Indeed, the use of community-service sanctions is increasing in the criminal justice systems of the industrialized countries, so it is even more paradigmatic than one could say a few years ago.

With these two examples, I can now proceed to argue against the three versions of the Standard View.

PUNISHMENT AS UNWANTED

Of all the versions, the worst one is that which makes *unwantedness* a defining characteristic of punishment. There are two subversions: One says that punishment is unwanted by the punishee; the other, that punishment consists of the kind of thing that is unwanted by people in general. I consider the first one first.

Unwanted by the Punishee. The Conscientious Punishee—someone who wants to atone or be reconciled—will see punishment as a convenient or even indispensable means of doing so. She will therefore want to be punished. Punishment, then, cannot be defined as something that the punishee does not want. Of course, there are many people who do not want to undergo punishment and do so only under coercion. But even then, the coercion—and hence the unwantedness—is not usually part of the punishment, but merely a means of ensuring punishment. If coercion were an integral part of the punishment, then no one could carry out his duty to submit to punishment. For those who submit willingly are not coerced. Hence, again, unwantedness cannot be part of the definition of punishment.

Generally Unwanted.   The second sub-version maintains that punishment consists, by definition, of something that people generally want to avoid. Our two prime examples suffice to refute this claim. These punishments involve prayer, works of charity, and useful community service. These are things that many ordinary people do every day and would not want to omit. There are other examples, too. A Marine sergeant may punish a disobedient recruit by requiring him to do twenty push-ups, but push-ups are not something that people generally want to avoid; on the contrary, many people choose to do them every day. A parent may punish a child by requiring her to stay in her room for an hour; but people, even children, often want to stay in their rooms for an hour. Perhaps even this child herself may want to stay in her room, though in this case the punishment is probably ineffective.

Here one is tempted to point out an important fact: Although many people often want to do push-ups, or stay in their rooms, the Marine recruit and the child typically do not want to do these things, at least, not when assigned as punishment. But this thought merely brings us back to the first sub-version, already shown to be inadequate.

PUNISHMENT AS UNPLEASANT OR UNDESIRABLE

Our two prime examples also defeat the claim that punishment must be unpleasant or undesirable. Prayer, charitable work, and public service are not particularly unpleasant things. Public service and charitable work may on occasion involve wretched toil (for example, working on a chain gang), but they may equally well involve such rewarding tasks as coaching a little-league baseball team. The idea that punishment *must* be unpleasant seems to arise from the legal paradigm's assumption that the typical punishee does not want his punishment, does not perceive or appreciate its expiatory or reconciliatory effect. Naturally, anything will seem unpleasant to a person who does not want it and does not even see why one would want it. But the conscientious punishee does want to submit to his punishment, and knows why.

Nor are prayer, charitable works, and public service bad for the person who undertakes them. On the contrary, they are worthwhile ways to spend time and can make someone into a better person.

"Well, prayer and the others may not be unpleasant or undesirable in themselves, but you forget the opportunity cost. The person who prays gives up the chance to dance and sing (which is more pleasant);

the person who does charitable work gives up the chance to eat and drink (which may be a better way for her to spend her time). If we count the opportunity cost, these punishments are, after all, unpleasant and undesirable. Or, as we might better put it, they deprive us of pleasures and goods that we might have had."

But even if we count the opportunity cost, we come out ahead. As for pleasure, the conscientious person feels remorse for his misdeeds and is happier if he submits to a deserved punishment. Of course, even the conscientious punishee would probably not want to be punished if he had done nothing wrong, or if he expected no good effect on the order of reconciliation. But, granted that he had done wrong and knows it, and expects reconciliation to come from punishment, then he will find the punishment pleasant and desirable. At worst, this objection only shows that punishment is not the most pleasant or most desirable alternative, which need not worry us.

"Well, perhaps prayer, charitable work, and community service are not unpleasant. But it is unpleasant to be forced to do these things."

True enough. But, as we have said, coercion is not part of the punishment. If a person is ordered to pay a fine, it is not required that the money be extracted against her will. There may not even be a threat of force. If Houdini is sentenced to a term in jail and stays in jail till the term is up, then he has been punished, even though he could escape without difficulty. Coercion, when necessary, is only a means of assuring that the sentence is fulfilled, not part of the sentence itself.

"Let me reformulate the last objection. The disvalue of punishment lies not in being forced to undergo it, but in losing the legal right to do otherwise. The right to control one's own life and possessions is precious, and any loss of it is a serious loss."

This is true. The loss of legal rights is a serious loss. Someone who has been sentenced to serve a term in prison has lost the legal right to do otherwise. But—much as in the last case—the loss of rights is not the punishment: Going to prison is the punishment. If Al Capone is sentenced to a term in prison but never goes, he has lost certain legal rights, but he has not been punished. What we mean by "loss of legal rights" is simply that it is legally permissible to punish the person.

"Yes, well, if someone goes to prison or says penitential prayers, the loss of rights is no part of the imprisonment or the prayers. But loss of legal rights is itself a punishment. This is especially clear when a reckless driver is punished by having his driver's license suspended. And to lose rights is to be deprived of a good. In particular, a conscientious person will feel bound by the limitations on her rights, and will comply: For her, loss of legal rights is worse than for the scofflaw Capone."

We can reply in two ways.

It is true, first of all, that loss of rights is a bad thing. So is loss of money. But this does not mean that every occurrence involving loss of rights is disvaluable: One might as well say that every purchase is a loss, since it involves loss of money. People often give up rights, usually in exchange for something else, but often without seeking anything in exchange. In particular, it can be a gain if I lose the legal right to do something I am personally committed not to do. If I don't want to do it and feel obligated not to do it, what good to me is the legal right to do it? It is only an unwanted temptation. (I am speaking of a short enough period so that one can later change one's mind.) Is it a loss for me that I do not have the legal right to commit murder? Hardly. A conscientious punishee is in just this kind of position: She feels that there is a rationale for punishment and accepts the duty to submit. She does not want to—indeed, feels obligated not to—avoid her punishment. So it is no loss to *her* if she loses the legal right to avoid her punishment.

Second, even in the case of less conscientious offenders, loss of rights may be valuable. A criminal may be dissatisfied with a life of crime, but may know no other or consider herself incapable of change. A loss of rights makes it permissible for the state to intervene and steer the criminal into a new way of life. (I assume that rehabilitation is possible, at least occasionally.) Both the criminal and those around her may consider her new life better than the old one. The medical theory of punishment, held by Plato, Aristotle, and Aquinas, justifies punishment in this way.

Hence, none of the three versions of the Standard View is acceptable. The proponent of that view, in a last effort, might offer a composite view: Punishment, he might say, is by definition *either* unwanted *or* unpleasant *or* undesirable. But clearly this maneuver gets him nowhere. The same two prime examples that served to defeat each version separately also serve as counterexamples to the disjunction of all three. There may be yet another version of the Standard View that might escape my objections; but the task of devising such a view I will leave to someone else. For now, I think we may regard the Standard View as unacceptable, and with this thought I complete the main argument of this chapter.

3. Additional Counterexamples

Aside from the two prime examples, there are many other counter-examples to the Standard View. Though not crucial to my main argument, these other counterexamples are of considerable interest. They fall into two categories.

DISVALUE NOT A NECESSARY CONDITION

First of all, there are examples of punishments that are not disvaluable, or not completely so:

Example 1.   A fine of ten cents (or, if one is rich enough, even ten thousand dollars) will probably not be unpleasant and may even present a welcome opportunity to rid oneself of unwanted loose change. (Isn't it a pain to carry all those pennies around?) Inappropriate punishment, perhaps, but a ten-cent fine is still a punishment.

A prison term of one minute may also cause no distress at all, and the proverbial slap on the wrist, if it is light enough, may also involve no unpleasure.

"But if someone is fined ten cents, or serves a one-minute term in Sing-Sing, or endures a mild slap on the wrist—or even if someone undergoes all three—why, that person hasn't really been punished at all! So your examples prove nothing."

There is something to this objection, but it does not really defeat my examples. The objector accurately notes that these tiny inflictions are totally inappropriate as punishment for the typical offense, legal or otherwise. And one may fairly express this by saying that the person subjected to them hasn't really been punished at all. But tiny punishments are not necessarily silly. There are offenses for which they are quite fitting and, if we look at such cases, we may no longer be tempted to retort, "He hasn't really been punished at all." A very short stay in jail, for example, may acquaint a first offender with the much more serious punishment that awaits her if she persists in offending. This kind of sentence would be especially fitting for someone whose character is not firmly set in its evil ways, someone whose offense represents a first, tentative foray into the unlawful. The threat of a substantial prison term will thereafter have a greater deterrent effect. Very short prison sentences are, in fact, sometimes given out by judges. The practice is usually called "shock sentencing." These shock sentences, however, are usually much more severe than those

I have mentioned, amounting to perhaps a weekend in prison. Most people would find such a term unpleasant and unwanted.

A tiny punishment may also serve a particular expressive function. As many have noted, punishment usually expresses condemnation or disavowal of the offense on the part of the punishing authority, and on the part of those whom the authority represents.[56] But on occasion the person assigning punishment may find that there are offenses that she cannot in good conscience condemn or disavow. This may happen especially if the standards under which the offender is condemned are unjust or archaic. Faced with an offender of this kind, a judge may impose a token punishment. The symbolic function of this punishment is ironic: It is a punishment that is not really a punishment, expressing a condemnation that is not really a condemnation. It is as if the judge were to wag his finger and say, "Naughty, naughty." In this way the judge manages to maintain his fidelity to the law while maintaining his own moral integrity.

In 1977 in New York City, one George H. Willig paid $1.10 as a penalty for scaling the World Trade Center.[57] Though this was a civil penalty and therefore perhaps not strictly a punishment, it illustrates the principle well enough. Willig entertained large numbers of people by a show of skill that could not but draw admiration. The court dealt with him in a way that expressed this admiration but also made clear its intention to enforce the law.

Example 2.   Even if we consider severe sentences, there are still people who do not find them disvaluable. Some people regard money as a burden and are glad to be rid of it. (Spinoza seems to have been like this.) Such people might be pleased at the opportunity to pay a fine. There are others who prefer prison to liberty. Some of these are indigents who commit crimes in order to get the free room and board that prison provides. Others are jailbirds who have been in prison so long that they no longer know how to live outside and fear being released.

Now, these two examples do not really count against the Standard View, since both involve deprivation of a good, albeit sometimes a small good. But there are others that do count.

Example 3.   Allenwood Federal Prison is said to be a very pleasant place, something on the order of a penal country club. (Even if it is not like a country club, we can easily imagine such a prison.) Now, a term in Allenwood may be an inappropriate punishment; many people thought so when, amid great publicity, some of the Watergate convicts were sent there. Nevertheless, it is definitely a punishment. Yet it consists of something that most people would find pleasant indeed: A sojourn in a place very much like a country club, where food and clothing are provided, and one need not work.

Someone may object here that it is unpleasant to be *forced* to stay in Allenwood. To this we may give the same replies that I gave to a similar objection in the last section. Indeed, this example differs from the prime examples only in that they involve sanctions that seem appropriate, while Allenwood does not.

Example 4.   Also relevant here are such punishments (previously mentioned) as push-ups administered by a Marine sergeant, or remaining in one's own room. These are, in themselves, neither pleasant nor unpleasant, desirable nor undesirable. For some offenses they are appropriate punishments, though they seem less so if they are wanted by the punishee.

These examples are, in themselves, of more interest than importance. Yet they serve to show that my prime examples of nondisvaluable punishments are not radically different from the more usual kinds, but form part of a continuum, which we may illustrate thus:

Penances	(1) Typically desirable things to do, even apart from offenses.
	(2) Typically wanted by offender.
	(3) Appropriate response to offense, even when wanted by offender.
Community-service sanctions	(1) Typically desirable.
	(2) Often wanted.
	(3) Appropriate even when wanted.
Allenwood Prison	(1) Typically desirable.
	(2) Not often wanted.
	(3) Inappropriate in most cases (?).
Push-ups, confinement to room	(1) Not undesirable.
	(2) Seldom wanted.
	(3) Inappropriate when wanted, except from conscience.
Serious fines, typical prison	(1) Undesirable.
	(2) Almost never wanted.
	(3) Typically inappropriate when wanted, except from conscience.

DISVALUE NOT AMONG SUFFICIENT CONDITIONS

So far I have concentrated on showing that disvalue is not a necessary condition of punishment. There are, second, examples that show that disvalue, when added to the other parts of the usual definition of punishment, does not yield a set of jointly sufficient conditions of punishment. We may take Hart's definition as our example; he defines the "standard or central case of 'punishment' " in terms of the following five conditions:

(i) It must involve pain or other consequences normally considered unpleasant.

(ii) It must be for an offence against legal rules.

(iii) It must be of an actual or supposed offender for his offence.

(iv) It must be intentionally administered by human beings other than the offender.

(v) It must be imposed and administered by an authority constituted by a legal system against which the offence is committed.[58]

Benn and Peters add the following:

[vi] The unpleasantness should be an essential part of what is intended and not merely incidental to some other aim.[59]

Now consider the following example: Johnson has committed a hideous crime—too awful to describe here. He is being tried before a judge. After the evidence has been presented and the arguments heard, the judge makes the following speech:

There is no doubt in my mind that you are guilty of the crime of which you have been accused, a crime so vile and execrable that every decent person must be revolted. [Johnson begins to sweat.] As a judge sitting on the bench, I feel constrained not to use the kind of language which adequately describes you. [Johnson's face turns ashen gray; he gapes blankly.] There is nothing at all in your conduct which speaks for leniency. But, evil as you are, the punishment prescribed by law is so vicious that I cannot in good conscience impose it even on someone like you; and the law gives me no discretion to reduce or alter the sentence. Though I personally have no doubt whatsoever as to your guilt, it would not be unreasonable if someone did doubt it. I therefore, with great reluctance, find you not guilty.

This speech is calculated to strike fear into the heart of the defendant since, until the last sentences, it appears as if he is to receive the vicious punishment. The speech fits the Flew–Benn–Hart definition of punishment: It is unpleasant for the offender; it is for an offense against legal rules; it is imposed upon the offender; it is administered intentionally by another human being, who is an authority constituted by the legal system against which the offense was committed; and the unpleasantness of the speech is part of the intended effect. But Johnson has not been punished. Fortunately for him, he has escaped punishment.

Now some may object: "Johnson *has* been punished. Even though no legal penalty has been imposed, we could call the judge's speech a moral punishment." Well, even if this is so, the example serves to undermine the Hart–Benn–Flew definition as a definition of *legal* punishment, which is how they meant it. And we can overcome the objection by noting that the trial itself (even apart from speeches calculated to terrify) fits Hart's definition: Standing trial is (i) an unpleasant experience (ii) imposed for an offense against legal rules (iii) upon the suspected offender because of his or her offenses; it is (iv) intentionally administered by human beings (judges and bailiffs) other than the suspected offender, and (v) imposed by a suitable legal authority. But a trial is surely not a punishment.

Of course, until the trial is over, the defendant is not officially deemed to be an offender. Since the definition requires that the punishment be imposed on a suspected offender, one might think the example fails. But we do not select people at random to stand trial for criminal offenses; we try only those who have been determined by less formal procedures to be worthy of suspicion. So the trial is a trial of a supposed offender.

This example, I confess, fails to meet the extra condition added by Benn and Peters: The unpleasantness of a trial is merely incidental to the aim of determining guilt or innocence. But this clause fails for other reasons. (For example, our aim in imprisoning a violent criminal may be to keep her off the streets and thereby protect the rest of us. Any unpleasantness involved is purely incidental to this aim. Yet this imprisonment is surely a punishment.)

The main problem with the Hart–Benn–Flew definition is, I suggest, the clause that makes pain or unpleasantness an essential condition. I have more to say about this in section 5.

4. The Psychology of Positive Punishment

Now, the reader might find no flaw in the arguments just presented, yet remain unconvinced. It is perhaps hard to picture to oneself the kind of person who would fit the Paradigm of the Conscientious Punishee and would actually be pleased with his punishment. One may think, "Well, there may be people who willingly endure punishment, but surely no one likes it. Even when people seem to like punishment, it smacks of suffering somehow, even if one is glad to endure it."

This conception is, in fact, mostly supported by writers on penance. We read their recommendations: The sinner is to make herself suffer. Fasting, exile, sackcloth, ashes, hairshirts: the person who enjoys these is obviously enjoying her self-affliction. It is certainly possible to make oneself suffer and take pleasure in the suffering— but that doesn't mean that the penitent is not suffering.

This view is reinforced by much of what one reads on the psychology of submission to punishment. One gets the idea of a vindictive agency within the psyche that delights in afflicting the true self: in Freud's words, "The super-ego torments the sinful ego with [a] feeling of anxiety, and is on the watch for opportunities of getting it punished."[60] This punitive agency of the psyche, moreover, is perceived as if it were an alien entity, pressing on the poor ego demands that the ego would prefer to have nothing to do with. Self-punishment, on this view, along with willing submission to punishment by others, is necessarily an ascetic exercise. Indeed, it has often been thought that a punitive psychic agency of this sort is the source of all moral motivation.[61] Even if the person seems to be enjoying things, she is at the bottom engaging in self-denial. Gomez, let us say, is carrying out a sentence of public-service work, working in a public park, planting trees and shrubs out in the fresh air. He seems to be enjoying it. He would probably say so, if we asked. But what he'd *really* enjoy is a week in Las Vegas, and he'd be there right now if his overbearing superego only let him. One day he tries. Though he succeeds in escaping the work crew, the superego hounds him with such great waves of anxiety and guilt that it's easier to come back to the spade and shovel. What we have is a whole economy of pain, suffering, and self-denial.

Something like this surely happens in many cases of willing submission to punishment. There is, though, another possibility. We can best start by turning to the handful of writers on penance who take a truly nonascetic approach. Thus they describe their experience:

> True repentance brings joy. If repentance is genuine, the person is joyful, though contrite and humble. If it is insincere, the penitent is melancholy and irritable.[62]

Why fast? If a man fasts with the idea of gaining a favor from Heaven thereby, it is a futile self-affliction, and it will be of no avail. If a man fasts for the sake of Heaven, is it not better to devote himself to learning for the sake of Heaven?[63]

The epitome of this line of thought is Abraham Isaac Kook:

Repentance is the healthiest experience of the soul. . . . [I]n this state the soul will feel the greatest natural pleasure.

Without the thought of repentance, its tranquility and assurance, man would be unable to find rest, and spiritual life would be unable to develop in the world. . . . [S]ince the primary basis of [a person's] perfection is the yearning and firm desire toward perfection, this desire itself is the basis of repentance, which constantly triumphs over his [imperfect] way of life and truly perfects him.[64]

One gets the impression of a truly joyful penance. But can we rely on these self-descriptions? Are these pious authors perhaps deluding themselves for a holy cause? Whether they are or not, we do find in the psychoanalytic literature a psychic function described in remarkably similar terms; in Freud's words,

One important function remains to be mentioned which we attribute to this super-ego. It [the superego] is also the vehicle of the ego ideal by which the ego measures itself, which it emulates, and whose demand for ever greater perfection it strives to fulfill. There is no doubt that this ego ideal is the precipitate of the old picture of the parents, the expression of admiration for the perfection which the child then attributed to them.[65]

Freud himself left this concept relatively undeveloped and did not always distinguish it clearly from the superego proper. It was taken up, however, by his disciples, who worked out its details in various ways. Though not all are consistent, the consensus distinguishes the ego ideal from the superego (in the narrower sense) in the following terms: We submit to the superego out of fear; to the ego ideal out of love. The superego sets boundaries, restrictions, and prohibitions; the ego ideal provides goals and positive aims. The superego says, "I will live up to the demands of my parents"; the ego ideal says, "I am like my omnipotent parents." Unlike the superego (in the narrower sense), the ego ideal does not strike the ego as an alien power: One might say, it is an identification, not an introject.[66] Erich Fromm makes a similar distinction between the authoritarian conscience and the humanistic conscience.[67]

Accepting this analysis of the ego ideal, we have a natural locus for the need for punishment that avoids the hostile aspects of more usual views. Few writers, however, have seen it in this light. Under the influence of the Paradigm of Legal Punishment and the Standard View, most find the ego ideal an unlikely candidate for the job. Psychologists have tended to view punishment as something that the ego ideal, by definition, would not bring about. After all, the ego ideal works by attraction, not by repulsion. Indeed, if we speak of self-punishment in an intrapsychic sense, it probably cannot be ascribed to the ego ideal. It is different with punishment in a social context. Here, a person, identifying not only with his parents but with the larger society (or indeed with God Himself, following Kook), strives to perfect himself as part of society and the world. The world, we know, is imperfect, but we work to move it toward perfection. If we ourselves are responsible for the imperfection, we work twice as hard, and this extra work is the punishment. (We work twice as hard to perfect ourselves: this is reform; and to perfect the world: this is restitution and penance.) Our two prime examples—community service and penance for sins—are perfectly intelligible on this model. The offender need not have a vindictive, guilt-provoking conscience to prod her. All she needs is a sense of the perfection and beauty that the world, and she as a part of it, are capable of. Her wrongdoing is a blot on the world, and on herself; attracted by a vision of a more perfect world, she wipes away the blot. She undertakes tasks that undo the effects of the misdeed, thereby undertaking her own punishment.

I must add a by now familiar stricture: The typical criminal will have no such sense of perfection, no such attraction. I am not suggesting—it would be a bizarre proposal—that we should treat typical criminals as if they had such motivations. But it is perfectly possible for a normally constituted human being to have such motivations, and that is all we need to show. If so, then we can understand how there can be punishment that does not partake at all of any form of disvalue.

5. Disvalue and the Justification of Punishment

Many authors have claimed that punishment requires justification because it involves the infliction of pain or other disvalue. But the justification of punishment differs, in important ways, from the justification of imposing disvalue upon someone. This provides another argument against the Standard View.

Punishment requires a justification, and most people would not be satisfied with a justification that simply points out the good consequences of punishment. (For example, the fact that incarceration can deter crime is not enough all by itself, in most people's eyes, to justify the apparent injustice of imprisoning people.) But the imposition of disvalue is different. Sometimes it requires virtually no justification; in other cases it is enough to provide a simple justification by pointing out the good consequences. For example, it is morally permissible for me to marry the person you wanted to marry, to paint my house purple, or to worship Baal. Any of these things may cause you great distress; you may not want them to happen; they may leave you worse off. Yet no justification is required. Or, at most, I must give a token justification: "Bernice and I freely choose to marry each other, and we have not promised not to; it is my house, and I may paint it any color I like; and my religion is none of your business." In each case these are things I am at liberty to do, and you have no claim against me that I not do them. This recalls the case of Johnson, the reprehensible criminal of section 3. People in general are at liberty to say nasty things to Johnson, so the judge may do so as well. This lecture is therefore not a punishment. In order to punish Johnson, the judge would have had to do something to him that would ordinarily count as a violation of Johnson's rights. It is the violation of presumptive rights that calls for justification, not the imposition of disvalue in itself. And a violation of presumptive rights would call for justification even if it did not cause the victim pain or other disvalue. (I would not, however, make violation of presumptive rights a general necessary condition for punishment in place of the disvalue condition; but that is a subject for the next chapter.)

To see the second point, note that it is morally permissible for me to take your food without your permission if I am starving, or to knock you down in the process of saving a drowning swimmer. These things may cause you all three kinds of disvalue: You will likely be displeased, you may not want such things to happen, and they may leave you worse off. Yet, in either case, a simple consequentialist justification is sufficient: "Lives were at stake, and they could not be saved except by hurting you in this less serious way." This kind of justification does not work in the case of punishment. The practice of imprisoning criminals may save lives, but most people consider it unsatisfactory just to tell the prisoner: "Lives are at stake, and we can save them only by imprisoning you, along with others."

Similarly, a simple consequentialist justification often suffices for individual acts of a legislature, even though they often help some people at the expense of others. Such acts are justified by two facts:

(1) A government with coercive powers is justified in general; and (2) the actions of the legislature on the whole benefit (nearly) everyone. But this reasoning does not seem adequate to justify penal legislation.

These facts about justification of disvalue and of punishment argue against the Standard View.

6. Concessions to the Standard View

The Standard View is false, but not completely without truth. How could it be so strongly held, if it did not contain some insight?

First, even though the Standard View is incorrect, it is still true that many punishments are imposed on people against their will. It is these that cry out for our attention: In this sense, they are the most important, and most urgently in need of justification. I speak here of legal punishment, which may lock a person away for years, or execute her, or even torture her. Parental punishment, too, must be remembered here, for a parent is a sort of absolute ruler, from whose decisions there is often no appeal, who can administer harangues and beatings. (Indeed, it is surprising that relatively few philosophers have considered this issue.) We cannot give up punishing criminals and children, nor can we expect them all to be conscientious punishees. These important cases of unwanted punishment will always be with us.

Moreover, the typical rationales of legal and parental punishment ensure that such punishment will usually be unpleasant. The usual purposes are retribution, deterrence, and reform. Retribution, by definition, is the returning of evil for evil or harm for harm. Deterrence takes place by the threat of harm. And reform is needed most by the unrepentant offender, who is exactly the one least likely to want it; so reformatory punishment, too, is typically unwanted. But these rationales are not necessary properties—much less defining properties—of punishment.

Yet further, the conscientious punishee accepts punishment because she appreciates its rationale. Criminals, however, usually do not appreciate the rationale for their punishment. Children usually do not have the maturity to understand the rationale for their punishment. So we cannot expect them to find their penalties desirable.

Second, even when we consider non-disvaluable punishment, there is still some truth to the Standard View. The activities involved in such punishment—prayer, charitable work, public service, push-ups, remaining in one's room, and so on—are not things that we usually have an impulse to do. Submitting to such punishments is not like eating, or engaging in sex. When we want to do charitable work, public service, and the like, our desire is usually reflective; we want to be a certain kind of person, or live up to certain principles, or achieve certain ends, and we act as we do in order to become that kind of person, or live up to these principles, or achieve those ends. Most of us, acting on impulse alone, would not be very charitable. But if we want to think of ourselves as kind and charitable persons, we will do charitable work. Most of us, acting on impulse alone, would serve ourselves and our friends, not the community. But if we think we have a duty to serve the community, we may do so. Most of us, acting on impulse alone, would not do push-ups. But if we have physical strength as our goal, we may do them. So one cannot usually submit to punishment just by giving in to an urge.

You might be tempted to make this into a defining feature of punishment by saying punishment essentially involves things that we have no impulse to do. But it is not so. Many people pray impulsively (for example, in times of stress or great joy); many people impulsively help the needy people they encounter. If these activities are undertaken as punishment, the fact that they are impulsively done does not seem to make them inappropriate as punishment. On the other hand, some punishments do seem to be spoiled if they are undertaken on impulse. If someone simply prefers prison and impulsively chooses to go there after a crime, the imprisonment does not seem like an appropriate punishment.

Third, even if a punishment is not painful, it can still be serious. It can be difficult, daunting, and exhausting. It can require the punishee to put his whole self into it. It can be a Herculean task without being a Sisyphean one. Indeed, it seems that the punishment for any serious offense would need to be serious in this way.

The concept of work provides a useful parallel. Work is human effort aimed at producing a result. It is not necessarily unpleasant, unwanted, or bad for the worker. But if work were done only by people who prefer not to do it, one can understand how disvalue would come to be seen as an essential characteristic of work. In fact, most people who work probably would prefer not to, and there is a tendency to use the word *work* in just this way. If someone thoroughly enjoys her job, people may say, "Why, that isn't work at all." Our word *travail* is the French word for work. But it would be wrong to write disvalue or unpleasantness into the definition of *work*.

Finally, even for the most conscientious of punishees, a penalty

will be desirable only in context—that is, if the person has committed an offense—and only because it is understood to produce
atonement, reconciliation, expiation, or the like. A person who willingly does community-service work as a penalty for crime would
probably not choose to do the same amount of work if she had not
engaged in crime. If she were innocent, she would resent being forced
to do that amount of work and would probably not feel happy about
doing it. So, in a limited sense, the penalty is something unwanted
and unpleasant: We want punishment only for the expiation (or the
like) of an offense, and we hope that we will not commit any offenses.
In other words, innocent people usually do not want punishment,
and they hope that they will never want it. But if, nonetheless, the
innocent become guilty, they will see punishment as exactly what
they need.

CHAPTER 4

What Is Punishment?

1. A Definition

IF PUNISHMENT has no intimate connection with pain or suffering, then what do I mean by *punishment*? If I not only break the connection to pain or suffering but bring in the full conscientious paradigm, it may seem that the concept of punishment, like a thick black cloud, has not been illuminated by the sunlight of inquiry but has been dissipated altogether. This is almost so, as I will explain momentarily. But now, pending that explanation, all sorts of strange thoughts may arise.

Suppose Rickard has committed a terrible crime. He is wracked with guilt. He therefore uses the money gained through crime to finance a vacation to Bermuda, hoping that this will make him forget his feeling of guilt. Is that punishment? Obviously not. But, on my theory, what is to prevent us from saying so?

Suppose Simms has done something wicked. She is wracked with guilt. She therefore performs a certain dance, something like a cake-walk, which she believes is the proper thing to do in such situations. After dancing, she feels cleansed and relieved. Is this punishment? It certainly doesn't seem so. But, on my theory, what is to prevent us from saying so?

Well, let's look. Look, in particular, at Hart's definition of *punishment*, which, as we have seen, is the most widely accepted. It is hard to believe that something so widely accepted by intelligent people could be entirely wrong, so I will cross out all the provisions that we have seen not to apply, and see what is left. (I am concerned here only with his definition of the standard or central case, leaving aside his comments on secondary and substandard cases.)

(i) [Punishment] ~~must involve~~ pain or other consequences normally considered ~~unpleasant.~~

(ii) It ~~must be for an offence~~ against legal rules.

(iii) It must be of an actual or supposed offender for his offence.

(iv) It must ~~be intentionally administered~~ by human beings other than the ~~offender.~~

(v) It ~~must be imposed and administered~~ by an authority constituted by a ~~legal system~~ against ~~which~~ the offence is committed.[1]

I have stricken out (i) for reasons described in Chapter 3: As we saw there, punishment need not involve pain or unpleasantness. I have stricken out (ii) because, as I argue in Chapter 2, there are important nonlegal cases of punishment. I have stricken out (iv) and (v) because punishment may be administered by the offender herself, even though she may not be—indeed, is usually disqualified from being—a legally constituted authority with the legal power to administer punishment in her own case.

We are left with (iii): Punishment "must be of an actual or supposed offender for his offence." This seems meager. Yet this one provision is what I will propose as a complete definition of *punishment*.

Of course, it needs some amplification.

The key word is *for*. One might take it to indicate that punishment regularly follows upon commission of an offense, or that knowledge of the offense motivates the punisher. But I take the word *for* to indicate that the offense provides a good and sufficient reason for the subsequent punitive treatment, or is at least thought to provide one. To expand this further,

> Punishment is (by definition) something done to or by an offender that is justified by prior commission of an offense, and generally not justified without it.

I intend the word *justified* to include both dimensions of justification: That is, the offense must provide a legitimation and a rationale for the punishment. Moreover, the word *something* is meant as generic, so, strictly speaking, the definition should begin:

> Punishment is (by definition) an instance of a kind of thing done to or by. . . .[2]

This definition is very similar to that given by James Doyle, who defines *punishment* as "the satisfaction of all the just claims invoked by the commission of criminal offenses."[3]

Punishment, then, is defined primarily by its justificatory connection with a prior offense. This connection is a matter of degree. A certain kind of treatment may be justified by a prior offense in only one of the two dimensions. Or it may be justified in many cases even when there is no offense. Such a kind of treatment is still punishment, but it is a less central case. The tighter this justificatory connection, the more certainly and properly can we apply the word *punishment*.

One feature of this definition calls for special note. Punishment, as here defined, must consist of treatment that is generally not justified without prior commission of an offense: This means that *at least one* dimension of justification is generally lacking for this sort of treatment or activity. The other one may be present. For example, it is generally legitimate for me to put an entire week's pay into the poor box and, in this sense, my action is justified; but I generally do not have sufficient rationale for donating that much money. Such a donation may therefore qualify as punishment, provided we can say why it *is* justified if I do commit an offense.

It follows that punishment, though not necessarily disvaluable, must be something out of the ordinary. It must be something that would generally, under ordinary circumstances, lack sufficient justification in at least one of the dimensions.

We may say, by way of metaphor, that punishment is to be defined as a *course-correction*. This way of viewing it is, I think, more illuminating than the strict and literal definition given above.

2. Applications

How does this definition apply to our two paradigms?

Let us look first at the Paradigm of Legal Punishment. Such punishment is, as will be recalled, imposed on an unwilling punishee. Now, if it is to fall under my proposed definition, this sort of treatment must usually be unjustified if imposed on people who have committed no crime. Notoriously, the various rationales for imposing punishment on criminals often apply also to noncriminals. Reform, for example, is appropriate for people of bad character even if they have committed no offense. And deterrence may be achieved by framing an innocent victim as well as by punishing the truly guilty.[4] The missing dimension of justification must therefore be legitimation. Punishment imposed by others upon the punishee must therefore involve treatment that would usually be wrong or unjust if imposed upon the innocent. That is, it must involve treatment that, if imposed on the innocent, would constitute a violation of their rights. This may be regarded as a corollary of the main definition, applying to punishment under a just or nearly just government.[5] Of course, if we are dealing with an unjust legal system, punishment cannot be defined in terms of violation of rights, since under such a system rights are violated as a matter of course. Punishment must then be characterized as a deviation from the norm in the treatment of citizens, justified by a prior offense. For example, a monarch may generally refrain from putting his subjects in the pillory, though they have no legal right that he refrain from doing so; pillorying may then be considered a punishment if administered for violations of royal commands. (Of course, it is then justified only by reference to the monarch's standards; in an absolute sense, it is probably unjustified, unless the monarch is exceptionally benign.) In the extreme case, a legal system may be so capricious that it is impossible to distinguish punishment from the usual horrendous course of life under such a regime. If people are routinely harassed, subjected to ex post facto laws and to laws that one cannot but violate, the concept of punishment has little use. Such has recently been the situation, for example, in El Salvador.[6]

How does my definition apply to the conscientious paradigm? Punishment under the legal paradigm involves treating someone in ways that would ordinarily be wrong or unjust, but such problems do not usually arise with regard to oneself. *Volenti non fit injuria:* It is difficult, and perhaps impossible, to think of ways of treating oneself wrongly or unjustly. The burden falls on the justificatory dimension of rationale: Punishment under the conscientious paradigm involves doing something that one would generally have no sufficient rationale for doing unless one had committed an offense. To recur to our metaphor, punishment here is a course-correction, which would be pointless unless one had deviated from one's course. Or, to put it yet another way, suppose that each person guides his life by a life plan. This plan gives a rationale for doing things that accord with it or promote it. Such a plan will, no doubt, involve a complex hierarchy of subplans. At the highest order, a person has a rather abstract plan that generates more concrete plans for various circumstances. (For instance, a high-order, very abstract plan might say, "Pursue a career." At a lower level, "If you enjoy plumbing, and plumbers are in demand, pursue a career in plumbing.") Among these concrete plans, preference is given to those that involve no violation of moral and other important standards that one accepts for oneself. (Our aspiring plumber should avoid a plan that involves counterfeiting a plumber's license.) But one must also provide contingency plans that tell what to do in the event that one offends against these standards. Submission to punishment is what happens when one of these contingency plans is invoked.

Of course, nothing said so far answers the question of what contingency plans one ought to make for oneself. Indeed, my basic definition of *punishment* leaves unanswered the question of what actions generally are justified by prior offenses. In leaving this question unanswered, it resembles definitions given by Doyle, Max Grünhut, and Unto Tähtinen.[7] This procedure may leave one unsatisfied, but it would be a mistake to include in a definition of *punishment* any particular justificatory theory of punishment. As we have seen in Chapter 3, section 6, this mistake has led to unsatisfactory definitions in the past. But I postpone a fuller discussion until the next section.

For the moment, we may take as an example a particular justificatory theory. Those who believe in God often believe that doing evil upsets one's relationship with God, while prayer can mend this relationship. If one has done evil, one has a rationale (beyond the usual ones) for praying, and prayers said for this reason constitute a punishment. They may be extra prayers, or prayers that differ from the usual. The same theory may be applied on a more down-to-earth level: If crime upsets a person's relationship with her fellow citizens and community-service work restores it, then a person who is guilty of a crime has a rationale (beyond the usual ones) for doing community-service work, and work done for this reason constitutes a punishment. This may be community-service work beyond what the person usually does, or of a different kind.

By contrast, recall the cases of Rickard and Simms and note how they are excluded by the present definition. Rickard takes a vacation in Bermuda. This is not punishment because, unless we adopt a bizarre value system, crime does not provide us with any special reason for taking a trip to Bermuda (though it may provide the means). One has plenty of reason to go to Bermuda anyway. Simms does a certain dance, something like a cakewalk. She does this dance only as a response to her own offenses, but, unless we adopt a bizarre plan of life or a bizarre theory of dance, committing an offense gives us no reason at all to perform a dance like a cakewalk. Of course, if Rickard had a theory that explained why going to Bermuda was particularly appropriate as a response to one's own crimes, but not otherwise, then the trip would be a punishment after all. (Recall that British criminals were once punished with trips to Australia.) And if Simms could say why wrongdoing made her dance appropriate, we could call that punishment, too.

When speaking of the legal paradigm, I pointed out that there are situations in which the concept of punishment has little application, for example, under a capricious tyrant. So, too, with the conscientious paradigm, there are cases when the concept is fairly useless. An ordinary person may punish himself, say, by doing community-service work; but if a fanatical person devotes his entire life to service of the community, then there is no room left for punishment on top of this. Such a person already does all that can be justified by the prior commission of an offense.

3. Definition and Justification

The present view holds that punishment must have *some* justificatory connection with a prior offense. Some writers have objected to this mode of definition.[8] Igor Primoratz, whose objection seems the strongest, brings up an example: "If a judge says that she is punishing an offender, but not because the latter has committed an offense, for that, in her eyes, is no reason at all . . . but because of the consequences the punishment is going to have, that would mean that the evil she is inflicting on the offender is not a punishment, but something else."[9] But this example does affect my present definition. Presumably, the judge—let us call her Judge Bentham—is acting under a system of law that provides penalties for crimes; that is, within the system, penalties are justifiably imposed on those who have committed crimes, and otherwise generally are not justified. If so, then what Judge Bentham imposes on the convict is in fact a punishment. Of course, Judge Bentham herself appears to be thinking of her action in other terms—"telishment," as Rawls says[10]—since she would (apparently) also impose it on the innocent if good effects would follow (and if she didn't think she would be thrown off the bench for doing such a thing).[11]

To get a workable example, we would have to consider a whole system of this sort. Suppose all the judges in Ruritania hold to the following rules:

1. Every person convicted of a criminal offense shall be imprisoned for a term of not less than six months.
2. No one shall be imprisoned if he or she has not been convicted of a criminal offense.

3. The commission of a criminal offense does not provide a reason— any sort of reason—for imprisoning a person.

Note that we cannot follow Primoratz and refer to good consequences in setting up this example. If good consequences follow on the imprisonment of criminals, but not of other people, then surely commission of a crime gives some reason for the penalty, contradicting the third rule of Ruritanian justice. It is hard even to imagine such a situation, but let us try. Suppose Ruritanians formerly believed that the great god Cthulhu had commanded them to put criminals in prison. They followed his command. Later, they stopped believing in Cthulhu, and now no one does; but the custom of imprisoning criminals survives. When judges are asked why they imprison criminals, they simply cite precedent. If it were up to their own discretion, they would not imprison anybody. But, clearly, even in this extreme example, there is a reason for judges to imprison criminals, namely, the decree of custom. (Or we might say, the principle of equal treatment requires that current criminals be treated the way criminals were in the past: a stronger reason.) This sort of explanation is not deeply satisfying, yet it suffices for many a case at law; and likewise it suffices to lay to rest the worries raised by Primoratz's objection.

Primoratz, as we see, says that punishment need have no justificatory connection with wrongdoing. I say that it must have *some* justificatory connection. Others go further and write some particular justification into their definition of *punishment*. Hobbes, for example, as we have seen, defines punishment as something justified by its deterrent effect. But this procedure cannot be right, either. Just perform a thought experiment: Suppose that we have adopted a definition of *punishment* that includes some particular justification, say, reform. Most likely, in our own society (in the thought experiment) criminals are punished by undergoing certain experiences that we think will reform them. Now suppose we come to believe that these experiences are really not reformatory after all, but we still treat criminals the same way—perhaps for some other reason, perhaps simply out of custom. Are we now to say that criminals in our society are no longer punished? That would be a cruel irony. "You must undergo this treatment," we say to the convict, "because you have committed a crime. We used to think that this sort of treatment was likely to reform you. Now we know better. Still, you must undergo it all the same, and you can't even complain that you are being punished, since 'punishment,' by definition, is something that is justified by its reformatory effects."

The point, of course, is not about reform, but is equally valid for any justification that might be suggested. If we keep the method of treating criminals but drop the justification for it (or adopt a different justification), we cannot say we have eliminated punishment. We must not, then, write any particular justification into a definition of punishment.

I began this chapter, as many philosophers begin, by looking for a definition of *punishment* in order to then try to justify punishment. But my attempt has boomeranged: Punishment turns out to be whatever is justified by a prior offense. So we must reverse the typical order of proceeding and approach the justificatory question first. Only then can we fill in this abstract and unsatisfying definition. Our first question, then, is: How should we treat offenders, including ourselves? What are we justified in doing to them that we are not justified in doing to people generally (again, including ourselves)?

Here we face another perplexity. Before, when we accepted the Standard View, we could say, "Punishment calls for justification because it involves pain or suffering," but now what? If there is nothing apparently wrong with punishment, there is no call for justification. Indeed, I have already refuted the charges traditionally brought against punishment: It need not involve disvalue (Chapter 3), nor need it involve using punishees as means rather than ends in themselves (Chapter 2, section 2, "The Status of the Two Paradigms"). So far from fretting over the great evil of punishment, we are now puzzled to know what is wrong with it.

What is wrong with punishment—at least punishment imposed by the state—is that it is illiberal. It may involve no disvalue to the punishee—indeed, may make her better off, even in her own estimation; it may treat her as an end in herself; she may even enjoy it; but it follows from my definition that it involves what would ordinarily count as a violation of rights. Civil rights in the liberal state grant to citizens the opportunity and means to choose and act upon their own plans of life, within broad limits. In the case of legal punishment, the state goes beyond these limits and restricts the criminal's right to choose and act upon her own plan of life; the state asks her to adopt a plan of life that she may not have chosen, and probably would not have chosen, for herself. And if she does not then adopt this plan, the state forces her to adopt it. The plan that the state chooses may be a perfectly good one, but it is a plan that the average citizen has the right to accept or reject.

Even in a liberal state, of course, some limitations are placed on citizens' plans of life. For example, we may not plan to murder or rob each other, or to evade our taxes.[12] The problem with punishment is not that the state places limitations on our life plans, but that it places greater limitations on our plans than are usually justifiable.

No one would deny that many punishments are painful, and pain calls for justification, but that is a problem about pain, not punishment. Many of the things that the state legitimately imposes on law-abiding citizens are as painful as serious punishments. (Consider the suffering of someone conscripted to serve in a just war.) And similarly for other forms of disvalue.

But if we insist too much on asking "What's wrong with punishment?" we show a misconception about justification. Things that appear to be wrong demand justification, but it is a mistake to think that these are the only things that need justifying: Things that are merely out of the ordinary also call for justification, though in a quieter voice. We have defined punishment as something out of the ordinary: For this alone it calls for justification.

But, finally, the present way of conceiving punishment hits the ball into the other court. Let someone propose a way of dealing with offenders; then we can look at it and see if there is anything objectionable about it. If there is, then that will call for justification.

PART TWO

A Theory of Punishment

CHAPTER 5

The Rectification Theory of Punishment

WE NOW turn to the actual task of justification. In this chapter and the next I offer a theory of punishment as rectification. The essentials of this theory can be stated quite briefly: Suppose there is in some country a system of equal basic rights, guaranteeing to all citizens a body of equal liberties. By doing certain forbidden things, a person can exceed the bounds of his or her liberties. The offender thus arrogates to himself or herself excess liberties; the scheme of equal rights is upset. In order to restore it, the person's basic rights must be restricted in an equal but opposite way. This restriction is the punishment.

The rectification theory must be distinguished from the concept of restitution. The aim of restitution is to compensate victims of crime or negligence. Certainly, victims should be compensated—I do not want to be taken to suggest that they should not. But even when the victim of a crime has been compensated, the criminal may still have arrogated to himself excess liberties. If so, rectification will still be required.

This theory falls into my category of equilibrium views (see Chapter 2, section 3). I use the term *rectification* (first) because it involves rectifying a disordered situation and (second) because the word *rectification* recalls in its etymology the word *rights*, referring to the matter that is to be rectified.

I present the rectification theory here in an abstract form—abstracted, that is, from any particular system of equal basic rights. It can be applied to almost any such system, moral, legal, religious, or whatever; and below I apply it to Rawls's theory. This abstract justification may seem in itself unformed and void, as indeed it is: A complete rectification-based justification will draw many details from the background system of equal basic rights to which it is applied. I have suggested that *punishment* is less unitary a concept than has been thought. This theme comes out here, too. I do not think there is one all-purpose theory that vindicates every justifiable punishment. Rather, there are various justifications that justify various punishments under various circumstances. I develop two of these (beyond the present one) in the pages that follow. For now, one should note that it is therefore no objection to my present view that it fails to justify a certain sort of punishment that one pretheoretically holds to be justifiable. Such a result is only to be expected.

I proceed according to the following plan. In sections 1–11 I set forth the basic features of the rectification theory. Then, in section 12, I compare it with some related views, principally that of Herbert Morris, and show how the rectification theory avoids some of the objections to which they are liable. In Chapter 6, I apply the rectification theory to some of the typical (and some atypical) problems of the theory of punishment and see if the theory does what we want a theory of punishment to do, according to the considerations of Part One of this book.

1. Equal Basic Rights

Let us now look in greater detail at the rectification theory. First of all, I must devote a few words to the concept of equal basic rights. The general conception of rights that I am using is essentially that of Hart, known as the *choice* or *will* theory of rights. According to this conception, to have a (moral) right is to be, as it were, a moral legislator over a certain sphere of action. In Hart's words,

> the possessor of [a moral right] is conceived as having a moral justification for limiting the freedom of another, and . . . he has this justification not because the action he is entitled to require of another has some moral quality but simply because in the circumstances a certain distribution of human freedom will be maintained if he by his choice is allowed to determine how that other shall act.[1]

Put another way, when doing those things to which one has a right, one need ask permission of no one. This being noted about rights generally, we may turn specifically to equal, basic, inalienable rights. By this phrase I refer to such of these rights as are important, and are distributed in a fixed and equal way, so that they can be neither acquired nor disposed of.[2] For example, the inalienable rights to life, liberty, and the pursuit of happiness (as posited by the United States Declaration of Independence) would count as rights of the sort in question. The distinction between basic and nonbasic rights is among those things to be developed by the particular theory of rights to which the rectification theory is applied. Locke, for example, posits his celebrated trio—the basic rights to life, liberty, and property; other rights, by contrast, are nonbasic, such as a monarch's right to rule her nation. Rawls draws the line differently, distinguishing between the equal basic liberties (granted by his first principle of justice) and rights to property (whose distribution is governed by the second). Rawls's system allows a legislature to abridge the second sort of rights, say, by taxing its citizens; but it may not abridge the first (for example, it may not restrict freedom of religion).

Now, any system that can be said to grant people rights must grant them *some* basic rights (in the sense just defined). Otherwise all the "rights" granted by the system are mere privileges, revocable at the wish of someone other than the right-holder. For example, if I say, "You may walk on my lawn," you then (in a weak sense) have a right to walk on my lawn; but at any time I may change my mind and say, "You may no longer walk on my lawn," and your right is no more. If all rights are like this, it hardly makes sense to speak of rights at all.

On the other hand, only some rights need be so strong. The rest can be protected by these strong, basic rights. To revert to my example, property rights can be abridged in various ways—by taxation, by eminent domain, and so on; but (in the United States) we have basic rights that limit the ways in which our property rights can be abridged. For example, if property is taken by eminent domain, the former owner has a basic right to compensation. We can expect, then, that a system of rights will grant a set of basic rights and another set of less basic rights.

A note on usage: When I speak of basic rights, I am using the word *right* in a normative sense. Thus, when I say that someone has such and such *rights*, I am making a statement about how he, and other people, *ought* to behave. (This *ought* may be moral, legal, institutional, or the like.) By contrast, I use the word *liberty* and sometimes *freedom* in a descriptive sense. They refer to the opportunities and powers granted to a person by others. Thus, when I say that someone has such and such *liberties*, I am making a statement about how he, and other people, *do* behave, or how they are *disposed* to behave. A person's rights protect his liberties; or, as we might say, the liberties are the object of the rights. And we observe someone's rights by granting that person the corresponding liberties.[3]

2. The Kernel of the Theory

Equal basic rights guarantee to each person a protected sphere of action, within which he or she acts as moral legislator: That is, each person is to be permitted to do certain actions without interference from others, and to bring it about that others shall perform or refrain from certain actions on their part. For example, persons in the United States have an equal basic right to move about freely in public places, so that my sphere of freedom of action includes taking myself to any public place whatsoever, and being free from physical interference in doing so. This right to free movement is not, of course, unlimited. It is restricted by such things as other people's right to physical integrity. That is, in moving about freely in public places, one must not injure others, or (in the words of the old saw) "your right to move your fist ends where my nose begins."

Given a system of equal basic rights, a person may violate the system in two ways: (1) She may encroach upon the protected sphere of others, or (2) she may enlarge her own sphere beyond its proper boundaries. In the first case (which many have considered) the violator must redress the imbalance by making restitution, restoring the original boundaries of the victim's sphere insofar as possible. If our violator injured the victim physically, she must pay for the victim's medical care, lost income, and pain and suffering. This duty of restitution is important. It is also not at issue here. Even if the victim's injuries have been made good—or even if there was no victim—the second way of violating the scheme of rights must be addressed. In this second case the violator's sphere of action has been improperly enlarged and must now be diminished by an amount that offsets the illegitimate enlargement, so that she ends up with a sphere whose volume is the same as everyone else's. This diminution deprives her of opportunities and freedoms that she otherwise would have enjoyed; certain courses of action are no longer open to her. The course of action she must now take constitutes the punishment. We may formulate this conception as the *Rectification Principle:*

> When a person has arrogated excess basic liberties by
> committing an offense, that person must then forgo an
> equivalent body of basic liberties by way of punishment.

Notice that the Rectification Principle introduces no special principle of punishment: It is merely a matter of trying to maintain the
preexisting system of equal rights. I therefore present little by way of
argument for the Rectification Principle. I only try to show that anyone committed to a system of equal, basic, inalienable rights is also
thereby committed to a system of punishments specified by the Rectification Principle. That being granted, the system of rectifying punishments is established on the same grounds (whatever they may be)
that support the system of equal basic rights. There are, of course,
questions as to the correct measurement of equality of rights, and
why such equality calls for the punishments I specify. Such questions
are considered in sections 3–5.

A good example of rectification-based punishment involves the
just-mentioned right of free movement. Suppose Smith is walking
down the street and punches Jones in the nose. Smith has thus exceeded her rights and enlarged her sphere of action beyond its proper
limits. If the equality of liberties called for by the system of equal
rights is to be restored, Smith's freedom of action must be restricted
in an equal but opposite way. Since she has enlarged her sphere of
action by disregard of the physical well-being of others, it would seem
appropriate for her to restrict her sphere of action in such a way as
to promote, rather than injure, the physical well-being of others, for
example, she might work without pay in a clinic.

Now, the phrase *sphere of freedom* is a metaphor, and is in need
of some expounding. By this phrase I refer to the sphere of action over
which a person's rights make her a moral legislator. In more literal
language, a person's sphere of freedom consists of (1) actions that she
may perform without asking permission of anyone, and (2) actions
that others may not omit without asking permission of her. In other
words, a person's sphere consists of actions—to be performed by herself or by others—that shall take place unless she wishes otherwise.
Some of these actions may in fact be omissions: For example, one
action in my sphere is that Smith shall omit punching me in the
nose. And the sphere is not closed under negation: For example, I
can require that Smith omit punching me in the nose, but I cannot
require the negation of this, that is to say, I cannot require her to
punch me in the nose.

There is still a certain ambiguity—an intentional one—to my
explication of the metaphor: The phrase *sphere of liberty* has three
senses, one normative and two descriptive. First, when I speak of
"actions that shall take place unless the person wishes otherwise,"
I may refer to those actions which, according to a particular system

of rights or other standards, *ought* to take place, unless the person wishes otherwise. Second, I may refer to those actions that *other people are actually able and willing to perform* for her, or to permit her to perform. Third, I may refer to those actions that *she is able and willing to perform*, or whose performance she is able and willing to exact from others. We may speak of these, respectively, as her allotted sphere of freedom; the sphere that others grant to her; and the sphere of freedom that she exercises. The distinction may be best illustrated by a parallel: If I own a piece of land, my allotted sphere is the area of land that the law entitles me to use, and from which the law excludes others without my permission. The sphere that others grant me is the area of land that others actually allow me to use and that they refrain from using without my permission. And the sphere that I exercise consists of that area of land which I am able and willing to use (perhaps if only by putting a fence around it). Both in the parallel and in the original case, all is well so long as the sphere of freedom that I exercise is contained within the sphere allotted to me, which in turn is contained within the sphere that others grant to me.

3. How to Broaden Your Sphere

How can a person broaden his exercised sphere of freedom?

One might be tempted to answer: "By doing something that he has no right to do or (as a special case) by exacting from others some action that he has no right that they do."

This is almost correct. The right answer is, I claim, that a person broadens his sphere by acting *as if he had a right* to do something that he in fact has no right to do. Two parts of this formula must be explained. First, by "acting as if one had a right to do some (specified) thing" I mean "doing things that a conscientious person would do only if she believed herself to have a right to do the thing in question." A person who acts as if she had a right to do something may have no belief about her rights, or may believe that she lacks this right. What matters is how she acts. Thus, a burglar who breaks into someone's home is behaving as if she had a right to be there, even though she may recognize that she has no such right.

Why does a person expand her sphere of liberty only by acting as if she had a right to do things (and not simply by doing them)? It is the "choice" theory of rights that answers this question. A right, according to this theory, allows a person to choose to do things (or not to do them) without asking anyone's permission. The liberty that such a right protects is the corresponding liberty of choosing to do things (or not to do them) without asking permission. So the only way of taking the kind of liberties that this theory is concerned with is by choosing to do things without asking permission—that is, by acting as if one had a right. The theory does not directly concern itself with other sorts of things that a person might do. A person might act without choosing to act—perhaps accidentally or unintentionally, perhaps under coercion. A person might seek permission before acting, making all the difference between a burglary and a social call. Such cases involve no arrogation of excess liberties.

To put it in other words: Having a right makes a person into a moral legislator over a certain sphere. We put rights into effect by making sure that people are actually able to "legislate" over their own spheres. Consequently, the only way to expand one's sphere is by legislating over a broader domain. For example, if I kidnap McCoy, it is as if I had laid down the decree, "Let McCoy be put in my physical power," a decree that is not properly within my competence. If I drive off with McCoy accidentally trapped in the trunk of my car, I have not legislated anything, so no arrogation of liberties is involved. And if I try, but fail, to kidnap McCoy, I have still arrogated liberties. It is as though I had issued the decree "Let McCoy be put in my physical power" but then proved unable to enforce it.

There thus enters a mental element, a requirement of *mens rea* (that is, "guilty mind") into the rectification theory. This theory assigns a penalty only to someone who has *chosen* to act.

One point needs to be reemphasized. It is irrelevant whether the person believes she has the right to do the thing in question. It is even irrelevant whether the person announces that she has the right in question.[4] What does matter is choosing to act without permission.

4. The Extent of the Broadening

Our theory, up to this point, offers a general justification for certain punishments: To maintain equal liberty, a person who has taken excess liberties must relinquish an equivalent body. Now, when we turn to the application of this scheme, two further questions arise:

(*Assessing the Offense*) How much, and in what way, does a given offense broaden the offender's sphere of freedom?

And once we have answered this, we must go on to add,

(*Assessing the Penalty*) What penalty will counterbalance a given expansion of the offender's sphere of freedom?

The present section addresses the Question of Assessing the Offense; the Question of Assessing the Penalty is the subject of the section to follow.

The Question of Assessing the Offense might at first seem easy, but we soon discover a problem. When someone commits an offense, her action can be described in many ways. Consider Smith again. Did she take only the liberty of punching Jones in the nose? Or can we better describe her as having taken the liberty of punching anyone in any part of the body? Or the liberty of harming anyone in any way? Or the liberty of doing whatever she wants? Or (to go in the direction of specificity) did she merely take the liberty of punching Jones in the nose at 11:15 A.M. on a Saturday with a fist-impact velocity of 20 feet per second? If Smith has arrogated the liberty to harm anyone in any way, she has broadened her sphere very expansively. If she has arrogated only the liberty to punch Jones in the nose at 11:15 A.M. on a Saturday with a fist-impact velocity of 20 feet per second, then the expansion of her sphere is exceedingly small. In one case, the punishment will be severe; in the other, extremely mild.

My proposal for assessing the offense is, in brief, as follows. In order to determine what body of excess liberties an offender has taken, we must treat her *as if she had claimed a right to do what she did*. We can then ask,

> (*Question of Interpretation*) What is the most plausible (to us)[5] normative theory that we can attribute to the offender that grants her a right to do what she did?

This question will prove more tractable than the Question of Assessing the Offense; and having answered it, we can then say that the offender has arrogated exactly those liberties specified in our answer to the Question of Interpretation. I consider these points in order.

But, first, three things must be made clear. First, this suggestion—that we should treat the offender as if she were claiming excess rights—is appearing now for the first time. In particular, the kernel of the theory does not depend on any such suggestion. It is being introduced now in order to answer questions of measurement. If one should reject the suggestion, the kernel of the rectification theory would not be undermined: We would need, however, a different answer to the questions of measurement. Second, I wish for now only to support the view that we should regard the offender *as if* she were claiming excess rights. Indeed, I argue below (section 8) that the offender has in fact claimed excess rights; but that stronger conclusion is not needed at this point.

Third, we must distinguish two senses of the phrase *claiming a right*. Consider two cases: (1) I tell my friends, "The Internal Revenue Service (IRS) owes me $1,000." (2) I file a tax return with the IRS showing that they owe me a refund of $1,000. Both of these actions might be called "claiming a right to a $1,000 refund," but it is only the second kind that interests us. If my friends accept my claim, I get their agreement, but if the IRS accepts my claim, I actually get the money. In general, we are concerned with rights-claims which, if successful, result in the claimant's actually getting whatever it is he has a right to. When I make this kind of claim, I bring about a change in status: I become a claimant. Hence, Joel Feinberg has distinguished this kind of claim by dubbing it a *performative claim*, as opposed to a *propositional claim*.[6] If made in words, a performative claim indeed involves a performative, for instance, "I claim this land in the name of King Ferdinand and Queen Isabella."

But why should we treat the offender as if she were making any sort of claim at all? She is, after all, merely doing something and may have given no thought to the issue of rights. To give answer, we must consider why we want a system of rights in the first place. One of the purposes of a system of rights, and especially of a system of basic rights, is to coordinate[7] the activities of a number of persons, allowing them to achieve their personal ends in peace and without undue interference from others; and they do this by adhering to the rules and principles that constitute the system of rights. Assume that such a system exists in some country—call it Fredonia. When something goes wrong, the Fredonians must apply or extend these principles to cover the new case; otherwise, their response will be uncoordinated, and they will not achieve their purpose.

In particular, when someone exceeds the bounds of his basic liberties, the Fredonians must decide how to respond. Suppose Nolan has stolen a Ming vase. The Fredonians can either let him keep it or try to get it back. More generally, when someone oversteps the bounds of his liberties, there are two basic possibilities: (1) The Fredonians can concede, and apply the rules and principles so as to allow the offender to accomplish what he set out to do. They have thus granted him the right to do it. (2) They can resist and try to rectify the offense, or at least protest it. The Fredonians must, then, either second the person's offense or oppose it. (To ignore it would seem to be a way of seconding it.) The offender's fellow citizens must thus treat him as if he were applying to them for an extension of his rights. In other words, they treat the offense as a rights-claim.[8] Note that this conclusion is drawn not from an examination of the offender

Nolan alone; rather, it follows from the fact that the majority are maintaining a scheme of rights, and they must react to Nolan's offense, fitting him somehow into the scheme.

Moreover, an offender wants to succeed in committing her offense and wants others to refrain from hindering her: That is, she wants to act as if she had a right to do it, and she wants others to recognize this "right." The thief, for example, does not merely want to hold someone else's money in her hands; she wants to be treated as if it were her money, that is, as if she had property rights in the money. By committing the offense, she puts others on notice that she intends to act in this way, and that they are to comply.

These considerations taken together show that within a system of basic rights, a person's action in violation of those rights affects others in such a way that they must consider it as if the offender were claiming rights in excess. This claim may be no part of the offender's plan; she may not have thought about her rights or may frankly admit that she is overstepping her bounds. Such facts are not relevant: In any case her fellow citizens must treat her as a claimant of excess rights. (Similarly, if someone files for a refund with the IRS, he is to be treated as claiming rights; and he is to be so treated even if he believes that he is not entitled to the refund.)

And why is this rights-claim that we attribute to the offender a fair measure of the liberties that she has taken? It is because in a system of equal basic liberties, the offender's fellow citizens must take action on the basis of what they can reasonably expect from her— on the basis of the sphere of freedom they reasonably consider her to have staked out. On this basis they must take action, perhaps giving up treasured liberties of their own or restricting important principles by which they govern themselves. So the scheme of liberties is in the end altered according to the claim of excess liberties that citizens attribute to the offender. It is thus appropriate for the rectification theory to use this measure of liberties taken.

For these reasons, then, we must treat the offender as if, by her offense, she were claiming certain rights. Which rights? We may best treat this as a semantical question. When we consider an offense, we may ask, "What is the meaning of this?" Or, more generally, "What is the significance of an offense when it is considered as a rights-claim? What relationship prevails between a given offense, and a given body of rights claimed?" The problem then becomes one of interpretation: We are to interpret the offender's action in the most reasonable way we can. As with the interpretation of words, the interpretation of nonverbal behavior is likely to involve indeterminacy, both in practice and in principle. No mechanical procedure is to be expected. As with the interpretation of words, we can state general principles, and persons of judgment can apply them.

Now, in putting forward a rights-claim, the offender is offering us a fragment of a normative theory. This normative theory must justify the offender's offense. The way to interpret the offense is, then, to ask the following question:

> (*Question of Interpretation*) What is the most plausible normative theory that we can attribute to the offender that grants him a right to do what he did?

—a question we have seen before. But now, having defined it as a question of interpretation, we can use principles like those applicable to any other interpretive task:

1. *Charity.* "In our need to make him [in this case, the offender] make sense, we will try for a theory which finds him consistent, a believer of truths, and a lover of the good (all by our own lights, it goes without saying)."[9]

In other words, we impute to the speaker or actor the most reasonable views that are consistent with what we know about him. Of course, if someone has committed an offense, it is hard to find him entirely a lover of the good, but we should not besmirch his name more than necessary. For example, we might attribute to Smith a claim of the right to assault other average human beings, but not infants, persons with disabilities, or the elderly. That could be claimed only by assaulting someone of the particular type. As a limiting case, if someone has committed no offenses, we treat him (for present purposes) as having claimed no extra rights at all. And if someone has committed only one offense, we treat him as having claimed the right to commit exactly one offense of that sort, even though he may have planned to commit more.

This principle of charity enables us to define more precisely the semantic relationship between the offense and the rights-claim. It is one of *exemplification*, in the sense of Nelson Goodman.[10] The offender must be seen as claiming the right to do what he did (under some description or other), but charity prevents us from ascribing to him any greater claim. Thus, the offense exemplifies a predicate of the form "act that may be done only by those with a right to do X." And our interpretive task becomes that of finding the right words to put in place of the "X."

> 2. *Universalizability.* The rights claimed by the offender must constitute a reasonable universalization of the offense, that is, they must constitute a normatively relevant class.

If the claim of rights is to have even a show of plausibility, we must be able to give some reason for it that supports a whole class of rights, viz., the right to do relevantly similar acts in relevantly similar circumstances.[11] Suppose Jones, our attack victim, has red hair and was attacked on a Monday. Even so, it would be implausible to treat Smith as claiming a right to punch red-haired people in the nose on Mondays. The color of a person's hair and day of the week are completely irrelevant to the question of whether one has a right to hit that person. Similarly, if White steals a silver spoon, he actually exercises only the right to hold the spoon in his hand, but we should see him as claiming the full range of property rights over the spoon, rather than merely the right to hold it in his hand.

> 3. *The offender's knowledge, purposes, and abilities.* We should not attribute to the offender a rights-claim that is made implausible by the offender's knowledge, purposes, or abilities at the time of the offense.

For example, it would be ridiculous to follow the suggestion made above and attribute to Smith a claim of the right to punch Jones with a fist-impact velocity of 20 feet per second. For Smith did not know that the impact velocity of her fist was 20 feet per second, did not care that is was 20 as opposed to 22 or 24, and, even if she did care, could not control it with such precision. Similarly, in a mugging for gain, it would be silly to attribute to the mugger a claim of the right to mug a particular person, since that would be irrelevant to his purpose; he could serve this purpose by mugging anyone with money.

> 4. *The context of action in which the offense takes place.*

This context may throw light on the criminal act by showing it to be part of a larger course of action. Smith, for example, might be thought to claim a right to do whatever she pleases. But this claim would be implausible if, aside from the assault on Jones, Smith leads an exemplary life.

> 5. *Simplicity.*

Other things equal, we prefer the simpler interpretation.[12] For example, suppose Johnson claims rights in a square field of 40 acres by sowing wheat in it. We might interpret this in two ways: (1) He claims rights in the entire 40 acres; or (2) he claims rights only in the portion of the field that he actually plows, sows, cultivates, or steps on, and only for the time that these activities are taking place. The second interpretation would give Johnson rights in an intricately and bizarrely shaped piece of land, a piece whose shape was in fact ever-changing; and this interpretation would permit others to use the parts of the original square field that remain unused by Johnson, so long as this does not interfere with Johnson's planting. But this second interpretation is clearly ridiculous. Simplicity favors the first interpretation.

5. Determining the Sentence

Having interpreted the offense as a rights-claim by which the offender arrogates excess liberties, we must determine an appropriate remedy. We can no longer put into effect the system of equal basic liberties in the literal and obvious way, for the past cannot be changed. We must, then, as a second best, find a body of basic liberties for the offender, including those extra liberties that she has taken, which will be in some sense equivalent to the original set of equal basic liberties she was to have. This equivalent set will clearly require her to give up certain liberties she would otherwise have had. We must, in particular, answer questions of quality and quantity: That is, What sorts of liberties should be given up? and What amount of them should be given up? These questions are considered in the following subsections.

Our answers here, though, must be general and programmatic, for any definite answer to these questions will depend very much on the specific theory of rights in question. Indeed, any theory of equal basic rights must include a theory of compensatory rights, for even without crime, there will always be cases in which the scheme of equal rights cannot be put into effect as planned: One must consider, for example, how we are to grant freedom of movement to a person with a physical disability. It is thus fitting to leave the bulk of this task to the specific theory of rights in question.

The most general principle is this: Since rights are in the first instance to protect the interests of the right-holder, in determining the sentence we consider the position of the right-holder, and not that of the victim, if any, of the offense. Not that the victim should be neglected. On the contrary, offenders should compensate their victims, but that is a separate question from punishment. I assume, then, that the offender has fully compensated anyone she has injured. We then go on to ask what kind of rectifying punishment she needs. The present method of sentencing thus differs from the traditional retributive principle, according to which we treat the offender as she treated her victim.

QUALITY

What sorts of liberties should be given up in order to compensate for liberties arrogated? Our answer will draw on two premises about basic rights: First,

The basic rights are not fungible,

that is, one sort of basic right is not an adequate substitute for another. This is so because each protects an important interest that must not be sacrificed for other interests. For example, an extra measure of freedom of speech cannot compensate for a loss of freedom of religion. The second premise:

The limitations on the basic liberties are not arbitrary, but serve important common interests.

Thus, for example, freedom of religion is not unlimited. The limitations on this freedom serve other important interests. The common human interest in remaining alive means that freedom of religion does not include, say, the right to perform human sacrifice. This is so even if there are worshippers of Molech who sincerely believe that their deity requires this kind of tribute.

Now, because basic rights are not fungible, the offender cannot restore a balance by giving up just any sort of rights; he must give up rights of the same sort that he took in excess. To put this another way: He must impose upon himself more stringently the same kind of limitations on his rights that he exceeded by his offense. Nor are these limitations arbitrary: They serve important purposes. Since we are trying to find an equivalent *whole set* of basic liberties for the offender, we must apply the same principles that govern the system of basic liberties as a whole. Thus, whatever purposes are served by the limitations that the offender violated must also be served by the more stringent limitations now to be placed upon him; and whatever general principles govern the assignment of basic liberties in the normal case also govern the assignment of basic liberties to the offender.

We thus get three principles to determine the kind of liberties to be forgone by the offender:

(1) The offender must impose upon himself more stringently the same kind of limitations on his rights that he violated by his offense.

(2) He must do so in such a way as to promote the purposes of these limitations.

(3) The sentence is to be determined in accordance with the same general principles—whatever they may be—that govern the entire system of rights.

Let us consider as an example the fistic Smith. She punches Jones in the nose. She has arrogated an excessive freedom of movement, so her freedom of movement must be restricted. One might think: Send her to prison. But this thought cannot be right, since going to prison will not promote the purpose of the violated limitation, which is the protection of the physical well-being of others. So Smith must, as punishment, do something that protects or promotes the physical well-being of others. Finally, if our system of basic rights includes as a general principle a right to a minimally decent level of health care, Smith's sentence must take this into consideration, so that, for example, it would be wrong to assign her to care for wealthy cosmetic-surgery patients in preference to those who might lack even basic care.

To take another example, consider the case of Thorpe, who commits election fraud: Say, he manages to cast two ballots. He has arrogated excess political liberty by violating the limitations that are imposed upon him by the equal political liberty of others. In accordance with the first principle, Thorpe must restrict his political activity in such a way as to promote the equal political liberty of all: He might be required to work in a voter-registration program. The second principle calls for promoting the purpose of this limitation on political liberty: Since this purpose is evidently equal political participation, Thorpe should work in registering underrepresented persons. And if there is some group whose underrepresentation is weakening its general enjoyment of basic liberties, the third principle would favor Thorpe's working with that group.

As is no doubt obvious, some degree of judicial discretion will be involved in applying these guidelines, as with any sentencing guidelines.

Now, these examples involve penalties of community service, and it can be seen that the rectification theory in general calls for such penalties. This feature of the theory follows from the second principle above (and to some extent from the third). For any sentence under the Rectification Principle is a restriction of liberties, and such restriction should not be arbitrary but should serve important common ends. Therefore any sentence should serve important common ends. In a way, indeed, an arbitrary imposition such as a fine or imprisonment does serve the important common end of security from crime, inasmuch as it deters others. But even so, it should always be possible to conceive of an equally burdensome sentence that directly promotes the purposes of the limitations that the offender exceeded, and such a sentence would be preferable under the second principle. Though the offender has arrogated excess liberties, though his liberties must be restricted, he is still a bearer of rights, and it would be a violation of these rights to imprison or fine him when an equally burdensome, though more directly productive, sentence could be found.

The rectification theory's support for community-service sanctions is a desirable feature if, as many people do, one finds such sanctions intuitively appealing as a fitting and just response to crime; for the theoretical basis of such sanctions has until now been tenuous and confused.[13]

Now, the Rectification Principle requires the offender to forgo certain liberties, but forgoing these liberties does not usually require one to do any single specific act. For example, Smith might reasonably work in any of a variety of medical institutions. And we can imagine an even greater latitude. To require one particular punishment rather than another would amount to a further deprivation of liberties beyond that required by the Rectification Principle. Such deprivation would be illegitimate without further justification.

QUANTITY

We now know what sorts of liberties should be excluded from the offender's sphere of freedom. We must next determine the extent of the exclusion. For example, should Smith work an hour in a hospital? A day? A week?

The answer to this question relies heavily on the underlying theory of rights. It is that theory which can tell us when a body of rights is equivalent to another. Indeed, as I have already suggested, it must have some answer. Questions like the present one arise not only in the case of punishment, but whenever things differ substantially from the norm. For example, persons with disabilities often cannot exercise many of their rights unless special provisions are made for them. A theory of basic rights must say what provisions are required. Similarly, people whose basic rights are abridged by accident may deserve compensation. A theory of basic rights must say what sort of compensation is required.

Nonetheless, we can say something more specific. The present task of measuring quantity is like the task of a judge in a torts case who must set a fair measure of damages for the loss of something that has no market value, such as a unique object. One approach in such cases is to ask hypothetically, "What price would be settled upon by a willing buyer and a willing seller of this object, neither being in immediate need of making the transaction?"[14] In answering this hypothetical question, we must imagine the buyer and seller as average, reasonable persons—in particular, we do not ascribe to them peculiar desires that would skew the results.

In the present case we can do something similar: We can ask, "What quantity of rights would a reasonable person willingly forgo in order to gain the right to do what the offender did?" In referring to a "reasonable person," we make abstraction from the offender's particular preferences and plans. We must do this because the distribution of basic rights must be independent of individual tastes: A person with expensive tastes should not for that reason have more rights, nor should a person of modest tastes have fewer.[15]

A fuller description of the reasonable person will depend on the particular theory of basic rights that one holds. Suppose, for example, we adhere to a theory like that of Rawls, in which the nature and extent of a person's basic rights are determined by asking what rights she would choose if she were placed in a suitably neutral position. (In Rawls's theory at least three such positions are involved: the Original Position, the [notional] constitutional convention, and the [notional] legislature.) We would turn to the legislature and ask, for example, "Not knowing your own tastes, and considering the principles hitherto adopted, how much medical service would you be willing to do in exchange for the right to punch someone in the nose?" Such a right would be quite useful; by threatening to punch, the right-holder could promote her plans in many ways. We can get some idea of the value of such a right by considering how much energy vengeful people often devote to their schemes of vengeance, which may involve physical attacks. The punishment for a punch in the nose should require one to exert at least that much energy.

6. An Objection: Future or Past Rights?

"This rectification theory is quite pretty," one might object, "but there is a problem. If the scheme of equal rights has been violated in the past, why should this affect the future? Better we should resolve *from now on* to maintain the scheme intact. To do otherwise is needlessly vindictive."

This objection presents a serious problem: If no solution is found, the rectification theory will be undermined. Fortunately, the problem is soluble. I give two replies: The first is universally applicable, the second only in an imperfectly ordered society.

First, I argue from the temporal nature of action. Actions are not instantaneous, but take place over time. Between the beginning and end of an action, some time, however brief, must elapse. Neither, therefore, can rights (which protect our freedom to act) be instantaneous. Rights, too, must be extended in time. It would be nonsense to talk of a right that someone has for an instant—say, at exactly eight o'clock, but at no instant before or after. In that amount of time nothing can be done, so this right is a sham, offering no protection at all.

Since rights are necessarily extended in time, we can measure rights, and speak of equality of rights, only with respect to some interval of time, however short or ill defined. Within this interval, we must be concerned with past violations or inequalities, or else we cannot say we are maintaining a scheme of rights at all. In particular, when we are in the middle of the interval, actions that have been begun in the past under color of right must be allowed to come to fruition in the future. We cannot say, "The past is past. Let's forget the past and do our best for the future." That would authorize a denial of rights. When people have rights, the past lives on—at least for a little while.

But how little is this while? If it is very short—say, a minute or so—its interest is mainly theoretical. But it is not so short, as we may see from the following.

Determining when persons have equal liberties is a problem of measurement. And the proper method of measurement depends on what we are measuring and why we are interested in it. So, for example, if I am interested in spending some coins, I will want to measure their face value. If I want to sell them to a coin dealer, I will want to know their market price. And if I want to put them in the fuse box, I will want to know their electrical conductivity in mhos. Rights, of course, are more abstract, but we can still ask the same questions. Now, why are we interested in basic, inalienable rights? Why do we value them? We have many reasons, but the foremost is this: They enable us to form and carry out life plans—conceptions of the good, as some philosophers like to say—and to develop and exercise a sense of justice. And thus it is proper to measure these rights *over a person's whole lifetime.*

Hence, if we wish to maintain equality of the basic inalienable rights, we must measure this equality over the entire lifetime of the right-holders. We cannot dismiss the past merely because it is past. We thus have our first reason for rectifying past violations of the scheme of rights.

Now, even if you reject this argument and maintain the "from now on" interpretation, there is a second reason. This "from now on" interpretation may be acceptable for a situation in which offenses are rare and unusual events. But it is not acceptable when offenses are a regular occurrence. Imagine, for example, the division of the proverbial pie. Let us suppose that everyone has a basic right to an equal share of the pie. But Otto takes an extra share. "Let bygones be bygones," says the official in charge of such things, "we will maintain the system of equal rights from now on." The next day another pie is baked and Otto once again takes an extra share. "Let bygones be bygones," says the official, "we will maintain the system of equal rights from now on." But by now it is clear that no system of equal rights is being maintained. Rather, Otto in fact enjoys greater rights than the others. This injustice could be corrected by giving Otto a smaller share to balance out his previous extra shares. Then we could say the system of equal rights was being maintained.

Thus, past takings of excess liberties ought to be rectified in the future, and not simply forgotten.

7. Suffering Not Essential

The Rectification Principle thus requires an offender to forgo any of a large variety of liberties, depending on the offense; and consequently the offender will be obligated to do any of a large variety of things that he might otherwise not have done. But only in the rarest of circumstances will the offender be obligated to undergo pain for its own sake, or to give up money or property for its own sake, or to be confined in prison, or to do other pointless, unpleasant things. Whatever is required of the offender must be designed to promote the principles underlying the theory of basic rights, and how could we promote such principles by undergoing pain, loss, confinement, or other disvalues? The disvalue would have to be sought either for its own sake or as a means to some end. Now, it is a rare system of rights whose basic principles call for the pursuit of pain, loss, confinement, or other disvalues as ends in themselves. On the contrary, the purpose of basic rights is usually to enable people to avoid pain, loss, confinement, and other unpleasant or pointless things. (Maybe there are some ascetic codes that constitute exceptions, but they are of little interest here.) These disvalues, then, must be means to some end. Now, the only prominent end which people in recent times try to pursue by means of disvaluable punishment is deterrence:[16] Disvaluable punishments may deter people from exceeding the bounds of their basic rights. So one might think that the Rectification Principle would support them. But it does not, or only rarely. As I have argued (Chapter 2, section 4), disvalue undertaken by the willing punishee does not serve as a deterrent. Now, disvaluable punishments imposed on unwilling punishees would, admittedly, promote deterrence; but, as I have also argued (Chapter 2, section 3), the punishment to be imposed on an unwilling punishee is merely that which he ought to undertake of his own accord, namely, in this case, a punishment not involving disvalue as such.

Of course, it is conceivable that we could treat unwilling punishees as an independent group and apply the Rectification Principle to them separately, prescribing for them a rectifying punishment involving disvalue as such. This would, indeed, promote deterrence. But it would be unjust in that it would prescribe nonequivalent punishments for similar offenses. For example, suppose that for burglary the conscientious are required to do one hundred hours of public-service work as a rectifying punishment. If we apply the Rectification Principle to the unwilling punishee with the aim of setting a deterrent punishment, the principle would prescribe that such a person should do the most nearly comparable thing that involves disvalue as such: Instead of doing public-service work, such a punishee should perform pointless toil, such as working on a rock pile for a hundred hours. But this sentence would be unfair: A hundred hours' work on a rock pile is a severer sentence than a hundred hours of public service, in which one can at least take some pride. So a lesser amount should be required—perhaps only ninety hours. Now the sentence is unfair to the conscientious people: They have to work a hundred hours, while the nonconscientious work only ninety. So we might give the conscientious person a choice: Either a hundred hours of public service or ninety hours of pointless toil. But this sentence is again unfair to the unwilling punishees, since they have fewer choices than the conscientious; this amounts to a severer sentence, as I argue in the preceding section. And we can reason similarly with regard to fines (as opposed to donation of money to charity) and other sorts of sentences. We can conclude, then, that the same sort of sentence must be assigned to all who are guilty of the same sort of offense, whether they submit conscientiously or not.

Even if we could justify imposing disvalue as such on unwilling punishees, it could be imposed only in a limited number of cases. For we ought at least give the offender a chance to submit willingly before imposing the harsher punishment. In other words, we say to the offender, "If you do not submit to the prescribed punishment, we will impose a harsher one upon you." If she then submits, she receives only the original punishment. These words addressed to the offender constitute a threat of coercion. So someone who submits under the *threat* of coercion still receives only the original punishment. The harsher punishment, involving disvalue as such—if it can be justified at all—may be imposed only on those who *actually must be coerced.*

But this dispute is a tempest in a teapot. Though the punishments assigned by the Rectification Principle are not calculated to deter, they have the effect of deterrence. For according to this principle, the specific limitations that the offender exceeded are to be imposed on her more stringently (by herself or others). A person likely to commit the offense is therefore unlikely to want to undertake the sorts of things involved in the punishment. For example, a person who is likely to commit vote fraud is unlikely to want to work without pay to register voters; a person contemplating burglary probably would not want to work without pay to prevent burglary or aid victims of burglary. Thus, this sort of punishment deters those who need to be deterred and fails to deter those who do not need to be deterred.

8. A True Claim of Rights?

As we left things at the end of section 4, we were considering the offender merely *as if* he had claimed certain excess rights, leaving open the question whether the offense actually constitutes such a claim. I wish to argue here, briefly, that it does, and that this justifies attitudes of indignation toward the offender. I make my argument brief because Alan Gewirth has argued cogently and at length that an act constitutes a claim of the rights necessary to perform that act. (His argument, though, is much more general.)[17]

To proceed, then: Why should we say that an offender has, by his

offense, claimed a right to do what he did? If we look at the case informally, it seems obvious that the offender does claim a right. Suppose
I grab a wad of hundred-dollar bills from your hands and show no
intention of letting you have them back. It seems superfluous for me
to add "This is mine"—that is, just grabbing the money and keeping
it is claim enough. I don't need to add a word.

But to consider the problem more formally, I argue as follows: I
will show that in a society that recognizes rights, behaving as if one
had a right to act in a certain way will, under most circumstances,
constitute a claim of a right to act in the specified way. (Recall the
definition of "acting as if one had a right," section 3.) My discussion
applies to rights sanctioned by custom or law; I am not assuming
that they are (or are not) moral rights. If we consider actual behavior,
we can see that the act of behaving as if one had a right and the act of
verbally claiming a right function the same way. Consequently, if the
meaning of words (and nonverbal expressions) depends on how they
are used, the meaning of acting-as-if-one-had-a-right is the same as
the meaning of the verbal claim of rights. In other words, the act is a
rights-claim.

An example can show that the argument is sound in at least some
cases. Consider the act of claiming one's baggage at an airport. At
some airports a passenger does this by handing over a claim check
and saying, "Please give me my baggage." In other airports the passenger simply goes up and takes her luggage, perhaps showing her claim
check to an official as she leaves. The only functional difference is
that in one case the passenger makes the claim in words, whereas in
the other she claims her property rights by exercising them.

To see that this is true more generally, we must consider what
characterizes the usage of rights-claims. I am dealing here with
claims of the sort that lead (if they are successful) to one's actually
getting the thing to which one claims a right. Now, how are such
claims used? We can pick out the most important aspects from the
baggage claim example: It is proper for me to claim baggage only if
it is mine;[18] when I claim my baggage, the normal result is that I
get my baggage; and it is reasonable for the baggage handler to ask
for evidence to support my claim. To generalize: I should claim only
rights that I really have; the normal result of a rights-claim is that I
actually get whatever it is I have a right to; and it is reasonable for the
addressee of the claim to ask for supporting evidence. It is easy to see
that acting-as-if-one-had-a-right functions in this way, provided the
action takes place in a society that recognizes rights, and provided
that people for the most part comply voluntarily with the system

of rights. In the first place, a person should act as if she has a right only if she really has the right in question. (This is true by definition.) Second, if I act as if I had some particular right, people, aware that compliance is voluntary, will assume that I probably do have the right, and they in turn—also voluntarily complying—will not interfere with me. If my right requires their cooperation, they will cooperate. So acting-as-if-one-had-a-right results in actually getting whatever it is one has a right to. Finally, people know that there are some cheaters, so when I act as if I had some particular right, it is expected and accepted that I may be asked for evidence—for instance, I may be asked to present a claim check for my luggage. Moreover, people who live in this kind of society are aware of these facts, so it is proper to say that they really are making a claim when they act as if they had some particular right. (They are not like the first-time auction attendee who scratches his ear and finds that he has made a bid.)

Now, one might object that a criminal cannot be claiming rights, since she usually acts furtively, whereas claims must be addressed to someone. But what the criminal often tries to conceal is evidence that her claim is unjustified, not the claim itself. If someone makes a claim by acting as if she had a right to something, that claim is addressed to everyone who is affected by her action. Thus, only a strictly self-regarding action would be subject to this objection, and there is good and independent reason for not criminalizing such actions.

If it be conceded that an offender, by exceeding the limits on his basic rights, actually claims excess basic rights, we can then say why serious crime is worthy of indignation. Typically, basic rights are those that a person has merely in virtue of being a person; and they are distributed equally, expressing the equality of persons. Someone who claims more basic rights than everyone else therefore claims a fundamental superiority over other people. He has not merely placed himself in a position that someone else is entitled to occupy; he has placed himself in a position that no one is entitled to occupy. He purports to make himself like the nobility of former days, who thought themselves fundamentally superior to commoners and arrogated rights accordingly, or like racial supremacists of today, who likewise have pretensions of superiority. We might fittingly style him a robber baron.

This conclusion would not follow if the criminal were not making an actual claim. In section 3, when we regarded the criminal merely *as if* she were making a claim, the argument rested on the community's need to maintain a system of rights. Maintaining this system

requires the community to *act* in certain ways (for example, to punish offenders), but it does not require the community to assume any
particular *attitudes* toward the offender. The attitudes just now mentioned are justified only if the criminal herself has evinced grandi-
ose attitudes on her part, which she does by actually making such
a claim.

9. Interpretation of the Punishment

Just as we have interpreted the offense as a claim of excess rights, so
also can we interpret the rectifying punishment as a renunciation
of this claim. On this view, we may tell the following story: The
offender claims excess basic rights by her offense and thus makes
herself out as fundamentally superior to everyone else. Even if she
makes full restitution, this intolerable situation is not rectified until
she renounces her claim and avows her fundamental equality. Until
she renounces her claim, we must view it as remaining in effect;
even though she makes restitution and refrains from wrongdoing, we
must see her as just biding her time until the moment comes when
she can successfully exercise her claimed rights.

The punishment therefore ought to be designed to act as a renunciation of the original claim. That is, the punishment should
be designed so that the offense and punishment together have the
effect of making no claim at all. Now, this provides some guidance
in setting the punishment, though nothing very concrete. It does,
however, suggest the following. Since the punishment as renunciation is a symbolic act, comparable to the act of speaking, it should
have the virtues that are desirable in symbolic acts. Among these is
sincerity. The punishment should therefore be of a kind that can be
wholeheartedly undertaken. And the punishee should do her best to
undertake her punishment with a proper attitude of sincerity.

10. How to Restrict Your Own Liberty

The rectification theory, then, requires offenders to restrict their own
liberty as punishment for their offenses. But now you might wonder:
"How can a person restrict his own sphere of liberty? A person's liberty can be restricted by others, acting against the person's will. But
a person acting autonomously does what he chooses. If he chooses to
work in a hospital rather than play golf, it is just a different choice. In

fact, no matter what we do, we do that thing and not anything else. So we might say that no matter what we do, we are always restricting our liberty to do every other incompatible thing."

Worries of this nature are very important for the rectification theory, in light of my insistence that willing submission to punishment is the primary case. So I must say how a person can restrict her own liberty and, in particular, how restricting one's own liberty to do some particular thing differs from merely refraining from doing that thing.

An example—an uncontroversial one, I hope—will help answer these questions. Suppose that I am a person who takes his promises seriously. I promise Deutsch that I will meet him at the movies at midnight on Friday the thirteenth. I thus restrict my liberty to do anything incompatible with going to the movies then.

How did I do this? Well, I accept it as a standing principle governing my behavior that those to whom I make promises have a right to my performance. This principle is a firmly entrenched part of my plan of life. Before making my promise to Deutsch, my plan of life accorded me the liberty (at least provisionally) to go to the movies, or to stay at home, or to set out for Katmandu, or any of a large number of things, some compatible with my showing up at the movies and others not. Indeed, my plan of life may have granted this liberty not merely through failing to specify what I should do at the fateful hour, but through actually specifying that the choice is to be left open until the time comes. But by promising to go to the movies at the specified time, I invoke a higher-order part of my plan: the principle of fidelity to promises. This overrules the lower-order provision of liberty at midnight, Friday the thirteenth, and thus my liberty is restricted.

So in order to restrict one's own liberty, the following conditions must, I suggest, be satisfied:

(1) One must have and largely follow a settled plan of life.

(2) This plan must allow for changes reflecting changes in circumstances, or in one's own preferences.

(3) The plan must be changed so as to require a particular course of action where it formerly allowed for a wider liberty.

This formulation answers the particular questions posed by my hypothetical questioner. First, the three principles make it clear how restricting one's liberty differs from merely choosing one thing at the expense of other things. For example, if I plan to be a firefighter,

but then change my mind and plan to be a cowboy, I have not restricted my liberty, but merely traded one plan for another. Or (more
relevantly) if on impulse I walk into the hospital and do volunteer
work, I have not restricted my liberty. Second, the principles show
how the questioner is proceeding on a false assumption: He suggests
that a restriction of liberty must go against the will of the person
whose liberty is restricted, but this is not so. This assumption is not
required by any of the conditions, and examples make it clear that
it ought not be required. If my promise to Deutsch was that I would
go to the movies with him, it is likely that going to the movies with
Deutsch is the thing that I most want to do at midnight on Friday
the thirteenth.[19]

Ideally, when persons restrict their liberty by way of a rectifying
punishment, they will do this because they accept the Rectification
Principle as a principle governing their own behavior. That is, they
will say to themselves, "I have done something wrong, thereby arrogating excess liberties. The Rectification Principle now requires me
to restrict my liberties so as to offset the arrogated liberties. I will
therefore do this." But even if this is not the case, the Rectification
Principle is still satisfied so long as the persons' liberty is actually
restricted.

11. Remission of Punishment

We may use the term *full measure of punishment*[20] to refer to the
sanction called for by the just-stated principles. (Unless otherwise
noted, the word *punishment* in this section refers to punishment as
prescribed by the Rectification Principle.) The question then arises:
Must the full measure of punishment always be inflicted or undertaken? Or may the punishment be partly or wholly remitted? Answers to this question have run the gamut. On the far right wing
we have the Kantian position that punishment may never (or almost
never) be remitted. On the left we have Sir David Ross's view that the
government has the right to punish a convicted criminal and may
at its pleasure either punish or remit. I take a stand somewhere in
between.

We may approach the question thus: Rectifying punishment is
merely the maintenance of a system of basic rights. There is a very
strong presumption that the system should be maintained, whether
in punitive or other contexts. To remit such a punishment would
amount to granting the offender a special privilege beyond her basic

rights. The question of remitting rectifying punishment thus resolves into the question: Should people ever enjoy special privileges beyond their basic rights? And to this the answer is: Yes, but not on a regular basis. If extra privileges were regularly granted, it could no longer be said that the system of basic rights was being maintained at all.

There are two ways in which a person could come to have special privileges beyond his basic rights. First, the limitations on his basic right may in a particular case be outweighed by other normative considerations. For example, a person might be so ill that he would be in danger of dying if he undertook the prescribed punishment. In that case his duty to submit is probably outweighed. But second, and more interestingly, the principles that underlie the system of basic rights may themselves call for a relaxation of the usual limitations. Several examples: (1) The purpose of a system of rights may be to protect certain interests, which occasionally can be much better served by relaxing one of the usual limitations. (2) A system of rights based on a utilitarian ethic (such as Mill's) will admit of exceptions when a greater good can be achieved by that means.[21] (3) A system of rights based on an agapistic[22] (that is, love-centered) ethic will admit of exceptions when exceptions will better promote the proper kind of loving relationship among the parties involved. Indeed, there is a point beyond which insistence on one's rights is inconsistent with the spirit of mutual love; we might say it would be pharisaic to go further.

It is here in this third category that the concepts of repentance, forgiveness, and mercy are most at home. If an offender sincerely repents, and if her fellows are moved by mercy and forgiveness, a relationship of mutual love can be maintained without punishment. (Punishment might in fact serve as a detriment.)

Rectifying punishments, then, may rarely be remitted. Does this mean that a government or other authority must seek out and convict all offenders to ensure that (with few exceptions) they are all properly punished? This, indeed, would be very difficult, and no one really tries to do it. Nor does the rectification theory oblige them to. As with other institutional duties falling upon individuals, the institutional authority may and must rely to a large extent on voluntary compliance, even though it knows that many people in fact fail to comply. Indeed, no (human) authority can pretend to discover every offense and every offender. On the other hand, when an adjudicating official has found someone guilty of an offense, she should only rarely impose less than the full measure of punishment. For such an official is making a declaration of what is required by the system of rights and other norms.

12. Affinities to Other Views

The rectification theory has affinities to many other views on punishment. It is most closely related to Herbert Morris's theory (as put forward in "Persons and Punishment") and may in fact be seen as a particularization of that view. In this section I sketch my theory's affinities with Morris's and show how the rectificatory conception of punishment overcomes the objections that beset Morris's view. I then discuss, much more briefly, some similarities between the rectification theory and views of punishment other than Morris's.

MORRIS

Morris's view is a kind of equilibrationism:

> It is just to punish those who have violated the rules and caused the unfair distribution of benefits and burdens. A person who violates the rules has something others have—the benefits of the system—but by renouncing what others have assumed, the burdens of self-restraint, he has acquired an unfair advantage. Matters are not even until this advantage is in some way erased. Another way of putting it is that he owes something to others, for he has something that does not rightfully belong to him. Justice—that is, punishing such individuals—restores the equilibrium of benefits and burdens by taking from the individual what he owes, that is, exacting the debt.[23]

Jeffrie Murphy and Michael Davis have expressed similar views.[24] Now, it is rather obvious how to derive the rectification theory from Morris's: We merely specify that the benefits and burdens with which we are concerned are the basic rights and the liberties they guarantee. The fair distribution of these rights and liberties is simply an equal distribution.

Along with this similarity between my view and Morris's, it should be noted that there are important differences. First, Morris's view is embedded (as the Rectification Principle is not) in a presupposed scheme of fair cooperation in which mutual sacrifices are required if benefits are to be produced for all.[25] This is true of Murphy as well, though not so much of Davis. Now, this presupposition does not formally enter the justification of Morris's view, as can be seen from the excerpt, but in spirit the presupposition permeates the whole essay. The tone sometimes is: "You have enjoyed the benefits, so now you must bear the burdens." Though quite reasonable, this attitude adds a distinct element that is not part of the Rectification Principle and subjects the theory to additional objections, as will be seen below. Second, Morris's theory applies generally to benefits consisting of "noninterference by others with what each person values."[26] This phrase evidently includes all generally valued things that the state tries to secure to people. The rectification theory, on the other hand, applies only to benefits that are distributed in a fixed and equal way, viz., the equal, inalienable, basic rights. The rectification theory could indeed be extended to any benefits and burdens that are distributed according to a pattern principle (to use Nozick's term): Any deviations from the pattern must be rectified. But there are many benefits, such as wealth and income, that are distributed according to procedural principles: So long as a just procedure is followed, *any* resulting pattern of distribution is just.[27] An equilibrium theory will fail if we try to apply it to such benefits, since there is no equilibrium to restore. (For more on this, see objection 1, below.)

The major objections to Morris's view are as follows.

Objection 1: The Nature of Self-Restraint.   Self-restraint is the burden with whose distribution Morris is concerned. Now, the term *self-restraint* is ambiguous in this context. We may interpret it either *subjectively* as the unpleasant psychological state associated with restraining oneself from things that one can do and wants to do; or we may interpret it *objectively* as obedience to law or other norms.

Now, those who hold a Morris-type view usually suggest that they are using the former interpretation. For example, Morris writes that "the burden consists in the exercise of self-restraint . . . over *inclinations*. . . . If a person . . . gives in to such inclinations, he renounces a burden which others have voluntarily assumed."[28] Punishment, an alternative burden, restores the balance. Two people, for example, may walk past an unguarded display of luscious apples. Both are sorely tempted; Hill steels herself and walks straight by, but Dale gives in and steals an apple. Dale therefore has an unfair advantage over Hill, not merely in the apple, but in the self-indulgence he exercised. But we run into trouble when we consider Cliff, who hates fruit and never needs to exercise self-restraint when passing fruit stands. It seems that Dale is unfairly burdened by comparison, and that Cliff thus has an unfair advantage. If equality of self-restraint is our goal, then Cliff must be punished along with Hill. More trouble ensues when we consider Woods, who is under suspicion and is always being tailed by the FBI. Under their strict surveillance, Woods never has an opportunity to steal an apple and thus never has an occasion to exercise self-restraint. Woods thus has an unfair advantage over Dale and ought to be punished along with Hill and Cliff, if equality of self-restraint is truly our goal. Moreover, let us consider Shore, who is a terrorist for the Symbionese Liberation Army. Shore would prefer to sit at home watching television but believes herself morally required to engage in terrorism. She overcomes laziness, fear of death, and strong moral scruples in order to do what she believes to be right. Shore thus exercises self-restraint far beyond that of the average person; self-restraint is involved in her very crime. Shall we say, then, that Shore should be rewarded for her exercise of self-restraint? Obviously not.[29]

What are we to make of this? Do those with weak inclinations to break the law have an unfair advantage over those with strong lawless inclinations? No; the fairness of the law cannot be measured by the relative amount of self-restraint that each person must exercise over his inclinations. On the contrary, we hold people to a great extent responsible for their inclinations.[30] What we require is that people, whatever their inclinations, conform their *behavior* to certain standards. Which leads us to the objective interpretation.

The objective version of the theory treats law-abidingness as a burden apart from any psychological states surrounding it. (Similarly, we say that possession of valuable property is a benefit, independently of the positive or negative feelings people may have about their property.) Everyone must bear an equal share of this burden, that is to say, must obey the entire law; and if some do not bear their fair share, they must bear an alternative burden, namely, a punishment.

We must here distinguish two subcases: The just distribution of this burden may be determined by a *pattern* principle or by a *procedural* principle. I will argue that if we consider a pattern principle, Morris's theory is reduced to the Rectification Principle, whereas if we consider a procedural principle, Morris's theory is implausible.

First, the pattern principle. Such a principle distributes things in some fixed pattern; each person's holdings depend on some unchanging personal characteristic. In a liberal democracy what burdens are distributed according to a pattern principle? These would seem to be nothing but the burdens of respecting the equal basic liberties of others, as embodied in a constitution and legislation; and the pattern is one of strict equality. All other benefits and burdens are transferable, and transfers will undermine any pattern that has been set up.[31] So in this case Morris's theory yields the Rectification Principle.

We turn to procedural principles. A procedural principle defines a just distribution in terms of the process that it results from. In the present case, then, a just distribution of benefits and burdens is whatever distribution the legislature happens to enact in accordance with its proper procedure. (We must exclude legislation that merely gives effect to the basic liberties, for such legislation is still to be judged by a pattern principle.) Now, Morris writes, "A person who violates the rules has something others have—the benefits of the system—but by renouncing what others have assumed, the burdens of self-restraint, he has acquired an unfair advantage."[32] This reasoning gets its plausibility from the assumption that the violator has the *same* benefits as others, or at any rate *equivalent* benefits, but fails to assume an *equivalent* burden. This assumption holds true if the principle of distribution is a pattern principle (as we have seen); but when benefits and burdens are distributed according to procedural justice, there is no pretense of giving each person the equivalent of what the others get; rather, each person gets whatever the system happens to give her. Some may get more, some less; there may not even be any way of comparing. Thus Morris's theory is implausible if applied to benefits distributed according to procedural justice, and simply yields the Rectification Principle if applied to pattern principles.

By way of digression, we may note the Kantian ambitiousness of Morris's view. For Kant, there is only one vice: exempting oneself from universal law. The vicious person hopes that others will assume burdens that she has renounced. Morris's theory is simply the penal counterpart of this view. Morris would have it that all crimes involve renouncing a burden that others are assuming. If only it were so! Some of us simply are luckier and find ourselves less burdened than others. To some extent, this imbalance needs correction, but only the most extreme egalitarian would say that every imbalance needs correction.

Objection 2: Theory and Practice. We might concede that Morris's view would justify punishment in a well-ordered society, in which benefits and burdens are fairly distributed; but in our less-than-ideal society, benefits and burdens are distributed unfairly. There is no equilibrium to restore.[33] If a hardworking but impoverished person steals twenty dollars from Donald Trump, one may admit that the thief should be punished, but it would only be a bitter joke if it were then claimed that this punishment restored some kind of balance of benefits and burdens.

Objection 3: Accounting Problems.   Morris's view, as an equilibrium theory, is subject to all the difficulties mentioned above (Chapter 2, section 4). For example, benefits and burdens ought to be balanced over a person's entire lifetime, not just for one transgression.[34] Consequently, extra burdens assumed in the past ought to allow a person to take extra benefits now, that is, to commit crimes or other wrongs. Moreover, if I choose to bear some of your burdens, why should I not be able to, just as I can pay your debts or take your turn driving the car pool? Thus, on Morris's view, I should be able to undergo punishment for you. Combining these two points, we would conclude that indulgences may be bought and sold, so that someone who had borne extra burdens in the past could have them transferred to a criminal's benefit-and-burden account in exchange for a fee from the criminal. Under such a system Al Capone could avoid jail by buying up "merit points" from the highly virtuous.

These, then, are the objections to Morris's view. How does the Rectification Principle overcome them? Basically, it does so by finding a special moral equilibrium that must be maintained and, if necessary, restored: namely, the equality of basic rights and of the freedoms they guarantee. In a just situation we may expect that some people will be happy, and some sad; some subject themselves to restraint, while others act freely; some have many resources, some have fewer; so that in many respects there is no order or equilibrium. Yet equality of basic rights is still to be maintained. A crucial feature of the basic rights is that they are nontransferable. This feature establishes an enduring order of equality in this sphere. Money and goods, on the other hand, can be bought, sold, or given away, so that there is no lasting order in the distribution of such things. If a wrongdoing involves these transferable rights only, we cannot, in punishing it, say that we are restoring equilibrium or order; there is no such order.

Accordingly, the Rectification Principle withdraws somewhat from the Kantian ambitiousness of Morris's position and does not claim that this one principle can justify punishment for every sort of wrongdoing, but only for some.

The objections can be answered specifically as follows:

Answer 1: The Nature of Self-Restraint.   The Rectification Principle is not directly concerned with self-restraint, but with equality of basic rights and of the freedoms they guarantee. Self-restraint will at times be required to maintain this equality, but then it is valued only a means. There is no call to distribute it in any particular way.

Answer 2: Theory and Practice. The Rectification Principle justifies punishment in any society or other situation that for the most part maintains an equality of basic rights. This is so even if the distribution of nonbasic rights is unjust. The basic rights are so much more important than other rights that it is reasonable to be concerned with their equality even at the expense of justice in other spheres.

Answer 3: Accounting Problems. In part, the principle of the objection may be conceded. If someone's basic rights were unfairly restricted in the past, compensating rights ought to be given in the present. Of course, a person who has been deprived of basic rights ought first seek redress through established means; but if this is impossible, the person may be justified in merely taking extra rights for himself. In doing so, however, she should not turn around and violate the basic rights of others: That would merely perpetuate the disequilibrium. Thus the Rectification Principle could sometimes justify crimes, such as crimes of civil disobedience or crimes undertaken to vindicate one's own basic rights, as long as the crimes can be committed without violating the basic rights of others. So the Rectification Principle *does* call for equilibrating a person's basic rights over an entire lifetime. But under a regime that generally protects people's basic rights, it can be assumed that people have generally enjoyed their full complement of basic rights up to the time they have committed an offense; so the offense can be punished without first investigating and summing up the offenders' prior rights-status. Moreover, the basic rights are not intersubstitutable. (For example, extra freedom of religion will not compensate for deprivation of freedom of the person.) This was seen in the method for selecting a suitable type of punishment under the Rectification Principle. Hence, it is unlikely that a prior deprivation of right will be of the correct sort to compensate for a present arrogation of excess rights.

As for the problem of one person's undergoing punishment on behalf of another, the answer should now be clear. Basic rights are nontransferable. The Rectification Principle will therefore not sanction vicarious punishments, still less the sale of indulgences.

Having responded to the objections to Morris's theory, we may conclude that the Rectification Principle saves it from them—at a certain cost, however, for it can no longer be claimed that the theory offers a general justification of punishment. As noted, many punishments fall outside the purview of the Rectification Principle. We must either say they are unjustified or else look for some other justification.[35]

HEGEL

The Rectification Principle has affinities to several other well-known views on punishment.

First, it offers one possible explanation of the Hegelian dictum that punishment annuls the crime. For according to the Rectification Principle, the offender, in doing wrong, makes a claim to excess rights and, in submitting to punishment, repudiates the same claim. So the crime is in one sense annulled. The claim is not merely abandoned: That could be done by refraining from similar wrongs in the future. Rather, by submitting to punishment, wrongdoers admit and announce that they never had the proper status necessary to make the kind of claim that they purported to make; and they therefore wish to have it considered null and void from the beginning. Recall, in particular, that the claim was *imputed* to the offenders, and this imputation may be defeated. If so, the claim has been annulled.

Naturally, one cannot bring it about that a past event shall not have taken place. But if that were what is required for annulment, then there would be no such thing as annulment.

MABBOTT ET AL.

The Rectification Principle also has an important similarity to a view expressed most articulately by J. D. Mabbott but implicit in the works of many legal theorists. According to Mabbott, it is *logically* true that a system of law involves punishment.[36] If, therefore, we are justified in having a system of law, we are justified in having a system of punishment. Now, this view tends to be undermined by the fact that there are theories of law that do not make punishment an essential component of a legal system. But the Rectification Principle proposes something similar to Mabbott's view. For according to this principle, punishment is a logical consequence not of law in general, but of a system of basic rights. Now, it is possible (all too possible) to have a legal system that does not grant its citizens basic rights. But any decent or justifiable system will grant them, and a system of punishment will follow.

ROSS

Here we have a case more of contrast than of similarity. Ross holds that if I violate your rights to life, liberty, or property, I ipso facto forfeit similar rights on my part; whereupon the state may punish me, by doing something that would ordinarily constitute a violation of those rights. Now, this differs from the Rectification Principle in that the principle does not look at the rights of others, and how they were violated, but only at the rights of the offender, and how they were exceeded.

Ross's view, as it stands, is open to a criticism against which the Rectification Principle is proof. If I violate the rights of some other people but then make complete reparation, it seems that, on the whole, I have respected their rights, though I have made individual lapses. What more is required? Why is there any call for punishment?

ANSELM

Saint Anselm offers in a way the closest antecedent to the present view. According to Anselm, when a creature sins, "he disturbs the order and beauty of the universe." But punishment restores the order and beauty.[37] With Anselm, however, this view is merely programmatic: He does not come to the point of saying how particular punishments contribute to the order of the universe. (One should also note that he offers two distinct theories of punishment. The one mentioned here is the second. It is presented as an explication of the first view in order to overcome an objection. But so far from supporting the first theory, the second theory is actually incompatible with it.)

THE MORAL EDUCATION THEORY

The rectification theory is in a way the obverse of the moral education theory. The moral education theory aims at internal rectification of the wrongdoer; the rectification theory aims at external rectification. When crime occurs, there is something wrong with the criminal and something wrong with the world. One theory tells the criminal to correct himself; the other tells him to correct the world. The rectification and moral education theories share a second feature: Both involve sending a message. Typically, the messages go in opposed directions. In moral education, society tells the convict,

"Mend your ways," hoping thereby to bring about a transformation in him. In rectification, the convict tells the world, "I am going to mend the world." Finally, both theories share the important feature that the punishment works well only if the punishee accepts the penalty as just.[38]

CHAPTER 6

———

The Rectification Theory: Application and Evaluation

$\mathbf{N}$OW THAT the basic features of the rectification theory have been set forth, I turn to some of its applications. After these, I briefly evaluate the theory by the standards set in Chapters 1 and 2. I begin with a general discussion of the kinds of offenses that fall in the domain of the theory (section 1). Having done that, I consider attempts and victimless offenses (section 2), the punishment of recidivists (section 3), community service as a penalty (section 4), the penalty of imprisonment (section 5), and penance for sins (section 6). Section 7, finally, contains the evaluation.

1. The Domain of the Principle

The rectification theory applies to offenses whereby an offender arrogates excess basic liberties. The question naturally arises: What kinds of offenses arrogate basic liberties, and what kinds do not? To borrow a figure from mathematics, we may rephrase this: What is the domain of the Rectification Principle? As I have suggested above (Chapter 5, section 4), this is best conceived as a question of interpretation: We are asking, What kinds of acts or omissions should we interpret as takings of excess basic liberties?

My answer in brief is this: An action counts as a taking of excess basic liberties if and only if the offender exceeds to a substantial degree the limitations intrinsic to his or her basic liberties. I discuss this criterion in two parts. In the first I explain why and how the offense must be substantial; in the second I explain why and how the offender must exceed limitations intrinsic to the basic liberties.

A SUBSTANTIAL EXCESS

Suppose Murphy is walking down the street, sees the unfortunate Jones, approaches him, extends her little finger, and touches him on the shoulder so softly that he is hardly aware of it. Suppose, too, that aside from this, Murphy has led a perfectly blameless life. Now, formally, this is exactly like the case of Smith, who punched Jones in the nose. But materially it is very different. It seems slightly absurd to require from Murphy anything beyond an apology, if even that. Yet the Rectification Principle might seem to call for a punishment.

In point of fact, our feeling of absurdity turns out to be correct. Recall the general principle of interpretation put forward in Chapter 5, section 4. This principle tells us to ask ourselves:

(*Question of Interpretation*) What is the most plausible normative theory that we can attribute to the offender [that is, Murphy] that grants him a right to do what he did?

In this case the most plausible theory is simply one that says that minor deviations count for nothing, or, to put it more pretentiously, *de minimis non curat lex*. This maxim establishes a small margin of tolerance. We then call on the principles of simplicity and charity, and attribute to Murphy the simplest and most praiseworthy claim permitted by this margin of tolerance. Namely, we interpret him to claim no extra liberties at all. (This process is like drawing a curve on a graph, given a series of points. If the points all fall fairly close to a straight line, we draw the straight line.)

But how minor is minor? How wide is the margin of tolerance? This question must be answered by the particular normative theory involved. In general, we may say that a deviation is minor if it has no negative effect on the values that the normative theory promotes. It is even more definitely minor if the attempt to rectify violations of that magnitude would have a negative effect on the values that the theory promotes. In such a case the cure is worse than the disease.[1]

A more vivid illustration may perhaps be drawn from a more concrete field. Suppose Victor, an employee of a hardware store, is to cut a piece of window glass with straight edges. He cuts the glass, but on one edge there is a notch measuring one micron. Should the boss reprimand Victor? If he did, it would only be a joke. For glaziers' purposes, a pane of glass with a one-micron notch *is* straight. It would not just be pedantic, but wrong, to say otherwise. It would indeed be a waste of time and materials for Victor to try to rectify his error by repairing the notch or by cutting a new pane of glass, for a one-micron notch in no way affects the performance of window glass.

Similarly, it would be wrong to say that Murphy had claimed excess rights so as to make him eligible for a rectification-based punishment. His prior blameless life we may picture as a perfectly straight line (the "straight and narrow"), and his encounter with Jones as a one-micron notch. It would be detrimental to the system of basic liberties if we tried to rectify this situation. Poor Jones, the victim, would have his rights restricted far more by having to testify in court than by the original offense.

This is not to say that it is right or permissible to violate the law in small ways, merely that such violations do not count as far as the Rectification Principle is concerned.

It should be noted that the reasoning for this claim is normative, and not just a matter of logic. It is conceivable—that is, logically possible—that there should be some normative system that counts *any* deviation as substantial, however small it may be. For example, according to Saint Anselm, any sin, even one glance contrary to the will of God, is infinite in weight and hence deserving of an infinite punishment.[2] If we apply the rectification theory to such a normative system, then the smallness of an offense is never a bar to a rectifying punishment. Such normative systems, however, seem unfit for human consumption: Such a minute examination of a person's conduct would be absurd and impossible.

LIMITATIONS INTRINSIC TO THE BASIC LIBERTIES

The second part of our criterion requires that the offender exceed some limitation intrinsic to the basic liberties. What does this mean, and what does it rule out? Our critic might think that nothing is ruled out. "Why, any offense constitutes an arrogation of excess basic liberties. If an offense involves any kind of physical motion, it is a claim of excess freedom of the person. If it involves speech or writing, it is a claim of excess freedom of expression. And so on."

This critic raises a serious problem. To solve it, we must distinguish between two sorts of limitations on our liberties. Some limitations are required by the very system of basic liberties. Thus Smith's freedom of movement is limited by other people's right to be free from physical attack. People's right to political liberty requires strict limitations on the liberty to stuff ballot boxes. If anyone exceeds limitations of this sort, the offense falls under the Rectification Principle.

Other limitations are imposed for other reasons. Some promote the common good in ways that go beyond the basic liberties—for example, an ordinance against walking on the grass in a public park.

Others are for administrative efficiency and convenience, including efficiency in enforcement. For example, many states have an "open bottle law" that forbids possession of an unsealed alcoholic beverage container in the passenger compartment of a moving automobile. What concerns us, of course, is not the fear that someone might be transporting unsealed bottles of bourbon. What we want to stop is people's drinking the bourbon while driving. But a prohibition on the former is much easier to enforce than a prohibition on the latter. Yet other limitations are simply matters of procedure. One must be cautious here, because some procedures are in and of themselves matters of justice, such as the voting regulations. In other cases, though, they are not—for example, people who want to hold a parade or demonstration may be required to get a permit. (Assume that the only criterion for granting permits is the avoidance of scheduling conflicts.) A person who violates such limitations has not arrogated excess basic liberties. For example, suppose that Nolan, without obtaining a parade permit, gets into his decorated limousine, puts an unsealed bottle of bourbon on the seat behind him, and leads a parade over the grass in a public park. There might be other reasons for punishing Nolan's behavior—but the Rectification Principle will not touch him.

In general, to fix the domain of the Rectification Principle, we must look one by one at the individual liberties that we consider to be basic—let us take freedom of association as an example. We ask ourselves: Which ways of exercising this liberty are most important? Here, certainly, we would include political and religious meetings, and gatherings of friends. We would probably classify meetings of organized crime syndicates as less deserving of this protection. We then ask: What constitutes a violation? Is it a violation if a permit is required? Is it a violation if the permit process is very inquisitive? There will undoubtedly be more than one possible answer to such questions. Whatever answers we settle on describe the bounds whose crossing constitutes an arrogation of excess liberties.

Within the basic liberties we will no doubt include the essential methods for exercising them: definitive procedures (such as voting procedures) and essential means (such as access to public spaces for meetings). Someone who violates these procedures or exercises improper control over these essential means has arrogated excess liberties and is liable to a rectification-based punishment.

In some cases a person can arrogate liberties without actually producing any bad effect. She can do this by endangering one of the basic liberties—for example, by reckless driving that (by good luck) injures no one. She can also do this by doing things harmless in themselves but harmful if done by many. For example, if only one polluter pollutes, the effect is negligible; but if many do it, people can be made seriously ill. So each individual polluter's emission may be considered an arrogation of excess liberties, even though no measurable harm can be attributed to one individual. Thus offenses of endangerment and offenses involving aggregative harm also fall under the rectification theory.

So much for basic liberties in general. One particular kind of liberty requires special notice: the basic liberties connected with property. We can start by asking: Does the crime of theft (along with other property crimes) fall under the Rectification Principle? One might be tempted to answer No. If I have $100,000, it is not in virtue of some basic right; if it were, then everyone would be entitled to $100,000, which they are not. So one might suppose that a thief who steals the $100,000 is not arrogating any basic liberties. But she is. Her crime invades my right to the secure possession of whatever property I happen to own, a right that sets limits on her right (Hohfeldian privilege) of acquiring property. So theft and property crimes in general are after all subject to rectification-based punishments.

There is, however, a point to the objection: Suppose gambling is prohibited because it is economically inefficient (as the Law and Economics people would have it), and not because it is thought to be immoral. If I nonetheless win fifty dollars from you in a poker game, I have not arrogated excess liberties: My crime did not interfere with your possession and use of your own property. I merely induced you to use it in a foolish and socially inefficient way. If any punishment follows, it is not based on the rectification theory. Only by interfering with your secure possession of property can I commit an offense that invokes the Rectification Principle.

The end result is a division of offenses corresponding closely with our distinction of felonies and misdemeanors. To beg no questions, I call them serious and minor offenses. Minor offenses include offenses of any kind, if they are small enough, and offenses—even if they are large in scope—that arrogate no basic liberties.

2. Attempts and Victimless Offenses

Attempted offenses and victimless offenses have long presented difficult and related problems for moral, legal, and religious theory. The problems are these: Why should an unsuccessful attempt, or a victimless crime, call down any punishment at all upon the perpetrator? No one, after all, was harmed. And if an attempt is to be punished at all, why should it be punished less severely than the successful commission of the offense? The rectification theory allows us to answer these questions.

WHY PUNISH THEM AT ALL?

There are two possible approaches to this question. First, one might argue that so-called victimless offenses (with which I include attempts) actually involve an obscure and overlooked victim. For example, an attempted crime creates fear in the general public, and thus all are victims, though there is no direct victim.[3] The second approach bites the bullet and admits that punishment is justified even in the total absence of a victim. Each approach entails its own typical problems. If we want to find a victim for every offense, we can certainly find one if we try hard enough; but this victim is often so strained and metaphysical that we blush to pronounce the word *victim* in this connection.[4] On the other hand, if we propose to punish victimless offenders, we risk advocating punishment for mere bad character, apart from any concrete wrong.

Now, the rectification theory clearly takes this second, bullet-biting approach. It does not look at harm done to others, but at excess liberties arrogated by the offender. Such liberties are typically arrogated at the expense of some identifiable other person, but not always. We have already seen the example of a person who arrogates excess political liberties by committing electoral fraud, with no actual victim. Much the same are crimes of endangerment and crimes involving aggregative harms. For the schemes of basic rights with which we are most familiar are designed on the whole, but only on the whole, to protect people's important liberties and interests. An individual act or forbearance required by the scheme may by itself contribute nothing; so an individual act or forebearance forbidden by the scheme may itself cause no harm at all to these important liberties.

Now, punishment under the rectification theory is not incumbent on people merely because they do what is morally forbidden; that would be unacceptably invasive. Rather, people become subject to punishment because they have upset the fundamental norms that make possible their mutual relationship as equals; and for this particular kind of immoral act the offender's fellows are justified in expecting her to submit to punishment. ("Well, upsetting this relationship is a kind of harm, and everyone is a victim." No, the relationship is valuable in itself, not necessarily to any of the partners. They may value it only as a means to their particular ends, or they may not consider it at all. If well maintained, it often fades into the background.)

WHY PUNISH ATTEMPTS LESS THAN SUCCESSFUL OFFENSES?

The easy part, then, is to show why, according to the rectification theory, victimless offenders should undergo punishment. The hard part is to say why the punishment for an unsuccessful attempt should be less than that for a successfully completed offense.

Our first try at an answer is as follows: According to the rectification theory an offender changes her status by committing an offense; it is in virtue of this new status that she has a duty to submit to punishment. Someone who tries but fails to commit the same offense has not changed his status in the same way. Therefore, he is not subject to the same punishment.

But this brings us back to the first problem. Why, then, punish at all? Well, the would-be offender has done *something* that involves an arrogation of excess liberties. If we foil a burglar in an attempt to burgle, we can justly ask, "What makes you think you have the right to enter my house?" We may demand of the would-be assailant, "What gives you the right to strike me?" But now here we are back in our first position. The would-be offender seems to have arrogated the liberty to perform the complete offense that she has attempted and so ought to submit to the full punishment prescribed for the complete offense.

But there is an important difference. Though both the attempt and the completed offense act as claims of the same sort of right, the attempter's claim is easier to revoke. The perpetrator of the successful, complete offense has claimed a certain right and exercised that right. The attempter has made the same claim but has not fully exercised it. The successful offender can revoke his claim only by undergoing a rectifying punishment; mere words will not suffice. Suppose he has committed a burglary. He has thereby expanded his sphere of freedom of action to include burglary; let him say what he will, he cannot undo this.

The mere attempter, on the other hand, has claimed the right to burgle (or whatever), not by actually committing a burglary, but by making preparations or taking initial steps that have their natural consummation in a successful burglary. It is thus possible for him to say things that cast a different light upon the preparations or steps, changing our interpretation of them. He can, namely, abandon the burglary and say, "No, I do not now, nor did I ever, have the right to commit burglary." This tends to undermine our interpretation of his actions as a claim of the right to burgle; the actions seem more like a lapse in behavior that the person has called short. The principle of charity now prompts us to favor the more lenient interpretation. Obviously, we are being very charitable indeed: People usually don't try to break into a house if they don't intend to get in. It is not, however, a crazy level of charity that we invoke, for quite often a person's moral scruples do not kick in until she is on the very brink of doing something she holds to be wrong. It would be better not even to set out to do such a thing, but abandoning it, even at the last possible moment, can bespeak a serious moral commitment. In this spirit, we can regard the attempter as making only a less serious claim of rights.

The attempter, however, *has* arrogated excess liberties. She has arrogated the liberty to do everything required for her crime, but not actually to accomplish the crime. This I call the *liberty to bluff*, and the right that guarantees such a liberty is the right to bluff. It is an odd sort of liberty: It is parasitic on the liberty actually to do the thing in question. A successful bluffer needs to make people think she is the real thing, not just a bluffer. If she lets it be known that she is a bluffer, the jig is up. Suppose I swing a sap and make it look as if I'm going to hit you. As it turns out, I miss (on purpose—but you don't know this). I say, "Gimme the dough, and make it snappy." You hand over the money because you fear being hit. It appears to you that I am willing to hit you with the sap if I need to. Only with hindsight, and by dint of charity, can we say I was arrogating only the liberty to bluff, and not the whole liberty to hit you with a sap.

Such, then, is the liberty claimed as a right by a person who attempts an offense. What sort of punishment is assigned by the Rectification Principle? To answer this we must ask: What measure of liberty would be given up by someone in exchange for the liberty to bluff? And to answer this we must ask: Of what use is the liberty to bluff?

We may say one thing right off: It is less useful than the liberty actually to accomplish the thing in question because it is properly included within the latter liberty. Hence we can reaffirm our practice of punishing attempts, but doing so less severely than accomplished offenses.

But to arrive at a more precise estimate of the punishment, we must find out what this liberty to bluff is good for. First of all, as suggested, it enables a person to *threaten* to do the thing in question. This liberty can come in quite handy, particularly if the threatened thing is painful or horrible. The liberty to threaten bodily harm is thus very useful, as is the liberty to threaten financial loss, destruction of property, or breaking and entering. The punishment for attempting to do such things should therefore be quite severe according to the Rectification Principle. Less useful are liberties to threaten aggregative harms or things that are prohibited only because of endangerment. For example, it is not so useful to have a liberty to threaten to drive above the speed limit, or to serve small amounts of alcohol to minors, or to sell milk without a license. One might imagine some use of such threats: "You'd better paint that eyesore of a house, Mr. Jones, or else I'll give little Billy a glass of sherry." The Rectification Principle would assign to such attempts little or no punishment. And, as mentioned above, all punishments for attempts would be proportioned to the credibility of the threat that can be made. The more likely the threatened outcome, the more valuable is the liberty to threaten and the more severe the corresponding punishment. So, for example, the right to threaten to break windows by singing loudly would evoke more skepticism than fear; the punishment for an attempt to do so would be correspondingly small. Attempts to do the obviously impossible incur no punishment at all. So the Rectification Principle would assign no punishment to a mad scientist who tried to destroy the world with a perpetual motion machine.

Another use of the right to bluff has been suggested. It might be valuable as a sort of insurance policy taken out by those who intend to commit real offenses. If they should fail in their intended offense, they would be immune from punishment.[5] But in the present scheme, at least, this use of a liberty to bluff is irrelevant. A conscientious person could never use the liberty in this way; hence it would have no value at all in this connection.

AN OBJECTION

"But it is unfair," one might object, "to punish those guilty of attempts less than those who succeed. Morally speaking, they are both equally guilty, both equally deserving. Whether one succeeds or fails at an attempted offense is determined purely by chance: Muggsy may have his burglary interrupted by the police, whereas Buggsy is not caught till he has cracked the safe. One assassin may fire and miss; another assassin, no better a marksman, may fire and hit through sheer luck; and a third may have his bullet stopped by a Bible sitting in the intended victim's pocket. Such factors are morally irrelevant and should not affect the amount of punishment that each must undergo."

This objection is appealing but does not in the end hold against the present view. Begin by considering a parallel case: Businessperson Green signs a contract a minute before the deadline for signing; businessperson Brown tries to do the same, but finds that her pen has run out of ink and is unable to sign before the deadline. Is it fair that Green reaps the benefits of the contract, while Brown does not? Yes—because Green has signed, and Brown has not. This is not a matter of desert based on one's merit as a person.

Similarly, a person who tries and fails to commit an offense might, in a way, be said to deserve the same as a person who tries and succeeds. But there is one important difference: One has committed the offense, and the other has not. If I were basing my theory on a principle of desert, then surely the attempter and the successful offender would deserve the same punishment. But the Rectification Principle is not based on desert, at least not on desert conceived as one's merit as a person.

Moreover, even if we require equal punishment for attempts and successful crimes, we still run into the same kind of discrepancies between desert and punishment. Let us consider Manya, a fanatical member of the radical Ruritania Liberation Front. When the Ruritania Liberation Front calls upon her to "execute" King Parsley, her fanaticism palls. She begins to feel ambivalent; she had not expected such heavy demands. Out of loyalty, she carries out the plan, squeezing out one bullet. By good or bad fortune, the bullet misses. Manya collapses from moral exhaustion. She cannot bring herself to fire again. Compare Manya with Commandante Jim, another assassin, a member of the counterrevolutionary Ruritania National Guard. The Ruritania National Guard calls on Commandante Jim to "execute" Comrade Marjoram, the dictator installed by the Ruritania Liberation Front. Commandante Jim coldly stalks Comrade Marjoram, fires once, misses, fires again, misses again, and succeeds finally in killing Comrade Marjoram only with the sixth bullet. If we consider desert, surely Jim deserves a harsher punishment. His character is much worse. In fact, it is Manya's relatively tender character that caused her attempt to remain merely an attempt, while the vicious Commandante Jim persevered until he succeeded.

Of course, Manya might equally well have killed King Parsley with a single bullet. This would have been misfortune, both for Manya and for Parsley. An element of pure luck would have entered Manya's life, making her eligible to be punished as a murderer, not merely an attempter. But even so, Manya's punishment would not be completely disconnected from her desert. Rather, it is loosely connected. (After all, she knew quite well that her bullet might kill.) Complete disconnection *would* be morally alarming. We can, for example, imagine a hideous society in which people are held criminally responsible for the unforeseeable consequences of their actions. I take a walk down the street and set in motion a Rube Goldberg causal chain resulting—quite unforeseeably—in the unfortunate death of Queen Rosemary. At once I am caught, tried, convicted, and imprisoned for life. That would be monstrously unfair. That is perhaps the sort of thing to which our objector is covertly appealing, when nothing of the sort is actually at issue.

3. Punishment of Recidivists

The punishment of recidivists presents a longstanding problem. Should the punishment for a second or third offense be more severe than the punishment for the first offense of the same sort? Good reasons pull us both ways. On the one hand, there are sound consequentialist reasons for punishing recidivists more severely. And even a retributivist might claim that a person who makes a habit of doing wrong is committing a greater moral evil with each subsequent offense than she did with the first one. On the other hand, people who commit like offenses should (it would seem) be treated alike, whether the offense is the first or the ninety-first.

The rectification theory comes down on the former side: It holds that recidivists should undergo a harsher punishment. I discuss the question in two parts. First, I consider those who commit a small number of offenses, and second, habitual offenders.

A FEW OFFENSES; WILLING SUBMISSION

Let us recall the case of Smith, attacker of Jones. She has just now completed her term of community-service work—let us suppose it was twenty hours—and is on her way home. Suddenly she sees Jones approaching. She tells herself, "I won't touch him," but he's such a hateful fellow that as he steps abreast, Smith's fist flies out and finds

Jones's nose once again. What now is her punishment? I will argue that it should be somewhat greater than her first punishment, since the second offense in a way nullifies the first punishment.

Why is this? Informally, we can say this: By punching Jones, Smith has in effect said, "I claim as my right the liberty to punch someone in the nose." By performing community service, she then says, "I revoke my previous claim." But by punching Jones again, she says, "And now I claim the right to do it again." Now, this third statement tends to undermine the second; specifically, it weakens or destroys its performative force as a revocation. This leaves the second rights-claim intact, and the first one fully or partially so; now both must be revoked. This will require a rectifying punishment greater than the original. Compare Galileo's celebrated statements on the heliocentric theory. He said, "The earth moves." The Pope made him recant. Legend recalls that after recanting, Galileo muttered, "*Eppur si muove*"—roughly, "It still moves." By reaffirming his original view, Galileo took away much of the force of his recantation.[6] It is almost as if he had never recanted at all.

Now, I think this informal account is basically correct, but it has two flaws. First, it does not tell us how severe the second (and subsequent) punishments should be. And second, it is open to an objection: Namely, if Smith, after her first offense has restricted her rights in the required way and has thus revoked her claim, how can *any* subsequent events undermine this revocation? Her later offenses make her seem hypocritical or fickle, but these character flaws do not call for punishment.

To answer this question and this objection, we require a more formal account.

Let us consider first the ideal case, in which Smith undertakes her own punishment of her own free will, without even the threat of coercion. Recall the nature of a rectifying punishment in such a case: The offender must restrict her own liberty, and this in turn means that she must have a settled plan of life by reference to which she restricts her liberty (see Chapter 5, section 10). But Smith's erratic behavior—offense, punishment, offense—indicates that she is not following such a plan. So her community service does not count as a restriction of liberty; it is probably only something done from a passing impulse of remorse. So she has not undertaken a rectifying punishment; she now must undertake the entire punishment for both offenses, which is forty hours of community-service work.

There is, however, a certain complication that may be made evident by a second example. Consider Smith II, whose case is just like that of Smith, except that her second offense occurs only after a lapse of forty years. Here, surely, the punishment of the first offense is not undermined. For in this case Smith II is for the most part adhering to a settled plan of life with regard to assaults upon others. The hard cases are the intermediate ones. Here we find persons who conform their behavior with regard to the offense in question to some degree to a plan of life, but not closely enough to erase all doubts as to the validity of the punishment. In such cases the duty to submit to punishment has been only partially fulfilled: Such offenders have restricted their liberty, but not restricted it enough. We would want to see whether they had the opportunity and motive to offend again. The more such occasions they live through without offending, the more closely they are sticking to a proper plan of life, and the more nearly satisfactory is their original punishment. Now, in this case, let us assume that the offender has a plan of life with regard to assaulting others—viz., "Don't assault others, but if you do, undertake suitable punishment"—and that she adheres to this plan on three occasions out of every four when she has reason and opportunity to deviate. It would seem reasonable, then, to count the original punishment— twenty hours' service—as three-quarters genuine restriction of liberty, and one-quarter mere impulse. So the punishment following the second offense is twenty hours for the second offense itself, plus five hours to make up the deficit in the first punishment.

Obviously, this account of how we determine severity can be considered only programmatic. How are we to enumerate opportunities to offend? How do we tell when there are reasons for offending? This is mysterious and must remain so for now. But the basic principle is, I think, quite clear, as shown by the examples of Smith and Smith II. Clarification of the details must be left for future inquirers.

A second complication arises from yet another example: Smith III punches Jones in the nose, does twenty hours of service, and then submits a fraudulent income tax form. Is Smith III a recidivist for present purposes? One tempting answer is, No, Smith III's second offense had nothing to do with the first. I think we should give in to this temptation. What liberty did Smith III arrogate by punching Jones? According to our main interpretive principle, we must ask: What is the most plausible moral theory granting Smith III the right to punch Jones in the nose? Well, generalizability would suggest that the right claimed is not restricted to punching, nor to Jones as a victim, but rather is a right to injure *someone* to a comparable degree of severity. But it would not be plausible to generalize to tax fraud. If we generalize this far, the theory becomes less acceptable, not more.

If Smith III, then, commits no more assaults, we may say that she is sticking to a plan of life by reference to which her punishment counts as a genuine restriction of liberty.

Second offenders must, then, submit to a severer punishment because the subsequent offense denatures the punishment for the first offense. This denaturing might be thought impossible, since it appears to involve backward causation, but the nature of any sort of behavior is dependent on the behaviors that precede *and follow.*

When I hum   only the notes that follow determine which song I have begun: It might be "Down by the Old Mill Stream," or "On the Isle of Capri," or equally well "I'm Going to Leave Old Texas." My intention at the time I start is irrelevant. So whether a given period of community service counts as punishment depends in part on what follows: offense or rectitude.

A FEW OFFENSES; COERCED SUBMISSION

We have been considering till now cases of punishment with no coercion. Things change a bit when we move to less-than-ideal cases in which the punishment involves an element of official coercion. Our offender Smith is this time made aware that if she does not perform the required service, something unpleasant will happen; or perhaps she is put under surveillance or confinement until the required service is done. In any such case her liberty has been restricted. So the requirements of a rectifying punishment have been partially fulfilled no matter what follows. But the essence of a rectifying punishment is service, and doing this service is up to the individual herself. Others may confine her, guard her, or threaten unpleasant alternatives, but performing the service requires a punishee to restrict her own liberty. If the punishee then goes out and commits the same sort of offense, this part of the punishment—the service part— is undermined just as before, though the confinement or coercion cannot be. The punishment for the second offense is therefore greater than the punishment for the first, but less than twice as great.

MANY OFFENSES

When a person commits a large number of offenses, the story is different.

Let us backtrack a moment. When a person commits an offense of a certain sort, I have taken him to claim the right to commit *exactly*

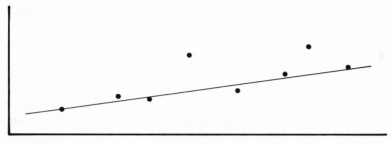

FIGURE 1

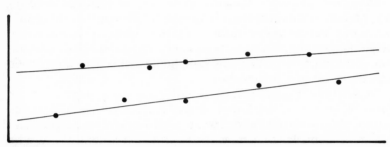

FIGURE 2

one offense of this sort. He might plan more, but that is irrelevant, and we give him the benefit of the doubt. Surely, the moral theory that allows for one deviation is much more plausible than the theory that allows for many. ("Everybody is entitled to one mistake.") Now, with a second or third offense a person might be seen as again claiming this same right. But if the person offends again and again, we can only see him as claiming the *general right to commit offenses of that sort.* The punishment is thus correspondingly greater. And if a person commits offenses of various sorts, he must be seen as arrogating the even broader right to do a large variety of forbidden things. And if a person shows no restraint at all, he has claimed the right to do as he pleases.

Now, how are we to judge these things? The problem is like that of drawing a line through plotted points on a graph. If most of the points lie on a straight line—the "straight and narrow"—we draw the line there and say that there are a few deviant points (see figure 1). But if there are many deviant points all falling nearly on some other line, then we draw that other line (see figure 2). Now, it is hard to articulate the precise standards for deciding how many lines to draw and where to draw them, but clearly such decisions are successfully made all the time.

4. Community Service

In many jurisdictions, both in the United States and abroad, community service has become popular as an alternative to the more traditional sanctions of imprisonment and fines.[7] The rectification theory of punishment provides a theoretical underpinning for this type of sanction and some guidance in setting the type and severity of the sentence. If community-service sanctions appeal to our moral intuition as a just form of criminal sanction, then the rectification theory gains considerable advantage. For most of the existing literature on community service is philosophically unsatisfying or even incoherent, as I momentarily show.

There are two primary problems with theoretical discussions of community service to be found in the literature—mostly in the criminological literature. The first is a philosophical naïveté and underdevelopment, leading to general confusion among those who consider community service. To the extent that a consensus exists among these writers, community service is usually considered to be a form of restitution. Therein lies the second problem. As I will argue, it does not even make sense to think of community service as a form of restitution.

As to the first problem, most discussions of community service simply list one or more aims of community-service sanctions (for instance, deterrence, rehabilitation, forfeit of unjust gain, and so forth). It is often unclear whether these are meant to be *justifying* aims, or whether they are merely good results that community service can achieve, or yet again whether they are merely some things that have motivated the creators of community-service sanctions. The state of affairs in the penological literature is aptly summarized by Sveinn Thorvaldson (who constitutes an admirable exception to the trend):

> It is obvious that the penal rationale of community service can be interpreted in many ways: for example, (1) simply as a means of keeping offenders out of prison; (2) as a means of rehabilitating offenders; (3) as a punishment for deterrent, retributive, or denunciatory reasons; and (4) as a means of reparation to the community for any material harm an offense might have caused to the state or for any harm arising from the violation of a law. Accounts of the versatility of CS [community service] are indeed ubiquitous in the literature. . . . [I]t is essential that

a researcher come to some more precise conclusions about what a program is supposed to do, or at least mainly supposed to do.

First, it seemed that it was the reparative element in CS that distinguished it from other sanctions. It was seldom clear in the literature, however, whether the reparation was merely regarded as a foreseen and desirable effect of CS or whether it was intended as an aim that justified it as a criminal sanction. . . . A close examination of the literature showed that CS could not be taken seriously as a predominantly punitive sentence that might serve the retributive, denunciatory, or deterrence sentencing aims. It was just not intended to make offenders suffer. . . . Nor was it of any real value as an incapacitating sentence, unless one assumed that these offenders tended to commit crimes on Saturdays between 9:00 A.M. and 4:00 P.M. . . . And the noncustodial aim (merely keeping more offenders out of prison) could clearly be accomplished by the expansion of any noncustodial penalty and did not necessarily justify developing a new sentence such as CS.

Finally, CS did not seem predominately rehabilitative in intent, at least as the term is traditionally defined. . . . Nor did anyone seem to be seriously suggesting (there were exceptions) that the duration of a CS order be based . . . on the offender's need for therapy.

One was driven to the conclusion that making reparation in the form of service to the community was intended, at least as far as its affects [*sic*] on offenders is concerned, to influence their broad social and moral attitudes.[8]

The confusion may be illustrated by such quotations as the following:

It is possible to conclude that the use of community service orders is preferable to incarceration. . . . [W]e are left with really only one justification for this programme, that of it being apparently a more humane form of punishment.[9]

Preliminary indications suggest that restitution [including community service] is used only in the rarest circumstances as an alternative to imprisonment.[10]

The theory of restitution is that once a person is convicted of an offense, that person will be rehabilitated or reformed if he is made aware of the loss caused by his criminal acts and is held responsible for remedying these acts.[11]

Compare this last quotation with Thorvaldson's statement, quoted above: "CS did not seem predominately rehabilitative in intent. . . . Nor did anyone seem to be seriously suggesting . . . that the duration of a CS order be based . . . on the offender's need for therapy." A similar confusion as to the aims of community-service sanctions seems to prevail also in the courts.[12]

Now, each of these aims has some plausibility, so it is not surprising that penologists disagree by supporting one aim or the other; what *is* surprising is that they agree almost universally upon the most implausible suggestion of all, namely, that community-service sanctions are a form of restitution.[13] Against this, I will argue that community-service sanctions (with minor exceptions) cannot be justified as a form of restitution, and indeed that in most cases they cannot even be conceived as a form of restitution.

But what is there to argue? The suggestion that community-service sanctions are a form of restitution seems simply wrong on the face of it: To make restitution is, by definition, to restore a victim to the status quo ante by means of money, goods, or services, whereas community service does not do this at all. If, for example, Smith robs me, how am I aided if she then does work in a public park? "The armed robber did not rob society; he robbed his victim. His debt, therefore, is not to society, it is to the victim."[14]

Moreover, the grammar of restitution is very different from the grammar of the community-service sanction. The main points of difference are two. First, restitution is the repayment of a certain sort of debt; but the requirement to perform community service, like the more general duty to submit to punishment, is very different in form from the duty to pay one's debts. This difference is discussed in Chapter 2, section 4, but for now the following points may be usefully recalled. Suppose I owe Smith a debt of restitution. My debt is canceled if my friend Rothschild comes along and pays it for me or hires someone else to perform the needed services. Or the debt may be equally well paid by an insurance company under a policy purchased in advance. But suppose now that I have committed a crime and have been convicted and sentenced to perform community service. No one would ever suggest that Rothschild may perform this service in my place, or that she may pay a third party to perform it, or that an insurance company may provide someone for the purpose. Such a suggestion would be absurd.

Second, the *way in which one incurs* a debt of restitution differs drastically from the way in which one acquires a duty to submit to the sanction of community service. I incur a debt of restitution by causing harm to someone's interests; no crime need be involved. I incur a duty to perform community service by committing a crime; it may be a victimless crime, involving no harm to anyone.

The concepts of restitution and of the community-service sanction thus differ greatly from each other. This difference sets a hurdle in the path of anyone who proposes to equate the two.

Advocates of community-service sanctions are, of course, not unaware of this problem. They try to make a case that the community (or the state as its embodiment) is in some way a victim of the crime and hence entitled to the compensation that is the victim's due. Three versions of this view may be found: (1) the community (or the state) is the *actual victim* of the crime; (2) the community (or the state) stands in as a *substitute victim;* or (3) the community (or the state) functions as a *symbolic victim.*[15] A full discussion of these would take more space than we can afford here, so I confine myself to some indicative remarks.

The first view is sometimes put forward as analytic, true by definition: A crime is, by definition, an offense against the law of the state; the state, therefore, is a victim of every crime. Now, this reasoning may not be literally incorrect, but it uses the word *victim* in an extended sense. The state is not the victim of a mugger in the same way as the actual muggee. If the state (in an extended sense) is a victim of the mugging, then (in the same extended sense) restitution to the muggee effectively compensates the state.

A more intelligent variety of this first version points to actual costs imposed by criminals on the public at large. For example, if burglaries occur, homeowners must install alarms, purchase insurance, and the like. These costs may be considerable, and it is for these that the criminal must make restitution.[16] But these costs are quite indirect. The criminal does not cause any direct harm to such "victims," nor does she threaten such harm, but merely gives them reason to believe that they may become the victims of similar crimes. If we applied this reasoning universally, the results would be absurd. For example, if I leave an icy sidewalk uncleared, someone may slip and fall, and I must compensate him. But then others, hearing of the accident, will have reason to believe that they may become the victims of icy sidewalks. Do I owe compensation to all of them? To say so would simply obliterate the distinction between victims and nonvictims.[17]

The second version of the restitution theory sees the community as a substitute victim. This is sometimes recommended when the true victim cannot be found, or when it is a matter of a victimless crime. But why should anyone ever compensate a substitute victim? If the culprit cannot be found, should we also exact compensation from a substitute culprit? The suggestion is almost too silly to consider. People are not interchangeable like that. If we are to compensate someone who has not been injured, the person proposing such an odd form of compensation bears a heavy burden of explanation.

The third version sees the community as a symbolic victim of crime. What seems to be going on here is a form of reform or rehabilitation: It is good for the criminal's character to bear the responsibility for repairing damage—and if not her actual damage, then someone else's. This might be so, but "restitution" is not the word for it. To call it restitution merely clouds our minds so that we cannot see what is going on.

There are possible replies to these criticisms, but they strike me as epicyclic, and I do not pursue them further here. The rectification theory, by contrast, gives a clear and straightforward account of community-service sanctions.

5. Imprisonment

The punishment of choice, according to the rectification theory, is community service. Now, one might wonder whether imprisonment, the current punishment of choice, would have any place at all. The answer is, Yes, but only as a means of enforcing some other penalty, and never as a punishment in itself. It may be that some other theory of punishment could justify imprisonment as a punishment for its own sake. The rectification theory does not exclude this possibility. But the theory itself will not justify imprisonment as a punishment.

IMPRISONMENT NOT JUSTIFIED AS PUNISHMENT

The rectification theory is an attempt to reestablish a scheme of equal, basic, nontransferable rights when the scheme has been upset by crime or wrongdoing. Now, the liberties guaranteed by such a scheme are not arbitrarily chosen, nor are the limitations on these liberties. Rather, they are chosen so as to protect and promote certain crucial goods. For example, freedom of religion allows each person an important spiritual autonomy; any attempt to impose an alien system of religious beliefs would undermine our very personality. Freedom of speech allows people—among other things—to be free of arbitrary coercive power by giving them an opportunity to influence the course of government. Obviously, and for good reason, we do not include among the basic liberties a freedom to play whatever card games one wishes, or a freedom of opera, allowing one to sing whatever operas one chooses. Nor are the limitations frivolous. These also protect and promote the same goods as the liberties themselves. For example, freedom of religion does not permit religionists to impose their forms of worship on others, even if their religion requires it. It would be logically possible to maintain such a scheme of freedom of religion. "All persons," we might say, "are free to maintain their religion, if they can withstand the other religions." This would be a sort of free market of religion. But this scheme would go against the purpose of the freedom. Nor would we adopt an arbitrary scheme, which would, say, give Protestants freedom of religion on Sundays, Catholics on Mondays, Jews on Tuesdays, and so on.

Now, in selecting a punishment, the rectification theory follows the same principles just outlined. The offender has acquired excess liberties, and her liberties must consequently be limited by an off-setting amount. But this limitation, too, must serve to protect and promote the same goods as the whole scheme of rights. Confining oneself to one particular room for months or years at a time could only by the wildest flight of fancy be conceived to promote such goods.[18] (Well, we might imagine a society that valued asceticism as a primary good. But that would be a fairy-tale society.) It is hard to imagine anything more pointless than confining oneself to one particular room for months or years at a time. When people on rare occasions actually do this, we suspect them of suffering from a mental illness, agoraphobia. Indeed, the original proponents of prison believed that confining oneself to one particular room for months or years at a time would promote reflection, penitence, and reform. But it is now well established that it promotes nothing of the sort.

If the rectification theory calls for the restriction of offenders' basic liberties, it does so only in such a way as to promote the equal basic liberties of all. Imaginative minds may devise many ways of doing this, but confining oneself to a room is surely not among them.

IMPRISONMENT JUSTIFIED AS A MEANS

The rectification theory thus never proposes imprisonment as a punishment in itself. But it may call for imprisonment as a means of ensuring that an offender submits to the appropriate punishment.

Let us say that Stone has robbed a bank and must perform certain community-service work as punishment. If Stone willingly performs this work and shows no sign of avoiding it, then it would be wrong to use coercive measures on him. That would be a further, unjustified deprivation of liberties.

But suppose that Wall, too, is subject to punishment and gives us good reason to suspect that he will try to avoid it. Then, as I argue in Chapter 2, section 3, the relevant community has a right, through its representatives, to inflict the punishment upon Wall, that is, to ensure that he carries out his allotted sentence. To do this, the community may need to keep him under the restraint of confinement. But this is merely so that we can observe him and ensure that he does not run away. The confinement must be as relaxed as is compatible with this goal, and must not be any more unpleasant than is necessary for the purpose.

6. Penance for Sins

The rectification theory justifies not only legal punishment but also penances for sin. Indeed, legal punishments under this theory may be aptly considered as secular penances.

RELIGIOUS RIGHTS

But the rectification theory makes essential use of the concept of rights. And you might think that the concept of rights, not to mention the concept of inalienable rights, is not to be found in the Judeo-Christian context that is the home of the concepts of sin and penance. This issue has been argued both ways.[19] Perhaps the most defensible conclusion is that traditional Judeo-Christianity gave great importance to particular human rights, so that we can say these faiths respected such rights, but they had no concept of a right in general. This is not the place for a full consideration, but the following remarks will, I think, make the point sufficiently clear for present purposes.

First, we can find at least one very clear example of an inalienable right in the Judeo-Christian tradition. The Old Testament system of land ownership quite clearly grants inalienable rights. Owners of land, under this system, could not sell their land; they could in effect lease it to another person, but it would return to them in the semicentennial Jubilee year.

Second, a more general argument. The following, I would say, are sufficient for a system of inalienable rights. (1) A system of norms permitting people to do any of a range of things, each at his or her own discretion. (2) A norm preventing a person from transferring or abandoning this permission. (3) A guarantee that the first two norms will not be revoked or altered. It seems clear that at least some branches of Judaism and Christianity fulfill all three criteria. Except under the most ascetic monastic orders, people are permitted to do, at their choice, any of a large number of things; sin occurs when the bounds of the permissible are transgressed. This permission cannot be transferred or abandoned. If God's law is thought of as eternal, then all three conditions are met, and we have inalienable rights.

The thing that poses the greatest difficulty here is the idea of grace. A bearer of inalienable rights is someone inherently deserving of respect and concern. If, however, we are saved only by grace, we are deserving of nothing and can have no rights. One indeed gets just such an impression from those Protestant denominations that emphasize the utter depravity of men and women. But even if we are saved only by grace, it is still possible that grace can be administered with justice: The whole system of inalienable rights can be seen as a gracious gift.[20] This point is made in Roman Catholic teaching by the distinction between congruous merit and condign merit, and among philosophers by Joel Feinberg's parallel distinction between desert as qualification and desert proper.[21] We can then say that we may not, in the strict sense, deserve inalienable rights, or that we may not merit them by condign merit, but we have them anyway.

The idea of inalienable rights, then, has a home in the Judeo-Christian tradition.

APPLICATION OF THE RECTIFICATION THEORY

The rectification theory now applies in a straightforward way. Sinners arrogate to themselves excess liberties. They must therefore restrict their liberties in a compensatory way. And, as before (Chapter 5, section 7), this restriction must be such as to promote whatever principles form the ground of the system of Divine law. The sanction will then be not community service, but Divine service.

This justification of penance can be seen as a particularization of the second justification given by Anselm in *Cur Deus Homo* (see discussion in Chapter 5, section 12). Anselm argues there that sin disturbs, whereas penance restores, the order and beauty of the universe.[22] But Anselm describes this beauty and order only in poetical language: "For if those things which are held together in the circuit of the heavens desire to be elsewhere than under the heavens, or to be further removed from the heavens, there is no place where they can be but under the heavens, nor can they fly from the heavens without also approaching them." We may now state this more prosaically: The order and beauty of the universe—insofar as human beings are responsible for it—consists in the state of affairs in which all people remain within the interlocking spheres of activity permitted them by God's law.[23]

Anselm himself, and other writers, often try to justify penance as our payment for injuries done to God. But we cannot injure God, except in some contrived sense of *injury*. The rectification theory of penance is thus superior to the repayment theory. (Compare the discussion of community service as restitution in section 4.)

7. Evaluation

Does the rectification theory do what we want it to do? The present section is devoted to this question. I here evaluate the theory according to the standards set forth in Chapters 1 and 2. I show that the rectification theory works equally well for the Paradigm of the Conscientious Punishee and for the legal paradigm. And I show that it provides both desired dimensions of justification, viz., legitimation and rationale (see Chapter 1, section 1).

THE CONSCIENTIOUS PARADIGM

In a nutshell we can say that the rectification theory accords with both paradigms of punishment for the following reason: A conscientious person who has exceeded the bounds of his liberties will for reasons of conscience restrict his own liberty so that he enjoys equal rights with others; a recalcitrant offender will have this restriction imposed upon him, to his dismay.

This nutshell, however, needs to be expanded. In this section I show how rectifying punishment accords with each of the seven features of the conscientious paradigm. These are, as we have seen, the following:

(1) Punishment consists of things that people often willingly accept or choose for themselves and is not particularly unpleasant, bad, painful, or the like.

(2) It is *undertaken by the punishee himself or herself*, who is

(3) *repentant* and *motivated by reasons of conscience*

(4) to *accept* the punishment,

(5) and is *active* with respect to the things that constitute the punishment.

(6) The *rationale* for punishment is *expiation* or *reconciliation*.

(7) The *typical* punishment is *religious*.

Features 1 through 5 are obviously in accord with a rectifying punishment; the others, less obviously so. I present first a brief overview of the obvious ones and then look more closely at the rest.

A conscientious person who accepts a scheme of equal, inalienable rights will not want to have goods or liberties in excess of those accorded to her by those rights. (Of course, she may have some desire for those goods or liberties: We do not have to suppose she is a saint. But her ruling desire in this case is not to transgress the bounds of her liberties.) She will not want to retain possession of goods that are not rightfully hers. The same is true not only of goods but also of more abstract things to which she has a right, namely, various liberties. If a conscientious person, despite her conscientiousness, has somehow arrogated excess liberties, she will want to right things and to have no more than is rightfully hers. She can do this only by restricting her own liberty, as discussed above. And until she does this, she will feel guilty and ashamed. From this sketch of the conscientious punishee, we can easily see how features 1–5 are met. Feature 1 requires that the punishment not involve disvalue to the punishee. And, indeed, this is so. For consider these two points. First, community service, the sanction of choice under the rectification theory, is not in itself particularly unpleasant or disvaluable to the person who does it. It is indeed the kind of thing that many people choose to do for its own sake. (Of course, many other people choose not to do it.) It would seem, then, that community service—considered in itself and from the point of view of the person doing it—is neither valuable nor disvaluable, except insofar as it is found so by the person doing it. And this fact suggests that such service is valuable and will be found pleasant, to the extent that it furthers the plan of life of the server. Now, second, the conscientous punishee's plan of life requires that she perform community service: This is what makes us call her conscientious. The service will thus be imbued with the pleasantness that comes with a release from feelings of guilt.

Community service, of course, is not a pleasure on the model of sex and good food. But neither is it an evil like confinement, torture, and the other things typically imposed as punishment.

Features 2 through 4 require that the punishment be (2) undertaken by the punishee himself or herself, who is (3) repentant and motivated by reasons of conscience (4) to accept the punishment. These three features are readily seen to apply to rectifying punishments. Now, a person who upholds and conscientiously adheres to a scheme of equal, inalienable rights will not want to have more than his share. If he has taken more than his share, he will feel repentant and will wish to rectify the situation. Even if no sentence is passed against him, he will feel that a rectifying punishment would be appropriate and perhaps even initiate it on his own account.

Feature 5 says that the punishee must be active with respect to the things that constitute the punishment. This again is easily seen to be true: Community service is something that we *do*, not something that is *done to us*.

Where do expiation and reconciliation fit into the rectification theory? The rectification theory interprets the offenses in its domain as claims of excess basic rights: It is in connection with such claims that expiation and reconciliation find their place. As said above, the basic, equal, inalienable rights are those that one has merely in virtue of being a person falling under a scheme of justice encompassing such rights. So persons who claim such rights in excess, claim to be more than just persons; they claim to be inherently superior beings. And this is not a mere verbal claim that a certain statement concerning rights is true; it is a performative by which the offenders alter their status with regard to their fellows: They acquire the status of *claimant of excess rights*.

These basic rights, moreover, form the foundation of the entire scheme of justice. If a scheme of rights is violated, it is a bad thing. But if the scheme of equal basic inalienable rights is violated, the foundations of justice are shaken.

These facts about the basic rights explain how the conscientious performance of a rectifying punishment can expiate or reconcile. Let us see first how it can expiate. Expiation, as discussed above (Chapter 2, section 1), may consist of two things: expurgation of guilt and propitiation of higher authorities.

Now, how can a rectifying punishment expurgate guilt? Or, for that matter, how can *anything* expurgate guilt? We cannot undo the past and turn the guilty into innocent. We can of course assuage *feelings* of guilt, but those are not at issue. The term *expurgation* suggests rather that the offender has become tainted and must be cleansed. (We thus sometimes read that sin stains the soul and penance removes the stain.) The kind of guilt that calls for expurgation is thus some persisting state of the offender that makes him deserving of ill regard or ill treatment.

Now, people who exceed the limits of their basic liberties put themselves into such a state: By the offense they acquire the status of claimant of excess rights. This status persists until it is changed, and certainly makes the offender deserving of ill regard. As we have seen above (Chapter 5, section 9), a rectifying punishment revokes the claim and restores the status quo ante. It thus expurgates the offender's guilt.

And how can a rectifying punishment propitiate the authorities? Well, if the authorities are committed to the maintenance of the scheme of basic rights (as they ought to be), then their anger will be aroused against anyone who undermines this scheme. If the offender then restores the scheme, the authorities will be mollified. This constitutes propitiation.

Finally, how can a rectifying punishment reconcile offenders with their fellows? Well, to give a simple answer, we need only adapt the one just given. Persons who consider themselves equals will rightly be aroused against one of their number who by his actions claims to be fundamentally superior. And such a claimant will probably in turn feel a certain alienation from his supposed equals. Since this fundamental equality underlies the scheme of justice, and since this scheme is the foundation of all sorts of interpersonal relationships, the relationships between the offender and his fellows will be strained and upset. I refer here to almost any sort of friendly and positive relationship—emotional, commercial, political, religious, sporting, and so forth. If the offender now turns around and revokes the claim, he makes it possible for the relationship to be restored.

This account is intended to be both normative and descriptive of people's behavior. People do, and have a good reason to, feel angry and alienated toward those who act unjustly in fundamental ways. And people do, and have a good reason to, permit themselves to be reconciled when the injustice is rectified.

The proposition that people actually behave this way would hardly seem to need substantiation. But social psychologists working under the rubric of Equity Theory have formalized this observation and provided some experimental support. Elaine Walster and coauthors have codified Equity Theory in four position statements, of which the third and fourth are:

Position III. When individuals find themselves participating in inequitable relationships, they become distressed. The more inequitable the relationship, the more distress individuals feel.

Position IV. Individuals who discover they are in an inequitable relationship attempt to eliminate their distress by restoring equity.[24]

Walster and her colleagues unfortunately use a gross and materialistic conception of *equity*, this being defined as proportionality of each person's inputs to his or her net outcomes (that is to say, benefits or rewards).[25] There seems to be no reason, however, that this conception cannot be refined.

Now, this way of conceiving of reconciliation is rather shallow.

Reconciliation, on this view, aims to undo bad feelings that one person may hold against another, or, more generally, to dissolve mutually hostile relationships. Although this dissolution of hostility undoubtedly permits more positive relationships to develop, it does not in itself involve the restoration of any such relationships. A stronger conception of reconciliation—one closer to ordinary usage—would involve the creation of good feelings and positive relationships.

In this stronger sense, too, rectifying punishment will promote reconciliation. For the punishee does not merely restrict her own liberty, she does so in such a way as to promote the general scheme of equal basic liberties. She is thus rightly seen as someone who is committed to the fundamental relationship of justice, and this rightly evokes the admiration, trust, and goodwill of her fellows. Nor is this scheme of equal basic liberties promoted in a merely abstract way. The punishee performs concrete services that promote the common good: She might promote health by providing medical care; she might help construct public facilities; she might help in the administration of justice. Any of these things will have two effects. First, such public services create a concrete and positive relationship between the offender and her fellows; she has done some particular thing from which they actually benefit. And, second, having performed this sort of service, the offender has placed a psychological barrier in the path of future offenses of the same sort. Having promoted health, or constructed public facilities, or administered justice, she will be reluctant to overthrow this effort by injury, destruction, or injustice to people or property. Things, alas, will not work this way all the time. But neither can we deny that people wish to preserve the result of hard, creative labor, even if the labor was not at the first undertaken by choice—consider the destruction, for example, of the fictional bridge over the River Kwai.[26]

A rectifying punishment, then, promotes reconciliation in the positive sense in several ways: by restoring the abstract fundamental equality of liberties and by means of the concrete public services that bind people together. The desire for this sort of reconciliation will give a special motivation to the person who values her fellows and desires their esteem—someone who is not satisfied with mutual noninterference but wants to share important common goals. If I steal a thousand dollars from a person who means nothing to me, it is enough that I give it back; but if I steal from my sister or brother or friend or compatriot or coreligionist—someone tied to me by fraternal bonds—there is a horror beyond this misappropriation, a horror that return of money may be insufficient to assuage: For how can I again sit at the same table or stand at the same altar or polling place with someone whom I have been willing to treat this way? And how can they sit or stand with me? Among brothers and sisters and true friends, love alone may well be enough to overcome the estrangement. But perhaps not, and almost certainly not in less intimate relationships. (The Prodigal Son is immediately forgiven; not so the Prodigal Next-Door Neighbor.) In these latter cases the offender needs to take some action to mend what she had damaged; and if these relationships rest on a fundamental equality of status as reflected in an equality of basic rights, then it is this equality that needs to be restored. The person who values such relationships, then, will be motivated to seek punishment not only out of devotion to principle but out of a desire to restore the kind of relationship that ought to prevail among compatriots, or coreligionists, or others sharing a common bond.

This idea, indeed, is not new. It is a commonplace that a criminal who dutifully serves his sentence has "paid the price" and ought now be readmitted into society. And it is another commonplace that the sinner who repents and does penance restores the loving relationship that ought to prevail between God and human beings. But it has been left unsaid why a price must be paid, and why a certain term in prison or a fine of so many dollars constitutes a fair price, and why a God of infinite love cannot love everyone (even a sinner), and how even a sinner is able to hate God, and how prayer and charitable deeds help to change this. The rectification theory can answer these questions.

But another question is raised in turn: What kind of relationship ought to prevail among compatriots, coreligionists, and so on? One answer: Whatever kind they mutually desire. This is the liberal answer. This answer, in the end, requires only mutual noninterference. Indeed, beyond this the classical liberal will require nothing, for our relationship with our neighbor is a component of our plan of life (or conception of the good), and this, says the liberal, is not to be dictated to anyone. So long as we respect our neighbors' rights, we do not have to love or even like them. The rationale of reconciliation is not available to the liberal political theorist, at least not categorically. The most she can say is, *If* you love your neighbor, *then* you should seek reconciliation in this way (but you do not have to love him). This is better than nothing, but it cannot work very well unless many people share a similar conception of the kind of relationship that ought to prevail among them. Indeed, in the sequel I will turn this into an argument against this doctrine of liberalism (Chapter 8).

We can now see why rectifying punishment, as performed by the conscientious punishee, will be typified by religious punishments. We have just seen that the rectification theory at least makes sense when applied to religious law, and indeed has been so applied (section 6). And we have seen that the theory provides an interpretation for the religious notions of expiation and reconciliation. And we have seen (Chapter 2, section 1) that religion, being a voluntary institution that promotes conscientious behavior among communicants, is the natural habitat for the conscientious punishee. Hence, rectifying punishment satisfies the seventh and last of the features of the conscientious paradigm.

THE LEGAL PARADIGM

Here we need not so much detail as with the conscientious paradigm, for punishment under the legal paradigm degenerates in predictable ways from the conscientious ideal. The defining features of this paradigm are, as we have seen, the following:

(1) Punishment consists of treatment that people typically wish to avoid (for example, it is unpleasant, bad, painful, and so forth).

(2) It is undertaken at the *initiative of someone other* than the punishee, who is

(3) *unrepentant*, and

(4) *wishes to avoid* the punishment, and is

(5) *passive* with respect to the things that constitute the punishment (that is, the punishment is inflicted upon the punishee).

(6) The *rationale* for punishment is *retribution* or *deterrence*, or perhaps reform.

(7) The *typical* punishment is *legal* punishment.

A conscientious person who is subject to a rectifying punishment will be painfully aware that he has arrogated excess basic liberties. Seeking justice and fraternal reconciliation, he will want to submit to a rectifying punishment. The unconscientious one, though, is unrepentant. He does not acknowledge that he has arrogated any excess liberties. A rectifying punishment will seem to him like so much pointless toil, a great disvalue. Hence follow directly features 1–5.

"But, as you yourself said, community service is not particularly disvaluable. This hardly seems like punishment at all, compared with imprisonment or fines."

The author of this objection should perhaps try working for days on end at some task that he considers pointless. No doubt it will seem disvaluable enough.

"But the punishee may happen to enjoy volunteer work in a hospital, or whatever penal task he is assigned."

This is not likely. For in a rectifying punishment a person must observe more stringently the very limitation on his liberty that he exceeded in the first place. If he is at all consistent, he will not enjoy this.

"But he may not be consistent." Well, in these paradigm cases I am dealing with people who are consistently one way or the other. That is why they are called paradigms. There are, of course, many cases that do not exactly satisfy either paradigm. Indeed, if every case were a paradigm case, there would be no point in singling out some cases as paradigm cases. In any case, convicts often do not even acknowledge their guilt, but just rue the misfortune of being caught and convicted. Such persons will not be able to see their punishment as a needed atonement.

I would probably find more merit in the objector's line of questioning if there seemed to be more ex-convicts doing volunteer work. But there seem to be few. Involuntary public service, I confess, involves less suffering than fines or imprisonment; but suffering is suffering. One should also note that fines and imprisonment involve less suffering than torture, dismemberment, and death. No doubt someone long ago argued that fines and imprisonment are so benign as to hardly count as punishment at all.

The only feature of the legal paradigm that might raise some question here is the retributive, deterrent, or reformatory rationale. If a rectifying punishment is imposed on an unwilling punishee, the primary rationale is retribution, in the sense of a return of evil for evil, justified apart from consequences. Retribution and expiation are here seen to be two sides of the same coin: Following the Catholic authorities, we might call this coin *satisfaction*. The rationale for rectifying punishment is thus in all cases satisfaction. In the conscientious, this takes the form of expiation; in the stiff-necked, retribution.

Deterrence and reform are secondary rationales. In forcing an unrepentant offender to perform public service, we hope that she will be reformed, or at least improved. (See the discussion, above, of reconciliation.) And since those most likely to offend are unlikely to want to submit, a rectifying punishment will function as a deterrent. But of these rationales, only retribution is inherent to the rectifying punishment of an unwilling punishee.

THE TWO DIMENSIONS OF JUSTIFICATION

In Chapter 1, I argue that punishment should ideally be justified along two dimensions, viz., the Right and the Good; or, in the terminology I adopted there, we should ideally provide a legitimation and a rationale for punishment. The rectification theory clearly meets this standard. For if anything at all is right, it is right that we should maintain a scheme of equal, basic, inalienable rights. And the rationale for rectifying punishment has just been set forth. Moreover, this rationale and this legitimation are equally valid for the conscientious paradigm and the legal paradigm. So, in sum, we have all the justification that was desired.

CHAPTER 7

Punishment and Contract

A CONTRACT theory of punishment, as we have seen (Chapter 2, section 5), is among the theories that can account for punishment under the conscientious paradigm. It would be a happy result, then, if we could incorporate the theory of punishment into a more general social contract theory. This is the task of the present chapter. Specifically, I find a place for punishment in Rawls's theory of Justice as Fairness. I proceed by taking the contract very seriously *as a contract*. Rawls's two principles of justice, as the text of a contract, are thus subject to the complications, reinterpretations, limitations, and reconstructions that are connected with ordinary contracts. By this method I will argue that the Rawlsian contract yields not one but three distinct justifications of punishment, namely:

1. Punishment is called for by the normal operation of the contract.

For example, the text of our social contract might have a clause saying "Persons who violate the foregoing provisions shall be fined X number of dollars."

2. Punishment is required by the contract as it is reconstrued (as it were by a court) to cover extraordinary circumstances.

Here the contract might say, "Everyone shall defend her country by serving in the army when called." Say Schultz is called but doesn't answer. By the time the authorities find her, the army doesn't need her any more. The contract is then reconstrued: Schultz is instead required to serve her country in a civilian capacity.

3. Punishment is required on the occasion of (partial or total) repudiation of the contract.

189

Here, for example, the contract may protect us against theft and assault. Someone who commits crimes may be thought to repudiate the contract. She no longer enjoys this protection and so may be fined or flogged as punishment.

The first way of deriving punishment from contract is the most obvious. Such a contract might contain explicit penalty clauses. Or it might avoid mention of punishment but contain more general language which, when interpreted straightforwardly and applied in ordinary circumstances, provides for penalties. Someone who becomes party to such a contract obviously commits himself to submit to the specified penalties. This view has been suggested by Cesare Beccaria, by Lawrence Kohlberg and Donald Elfenbein, by James Sterba, and by Rawls himself.[1]

The third way (leaving aside the second for a moment) is also fairly obvious. If one party to a contract repudiates it, refusing to perform, the other parties are released from their contractual obligations toward the repudiator. In the case of a social contract this permits them to treat him in ways that would otherwise be forbidden; this treatment constitutes a punishment.

The second way, though not obscure, is less obvious than the first and last. Real-life contracts often come to ill in ways other than repudiation. One party may perform only part of what was required, or may not do it in the proper way. Unforeseen circumstances may make it impractical or impossible to do what was called for. Such cases typically find themselves before a judge, who determines the parties' duties in light of the contract. One party may be required to pay the other a sum of money or on occasion to perform other actions. In any case, these are duties that arise from the contract, but they require the parties to do something quite different from what they apparently promised to do. The contract is not applied to this case in a plain and literal way, but is rather *reconstrued* to cover this unusual situation. A similar process, I will argue, takes place with regard to a social contract, opening a third door to punishment.[2]

I consider in this chapter these three contractual sources of punishment, determining the scope of each and the relations among them. I argue that only minor offenses may be penalized by the first method, and only extremely severe ones by the third, leaving the largest territory to be covered by the second.

The discussion in this chapter proceeds according to the following plan. Section 1 presents an overview of Rawls's theory and of the main conclusions of the chapter. In section 2, I outline a general methodology for nonideal theory: We are to adapt the original contract to cover nonideal conditions, rather than developing a totally new contract for such cases. This sets the next item on the agenda: In section 3, I develop principles of interpretation that allow the original contract to be applied outside its original range. Relying on these considerations, in section 4, I consider the content of the contract with regard to punishment. In section 5, using the principles of interpretation, I distinguish three sorts of notional societies suffering from different degrees of lawlessness, and I develop a distinct method for applying the contract to each of them: These three methods are the ones mentioned near the beginning of the chapter. Section 6 may be considered the heart of the chapter, for there I actually use these methods to derive the principles of punishment for the three nonideal notional societies. In section 7, I take the last step and show how the principles of punishment are to be transferred from the hypothetical[3] societies of the theory to similar nonideal societies of the real world. In section 8, finally, I consider what aspects of this chapter's approach can be extracted from their contractarian context.

Readers unfamiliar with Rawls's *Theory of Justice* may want to pass lightly over all but the first and last sections of this chapter, at least on a first reading.

1. Overview

The present chapter is based on the political theory that Rawls sets forth in *A Theory of Justice* and the Dewey Lectures, and develops in other works.[4] Rawls calls his approach Justice as Fairness. Justice as Fairness speaks of a social contract, but Rawls does not suppose that society is based on an actual contract, not even a tacit one.[5] The Rawlsian contract is hypothetical, or, to be more precise, notional.[6] Rawls describes an imaginary, idealized society that he calls a *well-ordered society*.[7] People in the well-ordered society have a strong sense of justice and (almost) always do what they believe justice demands. As Rawls puts it, in the well-ordered society there is full compliance. Moreover, members of the well-ordered society are in agreement as to what justice demands. Of course, they are not angels: Each has interests of her own that often conflict with the interests of the others, and each is willing to pursue these interests, even at the expense of others, to the extent that justice allows. The members' common conception of justice, however, and their readiness to honor its demands allow all disputes to be peacefully resolved. It is these imaginary persons, the members of the well-ordered society, who have entered into the social contract. In the course of this chapter I generalize this notion and define what I call the *contractual society*, which is like the well-ordered society but perhaps not so idealized. Although people in the contractual society mostly agree on principles of justice, their sense of justice is not necessarily as strong as that of the members of the well-ordered society. This less idealized notion gives us room to raise questions of crime and punishment.

Now, where do the members of the well-ordered society get the conception of justice that they hold in common? To them, it is the result of a contract—from their point of view, an actual contract. This contract was agreed to in a different imaginary setting, one that Rawls dubs the *original position*. The original position is a meeting, a sort of super-constitutional convention—"super" because it decides questions even more fundamental than those addressed in a constitutional convention. Every member of the well-ordered society is present in the original position.[8] To prevent rank special pleading, the parties in the original position put on a "veil of ignorance" that produces a sort of selective amnesia: As long as they remain behind the veil, they are deprived of all personal knowledge about themselves. They do not know their own likes or dislikes, talents or weaknesses; they do not know what social or ethnic group they belong to, what kind of family or friends they have, or even what period of history they live in. (Alternatively, we can think of each person in the well-ordered society as sending an agent to the original position to negotiate on her behalf. The veil of ignorance can then be put into effect by assuming that the agent has forgotten who his principal is and has no idea whose interests he is supposed to be supporting. This is perhaps an easier way to picture such a profound ignorance.)

Plunged as they are into this state of amnesia, what basis do the parties in the original position have for making decisions? They know, first of all, the general principles of the social sciences. Second, they think of themselves as having two moral powers: a sense of justice, and the ability to choose, reconsider, revise, and act on a plan of life;[9] and they regard the development and use of these powers as their most important and fundamental interests. Of course, they do want things like freedom and money, but only because freedom and money are needed for developing and using the two moral powers. Rawls uses the term "primary goods" to refer to liberties, money, and other things that are all-purpose means for developing and using the two moral powers.

These parties in the original position have convened to agree on principles of justice for the basic structure of the well-ordered society. They consider various alternatives, but Rawls predicts that they will settle on his celebrated *two principles of justice:*

> First [*Principle of Equal Liberty*]: each person is to have an equal right to the most extensive equal liberty compatible with a similar liberty for others.
> Second: social and economic inequalities are to be arranged so that they are both (a) [*Difference Principle*] reasonably expected to be to everyone's advantage, and (b) [*Principle of Equal Opportunity*] attached to positions and offices open to all.[10]

We are later told that the difference principle, which is somewhat ambiguous as stated, is to be understood to require that inequalities must be to the greatest benefit of the least advantaged.[11] The two principles are governed by two priority rules: The first principle has absolute priority over the second (Rawls calls it "lexical priority"), and the principle of equal opportunity has absolute priority over the difference principle.[12] The two principles contain two egalitarian clauses: the principle of equal liberty, and the principle of fair equality of opportunity. Together, these two clauses correspond to what I have been calling the basic liberties, or, as we may say, *basic liberties in the broad sense.* ("Basic liberties in the narrow sense" refers only to the liberties guaranteed by Rawls's first principle of justice.) The parties in the original position agree to these two clauses because the basic liberties (in the broad sense) are indispensable for developing and making use of the two moral powers. The parties agree to the difference principle on the basis of a variety of trickle-down view: If financial and other incentives are offered to productive persons, everyone—even the worst off—will benefit. This benefit, however, is not left to chance (as most trickle-down theorists would have it). Rather, the incentives must actually be set up so as to provide the maximum benefit to the worst-off group. From behind the veil of ignorance, this arrangement looks like a good deal, since each party in the original position is assured of the highest possible welfare floor, beneath which she cannot fall. Other arrangements might offer a greater probability of becoming wealthy and powerful, but to the parties in the original position this possible gain is outweighed by the risk of loss.

Once this agreement has been reached, the meeting in the original position disbands, and the parties go home to take up once more their positions in the well-ordered society. They follow the two principles of justice because they have actually agreed to them; they regard themselves as contractually bound.

We in the real world, however, have signed no such contract. If we regard the two principles of justice as binding, it is for a very different reason. We accept them because we want to act justly, and we believe that the sort of procedure just outlined is best suited for defining principles of justice. Since behind the veil of ignorance no one could favor herself or her friends, the result is fair: hence Justice as Fairness.

Thus far Rawls's theory. The theory is now applied to questions of punishment in three ways, as already mentioned. First of all, crime almost always upsets the operation of the difference principle. Crime does pay—or at any rate it is often attractive enough to compete with the rewards of honest toil. The effects of crime are like a tax—a tax that usually weighs most heavily on the least well-off. In a situation like this, the difference principle directs us to set up a system of incentives that will bring up the worst off as much as possible. Usually, the incentives that this principle calls for come in the form of power, wealth, and income, but in this case they are negative incentives in the form of fines. We want the worst off to be able to say, "Well, I'm badly off, but I'm better off than I would be if we didn't have a system of fines for criminal offenses." In fact, even if a member of the worst-off group has committed a crime, we want her to be able to say, "Well, I was badly off before, and now I've had to pay a fine, but even so I would likely be in an even worse plight if we didn't have a system of fines." Even criminals benefit when the general level of crime is reduced.

Punishments of this sort I will refer to as *deterrent*.

At this first level we are simply applying the contract in a straightforward way to a less than ideal situation: It calls for a system of incentives that maximally benefits the worst-off group, and that is exactly what we are providing. Not so at the second level. Here we are dealing with more serious crimes, crimes that involve arrogation of basic liberties (in the broad sense). When this kind of crime occurs, we assess a fine, as before; but that is not enough. The rectification theory now also comes into play. Now we are no longer applying the contract in a straightforward and literal way. The contract calls for a specific package of liberties. We can no longer give the criminal exactly that package. It is too late for that: She cannot simply put back the extra liberties she has taken. The best we can do is provide as near an equivalent package as possible. To do so we reconstrue the contract so that it gives us some advice as to what new package of liberties will be equivalent. This reconstrual is up to us: The parties in the original position did not anticipate that crime would occur, so they naturally made no provisions for it. The offender will, of course, have to give up certain liberties in order to get an equivalent package, and this relinquishing of liberty constitutes the punishment.

I refer to this sort of penalty as a *rectifying punishment*. The offender in this class, of course, also gets a deterrent penalty, but in deciding what that should be, we take into consideration the deterrent effect of the rectifying punishment, so that the two kinds of punishment together produce the optimal deterrence.

Some crimes, finally, may be so severe as to amount to a repudiation of the contract. These bring us to the third level. Here we include:

Murder, for the murderer eliminates one of the parties to the contract.

Treason—that is, aiding an enemy in time of war—for this seeks to eliminate the whole contractually based society.

Protracted engagement in a variety of serious crimes—for example, as by organized crime syndicates—since people who behave this way show no tendency at all to conform themselves to the contract.

Crimes that eliminate the capacity to choose that makes contracts possible—for example, assaults that leave the victim comatose.

Persons guilty of these offenses are subject to deterrent and rectifying punishments, as on the first and second levels. They have, however, repudiated the contract, and the rest of society cannot be expected to keep up its full contractual performance toward them. These criminals have taken themselves out of normal society and made themselves into something like enemies in wartime, or dangerous wild animals. Like animals and enemy soldiers, these criminals still have rights, which must be respected, but a much smaller set of rights than the others. The rest of society may defend itself against them by any means that respects this smaller set of rights. These rights serve as a limit on punishments even of this worst group of offenders. It would, for example, be wrong to kill a criminal—just as it would be wrong to kill a wild animal or enemy soldier—unless killing is the only way to prevent a comparable imminent harm; but such is presumably not the case once the criminal is safely in custody. This social self-defense may continue until the offender has been able to assure the rest of us that he is to be trusted enough to resume his role as an active party to the contract. In effect, this means imprisonment, both for social self-defense and for assurance: self-defense, in that the incarcerated criminal is prevented from committing crimes; and assurance, in that incarceration allows us closely to observe the offender and perhaps eventually decide (to the extent that we can ever decide) that it is safe to allow her some freedom. Penalties of this sort I call *self-defensive* punishment.

Although these most serious offenders have repudiated the contract, the contract remains valid, its operation being merely suspended (temporarily, we hope). This is certainly the case if we are speaking of the real world, as opposed to some imaginary notional society. In the real world, consent is not what obligates us to the social contract, nor is rejection of the contract able to obliterate it.

2. Methodology for Nonideal Theory

THE PARADOX OF CONTRACTARIAN THEORIES OF PUNISHMENT

Rawls deals mostly with ideal theory, as we have said: He assumes full compliance with the social contract. When we try to apply his theory to nonideal cases, all sorts of problems arise. The parties in the original position have made a contract for a society of fully compliant citizens. Can we take this contract for saints and apply it to sinners? Perhaps not.[13] Then maybe what we need is a contract made with the knowledge that crime will occur. If we examine this possibility, however, we discover a paradox. Either the prospective criminals are included among the deliberators in the original position, or they are not. If the prospective criminals are not invited to the original position, then those who are invited will be all too happy to impose the most gruesome punishments on criminals. If, on the other hand, the criminals are included in the deliberations, they will be able to distort the proceedings by threatening to commit crimes if the contract is not to their liking. This will give criminals an undue influence over the proceedings, a sort of extortion.[14] Not even Rawls's thick veil of ignorance will prevent this blackmail: Even our veiled individual knows that she *might* be a criminal, and she must weigh the interests that she would have as a criminal as seriously as the interests of honest citizens.

This is the basic paradox of contractarian theories of punishment. Social contract theory is plausible because we, as members of society, impose limitations only on ourselves. If the social contract is to deal with criminals, and possibly impose sanctions on them, then in fairness the criminals must be represented in the proceedings. In the Rawlsian original position, each party must be able to say, "*I* might turn out to be a criminal." But no sooner have these words passed his lips than he begins to rub his hands and grin, his eyes lighting up with larcenous glee: It dawns on him that he might *really be* a criminal. This is hardly the kind of person we want in our deliberations.

PROPOSED SOLUTION OF THE PARADOX

I propose the following four-step method as a solution to this paradox:

1. Parties in the original position select principles for a well-ordered society.
2. These principles are adapted to apply to a less-than-well-ordered society in which all offenders conscientiously make due amends.

(I leave open for now the question of what amends are due.)

3. These adapted principles are applied to similar societies even when not all offenders are conscientious.
4. The principles of step 3 are transferred to similar situations in the real world.

The general idea behind this method is that the nonideal is to be judged by the ideal; principles governing our behavior in nonideal conditions are to be adapted from principles governing ideal conditions. To give a homely example, by observing a good cook in a well-appointed kitchen, we can discern principles of good cooking. What should we do if we have only a dull-tongued cook in a poorly appointed kitchen? Well, what we should *not* do is derive special principles of poor cooking for the occasion. Instead, we want to derive principles that will enable the poor cook to produce a reasonable approximation of the good cook's cuisine, and allow him to become better at cooking. If nothing else, this last point shows the validity of the method. Special principles for poor cooks and persons lacking in virtue might serve well enough for the occasion, and in the case of cooking we might let it go at that. But when a person is deficient in virtue, it is incumbent on her to improve herself, to become more virtuous. So principles for the nonideal case must take cognizance of the ideal, at least as a goal toward which we must strive. This striving toward perfection, in turn, requires that we actually apply ideal principles, or principles closely approximating them, to the extent that this is possible and not unjust in our nonideal world. For if we become accustomed to nonideal principles that are substantially different from the ideal ones, we erect a barrier in the path of our progress toward perfection.[15]

Before we set to work applying the plan, some preliminary observations are in order. Only one of the four steps—the second—involves any substantial difficulty, but even for the easy ones we will want to see why they are easy. I present these observations in reverse order, starting in the real world with step 4. This step tells us that in some less-than-ideal situation, we in the real world ought to do what people in the contractual society ought to do under like circumstances.

To see why this is so, let us consider in detail why we are bound to the two principles of justice. Our duty to comply with them, as I have said, stems from the duty of justice.[16] The duty of justice, as described by Rawls, comprises two parts: "[1] This duty requires us to support and to comply with just institutions that exist and apply to us. [2] It also constrains us to further just arrangements not yet established."[17] The first part of this duty is static with respect to institutions; it assumes that some stable institution exists. The second part is dynamic, in that it directs us to change or establish institutions.

Now, what does the duty of justice require of us in the less-than-just real world? Well, the one dynamic principle is clearly applicable: It directs us to promote justice, that is, to bring about a situation in which all persons acknowledge and comply with the two principles of justice. But this principle does not tell us what method to use in promoting justice, nor does it specify what we are to do in the meantime.

The static principles ought to remedy this lack, but when we try to apply them, we run into problems. These principles direct us to comply with existing just institutions, that is, institutions satisfying the terms of the original contract. Now, the terms of the contract are embodied in the two principles of justice, but, as we have seen, these principles do not apply indiscriminately to every situation that may arise; and even where they do apply, they may require us to diverge from a plain and literal construction. So in order to find out what we must do in our imperfect real world, we must first find out what ought to be done in a less-than-well-ordered contractual society. The principles that govern the members of such a society also govern us in similar situations, the transfer being made via the duty of justice.

Step 3 tells us that principles governing a nonideal contractual society of conscientious people also govern a similar society that includes some nonconscientious people. That is: In the first case all those who commit offenses repent and make due amends, whereas in the second case those who commit offenses do not always repent, and the unrepentant make amends only when induced by incentives, or by the use of force. The same principles, I say, govern both cases. This point by now requires little comment, since it is the main burden of Chapters 1 and 2.

Step 2—the one difficult step—tells us to take principles for the ideal case and apply them to the less-than-well-ordered society. The difficulty has already been suggested: If the principles were chosen for a well-ordered society, why would one think that they should govern some other sort of society? That would be like taking principles selected for adults and applying them to children, or taking rules designed to govern baseball and applying them to football.

In a more systematic way some observations on the nature of contract argue for the same doubts. The justification of the practice of making contracts depends on the crucial assumption that the parties are well informed and plan rationally. In the real world we usually assume that adults do this and so hold them to their contracts even if the contractors have chosen things that seem bizarre or undesirable to us. But this assumption of rational, well-informed planning is overthrown if unforeseen circumstances arise. If the parties could not have foreseen the circumstances, then they were ill informed; if they could have but did not, then they were acting irrationally. In either case we can no longer apply the reasoning that called for the enforcement of contracts in such circumstances. You and I, for example, might agree to eat at Joe's Restaurant, having good evidence that it will accord with our desires. If, due to unforeseen circumstances, eating at Joe's no longer accords with your desires (or with mine), but perhaps even frustrates them, why should we be bound to do it? That would be perverse. So far from enabling us to make and carry out our plans, such a system would hinder us.

In ordinary contracts it is almost impossible to determine how much information the parties had. We usually assume that the parties supplied themselves with relevant information, unless there was outright fraud or deception. But when it comes to the original contract, the information that the parties have is strictly determined by the very definition of the original position. So there, ignorance is more of an excuse.

This reasoning is particularly apposite to punishment and the social contract. If the contract is designed for a well-ordered society, we will readily include provisions for all sorts of cruel and gruesome punishments. We know, after all, that in a well-ordered society there is no crime, and therefore no punishment; so we do not have to worry that we will suffer. But then we remove the veil of ignorance and find ourselves in a badly ordered society. In such a society we may find it reasonable or even nearly inevitable to commit crimes on some occasion. Now they come and propose to punish us: "You signed this contract," they say, "in which you agree quite specifically to submit to these awful and gruesome punishments if you should ever commit these specified crimes. You can have no complaint if we punish you now." But we do have a complaint. We were not making a contract with this sort of situation in mind. Indeed, if we had contemplated such a badly ordered society, we would have made a very different contract.

It is dubious, then, that the contract concluded in the original position should apply to any but a well-ordered society.

Furthermore, even if the contract is conceded to apply to less-than-well-ordered societies, it need not be the case that we are to apply it plainly and literally. This may be impossible, or may produce absurd results. If the aim of contracts is to enable people to advance their plans, a plain and literal application of a contract in an unanticipated situation may thwart this aim, rather than promote it. In this situation a contract may have to be reconstrued if it is to achieve the planned result. Justice may require the contracting parties to do something quite different from what they originally promised. An example from an actual contract might illuminate this principle. Suppose I build you a house which, when finished, turns out (through no intention of mine) to differ in trivial ways from the contractual specifications. Perhaps I used Brand A pipe instead of the virtually indistinguishable Brand B pipe. It may now be impossible to correct these defects except by tearing down the house and building anew. You might want me to do that (or, more likely, you might want me to give you enough money to do so yourself), and that is indeed what the contract says I must do, if we take it literally. But the court would award you only the difference in value between the house I promised to build and the house I actually did build.[18] Our plan, in specifying Brand A pipe, was to provide you with serviceable and reliable pipe; and this plan has been fulfilled. On the other hand, our plan in making the contract was certainly not to enrich you at my expense. These plans are best fulfilled by our doing something other than that which we originally promised. A strict and literal application of the contract is in such a case a hindrance to the aim of the contract.

So (to return to the social contract) even if it applies to a less-than-well-ordered contractual society, it may not apply literally, but may instead have to be reconstrued to meet this unforseeable circumstance. The application of the social contract to anything other than a well-ordered contractual society is thus not automatic but requires argument.

Step 2, then, will consume much of our effort.

This brings us at length to step 1. This step simply says that the parties in the original position select principles for the well-ordered society. Rawls himself has already carried out this step. Even so, some work remains for us. We must ask questions that Rawls, doing ideal theory, can leave aside. Just how well ordered is the well-ordered society? And what, if anything, does the contract made there say about punishment?

Having worked our way up to step 1, we now begin working our way down, this time actually carrying out the four-step method.

3. Making the Contract

THE RATIONALE OF CONTRACT

We begin by asking: Why should people in the original position be able to make a contract that binds members of the contractual society (well ordered or otherwise)? I do not intend to say anything new here, just to bring out some of the implications of what Rawls has said. With regard to ordinary legal contracts, we are often told (in varying versions) that the justification of the institution of contract is that it enables people to achieve their legitimate goals by means of reliable plans for the future. These goals often are unachievable without such plans. They could not be achieved by spontaneous action. Of course, this justification assumes that the contractors are well informed and plan rationally. Things are similar with regard to the original contract. The makers of the contract are exercising their autonomy in order to achieve their goals by means of reliable plans—or, I should say, irrevocable principles—for the future.[19] These legitimate goals are (according to *A Theory of Justice*) a large supply of primary goods or (according to the Dewey Lectures) the realization of one's highest-order interests in acting from a sense of justice and developing and pursuing a conception of the good.[20] Here I mostly follow the account of the Dewey Lectures. In either case the parties are motivated by a desire for primary goods—"things that it is rational to want whatever else one wants."[21] Whether we are dealing with social contracts or ordinary business contracts, these considerations seem sufficient to justify the practice of voluntary, binding agreements among persons.

THE PERFECTLY ORDERED SOCIETY

The next question we must ask is: How well ordered is the well-ordered society, the society for which the contract is designed? Is it perfectly ordered, or just pretty well ordered? The importance for nonideal theory is obvious. If the contract is designed for a less-than-perfectly-ordered society, then it is reasonable to apply it literally to similar situations in the real world. If the contracting parties are contemplating a perfectly ordered society, things are not so easy. Consulting *A Theory of Justice*, we receive little guidance. Rawls sometimes says things suggestive of a perfectly ordered society and at other times seems to have in view a lower degree of perfection. For the purposes of ideal theory this uncertainty is not a problem. The same two principles of justice are derived whether the contractual society is conceived as perfect or nearly perfect. But for nonideal theory the difference becomes important. James Sterba suggests that there can be considerable crime even in a well-ordered society.[22] I will argue for the opposite view: For theoretical purposes, the well-ordered society must be perfectly ordered.

We have already seen one reason for this. If the parties in the original position anticipate a less-than-perfectly-ordered society, they know that they may be criminals (or, more generally, that they may be unwilling to abide by the terms of the contract). If so, the noncompliant people in the contractual society will be able to extort favors from the parties in the original position. Except for the veil of ignorance, the situation is exactly that faced by one person who must enter into a contract with someone who does not have great respect for contracts. Suppose Adelman, whose word is his bond, is negotiating with Smith. Smith's word, however, is by no means his bond. It is no secret to either party that Smith will honor his contractual commitments only if they are not too inconvenient. Adelman is here at a distinct disadvantage. He and Smith may both be willing to enter into a mutually advantageous contract, but Adelman must consider the possibility that Smith may change his mind later. (Adelman could sue, but there are costs with that, too.) Smith, on the other hand, knows that whatever Adelman says is as good as accomplished. There is an imbalance here that undermines the fairness of the contract, and a parallel imbalance likewise threatens the fairness of Justice as Fairness. The parties in the original position must therefore assume full compliance.

We can find an additional answer if we come to see clearly why Rawls invokes the concept of a well-ordered society. We are most interested in two features of that society: strict compliance and favorable conditions. We need to know what role these features play in the theory.

In Rawls's words, "The notion of a well-ordered society articulates a formal and abstract conception of the general structure of a just society."[23] Just principles are those that would be selected for such a society. Rawls says less about the particular features we are concerned with. Concerning strict compliance, Rawls says, "This condition is to insure the integrity of the agreement made in the original position. . . . In reaching an agreement . . . they know their undertaking is not in vain: their capacity for a sense of justice insures that the principles chosen will be respected."[24] The same might be said for the prevalance of favorable conditions. They ensure the integrity of the agreement by guaranteeing that the parties are not only willing but also able to carry out the principles selected. But this reasoning still leaves us somewhat in the dark. Why must we suppose that a sense of justice motivates the parties and is nearly always effective? We could suppose that the majority are moved only by the threat of harm: This motivation would also produce an ordered society. And overall order is compatible with a substantial degree of noncompliance, so we might allow for that, too. It might indeed be said that we would get a more realistic result if we were to suppose the contract to be designed for this kind of imperfect but still ordered society.

Well, this would be fine, but it wouldn't be justice. Principles of justice are what we get when we select principles for people who are ruled by a sense of justice. If we select principles for other sorts of people in other conditions, we will get a very different sort of principle. This can be seen more strikingly if we look at principles from a different category. Suppose we wanted to put down some principles of violin playing. We would want to observe and talk with good violinists who want to play the violin. (They are motivated, we might say, by musical sense.) If we select principles for reluctant violinists, we might include such maxims as "Don't play unless you get a hefty fee and top billing." This might be a wise maxim, but one would never call it a principle of violin playing. It is a general prudential principle. Such maxims would be interspersed among true principles of musical artistry. Similarly, principles for people with a deficient sense of justice will include prudential principles such as "Bribe people to prevent harm to yourself." These principles are (like the violinist's fee) mere carrots and sticks whose function here is to induce just behavior, to whatever extent we can. This is seen most strikingly in Hobbes's *Leviathan*. He envisions people utterly without an effective sense of justice (as distinct from a pursuit of self-interest).[25] The principles appropriate for such a case are not at all like Rawls's, and not like anything we regard as principles for a just society. They guarantee no liberty and give the sovereign a free hand for arbitrary rule. To the extent that the contractual society deviates from full compliance, the principles chosen for it will be counsels of prudence, and not principles of justice. (The same reasoning applies to Rawls's supposition of favorable conditions. To the extent that unfavorable conditions interfere with just behavior, the principles chosen for such conditions will be counsels of prudence, not principles of justice.)

Now, justice does not rule out the use of carrots and sticks, but we must use them justly. How can we tell if we are doing so? Well, we must try to discern whether these carrots and sticks would be acceptable to a society of people ruled by the sense of justice. We thus come full circle. If we seek principles of justice, we must design them for a contractual society in which the sense of justice is *always* effective, and in which external conditions are so favorable that they *never* interfere with just behavior. This is what I have called a perfectly ordered society.

The perfectly ordered society, one should note, is not characterized by strict compliance per se. The definitive features are, rather, the strong sense of justice and the prevalence of favorable conditions. These of course lead to strict compliance; but strict compliance might also arise from compulsion, threats, hypnosis, behavior modification, or other means. Compliance achieved in this way does not make a society well ordered.

Note further that the members of a perfectly ordered society may be saints, but they are not angels. Although their sense of justice always prevails, they are subject to temptation and must work energetically to overcome it; and they succeed only under the favorable conditions that are assumed to prevail. An angel overcomes temptation even under unfavorable conditions. An angel perhaps is not even tempted. So the idealization of the perfectly ordered society should not lead anyone to complain that I am making a theory fit only for heaven.

THE PERFECTLY ORDERED SOCIETY: CONDITION OR ASSUMPTION?

We have said that the original contract is designed to govern a perfectly ordered society, but this is vague. If a case arising under the contract were brought before a judge, she would want to know: Are the contractual rights and duties *conditional* on the existence of a perfectly ordered society? Or do the parties merely *assume* that such a society will prevail, without making it a condition of their duties and rights? To illustrate this distinction: The text of the conditional contract might read as follows.

Contract 1

We, the undersigned, agree as follows: If we should find ourselves in a perfectly ordered society, we will adhere to the following principles of justice, viz., ...

In the second case the perfectly ordered society is an assumption:

Contract 2

We, the undersigned, being about to enter a perfectly ordered society, do agree and covenant to abide by the following principles of justice, to wit: . . . .

Now, what difference does this make? Contract 1 would be of no effect in any but a perfectly ordered society. If the parties took the trouble to make their duties conditional on such a state of things, it would be unreasonable to enforce it under other conditions. On the other hand, if the perfectly ordered society is merely something they assume will exist, it is an open question whether the contract ought to govern other situations.

The second possibility is the one we must accept. The reason has already been mentioned. In order to produce principles of *justice*, the parties must plan for a perfectly ordered society. They must not consider the possibility of noncompliance. (See section 2.) Now, the parties who frame and agree to Contract 1 obviously take cognizance of possible noncompliance and make plans accordingly. They cautiously agree to be bound only if compliance is perfect. And no doubt the very principles of justice they select will reflect this caution. (They might, for example, grant a narrower set of basic liberties in order to allow for the detection and prevention of crime.) A contract embodying principles of justice will take it as a *certainty* (for practical purposes) that the contractors are about to enter a perfectly ordered society.

This conclusion fits in with the Kantian interpretation of Justice as Fairness.[26] In offering this interpretation, Rawls suggests that the procedure of reaching agreement in the original position is a model for the Kantian procedure by which reason, unaffected by particular desires and ends, legislates for all rational beings. Our recent conclusion mirrors another feature of Kant's view. Kant's second formulation of the categorical imperative commands us:

> Act as if the maxim of your action were to become through your will *a universal law of nature.*[27]

Similarly, to the parties in the original position, the imminent existence of a perfectly ordered society is a matter of certainty on a par with the continued operation of the laws of nature. Their expectation that the contract may be violated is about the same as their expectation that the sun may fail to rise the next morning. They know, of course, that both are logically possible; but for purposes of planning, they may both be ignored. If they consider an imperfectly ordered society at all, it is only to dismiss it as impossible. The resulting contract thus has the form of Contract 2. This is fortunate, for Contract 1 would place a great hurdle in our path.

Now, even if it is taken to be a mere assumption, the expected existence of the perfectly ordered society plays a crucial role in the contract and the bargaining process. It is what lawyers would call the *basis of the contract:* "it creates a major part—an essential part—of the value of the one of performances that the parties agree to exchange, inducing one of the parties and enabling the other to reach the agreement."[28] (The "performance" is, of course, the act of abiding by the principles of justice, an act that may be worthless, indeed dangerous and foolhardy, in a badly ordered society. In the perfectly ordered society, moreover, the parties are symmetrically situated, so all are equally induced and enabled to reach the agreement.) If this assumption turns out false, we have a case of *frustration of purpose.* With regard to legal contracts, frustration of purpose will often terminate any further operation of the contract; but this is not invariably so, and the matter is not nearly so clear-cut as with failure of a condition.[29]

Now, just because lawyers do things one way, it need not follow that we ought to do things the same way when considering the original contract. But here it seems reasonable. This conclusion follows from the nature of contract as a device for making binding arrangements to further the plans of the individual parties. If the contractors' purpose were to be completely frustrated by an unexpected event, it would be lunatic to insist that the original provisions nonetheless be fulfilled. But when the contractors' purposes are not completely frustrated, nor even substantially frustrated, the contract still applies, even though the results are somewhat less than they had hoped for. The details here must be worked out as we go along. One thing, however, we can safely conclude: We can now rule out the extreme view that the contract applies to every conceivable sort of society. If applying the contract would lead to complete frustration of the contractors' purposes—if somehow the contract would undermine the development of the two moral powers—only a compulsive or fetishistic adherence to the contract could lead us to apply it.

4. The Content of the Contract

Next we must ask: What does the contract say about punishment? The answer, I argue, is, Nothing. That is, the contract contains no *explicit* provisions for punishment. The words *crime, punishment,* and the like do not occur in its text. We know, of course, that the two principles of justice contain no explicit reference to matters criminal. But neither are these things mentioned in the deliberations of the constitutional convention of a perfectly ordered society, nor in the promulgations of its legislature. Nor does the original position issue any other principles that refer explicitly to crime or punishment. It may happen that the more general contractual provisions turn out to require punishment without mentioning it explicitly. Indeed, I will argue that it is so. But explicit references are not to be found.

In this I differ from Rawls, who expects that a constitutional convention would set up a system of sanctions even for a well-ordered society.[30] I therefore first put forward the grounds for my contention and then account for my divergence from Rawls.

NO EXPLICIT PENAL PROVISIONS

As we have seen, the parties to the original contract expect to enter a perfectly ordered society, a society in which the sense of justice is always effective, and in which external conditions are so favorable that they never interfere with just behavior. And the parties feel as certain in this expectation as they do about the laws of nature. Since the contract is designed for this enviable state of affairs, it can contain no provision for coercive sanctions: The parties simply assume that none will be needed. Neither will the constitutional convention nor the legislature authorize any coercive sanctions, for they share this assumption. To these happy lawgivers, the idea of special provisions for crime would be filed away along with special provisions for people who exceed the speed of light and lead weights that rise when subjected to Earth's gravity.

Even if a provision for criminal sanctions were (somehow) included in the contract, it would be a mistake to act on it. For this would be a provision conditional on something conceded by all to be impossible. That is, it has the form

Let Y be done if and only if X occurs,

where X is conceded to be impossible. But this is just a picturesque way of saying,

Let Y never be done.

American Indian treaties—to consider an actual example—sometimes contained a provision making them valid "as long as the grass shall grow and the rivers shall run." Clearly, such language is not meant to invalidate the treaty on some scorching day when the grass and rivers dry up. It is merely a quaint way of saying that the treaty should be perpetually binding. In the same way we might imagine the original contract to include a clause like this:

Let persons be punished if and only if they have committed a crime.

But this could only be a roundabout way of saying,

Let no one be punished.

STABILITY IN A WELL-ORDERED SOCIETY

Now, why does Rawls suggest that even a well-ordered society will need penal sanctions? He gives the need for stability as a rationale:

> For although persons in a well-ordered society know that they share a common sense of justice and that each wants to adhere to the existing arrangements, they may nevertheless lack full confidence in one another. They may suspect that some are not doing their part, and so they may be tempted not to do theirs. The general awareness of these temptations may eventually cause the scheme to break down. The suspicion that others are not honoring their duties and obligations is increased by the fact that, in the absence of the authoritative interpretation and enforcement of the rules, it is particularly easy to find excuses for breaking them. Thus even under reasonably ideal conditions, it is hard to imagine, for example, a successful income tax scheme on a voluntary basis. Such an arrangement is unstable. The role of an authorized public interpretation of rules supported by collective sanctions is precisely to overcome this instability.[31]

Against this, I will argue, first, that the feared instability would not in any case occur; and, second, that even if it did threaten to occur, it would be prevented, in a perfectly ordered society, by noncoercive means.

Now, with regard to the first point, notice that Rawls makes his case plausible by tarnishing the character of the well-ordered society. The once virtuous citizens now seem to have become sullen and suspicious. Of course, in noting this fact, I am making no substantive argument. But it seems to illustrate my contention that one can derive punishment directly from the contract only by fudging the characterization of a well-ordered society (see section 2). Nonetheless, I must concede that even people of perfect goodwill can do wrong if they are misinformed, and this possibility is enough to set the ball rolling. Once such a situation develops, it might conceivably snowball into anarchy.

What would actually happen in a well-ordered society in such a case? Let us take Rawls's own example of an income tax. Suppose that many people do not pay the tax that they owe. Each feels somewhat justified, since it is known that evasion is widespread. What would happen? Well, these are people with a sense of justice; and the sense of justice, as described by Rawls, motivates its possessor not only to comply with existing just arrangements but also to further just arrangements that do not yet exist. Certainly, in a well-ordered society there will be one person who will do this by getting up in public and saying, "Our income tax, which we agree to be just, is nonetheless being evaded. You will agree with me, I am sure, that this is a bad situation. I am now therefore going to pay my tax in full [hands conspicuous bundle of cash to tax officer] and I urge you to do the same." Now the others will feel a little less comfortable about evading the tax. Certainly there will be another person who at that point will be willing to pay the tax that *she* owes. Her payment, in turn, will inspire a third person to pay; and so on. Indeed, it would be surprising if any taxes were left unpaid. If something like this scenario were not to occur, I do not think we could truly describe the people as having a strong sense of justice.

With regard to the second point, even in a perfectly ordered society there will be provisions for sanctions of a sort, viz., the sanction of public opinion. The threat of public exposure will prevent people from violating the rules. There might be police to investigate suspected crimes, and courts to try suspected criminals. If someone were convicted, the result would be made known to the public, but nothing further would be done. (Of course, in a perfectly ordered society, no one would ever be convicted.)

The sanction cannot be called coercive, because it simply consists in revealing an important truth about the criminal. Note in particular, *contra* Rawls, that an authoritative interpretation of the rules can be provided without subsequent coercive sanctions.

Indeed, a noncoercive system of sanctions is not only permitted but required by the definition of a well-ordered society. In such a society everyone has, *and knows that the others have,* an effective sense of justice. Now, how do they know this? They are not clairvoyant. If this knowledge is to be provided, there must be in place some mechanism for detecting, adjudicating, and publicizing acts of injustice. Of course, no injustice will be found; and this negative finding will confirm the citizens' belief that their society is in fact perfectly ordered; and, more importantly, it will confirm their mutual trust.

The only thing that one might question is this: Will people in a well-ordered society be concerned about public opinion? Will the sanction of public opinion affect them? It is conceivable that it might not. What if the society were full of independent-minded people—a congregation of J. S. Mills—moved by a sense of justice but willing to spit in the eye of public opinion? In that case, the sanction of public opinion would not work. I would argue, though, that the members of a well-ordered society will in fact be concerned about public opinion concerning matters of justice, and this concern is in fact an integral part of each person's sense of justice. This last suggestion might seem strange. One might think that such a concern for public opinion was merely a sort of vanity, a heteronomous motivation rather than a conscientious one. In the real world it is indeed so. But in a well-ordered society concern for public opinion is concern for the esteem of the morally discerning, not just of any person of unknown quality. This concern is needed if a person is to be just. Very often we do not have the detachment to judge our own case impartially; we must turn to others whose opinion we respect. And, partiality aside, the finitude of human beings forces us to rely on trusted moral advisors, just as we must rely on others for large parts of our scientific knowledge.

5. Principles of Interpretation

The original contract, as we have seen, is designed for a perfectly ordered society. We now need to see if we can take the second step of the four-step process: We need to see whether the contract can be applied to other sorts of societies. If it can, what kinds of societies can it be applied to? How, if at all, must the contract be adapted to apply to these societies?

How are we to answer these questions? Certainly not by posing them in the original position—that would amount to begging, not posing, the question. We must judge these questions from our own point of view, using the method of reflective equilibrium.

Our approach to this and similar questions has to be unsystematic. (If there were some systematic approach, we would have used it already in deriving the contract itself.) Nonetheless, we can lay down some general prima facie principles for interpreting the original contract. In the present section I put forward three of these, which I call the principle of *extrapolation*, the principle of *broad application*, and the principle of *plain dealing*. Between my discussions of the first and second principles I interpolate a "topography" of possible societies, well ordered and otherwise, and the ways in which the contract is to be applied to them.

THE PRINCIPLE OF EXTRAPOLATION

Under this name I refer to the following principle:

When the contract does not determine what is to be done in a certain situation, interpret it so as to maximize the ability of the contractors to make rational plans to realize their legitimate goals.

An example will illustrate this. If the contract is written down, typographical errors may occur. What to do? There may, first of all, be some doubt whether the error is in fact typographical, but let us assume that it is. There then seem to be three prominent possibilities: (1) Enforce the contract as intended; (2) enforce the contract as actually written; or (3) treat the contract as null and void. Option 1 seems obviously superior, but it is important to see why: If typographical errors invalidate or alter the effect of a contract, it is that much harder to make a contract that will accomplish what was planned. (Not that there is nothing to be said for options 2 and 3. Both ensure careful drafting of written documents, and option 2 in particular makes enforcement easier. In fact, all three rules seem to have been applied in court in various circumstances.[32] But when one is dealing with the original contract, the realization of the contractors' plan is more important than considerations of careful drafting or easy enforcement.) This example, I admit, is a bit contrived. But the use of such contrived examples seems unavoidable when we deal with such an extraordinary contract.

The principle of extrapolation clearly follows from our previous remarks on the nature of contract. The justificatory aim of the institution of contract, as we have said there, is to enable the parties, as autonomous persons, to achieve their legitimate goals by means of binding arrangements. Now, surely, if given a choice, we should arrange things so that this justificatory aim is achieved in the highest possible degree. So the principle of extrapolation seems to be no addition at all to the principle that authorizes the making of binding agreements. We may further note that the principle of extrapolation is at work in every application of a contract, even the most routine. For in choosing X and making a contract to get X, Smith (the contractor) has not fully anticipated X in every detail, still less the details of the circumstances in which X will occur. Smith is not omniscient; she cannot know all these things; and even when she knows them, she does not know what they will be like for her when they come to pass. So she could say, "This is not what I have chosen; I did not know it would be like this." But in that case no one could ever choose anything. Smith is laboring under a misconception about choice that parallels the skeptic's misconception about knowledge. So it seems that the very concept of *choice* and consequently of *contract* requires (something like) the principle of extrapolation.

Now, the principle of extrapolation may seem vague: Indeed, it is vague. And even when not vague, it may yield no determinate result. But it still gives guidance in many cases, as will be seen below.

The principle of extrapolation must be distinguished from two similar principles. The first of these involves a hypothetical choice:

> When the contract does not determine what is to be done in a certain situation, interpret it so as to achieve what the parties would have chosen if they had anticipated that situation.

The second involves the parties' well-being or happiness:

> When the contract does not clearly determine what is to be done in a certain situation, interpret it so as to maximize (or maximinimize)[33] the happiness of the parties.

Although these principles may have their place in more ordinary contexts, they cannot be justly applied to the original contract. There are two reasons. First, they are incompatible with the contract as an act of pure procedural justice. What is just is what they *did* choose, not what they *would* have chosen, nor yet what would make them happy, if they *were to* choose it. The principle of extrapolation, by contrast, helps us unfold the concept of choice and determine what it is that the parties have in fact chosen. Second, laying aside this first objection, we still face a related difficulty; our two alternate principles do not interpret the actual contract, but make a new one. It could be that happiness would be maximized by some unthought-of arrangement, described on unseen stone tablets. But the possibility of such an arrangement does not mean that their original contract can be interpreted as an agreement to obey the principles engraved on those tablets. Similarly, in reference to the method of hypothetical choice, if the parties had known about X and Y, they might have agreed to do all sorts of things having no connection whatever with their original agreement. If they had known about the upcoming sale at Bloomingdale's—to take an absurd example—they might well have agreed to go there. But that does not mean that their original contract can be interpreted as an agreement to go to Bloomingdale's.

Against the method of hypothetical choice there is another objection. The original contract is made behind the veil of ignorance: The lack of information is essential. It would defeat the whole contractual scheme if we were to start asking hypothetical questions about what the parties would have done, had they known . . . .

The principle of extrapolation, then, will be one of our guides in interpreting the original contract. It will help us decide both questions of applicability of the contract, and of its operation.

A TOPOGRAPHY OF CONTRACTUAL SOCIETIES

We have already considered and rejected the extreme view that the contract is applicable to every conceivable sort of society (see section 3). A different sort of extremist might hold that the original contract applies only to an absolutely perfectly ordered society; the sphere of applicability, in other words, is reduced to a single point. Our extremist might support this view by arguing that the purpose of the parties is frustrated by even the slightest deviation from full compliance, so that the contract is no longer applicable: If they do not find themselves in *precisely* the conditions they expected, if they do not get exactly what they bargained for under exactly the conditions they expected, they feel they have fallen hopelessly short of their aim. Now, this view seems quite improbable, and if we were considering an everyday contract, we would reject it out of hand. But in the case of an original social contract we must give it a closer look.

The main reason to reject this extreme view is that it would leave us with no binding contract at all. For a potential criminal could argue thus:

> The contract forbids me to rob, assault, defraud, and so forth. But this contract is valid only in a perfectly ordered society. Now, the moment I start robbing someone—indeed, the moment I decide to rob someone— society is no longer perfectly ordered, and so the contract will no longer be applicable; robbery, assault, and fraud will no longer be forbidden. So it is in fact permissible to rob, assault, defraud, and so forth.

There is something clearly wrong about this: The contract would be no contract at all. Rawls, on the other hand, specifies quite the opposite: The parties are said to convene in the original position under the assumption that their agreement will be binding and final,[34] an assumption that plays a crucial role in the contractual process. This assumption is not compatible with the view suggested by our extremist. Moreover, this extreme proposal would fly in the face of the principle of extrapolation: The parties in the original position need a robust contract, but the extremist is giving them a balloon that is likely to burst at the slightest provocation.

So the contract is applicable in at least some cases of less than perfect compliance. But we must still ask: Is it applicable in a plain and literal sense in such cases? Or must it be reconstrued to cover them? My answer is, The sphere of plain and literal applicability includes at least some nonideal cases. This point may be seen by an argument similar to one we have considered. Suppose that the contract were plainly and literally applicable only in a perfectly ordered society. In other situations the contract is applicable, but only as reconstrued. So if the contract says, "We agree to do X," we are bound to do X only in a perfectly ordered society; in other situations the contract requires us to do something else, let us say Y. Now, someone could argue:

> The contract requires me to do X, which I prefer not to do. But this contract is literally applicable only in a perfectly ordered society. In other societies I am required to do Y, which I would prefer. Now, if I fail to do X, the society is no longer perfectly ordered. So the contract, while appearing to require X, in fact gives me a choice between X and Y.

Now, there could be, and in fact are, legal instruments that do not require what they seem to require.[35] But this cannot be the case with the original contract. The parties to the contract have deliberated and decided to agree on the basis of the literal text of the contract. If this text is never literally applicable, then this was a case of misdeliberation. The original contract would then lose its claim to authority. Moreover, as before, the principle of extrapolation would be violated: Who would know how to plan if the plans were abruptly changed in this way? The contract is a guide to action, not merely a description of an ideal: and it is true by definition (or nearly so) that a guide presupposes the possibility of deviations from the true path. So the sphere of literal applicability must include at least some nonideal cases.

Now, it may be that the sphere of applicability is wider than the sphere of *literal* applicability. Indeed, I argue below that it is. So the situation may be graphically represented thus:

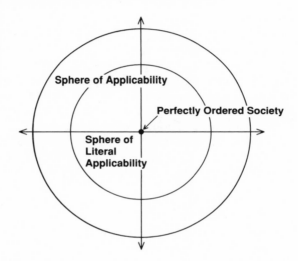

THE PRINCIPLE OF BROAD APPLICATION

As we have seen, the contract is not universally applicable, nor is it restricted to a perfectly ordered society. But how wide is the sphere of applicability? For all we know so far, it may be restricted to nearly ideal situations, or it may be expansive enough to include all but the rowdiest. A risk-averse critic might ask, Can we really apply it with justice to situations very different from that which the parties expected?

The answer, to a large extent, is Yes. We may be stretching things to apply the contractual principles to badly ordered societies, but what other principles do we have? None at all. Outside of the contract, justice is undefined. Unlike Locke, Rawls posits no state of nature with precontractual principles of justice. There is no just

status quo ante to which we can return if the contract proves un-
enforceable.[36] We must therefore apply the contractual principles as
widely as we reasonably can. We can, therefore, enunciate the *principle of broad application:*

> Interpret the original contract so as to apply to as wide a
> variety of situations as possible.

As with the principle of extrapolation, this is only a prima facie
principle; it may be outweighed by other considerations.

Note the sharp contrast here with ordinary contracts. An ordinary contract, when carried out, moves us from one just situation to
another. If something goes awry, we can almost always return to the
first situation. If, for example, I agree to buy a Veg-o-Matic for $19.99
and I find it has been misdescribed, we can return to the previous
state of affairs: I return their Veg-o-Matic, they return my money,
and justice is restored. Even if we cannot go back to the status quo
ante, we still have it as a reference point. The social contract does
not even give this. There is nothing to go back to. Indeed, in a sense,
outside the contract there is no justice.

The principle of broad application assures us that the contract
can be applied—literally or not—to a wide variety of situations. It
suggests that only the strongest of reasons will prevent its operation.

THE PRINCIPLE OF PLAIN DEALING

Now, just because the principles of justice are to be widely applicable, it does not follow that they are *literally* applicable over a
wide range. As will be seen, they must be reconstrued in many cases.
We can, however, state a principle governing the sphere of literal
applicability, which we might well call the *principle of plain dealing:*

> In the absence of sufficient reason to the contrary, assume
> that the contract applies plainly and literally to a given
> situation.

The burden of proof lies on the one who would argue that the contract does not apply in a literal way. The mere fact that the parties
promised to do something is a very strong prima facie reason for
them to fulfill their promise in a plain and literal way.

With these three interpretive principles, and with our other reflections on nonideal theory, we can now proceed to consider punishment and its relation to the contract.

6. Applicability of the Contract; Division of Offenses

Our next task is to determine the spheres of applicability of the contract. When is it literally applicable? When is it applicable by reinterpretation? And when is its operation suspended? There are many variables bearing on the answer to these questions, but here we are concerned only with one: the sense of justice. What is to happen when a society is perfectly ordered, except for a deficiency in the citizens' sense of justice? I ignore other nonideal conditions: incompetence, natural disasters, confusion regarding the law, accidents, and so on. There are three sorts of society that I wish to consider:

> *The Slightly Disordered Society.* In this society citizens' sense of justice is weak enough that they sometimes violate the difference principles, but not the basic liberties (in the broad sense).
>
> *The Very Disordered Society.* In this society the sense of justice is so weak that citizens sometimes violate the basic liberties, but on the whole each citizen still recognizes the principles of justice.
>
> *The Slightly Fragmented Society.* In this society a small number of people repudiate the principles of justice, but the number of these is small enough that it does not prevent the operation of the contract among the rest.[37]

(These brief descriptions need amplification, which I momentarily provide.) In the present section I argue for the following claims:

1. The contract applies literally to the slightly disordered society.
2. The contract, properly reinterpreted, applies to the very disordered society.
3. In a slightly fragmented society the operation of the contract is suspended with respect to those who have repudiated it.

After describing the three societies more precisely, I look at the division between claims 1 and 2 and then the division between claims 2 and 3.

THE THREE SOCIETIES

Now, the description of each society concerns the *character* of its citizens, and only secondarily their behavior. So we might more accurately say:

> In the slightly disordered society, citizens are of such a character that they may be expected to violate the difference principle, unless deterred by coercive sanctions,

and similarly for the others. A badly ordered society does not become well ordered just because its citizens are deterred from doing wrong by threats of evil.

Also important to notice: The citizens of each society suffer from no further defects in their sense of justice beyond those mentioned. Excepting those who repudiate the principles of justice, all are possessed of a strong and generally effective sense of justice: Their offenses are temporary aberrations. In particular, having committed an offense, they are willing to make due amends. These amends will include compensation to victims and (as we will see) submission to punishment, as well as apologies or whatever else is determined to be appropriate. Thus (except for repudiators) each citizen in a way has a full sense of justice: The sense of justice is not deficient in amount, it is just unevenly distributed. This full but badly distributed sense of justice allows us to overcome the basic paradox of the contractual theory of punishment: A contract suitable for the just will yield principles of justice but contain no provisions for punishment; a contract suitable for the unjust will contain provisions for punishment but will not establish principles of justice. The citizens of our disordered societies are in a way perfectly just and in a way not, so can play both roles at once.

The repudiators are a special case. They do not consider themselves bound by principles of justice. Some of them may have a change of heart and recommit themselves to the contract, but if they do not, the punishments to which they are subject (as we see below) are theoretically quite distinct. Such punishment is not so much an act of justice as a defensive measure in war.

Corresponding to the three sorts of imperfect societies, there are three sorts of offenses. The least serious are those that are to be expected in a slightly disordered society, involving violations of the difference principle: These I call *minor offenses*. Next come those graver offenses that are to be expected in the very disordered society: These I call *serious offenses*. And, finally, I reserve the title of *extreme offenses* for those that involve a repudiation of the contract itself, the kind of offenses to be expected in a slightly fragmented society.

BASIC LIBERTIES VERSUS OTHER PRIMARY GOODS

Let us move on according to the plan of this section. First we must ask: How does the contract apply to the slightly disordered society, as opposed to the very disordered society? Now, this dichotomy of societies rests on a dichotomy between minor and serious offenses; and this in turn rests on a dichotomy in the class of primary goods. According to Rawls the primary goods are:

(i) The basic liberties. . . .

(ii) Freedom of movement and free choice of occupation against a background of diverse opportunities. . . .

(iii) Powers and prerogatives of offices and positions of responsibility. . . .

(iv) Income and wealth. . . .

(v) The social bases of self-respect. . . .[38]

These fall into two categories: Some of these primary goods are to be distributed equally to all (i, ii, and v), whereas others may be distributed unequally (iii and iv). The former we may call *invariant primary goods*, and the latter *variable primary goods*. My claim is: The variable primary goods are fungible and alienable, whereas the invariant primary goods are neither.

Before going on to explain and support this claim, we may make a simplifying assumption: We shall ignore item v, the social bases of self-respect. Not that self-respect is unimportant. It is, however, supervenient on the others. A just distribution of the other primary goods constitutes a just distribution of the social bases of self-respect.[39] In particular, granting equal liberties to all shows that all have the same moral status and are worthy of the same degree of self-respect. Omitting the social bases of self-respect, we are left with two sorts of invariant primary goods: the basic liberties, and the fair equality of opportunity. These are what I refer to collectively as *basic liberties (in the broad sense)*.

Just what does the present claim mean? When I say that different goods are *fungible*, I mean that a certain quantity of one good may be substituted for a certain quantity of the other, leaving the person equally well off *as far as the contract is concerned*. A ten-dollar bill, for example, may be substituted for two fives or ten ones. The person herself may prefer the ten to the ones, and in general fungible goods may differ in important ways, but these facts do not count with respect to our definition. The fungibility of variable primary goods is seen in their measurement by an index. As far as the contract is concerned, the form in which these goods appear does not matter, so long as the index value is correct. One person may have a lot of accumulated wealth, another may have little wealth but an assured income, and yet another may have power and influence with only moderate income and wealth. If these three have equal primary-goods index values, they are equal in the eyes of the contract. With the basic liberties it is different. As I have already noted, a greater freedom of speech (for example) will not make up for a lesser freedom of religion. Each person is assigned a very precisely specified package of basic liberties.[40]

When I say that the variable primary goods are alienable, I mean that the contract provides ways in which people can acquire and dispose of them. A person can buy and sell goods, accede to positions of power and resign from them. By contrast, the contract provides no way for someone to acquire or shed basic liberties. They are thus inalienable. Note that here again we are judging things as far as the contract is concerned. It may de facto be possible for someone to buy his freedom, or sell it; and there may be people (do we not know some?) who are willing to do this. But the contract does not permit it. Note also that a person may lose her liberty by repudiating the contract. This does not conflict with the inalienable status of the basic liberties. The contract itself does not provide for losing one's liberty, and this is all that matters in calling the basic liberties inalienable.

What accounts for this fact about inalienability and fungibility? My answer, in brief, is this: The parties in the original position agree to make each primary good alienable or not, fungible or not, as suits their needs. Let us look at each one in turn.

First, we have the basic liberties (in the narrow sense). As far as can be told from the original position, each of the basic liberties is necessary in order for the parties to realize their nature as free and equal moral persons. For example, freedom of conscience is required in order even to develop a conception of the good. Now, in the contractual society, some people may have little use for some of the basic liberties and might be willing to waive them or trade them away for a mess of lentils. Such people may prevent themselves from developing new plans of life or from pursuing them, or they may lose their status as equal citizens. Foreseeing this from the original position, the parties to the contract prevent such untoward outcomes by making the basic liberties inalienable.

Second, equality of opportunity. The case here is similar. Without such opportunity, persons will be cut off from pursuing plans of life for which they may be suited. This condition constitutes a restriction on their plans of life: The parties in the original position would not consent to it, for the opportunity to develop and pursue a plan of life is part of a person's nature as a free and equal moral person.

Third, we come to powers and prerogatives. Here the same considerations weigh on the other side. Different plans of life call for different sorts of powers. Yet people must remain free to revise their conceptions of the good, and to pursue the revised conceptions. Offices and positions of power must therefore be alienable. Leary was once happy with the influential office of college professor but eventually wanted the position of guru. Fortunately, he could abandon one position and take up the other.

At the same time, positions of power serve as generalized means for accomplishing plans of life. To a large extent, one can accomplish with money the same things that one can accomplish with power. Hence positions of authority are intersubstitutable with wealth, income, and the like. And to the extent that one cannot accomplish exactly the same things, the principle of responsibility applies: Each person is responsible for her own conception of the good. Society must accord her a reasonable range of opportunities, and she, in turn, is responsible for pursuing her conception of the good within that range. It would be impossible for a society to present anyone with an infinite range of possibilities. Hence, again, positions of authority are intersubstitutable with other variable primary goods.

Finally, income and wealth. Here the case is obvious. Income and wealth are worthless, indeed inconceivable, apart from their value as media of exchange. That is, they are alienable. Aside from exchange value, they are of interest only to the numismatist and the scripophile; but the parties in the original position cannot assume that they are numismatists or scripophiles. Moreover, the various forms of income and wealth are (as far as the contract is concerned) fungible with each other, and with positions of authority. For any of these will give its possessor access to a large variety of plans of life.

Now, these conclusions about fungibility apply not only instantaneously but also over time: That is, variable primary goods that a person has now are fungible with goods that she can count on having in the future, or goods that she had in the past. Basic rights are not fungible over time. With regard to the variable primary goods, this fact is easy to see. I may have money now, or I may be assured of getting some in the future; I may have authority now, or I may be assured of having it in the future; in any of these cases I have in my hands effective means of pursuing a conception of the good. If I have money now but do not yet need it, I can save it. If I need money now and expect to get some later, I can borrow. Thus Rawls lists income and wealth side by side in his list of primary goods: Wealth can be seen as capitalized income, and income is liquidated wealth. On the other hand, future basic rights are not fungible with present or past basic rights. Consider, for example, the right to vote. An adult is entitled to vote once in every election. Suppose one particular adult, Heider, is told that she may vote twice in the present election but not at all in the next one. Heider has grounds for complaint. The same is true if she is told she may punch people with impunity today, but they may punch her tomorrow. The reason is that a person must at all times have the opportunity to maintain a sense of justice, and to develop, revise, and act on a conception of the good. Nothing can adequately compensate for the temporary absence of such things. (Of course, if someone is temporarily without basic liberties, we should try to compensate her as best we can, but such compensation is at best palliative.)

THE SORTS OF OFFENSES

Before proceeding with the argument, let us pause and look at some of the offenses falling into each of the three categories outlined above. Doing so will illustrate the previous discussion and enliven the discussion to follow.

First of all, what is an offense? An *offense* is characterized by three properties: (1) it is forbidden by law; (2) people can reasonably be expected to avoid it; and (3) officers of the law are authorized to intervene by force to prevent or interrupt offenses. This last condition distinguishes offenses from those lesser evils that elicit no interference from law officers save the immortal refrain, "Tell it to the judge."

Now, serious offenses are those by which one violates the principle of equal basic liberties, or the principle of equality of fair opportunity. In other words, serious offenses are those that disrupt the equality of basic liberties, in the broad sense. As I have argued above, I will interpret this to mean: Serious offenses are those by which one arrogates to oneself an extra share of the basic liberties. They thus fall under the Rectification Principle. Violating the basic liberties of another is, of course, one way of committing a serious offense. So among the serious offenses we have: assault and battery, religious persecution, interfering with the exercise of political rights, enslavement, kidnapping, and so on.

But one may also commit a serious offense without violating the basic rights of any particular person. For example, attempted murder is a serious offense, even though the intended victim's rights remain inviolate; and similarly for other attempts to commit a serious offense. But a person may also commit a serious offense without even trying to interfere with the liberty of another particular person. This can be done by interfering with the institutions and procedures that the basic liberties require. Thus, one may commit some forms of voter fraud,[41] one may obstruct justice, one may engage in official corruption. In each case there may be no particular victim whose rights are violated, yet a serious crime has undoubtedly been committed.

Now, what does this leave in the category of minor offenses? My definition of these offenses was this: They violate the difference principle without violating the other principles of justice. Minor offenses, then, are those that improperly rearrange people's holdings of variable primary goods. But there is a complication: Among the basic liberties is the right of secure possession of personal property. Rawls places himself in the Lockean tradition by making this one of the basic liberties.[42] So the thief or robber violates this right in her victim and unduly expands it on her own part. (She takes unto herself the liberty to control not only her own property but that of others, too.) So theft and robbery are among the serious offenses, not the minor ones.

A minor crime, then, must disrupt the just distribution of primary goods without interfering with security of property, nor with the rest of the system of basic liberties. This leaves as minor offenses a class of unlawful acts we have already considered: those too mild to fall under the Rectification Principle (see Chapter 6, section 1). Included here are offenses whereby one disrupts public amenities (that is, those not required by right) or violates requirements that serve efficiency or procedure.

A further conclusion follows from these distinctions: The minor crimes are reparable, the major ones not. More precisely, if a would-be criminal succeeds in committing a serious offense, the damage is irreparable (from the point of view of the contract); whereas if she commits only a minor offense, the damage is reparable. This is so because wealth, income, and similar primary goods are fungible, but the basic liberties are not. So if someone holds too much or too little of the variable primary goods, we can take some away, or give her more, so that the contract is completely satisfied. But if someone holds too great or small a share of the basic liberties, the situation cannot be fully remedied. One liberty is not fungible with another, nor even with the same liberty enjoyed at a later time. For example, if someone is unjustly injured, or imprisoned, or prevented from voting, nothing can fully make up this loss. But if someone has restricted access to positions of power or too little money, this situation can be fully remedied (so far as the contract is concerned). We merely see to it that the person gets more money or opportunities. (Of course, the person himself might not be satisfied with the compensation, or might even consider himself better off than before. As I pointed out before, this is not a present concern.)

ARGUMENTS FOR THE DICHOTOMY: (1) ARGUMENT FROM IMPOSSIBILITY

Having distinguished two kinds of offenses, we can now go on to consider why they relate differently to the original contract. The claim was this (you will recall): The contract applies literally to the minor offenses, but not to serious offenses. I now present three arguments for this claim: the argument from *impossibility*, the argument from *stability*, and the argument from *ability to plan*. The first two show that the contract is not literally applicable to societies in which serious offenses can be expected. The third shows that the contract *is* literally applicable to societies in which only minor offenses can be expected.

Now, the argument from impossibility is simple enough. In a very disordered society we must expect serious offenses. Since these are irreparable, it is simply impossible to carry out the contract in a literal way. A batterer, for example, has arrogated a greater freedom of the person than was his share. We cannot now bring it about that he has the same package of basic liberties as the others. Now, it is folly to interpret a contract so as to require the impossible. So the literal application of the contract is not appropriate in the very disordered society.

ARGUMENTS FOR THE DICHOTOMY: (2) ARGUMENT FROM STABILITY

The argument from stability is a little more complex in execution, though in concept it is simple. In brief:

(1) The contract applies literally only to stable societies

(2) A very disordered society is not stable.

(3) Therefore, the contract does not literally apply to a very disordered society.

Clearly, this argument requires some discussion.

Why is the contract literally applicable only to stable societies? And how stable must they be?

Consider the first question first. Remember that the parties assume in the original position that the society they are about to enter will be perfectly ordered. They must assume this if their contract is to define principles of justice: Otherwise, they will engage in prudential planning to protect themselves in the case of instability. This planning, as we have seen, allows potential criminals to have undue influence on the deliberations in the original position, and the resulting principles would not be principles of justice.

Now, I take *stability* to refer to a situation in which such prudential planning is not necessary. Either everyone sticks to the contract, or else violations are dependably corrected. What stability excludes is a progressive deterioration tending toward anarchy. The contract cannot be literally applicable to such situations. To apply it would frustrate the parties' ability to plan for themselves (to say the least). The effects would be disastrous. In a situation heading toward anarchy, it is foolhardy, even suicidal, to behave as if order reigned. If they had considered such a dire possibility, the parties would have made quite a different contract. They certainly would not have agreed on the contract as we know it. (They would have demanded fewer liberties and would have insisted on measures to promote law and order.) The contract therefore does not apply literally—perhaps not at all— to an unstable society.

One form of social instability involves the domino effect. Citizen A breaks the law. Citizen B now feels justified in doing likewise. Then C, hearing of B's violation, feels justified in a further violation. And so on. Rawls envisions such a possibility.[43] I want to look particularly at this sort of instability.

Now, what sort of offense committed by A will make B feel justified in committing an offense of his own? Well, we are assuming that these are for the most part persons of conscience, so we must ask: What kind of offense would actually justify B in committing an offense of his own? And, recalling that this is a contract theory, we can reformulate the question once more: What kind of breach of contract on the part of A would justify B in neglecting a contractual duty? To this question the lawyers have an answer: If A commits a *material breach* of contract, if her breach *goes to the essence* of the contract, B is justified in withholding at least a part of his contractually required performance; whereas if A's breach is minor, if she has *substantially performed* her contractual duty, then B is not justified in withholding any of his required performance.

Now, just because lawyers do this does not mean we should follow them. But we have good independent reason. Note first that the parties do not consent unconditionally or absolutely to the principles of justice. Rather, each promises to abide by the principles in consideration of a similar promise on the part of all the others. (This is but to say that the contract is, in lawyers' terms, *bilateral*.) So if Smith violates the contract, say, by physically attacking Jones, no one would say that the contract requires Jones to allow this. Certainly she may fight back. That is, her contractual duty not to attack Smith is temporarily suspended. But what if Smith's breach of the social contract is minor? Should we still say that Jones is justified in neglecting a part of *her* duty? It seems not. To allow this sort of reaction to minor violations would undermine the integrity of the contract. Smith is perhaps on the whole making a good-faith effort to carry out the contract and is mostly succeeding. If his minor breaches are made into an occasion for breaches by others, the result will be instability, or at least a deterioration in the level of performance. This reasoning is all the more persuasive considering that people in the societies we are considering are generally willing to make amends for their wrongs. So Smith will eventually make things up to Jones, and Jones knows this.

Where are we to draw the line between material and immaterial breaches of the original contract? What sort of offenses go to the essence, thus justifying a deviation in response? This line, I suggest, corresponds with the line between serious and minor offenses.

Consider first the plight of the victim of a serious offense: Her loss is irreparable; she is thrust into a situation that, by the contract, no one should have to endure. Certainly she is justified in suspending her performance of the contract in order to protect those liberties. On the other hand, consider the victim of a minor offense. Her loss is reparable—indeed, it *will* be repaired—and, in any case, she is not thrust into an intolerable situation. She may find herself in a lower socioeconomic condition, but this is a condition that many people must endure as a matter of course. She cannot well argue that her condition is so insufferable as to justify immediate action. She can wait until repentance or process of law restores her to her rightful situation. It therefore seems reasonable to draw the line as I have. The victim of a serious offense is herself justified in violating the original contract in order to prevent the impending harm. The victim of a minor offense is not so justified but must seek redress through lawful channels.

Now, this right to intervene in a serious offense does not reside only in the intended victim, but in all who wish to act on her behalf. So, for example, Jones may defend herself against physical attack, or Williams may step in to defend her. And anyone may step in to prevent the commission of a serious offense even if it is victimless.

It is now easy to see how the domino effect may proceed. *A* attacks *B*, who feels justified in counterattacking. *C* joins in to help *B*, *D* joins *A*, and so on. This perhaps should not really happen, but there is a problem of limited knowledge. *B* may counterattack only to the extent necessary to preserve his basic liberties. *B* must therefore call off his counterattack if *A* calls off his threat. But we never know if this is really true. *A* may cry "uncle," but this may just be a ruse. It is reasonable for *B* to continue his counterattack even after this point. But bystanders might now reasonably sympathize with *A* and come in on her behalf, and so starts the brawl.

Thus serious offenses may set off the domino effect, even if everyone acts conscientiously after the initial offense. Consequently, a society in which serious offenses are to be expected is prone to instability. The original contract therefore does not apply literally to such a society, which I have called very disordered.

ARGUMENTS FOR THE DICHOTOMY: (3) ARGUMENT FROM ABILITY TO PLAN

The previous two arguments show why the contract does *not* apply literally to a very disordered society. The next shows why it *does* apply literally to a slightly disordered society.

Note, first of all, that this sort of positive argument is less urgently needed than the negative ones. For the principle of plain dealing places the burden of proof on one who claims that the contract does not apply in a plain and literal way. It is not enough merely to point out that the situation is different from that which was expected.

But, beyond merely shifting the burden, we can present an argument of our own based on the principle of extrapolation. That principle, you will recall, directs us to adopt principles and methods of interpretation that maximize the contractors' ability to plan (section 5). This principle straight off favors literal interpretation when this is at all reasonable, since it is easier to plan if one knows that one's plan will be implemented literally. Now, in a slightly disordered society, things differ but little from the perfectly ordered society. The offenses committed are reparable, and the offenders all willingly compensate their victims and make other due amends. So the parties, even if they were to consider this situation, would not have to worry about harm to individual victims. The offenders, after compensating the victims, might indeed be somewhat worse off, and society as a whole would be somewhat less prosperous, but the scheme of basic liberties would remain intact. The situation, then, differs hardly at all from the perfectly ordered society. Under such circumstances the parties could do no better than to be ruled by the two principles of justice. Given their desire for income, wealth, and similar primary goods, the difference principle serves their ends as well as any principle could. And there is no reason at all to tamper with the principle of equal basic liberty, nor of equal opportunity, since we suppose these to remain inviolate. On the whole, then, it is reasonable to say that we are following the parties' original plan if we apply the two principles of justice literally to the slightly disordered society. And we can say this even though the slightly disordered society differs somewhat from the society they were expecting.

The same point can be made a bit more explicitly. When we interpret the contract, we must try to maximize the contractors' ability to plan. How can we do this? What counts as "maximizing their ability to plan"? In particular, what way of interpreting plans will maximize someone's ability to plan in the face of uncertainty and limited knowledge? We anticipate what we can, but we expect surprises. If a surprise does occur, the interpreter of plans faces a trilemma: She can carry out the plan literally, or adapt it, or ignore it. For us now, the third is not a live option, so in effect we have a dilemma. If we carry out the plan literally, we apply it to a situation for which it was not designed. If we adapt it, we do something other than what was planned. Now, in one case, the dilemma is easy to solve: Suppose the surprise is small, and the planner (had she anticipated it) would not have changed the plan. Then we carry out the plan literally. Otherwise, it would be very hard for a planner to plan. A rational planner knows that surprises must be expected; a rational planner knows it is counterproductive to spend an infinite amount of time planning and so must knowingly leave herself open to surprise. A rational planner would therefore want her plan to be flexible enough to cover such eventualities in a satisfactory way. Under the circumstances suggested, ability to plan is maximized by this method of interpretation.

Notice that this recommendation applies *only if* the surprise is small. I am not suggesting that we always do what the planner would have chosen, if she had anticipated the situation. As mentioned above, that would amount to making a new plan. But if things differ only slightly from what was expected, we can say we are carrying out the same plan. How small must the surprise be? Small enough so that neither it nor any smaller surprise would cause the person to change her plan, if she had anticipated it. So, for example, suppose that I ordered some 'Golden Delicious' apple trees and arranged for you to plant them in my yard when they arrive. The package comes, and, to your surprise, you find 'Red Delicious.' You know that I would have chosen to plant them anyway, so you plant them. You are following the plan. You know, however, that I would not accept 'Granny Smith' apples. If you received them and planted them, you would not be following the plan. Now, to consider a greater surprise, suppose the delivery person brings quince trees instead of apple. Perhaps I would be glad to have them and would have instructed you to plant the quince trees if I had thought of the possibility. Perhaps it would be wise of you to plant the quince trees. But you could not be said to be carrying out my original plan.

To return to the slightly disordered society: Our criterion would call for a literal interpretation of our plan—that is, of the two principles of justice.[44]

It might be well to point out just how small the differences are between a perfectly ordered society and the slightly disordered society we have been considering here. In the distribution of primary goods, as I have mentioned, there are two main differences: (1) An offender, after making amends for his offenses, may end up less well off than before. (2) Because of waste and destruction of resources, the slightly disordered society is less well off overall than a perfectly ordered society existing under similar conditions. From the original position, these differences will not be especially significant. The offender makes himself worse off, but people do that in any case: They drink themselves into hangovers, lose money at the race track, and so on. This would happen even in a perfectly ordered society, where the contract admittedly applies. (Here the tendency to commit offenses appears as a strange and somewhat expensive taste.) And, second, society on the whole is less prosperous because of the offenses, but this might happen anyway: A society could lack natural resources or technological developments, and these deficiencies would have the same effect. This could happen even in a perfectly ordered society, where the contract admittedly applies. (Here the tendency to commit offenses appears as an unfortunate fact of nature.) So a slightly disordered society, so far as primary goods are concerned, is just a special case of a perfectly ordered society. (It is not so if there are irreparable offenses.) The members of the slightly disordered society, moreover, have a sense of justice, which is almost always effective; and they are free to develop and revise their conceptions of the good.

The only remaining difference is this: In one case the people sometimes commit offenses; in the other, not. But this difference by itself should not stand in the way of enforcing the contract. It was not a motivating factor when the contract was made and so should have no relevance to its application.

REPUDIATION OF THE CONTRACT

We have now fixed the outer limits of the area of literal applicability. But outside this zone what are we to do? When can we apply the contract by reinterpretation, and when can we not apply it at all? As I have already suggested, we can reinterpret the contract to apply to a very disordered society; but its operation is suspended when we are dealing with those who repudiate the contract. I next fill in some of the detail of these claims and show why they are true.

Suppose some persons are completely lawless, repudiating the contract by their very deeds. Certainly our contractual duties toward them are suspended, if not indeed terminated. This conclusion follows from the reciprocal nature of a bilateral contract. As we have seen, we do not commit ourselves no matter what, but only on condition that the others comply. The principle of broad application dictates that we should be extremely forbearing in this regard: Only when someone's behavior amounts to a repudiation do we regard the contract as suspended. So in a slightly fragmented society, those who repudiate the contract may be treated as though they were not parties to it—at least until the suspension is reversed.

But what constitutes repudiation? Some have thought that any crime or offense constitutes a repudiation of the contract, for the offender in effect declares that the law has no authority over her. But this is not so. Suppose she has committed an offense, even a fairly serious one, but has otherwise obeyed the law. Well, on the whole she has conformed her behavior very closely to the contractual requirements. The offense is serious, but it does not constitute a repudiation.

This conclusion is reinforced by the principle of broad application. Outside the contract there is no standard of justice. We must therefore apply the contract whenever we can. We abandon it only when there is no choice. Repudiation, then, must consist of behavior that undermines the very possibility of a contract. Even here, the contract is not altogether abrogated: Though persons may repudiate, they cannot abolish the contract. Their action suspends many of the duties that we had toward them, but if they repent and somehow assure us of their repentance, they are to be readmitted. This is because the contract is made in the original position: When anyone in the contractual society comes and sincerely says, "I want to do what is just; what principles should I follow?" the answer must always be that she is to follow the principles of justice agreed upon in the original position. A real-life contract, because it is made in time, can be irrevocably abrogated by repudiation. Not so the original contract, which is eternal.[45]

As we have seen (section 1), four sorts of crimes fall into this category: murder, treason, persistent serious crime, and crimes that destroy the capacity to choose. Persistent serious crime, or "racke-teering," as I will call it for short, must involve a life of wrongdoing so abandoned that the person shows no tendency at all to respect principles of justice. If she happens to comply with them, it is only be-cause it suits her purposes better, and not at all because she respects them. Leaders of organized crime syndicates fall into this category. By contrast, a person who robs one person, or even two, may spend the rest of his life complying more or less closely with the demands of justice. I use the abbreviation "all but murder" to refer to the last category of these four, the crimes that destroy the capacity to choose that is required to make contracts. Here would be included assaults that leave the victim in a coma or persistent vegetative state; torture as well would probably fall under this heading.

Some have suggested that a less serious crime might constitute a *partial* repudiation of the contract. Society may then abstain from part of its contractual duty toward the offender. To bring in a paral-lel from our building contractor, if you are building me a house and stop when it is half completed and refuse to build any more, I must pay you (approximately) half the agreed-upon sum. But this is a false parallel. In the real world there is a status quo ante that serves as a standard of justice, namely, the state of things before you built any-thing for me, and before I paid anything to you. In the case of the half-finished house, we just interpolate between the status quo ante and the anticipated status quo post. But in the case of the original contract, there is no such status quo ante. The measurement does not make sense.

Short of the four extreme crimes, then, we apply the contract if we can find some way of interpreting it. And we can find such a way, which I discuss below (section 7). Of course, within a slightly frag-mented society the majority of people are not such extreme offend-ers. They have, by hypothesis, a fairly strong and normally effective sense of justice. Among them the contract operates normally, as if the society were not fragmented.

In conclusion, we may summarize the findings of this section as follows:

Type of Society	Defining Features	Applicability of the Contract
Slightly disordered	Violations of difference principle, followed by willing amends	Literal
Very disordered	Violations of basic liberties or equal opportunity, followed by willing amends	By reinterpretation
Slightly fragmented	A few persons repudiate	Suspended vis-à-vis repudiators

7. Applying the Contract

THE SLIGHTLY DISORDERED SOCIETY

Now that we have looked at the method of applying the contract to less-than-perfectly ordered societies, we can go on actually to use this method and apply the contract.

I consider the three sorts of imperfectly ordered societies, proceeding from the best ordered to the worst. The first to be considered is the slightly disordered society.

Here we apply the contract literally. We do not have to worry about the principles calling for equal basic liberty or equality of opportunity. These are not violated. There are, however, violations of the difference principle; or, to speak more precisely, violations of the laws and regulations promulgated in order to implement the difference principle. (The difference principle, it will be recalled, directs us to maximize the well-being of the least well-off group. See section 1.) We must concern ourselves with these violations. Under the circumstances of the slightly disordered society, what sort of laws and regulations should be selected in order to maximize the welfare of a person representing the worst-off group? Well, evidently, the welfare of this person can be increased if we provide penalties for offenders. So we need a two-tiered set of regulations: First-order regulations governing the distribution of (variable) primary goods, and second-order regulations governing those who violate the first-order regulations. (A defining feature of the slightly disordered society is that the second-order regulations are not violated; hence our hierarchy ends at the second order.) And we arrange the scheme of penalties so as to maximize the welfare of the worst-off representative person.

But who is the worst-off representative person? Usually we may conceive of this person as a member of the lowest socioeconomic class, someone who has the least income, wealth, and opportunity. But now we must add something: The worst off is the citizen who belongs to the lowest socioeconomic class and *who in addition suffers the worst penalty provided by law.* The system of penalties has become part of the structure: So the persons subject to the penalties must be included among the "representative persons." Otherwise, these people are excluded from the protection of the contract. Rational planners would not want this to happen to them. In the slightly disordered society it is a real possibility that a citizen may commit an offense, be subject to punishment, and submit to it. This is an integral part of the definition of this sort of society. If we exclude the punishees from consideration, we make them into scapegoats. Their punishment would not then be justified.

Unfortunately, authors who have written on this question have often excluded the offenders from consideration. Rawls, for example, says: "Now in setting up . . . a system of sanctions the parties in a constitutional convention must weigh . . . the danger to the liberty of the representative citizen measured by the likelihood that these sanctions will wrongly interfere with his freedom. . . . One who complies with the announced rules need never fear an infringement of his liberty."[46] But we must equally worry that the sanctions may *rightly* interfere with our liberty. (The person who pays a hundred-dollar fine has lost no less money than the person who is robbed of a hundred dollars.)[47]

The penalties justified by this scheme will require the offender to give up a certain amount of variable primary goods, that is, income, wealth, or positions of authority. In other words, someone who offends against the difference principle must either pay a fine or give up some privilege or power. The penalties may not involve a loss of basic liberties.

We thus get a system of deterrent punishments forming an integral part of a greater scheme of incentives. The very point of the difference principle is to maximize the well-being of the worst-off representative person by means of a system of inequalities of wealth, income, and power. The fines and forfeits now under discussion are merely one tool to be used in pursuit of this end.

Of course, in the slightly disordered society people are deterred not by the fear that punishment will be imposed upon them, but by the mere knowledge that by committing offenses they become eligible for punishment. They know that eventually conscience will move them to submit to the required punishment; rather than do that, they may avoid crime altogether. (See Chapter 2, section 4.)

THE VERY DISORDERED SOCIETY

In the case of the very disordered society, the contract cannot be literally applied, but must be reinterpreted. Punishment then follows in accord with the rectification theory. The offender has arrogated excess basic liberties and must forfeit some liberties to compensate. He ends up with a different package of basic liberties than that which the contract calls for: Herein lies the reinterpretation.

How do we determine what punishment a person should get as rectification for a given serious offense? The answer has already been given (Chapter 5, section 5), but here we may add some details. We want to know what new package of basic liberties is equivalent (as nearly as possible) to the original package. Since these rights originate in the contract, it is to the contract that we must turn in judging the equivalence. The contractors choose the basic liberties because they are useful and necessary for the development and exercise of the two moral powers. A reasonably equivalent package, then, is one that is equally useful and necessary for that same purpose. And we can determine this by asking: Would the parties in the original position be indifferent between these two packages of basic liberties?

Now, beyond upsetting the balance of basic liberties, a serious crime will probably have bad economic effects (or, more generally, bad effects on the supply of variable primary goods). Someone who commits such an offense is therefore subject to the same sort of deterrent penalties as applied to the minor offenses. The object is still the same: The penalties are to be arranged so as to benefit the worst-off representative person, but here the worst-off representative person appears in a different guise. Here it is the person at the bottom of the socioeconomic heap who is in addition victimized most seriously by crime. Why this difference? Well, with minor offenses, there either was no victim, or the harm was reparable. So there was no lasting harm to the victim. But now, when we are dealing with serious offenses, there is likely to be a victim whose basic rights are irreparably infringed. The absolute ("lexical") priority of the basic liberties makes this infringement a very serious matter. Such a victim is worse off than anyone who suffers a mere financial loss, or who loses a nonbasic liberty. So when we are making out a schedule of deterrent penalties for serious offenses, it is usually the victim we must keep in mind when trying to maximize the well-being of the worst off.

NO COMMERCE IN BASIC RIGHTS

"The first principle of justice," says the critic, "guarantees to each person the greatest system of basic liberties compatible with a like liberty for all. Now, in the very disordered society the basic liberties of some are abridged by criminals. We should therefore interpret this principle as a maximin principle. We should deprive criminals of basic liberties—beyond the amount your theory calls for—so as to maximize the basic liberties of those who have the least—namely, the criminals. More specifically, we are to use deprivation of basic liberties as a deterrent against serious crime."

To this critic we may reply: Your suggestion is not implausible, but you forget one thing: Unlike the variable primary goods, the basic liberties are to be inalienable. This means that no person should be able to deprive himself of basic liberties by his own voluntary act. Inalienability is essential to the basic liberties.

Moreover, if basic liberties can be alienated by a criminal act, surely they can be alienated by a lawful act. It would seem, then, that the basic liberties should be fully alienable to all; for this would result in Pareto-improvements with regard to liberty (that is to say, at least one person would end up with a package of liberties that she prefers to her original package, but no one would end up with a package of liberties that she prefers less than her original package). A person, for example, who tired of freedom, might sell herself into slavery in exchange for an annuity. A poor person might sell his vote to a political manipulator. (Of course, we would make all these arrangements revocable, in recognition of the importance of these liberties.) But this scheme strikes one as unacceptable, so it should be unacceptable with regard to criminals. We should not let a person trade possible criminal gain against possible loss of basic rights. Even if the trade is to society's advantage, we must forgo it: Basic liberties are not articles of commerce.

"Quite so; but let me rephrase my objection. We should not view the criminal as trading away her basic liberties. Rather, these liberties are themselves conditional. Indeed, the ultimate description of the basic liberties in a given society will be fearfully complex, and full of clauses saying that *this* may be done under conditions A, but not under conditions B. Now, what I propose is just one more condition: Everyone is to enjoy the liberty to (move about freely if one has committed no crime, or to move about less freely if one has committed a serious crime). And the various degrees of freedom of movement are to be arranged so as to maximize the basic liberties of those who have least. Now, this conditional liberty cannot be traded away, but one clause or the other can be activated by the person's conduct."

This reply is more cogent, and to answer it we will have to dig deeper. First, we must remind ourselves why we are to have *equal* basic liberties from the point of view of the representative equal citizen. It is because we evaluate a scheme of basic liberties from the point of view of the representative equal citizen. (And this, in turn, is because the basic liberties are needed equally by all for the development of the two moral powers.)[48] So even if we thought of the first principle of justice as a maximin[49] principle, it would still result in equal liberties, for we are considering only one relevant social position. More pointedly, we are to maximize the basic liberty of the representative person with the least basic liberty—but there is only one representative person.

Second, we must examine the distinct ways in which the contract is applied to the slightly disordered society and the very disordered society. In the slightly disordered society the contract is literally applicable. How do we apply it? The situation is not one that had been considered at the beginning, so it is not immediately obvious what we are to do. We begin by framing a description of the new situation in terms that make the contract applicable. Doing so involves an expanded set of relevant social positions. In the case of the well-ordered society we considered a hierarchy of socioeconomic classes. In the slightly disordered society we have in addition a classification based on subjection to punishment. In the slightly disordered society the least advantaged representative person is the one who is at the bottom of the socioeconomic ladder and who also suffers the worst punishment provided by law.

In the case of the very disordered society we cannot proceed this way. We are faced with a situation to which we cannot, and ought not, literally apply the contract. So we search for some interpretation of the contract that we *can* apply literally to this anomalous state of affairs. And our solution was this: Instead of "equal basic liberties for all," we read, "if not equal, then equivalent basic liberties for all."

You, however (you, our loyal Critic), have proceeded as if we were still dealing with the former case, the case of the slightly disordered society. You assumed that the contract was literally applicable to the very disordered society and then sought a proper description of the social positions in this society. Whereas in the perfectly ordered society and the slightly disordered society we had but one relevant class—the class of equal citizens—you here found many: The class of law-abiding citizens, and the various classes of felons. You then applied the first principle of justice, considering it (quite legitimately) to be a maximin principle. The result is a hierarchy of classes with regard to basic liberties. It would be demagogic—though not incorrect—to refer to these as first-class citizens, second-class citizens, and so forth. Under this description the theory seems self-refuting.

Now, one might worry that the serious criminals would be insufficiently deterred from crime. But, as I have noted, they can still be deprived of variable primary goods—wealth, position, and privilege—as a deterrent measure. And this deprivation will no doubt be an effective deterrent.

DETERRENT AND RECTIFYING PUNISHMENTS COMPARED

Here I want to point out one important similarity and one important difference between the two sorts of punishment just discussed.

The similarity: Just as deterrent punishment is an integral part of the system of incentives required by the difference principle, so also is rectifying punishment an integral part of the scheme of equal basic liberties. Both sorts of punishment arise when we apply the two principles of justice to situations of less than full compliance. No fundamentally new principles of justice have been introduced. But the parallel is not complete. When we have a minor crime followed by a fitting deterrent punishment, the provisions of the original contract have been fulfilled—perhaps not in the best way, but fulfilled just the same. When, on the other hand, a serious offense is committed, followed by appropriate rectifying (and deterrent) punishment, the contract has not been fulfilled. The offender may do her best to remedy her breach of contract, but it is not fully remediable. (A parallel case that may be helpful: Often, in the score of a musical piece, we encounter a passage very difficult to perform; and often a thoughtful composer indicates in small notes an easier alternative, marked *ossia*. Now, someone who plays the *ossia* passage has in fact performed the piece, though not in the ideal way. Contrast this with the person who botches, and plays wrong notes. He may recover himself so the performance can go on successfully. But he has failed to give a true performance of the piece in question.)

So much for the similarity; now the difference. Recall that the variable primary goods are transferable whereas the basic liberties are not. This distinction induces a similar distinction between punishments. Deterrent punishments consist of fines or deprivations of privileges. These being transferable, the burden of punishment can be assumed by someone other than the punishee. If I must pay a hundred-dollar fine, my friend Rothschild can come and hand me one hundred dollars. If I am deprived of the right to drive on public roads, Rothschild can have his chauffeur drive me. The burden of this kind of punishment can always be assumed by Rothschild. But if my punishment involves forfeiting a basic liberty, Rothschild cannot assume my burden. If I must perform one hundred hours of community-service work, I cannot discharge my duty by getting Rothschild to do the work. If I must spend one hundred days in prison, I cannot get off the hook by getting Rothschild (or his flunky) to spend one hundred days in prison.

One sort of punishment, then, is assumable; the other, not. This fact bears on the ignominiousness of the two sorts of punishment. If my hundred-dollar fine may be assumed by Rothschild—blameless, upstanding Rothschild—then the fine cannot be a sign of great moral turpitude. But a term of community-service work, or a prison sentence, falls on the offender alone and cannot be assumed by anyone else. The offender then is more particularly stigmatized. This distinction gives us one interpretation of the penalty–punishment distinction. It is in harmony with what Joel Feinberg says about the same distinction. He holds that "punishment" proper has a reprobative quality that "mere penalties" lack.[50]

Now, one might think that assumability is a bad feature in any sort of penalty, that the burden should fall on the offender and on no one else. But this thought would not be completely correct. The aim of our system of deterrent penalties is to help implement the difference principle. Does it violate the difference principle if one person gives a gift of money to another? Almost certainly not. The fact that the recipient has just committed an offense would not seem to make any difference. (Of course, it *would* be bad if Rothschild were paying people to commit offenses—but that is another story.)

THE ASSURANCE THEORY; REPEAT OFFENDERS

At this point it will be convenient to recall the assurance theory and discuss its consequences for repeat offenders. As you will recall (Chapter 2, section 5), the assurance theory places on offenders the duty to assure their fellow citizens that they (the offenders) will not offend again.

How does the assurance theory come to apply to contractual societies? It is a consequence of the publicity requirement.[51] In an ordered society those who have a sense of justice are known to have it; and those who lack it are—through their own confession or the work of the police—known not to have it. If offenses occur, we may reasonably suspect that the offenders lack some elements of a sense of justice; and we may reasonably fear that they will offend again. If the offenders wish to remain members of the society, they owe us some assurance that they have the requisite sense of justice. True repentance is not enough; some public sign must be provided.

What kind of assurance is sufficient, and how much? It would seem that we must rely on statistics to judge this. That is, an offender should provide assurance such that the probability of her offending again (given this assurance) is the same as the probability that a non-criminal would commit that kind of offense in the first place. And these probabilities are to be judged by public statistics concerning illegal behavior. Aside from this statistical method, the only other possibility would seem to be based on a personal knowledge of the offender. But this would require the offender to reveal more than she ought to have to reveal, and would not be very reassuring to those who did not know her personally. So the statistical measure is to be preferred.

The assurance theory does not call for a specific penalty to be superadded to other penalties that the person may already owe. Rather, the assurance theory judges the total of the penalties owed by the offender and requires that this total penalty provide the necessary assurance. It may be that rectifying and deterrent penalties already provide the assurance. If so, nothing further is required. If not, some extra assuring measures must be taken.

Having considered these preliminaries, let us see how the assurance theory applies to the slightly disordered society and the very disordered society. (I discuss the slightly fragmented society in the following section.)

In the slightly disordered society it will probably be enough for the offender to say, "I'm sorry; I won't do it again." The offenses committed in the slightly disordered society are minor and stem less from malice than from inattention. In extreme cases we might require an additional penalty for second offenders. Such a penalty would have to satisfy the difference principle: It must help maximize the well-being of the least well-off representative person. But this person is likely to be the one who suffers the penalty. Since the offenses involved cause only minor, remediable harms, the additional penalty for repeat offenders would probably cause more suffering among the worst off than it would prevent. It would, in such cases, be unjustified.

There might, however, be some who are subject to a particular temptation; they might have an irresistible urge to park in illegal parking spaces. In such cases an additional penalty would probably be justified. Most likely, it would not be imposed until a definite pattern of offenses became apparent.

When we turn to the very disordered society, we see that the crimes there are likely to cause more serious, irreversible harm to persons and institutions. A more effective form of assurance will be needed. Now, one form of this assurance is integral to the rectification theory itself. For under that theory, as I have argued, a series of offenses of a given sort constitutes a more grievous offense. The penalty is accordingly more serious, and this fact might by itself serve as a sufficient assurance. If not, the deterrent portion of the penalty might be increased for those who offend more than once. In determining the sentence, here our aim (as before, section 6) is (first) to assure equal basic liberties to all and (second) to enforce the difference principle, maximizing the variable primary goods of those who have least.

THE SLIGHTLY FRAGMENTED SOCIETY

We now turn to the slightly fragmented society, the last of the model societies that we are to consider. The slightly fragmented society is defined by the presence of some who by their actions repudiate the contract, but few enough of these so that the contract operates normally among the rest. There are two cases to consider: In one case the offender repents and wishes to reenter the contractual society; in the other the offender is stiff-necked.

To take up the first case: Suppose the offender wants to reenter the contractual society. How can the society dare to readmit such a dangerous and unpredictable person? Invoking the assurance theory, the repentant offender must take extreme measures to assure the rest of society that it is safe to readmit her. Now, as we have just seen, those who commit serious crimes without repudiating the contract need not forgo any basic liberties (beyond those governed by the Rectification Principle); criminals of this sort have still shown a considerable sense of justice, and we may rely on them to obey the law for the most part. Their assurance is a pledge to pay an additional penalty should they repeat their offenses. But the present case is different. The repudiator has undermined the very basis of the contract; we cannot expect her to obey it. And by taking herself out of the contractual society, she has waived the rights that she enjoyed under the contract.

So the assurance that she is to provide may involve forgoing basic liberties; and, indeed, how could any lesser measures adequately reassure us? Only close supervision of the offender can reassure us of her future good behavior. The appropriate assurance, then, is a term in prison. So far as assurance is concerned, imprisonment might gradually be replaced by less stringent forms of supervision, such as work-release, intermittent sentences, and finally probation.

Having submitted to this measure of assurance, the repentant criminal is now at least tentatively readmitted into the contractual society and so is governed by the contract. Accordingly, she owes a rectifying punishment. This punishment will be quite severe. The four crimes involved are murder, all-but-murder, treason, and racketeering. In each case the criminal makes herself, as it were, a god with respect to her victims. If the criminal enlarges her sphere of liberty by making herself a lord over others, then she must restrict her sphere of liberty by making others be lord over her. That is, she must make herself into a virtual slave. But no arrogation of rights, however great, could require the penalty of death. For the degree of the penalty is to be measured by what one would forgo in exchange for the liberty to commit the crime (Chapter 4, section 5), and no rational person in the original position would forgo life in order to gain other liberties. So the penalty for these extremely serious crimes is to consist of some sort of subjection to the will of others, and this in practice means imprisonment with little freedom to lead one's own life. And the term of years is likely to be great, for a rational person would give up immense things for the liberty to commit such huge crimes.

The repentant criminal, then, has a duty under the Rectification Principle to submit to a long term of imprisonment, putting herself at the service of the community. This merely reinforces the conclusion we reached with regard to assurance.

We now turn to the second case: those who do not repent. In an informal way we can reason as follows. Certainly, these criminals are not entitled to any better treatment than those who do repent. So their penalty must be at least as severe. Like the repentant, they owe us the same duty of assurance, which (they being unwilling) we may extract from them. But in their case this assurance will require a closer confinement and supervision than it would in the case of the repentant.[52]

Furthermore, these extreme criminals have taken themselves out of the contractual society by attacking it at its very foundations. They have thereby forgone at least some of the contractual protection that they once enjoyed. The lawful members of society may therefore treat them somewhat in the manner of invaders or wild animals. This means that we may deprive them of basic liberties, not only to restrain them from committing further crimes but to deter others: That is, we use them as means to our end of reducing serious crime. Herein they differ from the repentant, who lose basic liberties solely on their own account. The penalties imposed should be the minimum required to protect the basic liberties of citizens and (once this is done) to maximize the (variable) primary goods of those citizens who have least.

Such is the informal account of punishment of unrepentant, extreme criminals. The matter deserves a more formal consideration, which follows immediately. But even here the account must be sketchy and programmatic. For (as will soon be evident) the question opens up whole new areas of social contract theory.

We begin by asking: What does the contract provide for those who repudiate it? The question is paradoxical. Those who repudiate the contract are not governed by it. What it specifies is irrelevant to them. Nor does it seem that any reinterpretation, however vulcanized, could apply to those who reject the contract and its interpretations altogether. On the other hand, the social contract theorist has nothing but the contract.

We might resolve the paradox by recurring to noncontractual methods, but it would be better to retain the contract conception if possible, and this turns out to be possible, by way of renegotiation. These serious criminals are to be considered as people deficient in one of the two moral powers. They lack a sense of justice. (Though they might in a sense possess this power, they at any rate do not use it; so they may be considered as lacking it.) These criminals are thus of a kind with animals, the mentally disabled, the comatose, and (in a way) even children. All these creatures must somehow be fitted into the scheme of justice, though none is capable of a sense of justice, nor perhaps even a conception of the good. We may refer to such people as *moral incompetents.*

Imagine the following scenario: In a well-ordered society there suddenly appear a number of moral incompetents. Though capable of feeling joy and misery, they cannot be counted on to act in accordance with a conception of justice. What to do? One might want to *force* them to comply with the contract, but this would require such close supervision and control that they would lack most basic liberties. Indeed, the suggestion is probably impossible, for it would amount to forcing an animal to be human, or a child to be an adult: They do not have the capacity. More reasonable to return to the original position, along with these incompetents (or their competent representatives). Once behind the veil of ignorance, all are competent to conclude a contract. They know that some among them are, in reality, morally incompetent, though they do not know who will fall into this class. The parties know that a contract has already been concluded, yielding the two principles, and they concede it to be binding in the contractual society among those who have the full moral powers. They concede, too, that the original contract is binding on the incompetents as an ideal: To the extent that it can be put into effect for the incompetents, it must be. All the parties in this reconvened original position must decide unanimously on principles by which the morally competent are to treat the morally incompetent.

In this position the parties regard themselves as all of equal moral status; but some of them have suffered a misfortune—they are morally incompetent, though this fact is now masked.

The reasoning of the parties proceeds as follows. The morally incompetent, lacking a sense of justice, cannot conform their behavior to principles of justice. Their behavior toward others may be considered a series of natural events, rather than a series of human actions. It can be controlled only by measures imposed from the outside: either direct coercion, or the threat of punishment and the prospect of reward. A being so deficient in the sense of justice logically cannot have rights in the same way as normal human beings. Most rights—in particular, most of those constituting the basic liberties—can be claimed, waived, or exercised; and claiming, waiving, and exercising rights are actions directed toward others. But the incompetent's behavior toward others we are considering as a natural event that can be controlled only by the intervention of others. So the morally incompetent cannot have rights of a sort that need to be claimed, waived, or exercised.

Of course, in a weaker sense, moral incompetents can have rights: That is, they have a moral status that entitles them to certain treatment at the hands of moral agents; and it is an injustice to the rightholder if he is not treated this way. Thus children have a right to an elementary education, animals have a right not to be tortured, and so on. (Note that children get educated in spite of the fact that most of them would rather play baseball; this indicates the nature of their right to an education.) The rights of the morally incompetent are of a kind that can be exercised by others in their behalf.

As far as the basic liberties are concerned, this means that the morally incompetent can have but few. The rights to freedom of speech and of movement, for example, are of the kind that must be exercised, so the morally incompetent do not have such rights. Probably they have only the rights not to be killed or injured or made to suffer; the right to the basic necessities of subsistence; and the right to due process of law.

Of course, depending on their condition, even many of the morally incompetent appreciate the opportunity to speak freely, to move about, and to do the other things that the basic liberties usually guarantee. But for the incompetent, these opportunities are merely goods, to be included in an index of their primary goods. They do not enjoy them as a matter of right. Indeed, even their possession of wealth and similar primary goods is different from possession by normal persons. The morally incompetent must be controlled by material incentives and direct coercion. Whatever goods they possess, beyond those required for a minimally decent subsistence, are subject to forfeit as part of this system of control. So for example, a child may have a toy, but the toy may with justice be taken away as a punishment if the child has injured a playmate.

Keeping in mind this description of the morally incompetent, the parties proceed to draw up their contract. They would first like to provide greatest equal basic liberties for all, but the incompetent are logically unfit subjects for most of them. So they grant to the morally incompetent those rights to which they are susceptible.

Second, they must make special provision for the enforcement of this scheme of liberties. In ordinary circumstances they could depend on the sense of justice for an at least approximate enforcement of the basic liberties. But the morally incompetent have no tendency at all to comply with this scheme. So the pattern of incentives and coercions is set up to induce them to comply. If we were dealing with normal persons, we would prefer incentives to coercion, since incentives preserve a greater measure of liberty; but for the morally incompetent the basic liberties are not distinguished from the other primary goods, so there is no such preference: We do whatever leaves them best off. (I exclude, of course, the few basic liberties that even the incompetent retain.) This scheme of enforcement has absolute (as Rawls would say, "lexical") priority over the distribution of wealth and other primary goods (to be considered momentarily). For in the presence of moral incompetents we cannot be said to have established a system of liberties at all unless we provide for their enforcement. The priority of enforcement has two major consequences: First, the incompetent are liable to lose all their primary goods except those necessary for decent subsistence; and, second, all must forgo at least some primary goods to pay for the scheme of enforcement.

It is to be noted that the scheme of enforcement prevents the morally incompetent from abridging their own basic liberties, as well as others'. The scheme may be applied paternalistically, especially to children and the insane.

The third step in constructing the contract is an agreement on the remaining primary goods. Here the difference principle will no doubt be selected. There are serious questions as to how we may measure and index the primary goods of the morally incompetent so as to compare the incompetent with each other and with the competent. For we are dealing with different sorts of primary goods in each case. But for the present I will gloss over this difficulty and assume that some index can be constructed.

Considering, then, these basic features of this contract with the incompetent, let us apply it to the extreme offenders of the slightly fragmented society. By the first clause of this contract, the extreme offenders are granted only a small bundle of basic liberties. By the second clause, citizens are directed to set up an enforcement scheme that will secure the basic liberties of all. These two features call for a scheme of self-protective punishments that violate what would ordinarily be the basic liberties of extreme criminals, though they retain a smaller set of basic liberties. This is as we concluded above in the informal account of this subject. Finally, the third clause of the renegotiated contract directs us to maximize the primary goods of the worst-off class of moral incompetents.

All the distinctive punishments of repudiators can be characterized as measures of social self-defense. It is a practice very different from the negative incentives attached to minor offenses. In a slightly disordered society, we avoid minor crime because we know we will otherwise become liable to pay a fine; and we know that we *will* pay it. Having the offender pay for his offense in this way is an integral part of the social system, just like having a purchaser pay for what she buys. When we impose deterrent measures on the stiff-necked repudiators, we can be all but certain that they *will not* cooperate with us in imposing them. These punishments are measures imposed on persons outside the social system to protect those who are within it. Even the confinement of the repentant repudiator is a matter of social self-defense, although it is a nonviolent form of it. We keep him in custody, because—as in the case of a tiger in a zoo—we fear what he would do if he were released, and he has no way in the short run of reassuring us.

8. Transfer to the Real World

These, then, are the penalties that are to prevail in the various contractual societies—slightly disordered, very disordered, and slightly fragmented. Two steps remain separating us from the real world.

In our two disordered societies everyone has a strong sense of justice, so that all offenders repent and try to make amends for their crimes. What should be done, now, in similar societies where the same sorts of crimes occur, but the offenders do not always repent? If we follow the principles established in Chapters 1 and 2, the answer is that we then force the unrepentant offender to undergo the same punishment that the repentant offender undergoes willingly. In our discussion of the slightly fragmented society we have already treated separately the repentant and unrepentant. So we know what is to be done in contractual societies where some offenders are unrepentant.

Such societies resemble our world, the real world. The principles for them, therefore, are the principles for us.

This concludes our contractual account of punishment.

9. Hamlet without the Prince

The results of this chapter are based on a very specific social contract theory. One might wonder to what extent these results can be appreciated without the theoretical background. Can there be a social contract theory of punishment without the social contract?

Indeed, much of the theory can be saved. Imagine a society meeting the following criteria:

It assures each of its citizens a set of basic, inalienable rights.

These may be limited to normal, adult, noncriminal citizens.

It has a market economy whose existence is justified on grounds of efficiency.

That is, the citizens are followers of Adam Smith, not Robert Nozick. They do not consider a full complement of economic rights to be part of their set of basic rights. Of course, there are differing measures of efficiency, and such a measure may include some distributive criterion, such as Rawls's difference principle. The point is that the economic system is valued to the extent that it succeeds in achieving productive–distributive goals.

The society regards certain extreme offenses as putting the offender beyond the pale.

If these three conditions are met, a system of punishment very similar to that of this chapter can be upheld. Under imperfect compliance, negative economic incentives—that is, fines—will be required to achieve the goal of productive–distributive efficiency. These deterrent punishments will fall out as a consequence of the society's accepted economic principles as applied to nonideal cases. If the scheme of basic liberties is violated, a rectifying punishment will be called for. And if a person commits crimes severe enough to put him beyond the pale, socially self-defensive measures will be appropriate. Conscientious persons who accept the three basic principles will likewise accept punishment when it falls due to them under the principles.

It is hard, of course, to give any firm idea of the criteria for assigning penalties under such nonspecific assumptions. Unless we know the way productive–distributive efficiency is measured, we have no idea what kinds of penalties will promote it; and similarly for the other principles. What remains is a theory that tries to see punishment as part of the normal functioning of a necessarily imperfect world, like the kick that dislodges the bottle from the Coke machine. In the end, this cannot always be done: Extreme offenses do not allow themselves to be viewed this way. We can hope, however, for a society where there are serious offenses, but no extreme ones; and this is not an unreasonable aspiration.

CHAPTER 8

Punishment, Contract, and Fraternity

IN THIS final chapter I touch briefly on some interconnections between punishment, the social contract, and the political ideal of fraternity. I am concerned here with the rectification theory of punishment viewed in the context of social contract theory; I will call this the *contract-rectification* theory.

What I suggest is this: Liberalism sees society as a collection of individuals, not a community. Each person is free to choose and act on her own plan of life, which may leave her completely indifferent to the others. So long as she does them no harm or injustice, she is in the right. The rectification theory, however, requires a stronger sense of community, one bound by the relation of fraternity. If we view the question in terms of social contract theory, we can say that we view the contract in a certain way: It does not merely create duties to do and omit certain actions; it also creates a relationship of fraternity among the parties, in much the same way a marriage contract creates a much stronger relationship. Serious offenses undermine this fraternal relationship. Rectifying punishment is usually necessary to restore the relationship of fraternity. For this reason a guilty person must submit to such a punishment. The restoration of fraternity is the offender's rationale for submitting to punishment. Without this rationale, submission to punishment will seem unmotivated.

1. An Objection

We may begin by looking at a possible objection to the contract-rectification theory. Suppose Brown has committed a fairly serious crime, the sort that usually falls under the Rectification Principle.

Perhaps he has stolen something from Green. But Brown has re-pented and made full restitution to Green. Now, according to my theory, he has arrogated excess basic liberties and must still submit to punishment to restore the equality of basic rights. But (one might object) why should this matter to the rest of us? So long as Green has been fully compensated and our own basic liberties are unim-paired, why should we care if Brown has enjoyed more? Isn't this just baseless envy?

We could answer curtly: No, it is not envy. The contract calls for equal basic rights, and the contract must be enforced. Envy might ally itself with contract fidelity as a motive for this, but the envy is irrelevant.

From the punishee's point of view there is a corresponding prob-lem. He has compensated Green, he has resolved to be better in the future, he has even made arrangements to ensure that he will keep this resolution—why do anything more? Would not any additional measures just amount to neurotic guilt, pointless breast-beating?

Again, the curt answer: No, it is not neurosis. The contract calls for equal basic rights, and the contract must be honored. Feelings of guilt might ally themselves with contract fidelity, but the guilt feelings are irrelevant.

This curt answer, though correct, is too shallow. Why (our ob-jector might continue) does the contract itself call for equal basic liberties? And here we must stop and think. Rawls's most general conception of justice is a sort of maximin[1] principle:

> All social values—liberty and opportunity, income and wealth, and the bases of self-respect—are to be distributed equally unless an unequal distribution of any, or all, of these values is to everyone's advantage.[2]

Why should we not apply this principle to the basic liberties? Why should we not distribute the basic liberties unequally if by doing so we could increase the basic liberties of all? Mill, indeed, suggests just such a thing.[3] This interpretation of the contract would abolish the equality of basic liberties; or, more precisely, people would enjoy equal basic liberties only in the original position, but not in the well-ordered society or the real world. Equality of basic liberties would be completely metaphysical. This objection, if it stands, would be fatal to the contract-rectification theory. This theory can work only if there is a fixed, equal distribution of basic liberties.

Now, the proposition that people should have equal basic liber-ties is enshrined among the verities of liberal political thought and, I think, deservedly so. If any political maxim is true, it is this one.

But the derivation of equal basic liberties turns out to be surprisingly difficult for a social contract theory, especially for Rawls's. The provisions of the contract derive their force from considerations of pure procedural justice: *Whatever* is agreed to from the original position is just. Equality of results is not guaranteed. Indeed, if Rawls argues for inequality in the distribution of wealth and similar primary goods, it is hard to see why similar arguments should not establish inequality of basic liberties. In general, if an unequal arrangement can result in a greater liberty for all, it seems that the contractors must adopt it.

Rawls does in fact consider this possibility briefly.[4] He examines Mill's suggestion that well-educated persons should be given more votes than the general populace. And we can imagine other situations. A male supremacist might argue that by giving a more extensive liberty to men, we actually increase the liberty of men and women alike. (Women, he might say, are burdened by the task of bearing and raising children. They cannot carry out this task and at the same time exercise the full complement of economic and political rights. By vesting some of these rights in men alone, we can secure for women a greater measure of other basic liberties. This reasoning strikes me as completely wrong, but it is a serious sort of argument.) And, indeed, this sort of argument sometimes does seem to work: For example, we give children fewer rights than adults so that in the long run the rights of those who are now children will be maximized. If we gave children the full complement of adult basic liberties, they would likely use these liberties so badly as to jeopardize their liberty in the future.

The general form of this argument is as follows: We have a society of equal moral persons. But we find that they fall into two groups. One group, though in no way morally superior, has some characteristic that enables it to use a greater share of basic liberties so as to increase the liberty of all. We therefore divide society into two groups and then apply the maximin principle with respect to basic liberties—that is to say, we arrange things so as to maximize the liberty of the group that has less.

We are, then, dealing with a serious problem. How can Rawls's theory, or any social contract theory, yield a strict equality of basic liberties for all competent adults?

Rawls himself relies on considerations of self-respect: An unequal distribution of basic liberties would tend to diminish the self-respect of those with the lesser liberty.[5] Certainly it is so, but something seems to be missing from the account. If an unequal liberty were indeed called for by the principles of justice, why should those with less liberty feel ashamed, any more than the poor need to feel ashamed before the well-to-do? After all, they were all treated with equal respect and consideration in the original position. With the method of pure procedural justice, equal outcomes cannot be assured, nor does inequality stigmatize those in lower positions. Those who are less wealthy have no good reason to feel ashamed when they contemplate the Rothschilds. Ordinary citizens have no good reason to feel ashamed when they consider senators and presidents. A lesser liberty would be good grounds for shame only if it were unjust. We now seem to be in a circle: Unequal liberty is unjust because it undermines self-respect, and it undermines self-respect because it is unjust.

Lest dizziness supervene, let us turn aside from this circle and turn for a while to the topic of contract, which, I believe, can extricate us.

2. The Social Contract as Relational Contract

When parties enter a contract, as I have suggested, they may not only create rights and duties; they may also create a certain sort of relationship among themselves, a relationship that cannot be exhaustively described by any list of rights and duties to undertake specific actions. The most obvious example is marriage. When bride and groom enter into a marriage contract, they do not wish merely to create in each other certain specified contractual rights and duties. They wish to become husband and wife; they hope by their contract to establish a loving and committed relationship. Similarly, though less intensely, businesspersons who sign a partnership agreement do not merely bind themselves to a list of duties and rights; they hope by their contract to create a prosperous and harmonious working relationship. Now, these relationships, these personal connections, are of the essence of these contracts; they are not just pleasant side-effects, or external means to the end that is internal to the contract. The husband or wife who acts to undermine the loving and committed relationship is acting in bad faith with respect to the contract, though no clause can be cited that specifically forbids what is done. Similarly, a business partner who tries to undermine the relationship of trust and harmony is acting in bad faith with respect to that contract.[6]

As far back as Burke we can find the idea that the social contract is more than just a discrete exchange of specified performances among parties who are otherwise uninvolved:

Society is, indeed, a contract. Subordinate contracts for objects of mere occasional interest may be dissolved at pleasure; but the state ought not to be considered as nothing better than a partnership agreement in a trade of pepper and coffee, calico or tobacco, or some other such low concern, to be taken up for a little temporary interest, and to be dissolved by the fancy of the parties. . . . It is a partnership in all science, a partnership in all art, a partnership in every virtue and in all perfection. As the ends of such a partnership cannot be obtained in many generations, it becomes a partnership not only between those who are living, but between those who are living, those who are dead, and those who are to be born.[7]

Burke, of course, is headed in a very different direction than our thoughts in this chapter, but his point is well taken, that the social contract is not merely a tit-for-tat but a sort of partnership, if not in all art and every virtue then at least a partnership of people who live, and often must live, their whole lives together. No one, of course, would suppose that the Rawlsian social contract is a trade of pepper for coffee, but it could conceivably be seen as an insurance contract, with the state as a life and indemnity company, whose body is in Washington but whose soul is in Hartford. Let us take a look, then, at this aspect of contracts in the everyday world.

DISCRETE VERSUS RELATIONAL CONTRACT

Ian Macneil has distinguished these two sorts of contract as *discrete* and *relational*.[8] The typical discrete contract involves an instantaneous exchange of one item for another by persons who (apart from this exchange) have nothing to do with each other. On the other hand, "in relational contract personal relations are what the sociologists call primary relations. They involve the whole person, are unlimited in scope, are unique, and are nontransferable."[9] Marriage is Macneil's most typical example,[10] but he also mentions "IBM, the UAW's relations with General Motors, Lockheed–Defense Department relations, a McDonald's hamburger franchise and a shop in Harlem with two employees."[11] The distinction is one of degree, not of kind: It sets up a spectrum rather than a dichotomy. Indeed, there seem to be no purely discrete contracts, since any contract presupposes a minimal degree of mutual trust and respect.[12]

Now, it is miraculous but not surprising that persons can by means of a contract create such intimate relationships. Contract, as I suggested earlier, is a device by which persons can secure their future plans by means of binding arrangements. These arrangements, in the case that most readily comes to mind, require the doing of specific, named things; but why should they not also require persons to enter into and maintain certain personal relationships? There are goals that can be achieved in no other way. This is especially so if the matter at hand is to last a long time and may encounter unforeseeable circumstances. Our business partners, for example, may expect to work together for many years. They might wish they could foresee every relevant possibility and provide for it explicitly in their partnership agreement, but this sort of contract would be beyond human powers. The best they can do is to bring about a situation of mutual trust and concern. In general, the parties to a contract of this sort (as I see it) agree to nourish within themselves dispositions to act and feel in certain ways toward the other parties. This may seem odd: We cannot will character traits into existence. But we can develop and preserve them. Thus, for example, our married couple do not merely *happen* to love each other; they work to maintain their love, and they consciously refrain from things that would undermine it. And business partners, in their less consuming way, work to preserve their trust and harmony.

There are, then, these two sorts of contracts. How can we tell what sort of relationship a given contract requires of us? The terms of the relationship may sometimes be explicitly stated, as when brides and grooms promise to love, honor, and cherish one another. But the terms also may not be explicit, for these words are not essential to the marriage ceremony. People who wed without saying them are just as truly wed as those who do specifically promise to love, honor, and cherish. Moreover, even the most discrete contract presupposes a minimal degree of trust between the parties. It would seem, then, that there are no general guidelines; the nature of the relationship must be inferred from the circumstances of each case.

Let us now apply these conclusions to the social contract. Corresponding to the two sorts of contract we have two possible interpretations of the social contract: discrete or relational. (Actually, there are many possible interpretations, but I simplify for now.) I assume, with the liberal, that the social contract contains no explicit relational elements: It says nothing about pursuing common goals, or maintaining elements of the culture, or loving one another—at least, not in so many words. Nonrelational language, however, may still create a substantive relationship. In this case, which interpretation is more appropriate? And what sort of relationship do the parties create by entering into the social contract?

One factor favors the relational interpretation of the contract. The parties are embarking on a venture—a partnership—that will last their whole lives and involve many aspects of their lives. They cannot predict what may happen and provide accordingly. As Macneil suggests, in a situation of this sort a relational contract is usually indicated. On the other hand, the parties value their ability individually to choose and revise a plan of life: Indeed, they see this as an essential part of themselves.

FRATERNAL EQUALITY

To decide the issue we must look more closely at the relationship that the contract supposedly creates. The parties consider themselves equal moral persons, possessed of the two moral powers (a sense of justice and the capacity to choose a plan of life); each considers each to be an independent, equal source of self-validating claims. The appropriate relationship for such persons is, I suggest, one of fraternal equality. This is a relationship that embodies in each person's character, to the extent possible, the procedures of the original position. The relationship consists of dispositions to feel and act in certain ways toward others, as well as an understanding of the reasons for doing so. Persons in such a relationship are disposed to feel, act, and think about each other as equal moral persons. Three things in particular are required:

All persons *feel* that they are the moral equals of the others.

In Rawlsian terms, they feel equal with the others in respect of the two moral powers.

All persons make it at least a minimal part of their plan of life that the others should flourish, each according to his or her own plan of life.

They do this not merely in an abstract way; they actually make an effort—at least a small effort—to bring about this general flourishing, and they feel pleased and satisfied when it occurs.

They regard their moral equality, and the fact of their fellow citizenship, as a good reason—and usually a sufficient reason—for maintaining the interconnection of their plans of life.

This sort of relationship is deserving of the name "fraternity" for two reasons: (1) Like ideal brothers and sisters, fraternal fellow citizens feel that they are all of one kind; none is superior (like a parent) or inferior (like a child). (2) Like ideal brothers and sisters, fraternal fellow citizens are motivated, at least to a small extent, to support each other in their pursuit of their individual plans of life; and each respects the right of the others to plan individually for themselves. On the other hand, unlike biological brothers and sisters, fraternal fellow citizens do not usually know each other intimately, nor do they feel required to do so.

This conception of fraternity might be called a minimalist communitarianism. It is communitarian in that it posits a bond of feeling and a common goal shared by the members of society. It is minimalist in that it posits no substantive common goals or feelings. All it requires, essentially, is that each person should consider herself better off when others are enjoying success at making and carrying out a plan of life. What it excludes is complete indifference: We might say it excludes "spit in your eye" liberalism, the doctrine of a person who says, "I'll obey the law and do what justice requires, but I don't care whether you live or die." Only a few in the liberal tradition actually advocate anything like this; Ayn Rand probably comes closest when she touts the "Virtue of Selfishness."[13] But neither does liberalism have the resources to condemn this profound indifferentism, since the individualism that lies at the heart of liberal thought prevents taking such a stand. Indeed, the spit-in-your-eye attitude seems to arise all too often.[14]

For the fraternalist, society is like a jazz ensemble: Each member's performance is her own, shaped by her own standards, not dictated by the others; but it makes sense only in the context of what the others play. Each person's performance is highly individualistic, yet bound up with the others. More strictly speaking, fraternal society is not like a jazz ensemble, but like a jazz festival—even more strictly, a festival of improvisational performers of all kinds in ensembles of any number.[15] Each performer, and each group of performers, is intensely individualistic, yet each considers her performance enhanced by the presence of the others. Louis Armstrong helps us appreciate Charles Parker. The beginner is inspired by the virtuoso, and the virtuoso receives satisfaction from contemplating the beginner. (I do not mean that she gloats: Rather, the beginner's aspiration helps the virtuoso appreciate what she has accomplished, something she might easily come to take for granted.) Even *that awful stuff*—fill in your favorite kind—helps us appreciate the good, and (in a certain frame of mind) fills us with admiration at some people's ability to find value in productions that seem totally worthless to us.

One might ask: What about the tuba player or the amplified rocker who completely drowns out the clavichord? More generally, what about people whose projects can succeed only if some of the others fail? Life, after all, is not a festival. Among fraternal equals no one indeed will desire the failure of others as an end in itself, but there will certainly be incompatible projects and plans of life. What distinguishes fraternal equality is not the absence of conflict, but the response to it: Fraternal equals will feel distress at the incompatibility of their projects, for they want all to be able to succeed, each by her own plan. They probably will not go so far as to abandon their own projects, and they will no doubt hope that incompatible projects will fail. Yet at the same time they work to harmonize everyone's plan of life, at least to some extent. They hope for the ingenuity to devise a new plan of life that will harmonize with others while not betraying themselves.

This conception of fraternal equality may be thought of as a non-Kantian version of Kant's concept of the kingdom of ends. In the kingdom of ends, persons follow rules that are aimed at harmonizing the ends that each person chooses for herself. Each person in such a kingdom, we might say, perceives all the others as ends in themselves. Among fraternal equals it is the same, except that they do not only perceive each other this way: They also *feel* the dignity of each person as an end in herself, and they are moved to act this way from inclination as well as from conscience. In the Kantian kingdom of ends, we feed the hungry because we know it is right and we want to do what is right. The same is true if we are fraternal equals, but in addition we feed the hungry because they are hungry, and because it pains us to see them hungry. Fraternal equality breaks down the Kantian wall of separation between conscience and inclination.

I make no assumption about the intensity or the bindingness of the dispositions that constitute fraternal equality. Among the members of a small, close-knit group, such as an actual family, there may be strong feelings of attachment and a ready willingness to go to great lengths to assist the others; and the family members may believe that such dispositions are obligatory for members of a family. There can also be more loosely knit groups where the emotional bonds are weaker and more rarely felt, where each will help only a little, and where these attitudes are considered appropriate but not mandatory. Surely the larger society will be closer to the latter than to the former.

It is useful to compare fraternal equality with related notions. Under *liberal equality* (or, if you will, *atomistic equality*) people are equal in fundamental status and rights, but their plans of life are strictly a private matter. Under fraternal equality people are equal in fundamental status and rights, but they consider it appropriate that their plans of life should be harmonized in this purely formal way. Under *conservative equality* people (again) are equal in fundamental status and rights, but here they acknowledge substantive requirements on their plans of life. We can likewise have *atomistic inequality* and *conservative inequality*, which are like their egalitarian counterparts except that persons differ in their fundamental status and rights. *Fraternal inequality* seems to be a contradiction in terms; the proper term is *paternalistic inequality*. Under paternalistic inequality persons differ in fundamental status and rights, with corresponding conative and emotional dispositions. On the part of those with the higher status, there is noblesse oblige; and among the lowly, humble gratitude and deference.

DERIVATION OF FRATERNAL EQUALITY

Why should the social contract be interpreted as calling for fraternal equality? There are two reasons. First, persons in the original position define themselves as bearers of the two moral powers: the sense of justice and the capacity to have a plan of life. Their most fundamental interest is in developing and exercising these powers. Now, certainly, the two moral powers can be better developed and exercised in a situation where other people are pleased to see us develop them, and are willing to help, as opposed to a situation in which no such help and sympathy can be expected. So there is a preference for the relational interpretation of the contract.

This first reason, though, is not sufficient by itself. It is as compatible with paternalistic inequality as with fraternal equality. As we have already seen, it is perfectly consistent for a contractarian to say: "One group of people, though not fundamentally superior, are better able to protect basic liberties—both their own and others'. Consequently, we adopt a contract that gives them more basic liberties, so that even those with less liberty are still freer than they would have been under a regime of equality. We then simply adopt the relational version of this contract: The higher group are to cultivate the sentiment of noblesse oblige, while the lower group are to be humbly grateful."

The contract should, then, be interpreted relationally, but we still have concluded nothing about equality. This conclusion follows from the second line of reasoning. We start by introducing the concept of a *fully specified contract*. A fully specified contract is one that makes explicit provision for every possible contingency. Of course, no actual contract can be fully specified. A purely notional contract could be fully specified, but, significantly, Rawls's contract is not. Indeed, as we have seen, it is essential to the contract that the parties in the original position *fail* to anticipate certain contingencies. For example, they cannot even consider the possibility that crime would exist. Moreover, the text of the contract must be brief and simple enough so that people can understand, appreciate, and act on it; whereas no human being could understand a fully specified contract, except in a superficial way.

To illustrate our discussion of this point, I will compare several aspects of the social contract with corresponding aspects of a contract for a business partnership. Let us suppose, then, that Alexander, Nicholson, and DelTredici have entered into a partnership. They have written up and signed an agreement of partnership, in which they have equal status. Like the social contract, this agreement is not fully specified. I assume, too, that it is a relatively well-ordered partnership, paralleling Rawls's well-ordered society: The partners all are sincerely committed to their agreement.

The social contract, as we have said, is not fully specified; it contains gaps. We must find some method of filling them that assures (as much as possible) a just result. One thing that can serve this need is the existence of fraternal equality among the parties. If each party values the flourishing of the others as equal moral persons, each according to her own conception of the good, then they will be inclined to agree on measures that will promote this sort of flourishing. Similarly, our trio of partners must find a way to fill in the gaps in their agreement. They will be able to do this if each values the flourishing of the others as equal partners, each according to his own conception of business success. It would be a glaring case of bad faith if someone entered such a partnership with the end of enriching only himself, with complete indifference to his partners' success or failure. Exactly the same can be said of the social contract. Of course, in both cases, each person values her own success more, probably much more, than the success of the others: Still, she regards herself as completely successful only if they, too, are successful.

Here we already get the equality that we could not derive from the previous argument. The contracts are contracts of equals: Only a relationship of equals, such as a fraternal relationship, is compatible with such a contract. Contrast, for example, a paternalistic relationship. The paternalist thinks that she knows what is good for you better than you do yourself. If one party takes a paternalistic attitude toward the others, she will promote her own flourishing, as she conceives it, along with that of the others, again as she conceives it. They, in the end, will be less able to form and act on a plan of life (or a business plan). Among our business partners, Nicholson, perhaps, thinks he knows best: "Those others," he says to himself, "lack foresight. They want to maximize short-run profits, but I want to build up a business over the long run. They are lucky they have me around to protect them from their own rashness." Alexander and DelTredici, as one might guess, do not see it that way. They have a lot of bills to pay, and they need the income now. Nicholson is not taking them seriously, contrary to their supposed status as equal partners. In the realm of the social contract, especially a liberal social contract, each person's plan of life must be taken seriously, and not simply overruled by someone who claims to have greater foresight.

Of course, fraternal equality is only one possibility for filling in the gaps of the social contract. It might be argued that another possibility is better. The requisite dispositions, for one thing, are hard to develop. Perhaps we should instead establish formal procedures to fill in the gaps: legislatures, courts, and executive departments, which are elected or appointed in definite ways, follow a constitution, and so on. (Our partners, similarly, might agree to settle uncertainties by a majority vote.) Certainly these measures are not to be rejected: They are necessary and desirable. They will not, however, supplant the relationship of fraternal equality. On the contrary, I claim, they presuppose and require such a relationship. Fraternity is required in three distinct ways.

First, we require fraternity just to set up acceptable procedures. An acceptable procedure must promote the interests of all. The best way of doing this will vary from case to case, and what works well in one situation may be disastrous in another. In the absence of fraternity, we cannot know and act to promote the interests of all and consequently cannot set up acceptable procedures. This claim may be thought implausible, but consider our business partners. In the abstract, one might pick majority rule as the best procedure. In many cases, this procedure will in fact be suitable. Suppose, however, that Nicholson and Alexander (as it turns out) agree on almost everything, whereas DelTredici tends to differ. Majority rule would be tantamount to oppression of DelTredici. A rotating chairmanship would likely be better. But we cannot tell what procedure is better unless we regard each of the partners with fraternal equality: We must understand the interests of each partner as he himself understands them, and we must take each partner's interests equally seriously.

Parallel problems arise in the political sphere: We could have a parliamentary system or a United States–style legislature. We could require a simple majority to enact laws in the legislature, or we could require a supermajority in some or all cases. We could elect one representative per district, or we could employ a system of proportional representation. Such questions are sometimes academic, but sometimes go to the heart of justice. We can note, for example, the perplexing problem in the United States of devising legislative districts that will not unjustly dilute the voting power of blacks. If blacks are few, should the redistricters create one district in which they form the vast majority and so can be relatively sure of being able to elect a candidate reflecting their interests? Or should they create several districts in which blacks form a large plurality, so that they could form coalitions to elect several candidates? The candidates elected in the latter case would probably be less single-mindedly devoted to the black constituency, but blacks might elect so many more representatives that they are better off in the end. Or does justice require something entirely different, like the use of proportional representation in such cases, so that the legislature represents interests instead of districts? Again, the persons deciding these questions must have a fraternal attitude toward all their fellow citizens, so they can appreciate and take seriously the interests of each person, as conceived by that person.

One might think that impersonal respect for all persons—an attitude compatible with a nonrelational contract—would be sufficient for this purpose, without the deeper relationship of fraternity. We have, of course, already ruled out the discrete interpretation of the contract, so the point is moot, but it is useful to review it. Impersonal respect for all persons may indeed often be sufficient, especially if society is relatively homogeneous. Often, however, impersonal respect for the interests of others will lead to inappropriate and condescending measures. Legislators and designers of institutions must have some idea of the harms they inflict or benefits they confer. They must know how their actions will promote or retard the plans of life of their constituents (and any others for whom they are responsible). They must know not only what my plan (or yours or Jones's) tells me to do; they must also know how I may be hurt, or elated, or perplexed, or satisfied, or outraged, or left indifferent as a result of their action. They must, in short, know what it is like to be a person with the kind of life plan that I have adopted: In other words, they must consider me with some degree of empathy. Suppose that procedures for eminent domain are being set up. Suppose that the responsible committee consists of people who have never lived in one place long enough to form an attachment to it; perhaps they are simply not so inclined. They need to realize that for some people, losing their home is like being stabbed in the heart; and they must take this seriously. Could an unempathetic person do so? Well, perhaps on this one occasion our unempathetic person—a cold fish—might take this interest seriously. He might consider the case carefully, consult with others, and conclude, "I assign my own desire for political success—my driving ambition—a value of 500; and I assign old Mr. Northup's desire to stay put in his house the same value." We cannot, however, rely on our cold fish to do this on a regular basis. In most cases it will not even occur to him that he has harmed someone seriously until it is too late to correct. It would be as if someone were to try to drive by explicit maxims: "Here is a pedestrian in my path. Whenever I see a pedestrian in my path, I will apply the brakes. Therefore, I will now [*Thump!*] apply the brakes." What we need is someone who can *react* appropriately, with driving skill or with empathy, as the case may be.

Actually, it is hard to see how our cold fish could reach the right conclusion even on one occasion. How could he ever come to know how deeply Mr. Northup values the old Northup place? He himself has no such topophilia and is inclined to think that Northup is simply a histrionic grouch, someone who enjoys complaining about trivial issues as if they were of the utmost importance. Not that empathy will always enable us to distinguish correctly—but lack of empathy makes it hard to take it seriously when someone voices desires and feelings that we ourselves have never experienced.

This point, of course, is merely a variation on Mill's criterion for evaluating various sorts of pleasures. Mill says: The competent judge is the one who is familiar with the pleasures he is evaluating. One cannot, of course, be familiar with everything, but one should at least be able imaginatively to project oneself into the position of someone who has experienced the thing in question.

Our designer of procedures, then, must regard her fellow citizens with universal empathy. She must, further, take each person's plan of life equally seriously, as the plan is understood by the person herself, and be disposed, at least to some extent, to promote it. In sum, she must be connected to them by bonds of fraternity.

Of course, this fraternal concern for plans of life does not mean that the designer of procedures must cater to each person's plan of life, however demanding it may be. It does mean that the designer must avoid unwittingly trampling on someone's cherished plan and must use the available resources efficiently to promote those plans that people have, or are likely to have, and not waste resources on plans that no one is likely to adopt.

Once the procedures are set up, fraternity is still required for their proper use. We are accustomed to the idea of checks and balances, means of preventing bad men and women from putting a system to bad use. Checks and balances are of the first importance, but one must not lose sight of Gandhi's rather sarcastic words on the topic: "Everybody is looking for a system so perfect that no one inside has to be good."[16] Such a system is not likely to be found. Consider our business partners, who have by now set up a rotating chairmanship— say, on a monthly basis. What will happen if each monthly chair pursues his own interests exclusively, or even the common interest as he himself conceives it? In January, Nicholson will pursue long-run stability and try to lock in his plan; in February, DelTredici will launch a marketing campaign to boost the month's sales; in March, Alexander will try to improve productivity and eliminate waste. There are two possible outcomes: Policy may be so erratic that no one's aims are well served. Or, if there is a consistent policy, it is unlikely to incorporate equal concern for each person's interest. What is needed is a fraternal attitude toward the interests of the others. So, too, in the state—let us say, in the legislature—each representative must be aware that the body of which she is a member is a device for realizing the principles of justice. To the extent that these require respect for each person's plan of life, the legislators must know what is important to all constituents (indeed, all who are affected by the legislature), just as was the case when the legislative procedures were being set up; and they must see their job as the promotion of those interests in accordance with the principles of justice. For the same reasons as before, fraternity is required.

Finally, the general population must also be bound by fraternal ties if they are to act appropriately upon the pronouncements of the state. If they are not at all bound by fraternal ties, they will be unlikely to accept the enactments of a legislature of the sort described. Even if they do accept these enactments, another problem will arise in the absence of fraternity among citizens. Consider what would happen in a society full of what I have called spit-in-your-eye liberals. They obey the law scrupulously, and faithfully adhere to principles of justice as they understand them. Aside from that, they pursue their own interests with utter indifference toward all but themselves and their friends. Their adherence to principles of justice may be admirable, but it is of little help here, since we are dealing with cases where justice has gaps, and there is no agreement as to what it requires. Surely, in such a case our spit-in-your-eye liberals will make trouble faster than legislators can pass laws against it. Imagine a regulation requiring safety features on certain home appliances. Some manufacturers will surely relabel their home vacuum cleaners as industrial vacuum cleaners. A new regulation extends the requirement to industrial appliances; some manufacturers design an appliance that meets the requirement without solving the safety problem.[17] And so on. The arm of the law can prevail only if those subject to the law regard each other with a sense of fraternal equality and try to harmonize their plans of life at least enough so that they are not constantly seeking new forms of trouble to inflict on each other.

Fraternal equality, then, is the best way to assure all citizens of the greatest opportunity to develop and exercise their sense of justice and their capacity to choose a plan of life.

One might object, with Rawls, that it is unrealistic to expect "ties of sentiment and feeling . . . between members of the wider society."[18] An example, however, shows that such ties are quite common: If one studies the fans of, say, the Boston Red Sox along with the fans of rival teams, one finds that large numbers of people—probably enough to populate a medium-sized country—who have little else in common can be united by strong ties of sentiment and feeling, both positive and negative.

More to the point, however, is that feelings of fraternity are not based on intimate mutual acquaintance, but on general principle. Fraternal fellow citizens consider that their status as fellow citizens is a good and normally sufficient reason for maintaining these feelings. It would, indeed, be unrealistic to expect intimate personal acquaintance. It does not, however, seem unrealistic to suppose that a person should feel pleasure in the knowledge that her fellow citizens are prospering in their individual plans of life, and should be willing to support them in this. I might note that fraternal love among literal brothers and sisters is also based on principle. This can be seen at the reunions of long-separated siblings. One may not know the other, or even that the other exists; yet they take their common descent as a good reason for the strongest of feelings toward a perfect stranger.

Fraternal citizens, then, maintain a general disposition toward all who meet a certain description and do not have individual relationships with each of them. With this objection removed, we can view the social contract as a relational contract establishing a fraternal bond among the parties.

3. The Fraternal Society

How is fraternity actually put into effect?

The most crucial point is that fraternity is not another provision added to the text of the contract. It is part of the way we interpret the contract. Fraternity thus has a normative status, but it is not mandatory. It is considered fitting and appropriate for persons to adopt and maintain a fraternal attitude toward each other; but if they do not, they have not violated the contract. The spit-in-your-eye liberal, or even the misanthrope, is immune from corrective measures as long as she adheres to the principles of justice that are contractually agreed upon.

This conclusion, however, applies only to those with the two moral powers—a sense of justice and capacity to plan one's life. These capacities are the basis of the contract, and of our fraternal conception of it. If some persons are seriously lacking in these capacities, they may be guided toward the fraternal norm. Thus we bring up our children, and thus, too, if we choose, may we treat serious criminals. As we have seen, the principal thing about punishment that calls for justification is not that it is painful or bad, but that it is illiberal. When someone undergoes punishment, his choice of life plans is restricted, whether by himself or by others. Given the present conception, it is proper to steer the criminal toward greater fraternity, which is one aim of the rectification theory.

Although the fraternal plan of life cannot be enforced (except on those deficient in the moral capacities), the state can promote it and can discourage incompatible plans of life. There thus arises an exception to the usual liberal verity that the state may not favor or discourage any particular plan of life. Perhaps the state could go so far as to limit the expression of hateful ideologies, as, for example, the advocacy of Nazism is limited in the Federal Republic of Germany. Surely, such expression could at most be limited, and not simply forbidden, and even limitations might be too dangerous to allow in practice. At the least, it could be considered an aggravating factor in other crimes if their purpose was to express or promote attitudes of hate or contempt toward persons conceived of as morally inferior in a fundamental way.

4. The Questions Answered

We can now answer the questions posed earlier.

EQUAL BASIC LIBERTIES

Persons who view themselves as parties to the contract, as we have conceived it, will see their basic rights not only as a set of requirements and prohibitions but as the formal embodiment of their fraternal relationship. Even if an inequality of basic rights were useful, they would regard it as ruled out. Citizens are to nourish within themselves a character that disposes them to feel and to act toward each other as equal moral persons. Equal moral persons are those who possess the two moral powers, and the basic liberties are needed to develop and exercise the two moral powers. They must therefore be equally distributed.

Consider, on the other hand, how things would stand with an unequal basic liberty. One group could say to the other: "We have greater basic liberties than you, so that you can have greater basic liberties than you would otherwise." This epitomizes the proper attitude of a parent toward a child, or the old sentiment of noblesse oblige. The group with greater liberties are trustees for the rest, since their greater liberty exists for the sake of the rest. It would be hard for those in the lower group to avoid feeling morally inferior, nor can they easily maintain a disposition to support the flourishing of the better endowed. Those in the lower group may well say to themselves, "I am equal to them, and was treated as an equal by the deliberations in the original position. But, apparently, I can do little to help them, though they can help me." The result is likely to be either a sullen resentment, or else the most earnest efforts of the "inferior" to serve the "superior." Fraternity would surely decay.

Is it not possible, though, even in such a situation, for people to be so aware of their metaphysical equality that their actual inequality is outweighed? A member of the less-favored group could say to himself, "My equality was embodied in the original position. I have fewer basic rights than Jones, but he is my equal, and we are all brothers *sub specie aeternitatis*." Indeed, it is possible, but it is wrong to expect such a response. It is precisely the relational nature of the contract that rules out inequality of basic rights. If we were to conceive of ourselves as not essentially connected to each other, if it were not important for us to nourish feelings of mutual concern and respect, then the fact that you have more basic liberties than I do would be of no concern to me, any more than it would be of concern to me that someone on Mars was enjoying a greater liberty. But here you are, right here: I must encourage myself to maintain a fraternal relationship with you, to wish you well, according to your own view of what is good for you, and be disposed to help you. Now, we agree that the most important aspects of the self are the two moral powers, and that you, with the greater liberty, are ipso facto flourishing more than I am. If you are a good fellow, you will disavow this advantage and make efforts to secure equality for all; then I can return your good wishes. If, however, you accept the status quo, things are different: You do not merely *happen* to have a greater liberty; it was *planned* that you should have a greater liberty, and you are endorsing the plan. You tell me, "It is for your own good." Perhaps you even convince me. In that case no restriction is needed, or at any rate less restriction, and there is no occasion for resentment. If, on the other hand, you fail to convince me, you have me tied down, bound and trussed, allegedly for my own good, though you cannot persuade me of that supposed fact. You predict that if I and persons like me are not restricted in this way, we will eventually have even less liberty than we do now. I myself am thoroughly convinced of the opposite. In this case you do not merely happen to have a greater liberty, nor is it merely planned that you should have it: You and your cohort are actually thwarting me in my quest for liberty, which is my quest to exercise the two moral powers, which is the quest to be myself. In other words, you are subjecting me to a moral evisceration. I can in extremis imagine myself cooperating with you, even in this, out of lack of a better alternative: I can take it, but you can't make me like it. But now I am to wish you well! It would be a profound act of self-degradation. Fraternity is not one-sided: I can easily wish well to my well-wishers, and even to those who are indifferent. But to wish well toward those who thwart my most fundamental interests or who accept the benefits of their being thwarted—that is beyond the call of duty. It is not fraternity, but masochism.

We can draw a useful parallel with the case of a corporate employee. It's a bad situation, let us assume. They exploit her, and she exploits them. They pay her more than she could get elsewhere, but as little as they think they can get away with. She tries to expend the least effort for the most income. This arrangement is far from ideal, but no one says the parties have to like or respect each other, or be motivated by a desire to serve the other. So they can stand it. Things are different—and more like the unequal liberty case—if the employer expects loyalty and devotion but offers none in return. In that case the employee is suffering a great indignity. If the pay is good, it might be worth accepting—after all, one can always quit; but one cannot always quit society, nor should one be forced to. It is a great wrong if society imposes such an indignity on its citizens.

Rawls's account was correct, then, though incomplete when it gave self-respect as the reason for the equal distribution of basic liberties. Inequality of basic liberties by itself need not undermine self-respect. It does undermine it if the person is being deprived of liberty for no reason that he can accept and at the same time is expected to cherish feelings of fraternal equality toward those who are depriving him. If my face is slapped, I can maintain my self-respect: It is quite another thing if I am told I must have my face slapped and like it. In the nightmare fantasies of horror novelists, one stock character is the military school officer who beats a new cadet; supposedly it is for some infraction, but in reality the cadet is innocent. And after each blow, the cadet is forced to say, "Thank you, Sir!"

Indeed, a nightmarish fantasy.

Fraternity, then, binds all citizens together, so that when we try to determine the relevant social positions for the distribution of basic liberties, we find there is only one. To separate a fraternal society into two or more groups would go against their manifest nature. When now we come to apply the maximin principle and find only one group, the result is strict and universal equality of basic liberties.

PUNISHMENT

After our long excursion concerning basic liberties, we return to the topic that set us off in the first place. According to the rectification theory, a person who commits a serious crime arrogates extra basic liberties and thereby makes himself out to be a fundamentally superior being—a robber baron or crime lord, as we might say. The arrogation of basic liberties upsets the scheme of basic rights and the liberties that they guarantee. The claim of fundamentally superior status undermines the fraternal relations that ought to prevail among fellow citizens. A rectifying punishment now serves a corresponding dual purpose: It restores the equality of basic liberties and, by revoking the claim to superior status, makes it possible for self-respecting persons to restore the fraternal equality between them and the offender.

It sounds here as if we were speaking of two distinct things, fraternal equality and equality of basic rights, but they are in reality just two sides of the same coin, or, better, two flowers on the same plant. The true fundament here is the equality of persons as moral beings.

We can now at last answer the objection raised at the beginning of the present chapter. Our criminal, Brown, had stolen something from Green. But Brown has repented and made full restitution to Green. The rectification theory says that he has arrogated excess basic liberties and must still submit to punishment to restore the equality of basic rights. But if Green has been compensated and our own basic liberties are unimpaired, why should we care about the rectification? We care because we feel that we ought to maintain fraternal relations with Brown, yet we degrade ourselves if we maintain such relations with someone who arrogates a greater basic liberty. Once Brown has undergone a rectifying punishment, he has renounced his claim of greater basic liberty and of fundamentally superior status. We can now restore fraternal relations without losing our self-respect.

We see here an additional reason why the rectification theory calls for penalties of community service. A fraternal fellow citizen considers herself better off if the others are flourishing, each according to her own plan of life. The offender, then, restores fraternity by doing something that helps her fellow citizens flourish. Indeed, because her penalty serves to promote the scheme of basic liberties, she is in a sense helping everyone, each according to her own plan of life: For the basic liberties are held by all and are useful for any plan of life one might choose. Of course, not everyone will receive a specific benefit as a result of the offender's rectifying penalty, but the penalty contributes to a scheme of rights in which everyone senses a proprietary interest. Everyone, therefore, considers herself benefited by the penalty.

It is the relationship here that is crucial. We are in a difficult situation, because we must live together with the offender and adopt some sort of attitude toward her, even if it is only an attitude of indifference. (That, indeed, is probably the hardest attitude of all to maintain.) If she were only to disappear, never to be seen again, we could forget about her and feel no reason to care, no reason to be angry or regretful. Our being forced to live together with her gives the rectification theory its impetus.

Most criminals, sad to say, probably feel no need for this kind of reconciliation with the world. Some have no vision at all of a society of fraternal equality; they are the *Homo hobbesianus*. Some have the vision but blame others for their falling-out with society, seeing themselves as mere hapless victims. Some seem so full of pain and rage that they see nothing but pain and rage. Our fraternal seeds fall on a rocky and infertile field, and we need no agronomist to tell us that only an occasional one here or there will sprout and grow. Yet if criminals are not likely to restore the fraternal relations that they have made impossible, still their example shows us the need to maintain the fraternal relations that we, the noncriminals, too often take for granted.

APPENDIX

Rights-Claims and Acting as if One Had a Right

I HERE present a more formal argument to show that when a person acts as if she had a right to X, she thereby actually claims a right to X. *Acting as if one had a right* is defined as in Chapter 5, section 3, and *claiming a right* refers to performative claims (not propositional ones), as discussed in the same section.

I take it as a premise that the illocutionary force of a (verbal or nonverbal) expression is a function of its use. I discern the following to be the most important characteristics of our use of a rights-claim to X, made by person A and addressed to person B:

1. The claim presupposes that A actually has a right to X; that is, the claim is in order only if A has this right.
2. The claim normally results in A's getting X.
3. Once the claim is made, it is normally mandatory for B to make it possible for A to have X.
4. B may ask for evidence that A actually has the right in question.
5. B is excused from complying if A actually lacks the right to X, or if X cannot be provided, or if it is possible but wrongful to provide X, etc.

"Normally" here refers to circumstances in which everything is in order: A actually has the right and B knows that A has it; none of the excusing conditions are present; and so on.

I next show that in a society that recognizes rights, the act of behaving as if one had a right functions in this way under most circumstances.

First, as a matter of practical necessity, the scheme of rights must be administered largely by voluntary compliance: That is, people usually figure out what rights they and others have without going to a judge, and they observe the rights of others and the limits of their own rights even when not subject to the police officer's watchful eye. Moreover, people must be aware of this voluntary compliance and expect it to continue. Otherwise, this voluntarism would soon degenerate into a more-or-less Hobbesian war of all against all. They also know that some enforcement measures are needed.

Now, suppose that under such circumstances person A acts as if she had a right to X. Since voluntary compliance is usually expected, people will assume that A actually has the right to X; otherwise she would not act that way. Moreover, since voluntary compliance is not only expected but offered, most people will act toward A as if she had a right to X: They will not interfere with her having X, and (if they are the addressee of her right) they will do what is required to make sure she gets X. For example: If A walks into a store and offers money to pay for goods, she is behaving as if she had property rights to the money; the store personnel will accept the money as payment for the goods, and bystanders will not interfere.

If people behave in this way, the five conditions listed above are met. Condition 1 is true by my definition of "acting as if one had a right." Condition 2 is satisfied, since B and others usually allow A to have X. Condition 3 is met, since people for the most part comply with the scheme of rights; so that when A acts as if she had a right to X, it is usually because she does in fact have a right to X, and it is therefore mandatory for B to supply it. Next, since compliance is known to be good but not perfect, B is likely on occasion to ask A for evidence before doing what is required by A's alleged right, and this act will be generally regarded as a proper request, since it is known that some enforcement is needed. Thus condition 4 is met. Finally, since we are dealing with a community that observes rights, and since community members regard A's action as a sign that she has a right to X, they will observe the excusing conditions that apply to rights generally as detailed in condition 5. Thus all five conditions are met; they truly describe the practice of acting-as-if-one-had-a-right as found in the society in question. Therefore, acting as if one had a right to X will usually constitute a claim of a right to X. The criminal, moreover, is aware of these practices, and hence it is appropriate to say that he is making such a claim.

NOTES

Introduction

1. I have previously referred to this as the "rectificatory theory." See Jacob Adler, "The Rectificatory Theory of Punishment," *Pacific Philosophical Quarterly* 69 (1988): 255–281. The word *rectificatory* turns out to be too difficult to pronounce.

2. See Chapter 1, note 67.

Chapter 1. Why Submit to Punishment?

1. John Rawls, "Two Concepts of Rules," *Philosophical Review* 64 (1955): 3–32.

2. Joel Feinberg, *Harm to Others* (Oxford: Oxford University Press, 1984), p. 6.

3. See any text on Constitutional law, e.g., Gerald Gunther, *Cases and Materials on Constitutional Law*, 10th ed. (Mineola, N.Y.: Foundation Press, 1980), ch. 10. For a more extensive treatment, see Polynos G. Polyviou, *The Equal Protection of the Laws* (London: Duckworth, 1980).

4. H. L. A. Hart, "Prolegomenon to the Principles of Punishment," in *Punishment and Responsibility* (Oxford: Clarendon Press, 1968), pp. 8–11.

5. Plato, *Gorgias*, 478ff.; *Laws*, 5.375f.; Aristotle, *Nicomachean Ethics*, 1104b15–20.

6. Plato, *Gorgias*, in *The Collected Dialogues*, ed. Edith Hamilton and Huntington Cairns (Princeton: Princeton University Press, 1963), 480a–b.

7. This metaphor is so commonly encountered that it defies enumeration. Some examples: Julianus Pomerius (ca. A.D. 500), *De Vita Contemplativa*, II.vii.1, in *Patrologiae Cursus Completus, Series Latina* (hereafter, *Patrologia Latina*), ed. Jacques-Paul Migne (Paris, 1844–64), 59:451; decrees of the Council of Chalon (ca. A.D. 640), cited in Oscar D. Watkins, *A History of Penance* (London, 1920; rpt. New York: Burt Franklin, 1961), p. 759; Saint Thomas Aquinas, *Summa Theologica*, Part I–II, Q. 87, art. 3, obj. 2 and reply (regarding divine punishment) and Part III, supp., Q. 15, art. 1 (regarding penance); cf. Saint Thomas Aquinas, *Summa Contra Gentiles*, bk. 3, ch. 144; Peter Abelard, *Ethics*, trans. D. E. Luscombe (Oxford: Clarendon Press, 1971), p. 77.

8. The writer is Origen. See Ernest F. Latko, *Origen's Concept of Penance* (Quebec: Faculté de Théologie, Université Laval, 1949), p. 8.

9. For a general discussion of Christian penitential practices, see Watkins, *A History of Penance*. There appears to be no comparably comprehensive Jewish work, but see the *Encyclopedia Judaica* (1972), s.v. "Repentance" and bibliography thereto, which can be supplemented now by Ivan G. Marcus, *Piety and Society* (Leiden: Brill, 1981), chs. 3 and 8.

On penance as a form of punishment, see, e.g., Saint Anselm, *Cur Deus Homo*, bk. I, chs. 11–15, 19–20, in *Basic Writings*, trans. S. N. Deane (La Salle, Ill.: Open Court, 1962); Saint Thomas Aquinas, *Summa Theologica*, Part III, supp., Q. 15, art. 1; Abelard, *Ethics*, p. 109.

10. See, e.g., Abelard, *Ethics*, pp. 88–109; Watkins, *A History of Penance*, p. 751.

11. Watkins, *A History of Penance*, pp. 768–769. For examples of those who consider penance mandatory, see Hermas, *The Shepherd*, similitude 7, English translation by Kirsopp Lake with Greek original in *The Apostolic Fathers* (London: William Heinemann, 1913; New York: Macmillan, 1913), 2:183–187; Saint Thomas Aquinas, *Summa Theologica*, Part III, Q. 84, art. 7.

12. Julianus Pomerius, *De Vita Contemplativa*, bk. 2, ch. 7, para. 2, in Migne, *Patrologia Latina* 59: 451; English version under the title *The Contemplative Life*, trans. Mary Josephine Suelzer, Ancient Christian Writers, vol. 4 (Westminster, Md.: Newman Bookshop, 1946), pp. 69–70; Saint Caesarius of Arles, Sermo 104, paras. 5–7, in Migne, *Patrologia Latina* 39:1948; English version: Saint Caesarius of Arles, *Sermons*, trans. Mary Magdeleine Mueller, vol. 2 (Washington, D.C.: Catholic University of America Press, 1964), Sermon 179, pp. 452–454. See also Saint Caesarius, Sermo 249, in Migne, *Patrologia Latina* 39:2208; English version: Saint Caesarius of Arles, *Sermons*, trans. Mary Magdeleine Mueller, vol. 1 (New York: Fathers of the Church, 1956), Sermon 56, para. 3, pp. 280–281. (Migne attributes these sermons to Saint Augustine.) See also Watkins, *A History of Penance*, p. 753.

13. Origen and Tertullian are of this view. For Origen, see Latko, *Origen's Concept of Penance*, p. 11; for Tertullian, see his *On Penitence*, chs. 9 and 12, in Tertullian, *Treatises on Penance*, trans. William P. LeSaint, Ancient Christian Writers, vol. 28 (Westminster, Md.: Newman Press, 1959). Tertullian is startlingly graphic in ch. 12: "If you shrink from exomologesis [i.e., public confession and penance], then meditate in your heart on hell which exomologesis will extinguish for you. . . . What shall we think of that great vault of eternal fire when some of its tiny vents shoot out such bursts of flame that nearby cities are either all destroyed or, from day to day, expect this same destruction. The most majestic mountains burst asunder giving birth to their engendered fire and . . . although they are consumed, yet never are they extinct." See also Bachya [Bahya] ben Joseph ibn Paquda, *Duties of the Heart*, Treatise on Repentance, ch. 3, trans. Judah ibn Tibbon and Moses Hyamson (New York: Bloch, 1925; rpt. Spring Valley, N.Y.: Feldheim, 1970), 2:136–137.

14. See, e.g., Abelard, *Ethics*, pp. 76–90, and Saint Thomas Aquinas,

Summa Theologica, Part III, supp., Q. 2, art. 1. Saint Thomas concedes that penance done without the love of God does have a limited efficacy and notes that there is controversy over this question. See also the *Sefer Hasidim* ["Book of the Pious"], trans. Sholom Alchanan Singer, in *Medieval Jewish Mysticism* (Northbrook, Ill.: Whitehall, 1971), secs. 62–63, pp. 61–62; cf. Moses ben Maimon (Maimonides), *Mishneh Torah*, vol. 1: *The Book of Knowledge*, trans. Moses Hyamson (Jerusalem and New York: Feldheim, 1981), Laws of Repentance, ch. 10, pp. 92a–93a.

15. Saint Thomas Aquinas, *Summa Theologica*, Part III, Q. 84, art. 7.

16. See R. W. Carlyle and A. J. Carlyle, *A History of Mediaeval Political Theory in the West*, 6 vols. (New York: G. P. Putnam's Sons, 1903), 1:129–131, and references there; 3:103, 182–183. See also Saint Thomas Aquinas, *Summa Theologica*, Part II–II, Q. 108, art. 1, and *Commentary on the Ethics*, trans. Charles I. Litzinger, in *Medieval Political Philosophy*, ed. Ralph Lerner and Muhsin Mahdi (Glencoe, Ill.: Free Press, 1963; rpt. Ithaca, N.Y.: Cornell University Press, 1972), bk. 10, lesson 14 (pp. 286–290).

17. See Carlyle and Carlyle, *Mediaeval Political Theory*, vol. 1, part 3, ch. 13 (pp. 147–160), and references given there.

18. Saint Gregory the Great, *Libri Moralium in Job*, bk. 25, chs. 15–16 (olim 19–23), secs. 33–41, in Migne, *Patrologia Latina*, 76:342–347; English version under the title *Morals on the Book of Job* [trans. Charles Marriott] (Oxford: John Henry Parker, 1844–1850), 3:124–131.

19. Carlyle and Carlyle, *Mediaeval Political Theory*, 1:148–153; Saint Augustine, *Concerning the City of God: Against the Pagans* (Harmondsworth, England: Penguin, 1972), bk. 5, ch. 19 (p. 213); Saint Gregory the Great, *Libri Moralium in Job*, bk. 25, chs. 15–16 (olim 19–23), secs. 33–41, in Migne, *Patrologia Latina* 76:342–347; English version, 3:124–131.

20. See Carlyle and Carlyle, *Mediaeval Political Theory*, vol. 1, ch. 14; Saint Thomas Aquinas, *Summa Theologica*, Part II–II, Q. 104, art. 5–6.

21. With regard to this topic, see, in addition to citations above, the following chapters of Carlyle and Carlyle, *Mediaeval Political Theory*: vol. 1, chs. 13, 14, 17, 18; vol. 2, part 1, ch. 8; vol. 2, part 2, chs. 2–4, 7; vol. 5, part 1, ch. 6; vol. 5, part 2, ch. 4; vol. 5, part 3, ch. 4; vol. 6, part 1, chs. 3, 5.

22. Latko, *Origen's Concept of Penance*, p. 8; Saint Thomas Aquinas, *Summa Theologica*, Part I–II, Q. 87, art. 7 and Part III, supp., Q. 15, art. 2. It should be noted that the title of the former article is sometimes translated misleadingly as "Whether Every Punishment Is Inflicted for a Sin?" As is clear from the text of the article, a better version would be, "Whether Every Pain Is Inflicted for a Sin?" *Babylonian Talmud*, Shabbath 55a; English trans., ed. I. Epstein (London: Soncino, 1935). Solomon Schechter, "The Doctrine of Divine Retribution in Rabbinical Literature," in his *Studies in Judaism* (Philadelphia: Jewish Publication Society of America, 1958), pp. 105–122; see esp. pp. 106–117.

23. On psychological egoism and hedonism, see *Egoism and Altruism*, ed. Ronald Milo (Belmont, Calif.: Wadsworth, 1973).

24. I add the name of Hobbes to this list only subject to qualification.

There is, in fact, a lively debate as to whether Hobbes is really a psychological egoist at all. See Bernard Gert, "Hobbes and Psychological Egoism," *Journal of the History of Ideas* 28 (1967): 503–520, which is reprinted (along with other relevant essays) in *Hobbes's Leviathan: Interpretation and Criticism*, ed. Bernard H. Baumrin (Belmont, Calif.: Wadsworth, 1969), pp. 107–126. We need not decide the question here: It is enough that many influential writers have taken Hobbes to be a psychological egoist, or, indeed, *the* psychological egoist. See, e.g., Joseph Butler, "Upon Human Nature," which is the first of his *Fifteen Sermons Preached at the Rolls Chapel* (London, 1726), rpt. in Joseph Butler, *Five Sermons* (Indianapolis: Bobbs-Merrill, Library of Liberal Arts, 1950), pp. 19–32, and in Baumrin, *Hobbes's Leviathan*, pp. 16–25. To be strictly accurate, I should request readers to append mentally the phrase *as conceived by Butler* to every occurrence of the word *Hobbes* in this chapter.

25. For a behaviorist discussion of punishment, see James Q. Wilson and Richard J. Herrnstein, *Crime and Human Nature* (New York: Simon & Schuster, 1985), esp. ch. 2.

26. See Gary S. Becker, "Crime and Punishment: An Economic Approach," *Journal of Political Economy* 169 (1968): 1976; A. M. Polinsky, *An Introduction to Law and Economics* (Boston: Little, Brown, 1983), ch. 10, and bibliography, p. 129; R. A. Posner, *Economic Analysis of Law*, 2d ed. (Boston: Little, Brown, 1977), ch. 10; Posner, "Utilitarianism, Economics and Legal Theory," *Journal of Legal Studies* 8 (1979): 103–140, and App. A, pp. 136–137.

27. John Locke, *A Letter Concerning Toleration* (first published 1689; Indianapolis: Bobbs-Merrill, 1955), p. 17.

28. Thomas Hobbes, *Leviathan* (original ed., London: Andrew Crooke, 1651), ed. C. B. Macpherson (Harmondsworth, England: Penguin, 1968), Part 2, ch. 21, pp. 112–113 of original edition. Hobbes not only says that no one willingly submits to punishment; he goes so far as to say that it is permissible to resist punishment, by force if necessary. (See below, section 3.) Jeremy Bentham, *An Introduction to the Principles of Morals and Legislation* (New York: Hafner, Macmillan, 1948), ch. 15, secs. 3–4. Sigmund Freud, *The Ego and the Id*, in the *Standard Edition of the Complete Psychological Works of Sigmund Freud*, ed. James Strachey, vol. 19 (London: Hogarth, 1961), p. 25, and *Civilization and Its Discontents*, in the *Standard Edition*, vol. 21 (1961), pp. 76–77, 136.

29. Immanuel Kant, *The Metaphysical Elements of Justice*, trans. John Ladd (Indianapolis: Bobbs-Merrill, Library of Liberal Arts, 1965), p. 105, which corresponds to p. 335 of Kant's *Gesammelte Schriften*, ed. Königlichen Preussischen Akademie der Wissenschaften [Royal Prussian Academy of Sciences] (Berlin: G. Reimer, 1902–); hereafter, "Prussian Academy ed."

30. More strictly: If I rob, my maxim is, "When in need of money, rob." In order to punish robbery, I must be convinced that robbery is bad: In other words, I must hold the maxim, "Never rob." I cannot hold both maxims at once. What is more, in order to punish someone for a crime, I must apply to

him his own maxim. To the robber we say, "You hold that a needy person should rob, so that is what we will do to you." But if now I try to punish myself, I get stuck: I say to myself, "I will apply to myself my own maxim. My maxim *now* is 'never rob.' So I will punish myself by not robbing myself."

31. If there exists anyone unfamiliar with the reference, consult "How Mr. Rabbit Was Too Sharp for Mr. Fox," in Joel Chandler Harris, *Uncle Remus: His Stories and His Sayings* (New York: D. Appleton, 1880), reprinted in *The Complete Tales of Uncle Remus* (Boston: Houghton Mifflin, 1955), pp. 12–14.

32. Herbert Fingarette, "Punishment and Suffering," *American Philosophical Association Proceedings and Addresses* 50 (1977): 508–511. Henry Weihofen, "Punishment and Treatment," in *Theories of Punishment*, ed. Stanley Grupp (Bloomington: Indiana University Press, 1971), p. 259. Tziporah Kasachkoff, "The Criteria of Punishment: Some Neglected Considerations," *Canadian Journal of Philosophy* 2 (1973): 364–366. Richard Wasserstrom, "Retributivism and the Concept of Punishment," paper presented in the American Philosophical Association symposium on "The New Retributivism," December 27, 1978, at the Eastern Division meetings of the association, Washington, D.C.; a summary of Wasserstrom's paper appears in the *Journal of Philosophy* 75 (1978): 620–622, although the point in question is not to be found in the summary. Kathleen Dean Moore, *Pardons* (Oxford: Oxford University Press, 1989), pp. 101–102.

33. G. W. F. Hegel, *Philosophy of Right*, trans. T. M. Knox (Oxford: Clarendon Press, 1942), para. 100 and Remark thereto (pp. 70–71).

34. Ibid., para. 104 (p. 73); cf. paras. 24 and 25 (p. 31) and Remark to para. 119 (p. 82).

35. Ibid., para. 100 (p. 70); cf. Addition to para. 33 (p. 233).

36. Ibid., Addition to para. 101 (p. 247), emphasis added.

37. S. I. Benn, "An Approach to the Problems of Punishment," *Philosophy* 33 (1958): 329.

38. W. D. [Sir David] Ross, *The Right and the Good* (Oxford: Clarendon Press, 1930), p. 63; cf. Herbert Morris, "Persons and Punishment," *The Monist* 52 (1968): 475–501, reprinted in his *On Guilt and Innocence* (Berkeley: University of California Press, 1976), pp. 31–63; see esp. p. 32. All subsequent references to Morris are to this reprint.

39. A. M. Quinton, "On Punishment," in *Philosophy of Punishment*, ed. H. B. Acton (London: Macmillan, and New York: St. Martins, 1969), p. 57. Ted Honderich, *Punishment: The Supposed Justifications*, rev. ed. (Harmondsworth, England: Penguin, 1976), p. 70. An interesting discussion of the idea of a "right to punishment" is found in Igor Primoratz, *Justifying Legal Punishment* (Atlantic Highlands, N.J.: Humanities, 1989), pp. 98–108.

40. C. S. Nino, "A Consensual Theory of Punishment," *Philosophy and Public Affairs* 12 (1983): 289–306; Sir Walter Moberly, *The Ethics of Punishment* (London: Faber, 1968), pp. 131–143; Jean Hampton, "The Moral Education Theory of Punishment," *Philosophy and Public Affairs* 13 (1984): 208–238.

41. See, generally, Morris, "Persons and Punishment."

42. Ibid., p. 41.

43. A. R. Manser, "It Serves You Right," *Philosophy* 37 (1962): 303.

44. *Babylonian Talmud*, Shebu'oth 21a. See also *Babylonian Talmud*, Makkoth 13a–b. Such proceedings took place as recently as the seventeenth century. A vivid account, from the punishee's perspective, is presented by the noted heretic Uriel d'Acosta in his autobiography, *A Specimen of Human Life* (New York: Bergmann, 1967), pp. 21–27, esp. pp. 25–26. Acosta emphasizes the requirement of voluntary submission—indeed, the religious court had no power to coerce him.

45. Schneur [Shneur] Zalman of Liadi, *Likutei Amarim* ["Selected Discourses"] (also known as the *Tanya*) (Vilna: Romm, 1899), reprinted with English trans. Nissan Mindel et al. (Brooklyn: Kehot, 1984), Part 3 ("Igeret Hateshuvah"), ch. 9, p. 197 (= 99a) according to the two pagination systems of the Vilna edition, both reproduced in the Brooklyn edition. Schneur Zalman cites the *Tanna de-Be Eliyyahu* as the source of the quotation, but neither the translator nor I have been able to find it there (*Tanna Debe Eliyyahu: The Lore of the School of Elijah*, trans. William J. Braude and Israel J. Kapstein [Philadelphia: Jewish Publication Society of America, 1981]). *Likutei Amarim* is the fundamental document of the Lubavitcher Hasidim.

46. I say *he* here, and not *she*, because the ruler was almost always a male.

47. See, e.g., Locke, *A Letter Concerning Toleration*, pp. 18–20.

48. Immanuel Kant, *The Metaphysics of Morals*, Introduction, sec. III ("Of the Subdivision of a Metaphysics of Morals"), Prussian Academy ed., pp. 218–222. English translation: *The Metaphysical Elements of Justice*, trans. John Ladd (Indianapolis: Bobbs-Merrill, 1965), pp. 18–21.

49. Many readers will here note a similarity with H. L. A. Hart, *The Concept of Law* (Oxford: Clarendon, 1961), ch. 5. There are, as well, two differences. First, Hart is defining a "legal system," legitimate or otherwise, whereas I am defining a "legitimate state." Second, Hart says that the subjects must take "the internal point of view" toward the official rules—that is, they must accept them as morally binding, while I say that the rules must actually be morally binding. We might say that Hart's definition gives us the sociological conception of legitimacy, while mine gives the moral conception. This second distinction is the more important to our present concerns and is discussed further below.

50. Note the sinister effect produced by B-movie dictators and their lackeys when they say to their victims, "You will do such and such." This means, of course, "We have ways of making you do such and such." Precisely the same effect is produced in criminals if we say to them, "You will go to jail," unless we also address them as persons and say, "You must go to jail."

51. This tendency has been noted by Herbert Morris. See "Persons and Punishment," pp. 31–58. The position is explicitly advocated by D. Daiches Raphael, *Moral Judgement* (London: George Allen and Unwin, 1955), p. 70, excerpted under the title "Justice" in *Philosophical Perspectives on Punishment*, ed. Gertrude Ezorsky (Albany, N.Y.: State University of New York

Press, 1972), p. 142; and by W. G. Maglagan, "Punishment and Retribution," *Philosophy* 14 (1939): sec. 5.

52. See, e.g., Gresham M. Sykes and David Matza, "Techniques of Neutralization: A Theory of Delinquency," *American Sociological Review* 22 (1957): 664–670.

53. Herbert L. Packer, "The Practical Limits to Deterrence," in *Contemporary Punishment: Views, Explanations and Justifications* (Notre Dame, Ind.: University of Notre Dame Press, 1972), p. 106.

54. Most notably, John Austin, *The Province of Jurisprudence Determined* (1832), ed. H. L. A. Hart (London: Weidenfeld and Nicolson, 1954), lecture 1.

55. See notes 56 and 60.

56. See T. D. Weldon, *The Vocabulary of Politics* (Baltimore: Penguin, 1953; rpt. New York: Johnson Reprint, 1975), p. 57; John R. Carnes, "Why Should I Obey the Law?" *Ethics* 71 (1960): 14–26; Thomas McPherson, *Political Obligation* (London: Routledge & Kegan Paul, 1967), pp. 59–65.

57. This definition is adapted from S. I. Benn and R. S. Peters, *The Principles of Political Thought* (New York: Macmillan, The Free Press, 1965), p. 351. This book was originally published under the title *Social Principles and the Democratic State* (London: George Allen and Unwin, 1959). I have largely followed Benn and Peters in terminology.

58. Cf. Benn and Peters, *Principles of Political Thought*, p. 23.

59. Saint Thomas Aquinas, *Summa Theologica*, Part I–II, Q. 96, art. 6.

60. See A. John Simmons, *Moral Principles and Political Obligations* (Princeton, N.J.: Princeton University Press, 1979), esp. ch. VII; and M. B. E. Smith, "Is There a Prima Facie Duty to Obey the Law?" *Yale Law Journal* 82 (1972–73): 950–976.

61. John Locke, *Second Treatise of Government*, in *Two Treatises of Government*, ed. Peter Laslett (New York: New American Library, 1960), sec. 20. Cf. secs. 90–94, 123–131. See also John Rawls, *A Theory of Justice* (Cambridge, Mass.: Harvard University Press, 1971), pp. 133–134, and—for an especially forceful statement of this conception—Bruce Ackerman, *Social Justice in the Liberal State* (New Haven, Conn.: Yale University Press, 1980), esp. ch. 1.

62. See, e.g., Immanuel Kant, *The Metaphysical Elements of Justice* (1797), trans. John Ladd (Indianapolis: Bobbs-Merrill, 1965), Introduction; and John Stuart Mill, *On Liberty* (1859), ed. Currin V. Shields (Indianapolis: Bobbs-Merrill, 1956), ch. 3.

63. See Ronald Dworkin, "Justice and Rights," in *Taking Rights Seriously* (Cambridge, Mass.: Harvard University Press, 1978), 180–183. Cf. John Rawls, "Reply to Alexander and Musgrave," *Quarterly Journal of Economics* 88 (1974): 634, item 6.

64. We might add that this legal requirement must be established by a fair and open procedure and must be promulgated in such a way that people have a fair opportunity to act on it.

65. Cf. Rawls, *A Theory of Justice*, p. 134. Hobbes, of course, would con-

sider the described situation perfectly acceptable: See *Leviathan*, pp. 192, 270 (pp. 66 and 112–113 of original ed.), quoted below in section 4. But in a Hobbesian commonwealth one could hardly say that the rule of law prevails. Hobbes says, notoriously, that subjects can never accuse the sovereign of injustice, and—with particular relation to the present case—that the sovereign may punish "arbitrarily": "To the Soveraign is committed the Power of . . . Punishing with corporall, or pecuniary punishment, or with ignominy every Subject according to the law he hath formerly made, or if there be no Law made, according as he shall judge most to conduce to encouraging men to serve the Commonwealth, or deterring them from doing dis-service to the same" (*Leviathan*, pp. 232–235; pp. 90–92 in original ed.).

66. Under U.S. federal law, for example, a person who breaks out of prison is guilty of the offense of escape and may be fined up to $5,000, or imprisoned for up to five years, or both. See 18 *United States Code Annotated* (hereafter, *USCA*) sec. 751(a). A person who is delinquent in paying a fine may have an additional monetary penalty imposed or may be charged with the offense of criminal default. The penalty for the latter is a fine of up to $10,000, or imprisonment for up to one year, or both. See, respectively, 18 *USCA* secs. 3612(f)(1) and 3615 (version effective as of November 1, 1986). For representative state statutes, see, e.g., *McKinney's Consolidated Laws of New York Annotated*, Penal Law, secs. 205.00–205.18 (regarding escape), and, in the same work, Criminal Procedure Law, sec. 420.10 (2).

I am grateful to Linda Malone for pointing me toward these statutes.

67. With regard to the concept of a *claim-right,* see Introduction; for a fuller account, see Wesley Newcomb Hohfeld, *Fundamental Legal Conceptions*, ed. Walter Wheeler Cook (New Haven, Conn.: Yale University Press, 1919).

68. See, e.g., C. S. Nino, "A Consensual Theory of Punishment," *Philosophy and Public Affairs* 12 (1983): 289–306. A consensual theory of punishment is also implicit in Cesare Beccaria, *On Crimes and Punishments*, trans. Henry Paolucci (Indianapolis: Bobbs-Merrill, Library of Liberal Arts, 1963), ch. 2.

69. See Joel Feinberg, "The Expressive Function of Punishment," *The Monist* 49 (1965): 397–423; rpt. in Joel Feinberg, *Doing and Deserving* (Princeton, N.J.: Princeton University Press, 1970), 95–118. Subsequent citations refer to the pagination of the reprint.

70. Ibid., pp. 96–98.

71. Hobbes, *Leviathan*, p. 192; p. 66 in original ed.

72. Ibid., p. 270; pp. 112–113 in original ed.

73. See note 65.

74. As of this writing (1990), the possibility of change is just beginning to appear.

75. A similar point was made by Beccaria with regard to the death penalty. See Beccaria, *On Crimes and Punishments*, ch. 16, p. 45.

Chapter 2. Two Paradigms of Punishment

1. A more formal definition is as follows:

A conception C is reasonably called paradigm of X to the extent that it is important for our understanding of X by reason of fulfilling one or more of the following conditions:

(a) C describes a *standard X;* that is, a large proportion of all Xs correspond closely to C.

This "large proportion" need not be a majority, particularly if the concept X has a number of distinct paradigms. For example, *coins* and *bills* are paradigms of the concept of *currency.*

(b) C describes an *ideal X;* an X corresponding to C would be an extremely good X.

(c) C describes a *regular X;* that is, C exemplifies to a high degree the natural laws and regularities pertaining to Xs.

An object can be called a paradigm case of X if it satisfies some paradigm of X.

If this definition differs in any case from the informal one, the formal one should be understood to apply.

2. Hilary Putnam, "The Meaning of 'Meaning,' " in *Philosophical Papers,* vol. 2: *Mind, Language and Reality* (Cambridge: Cambridge University Press, 1975), pp. 247–252.

3. For documentation of such cases, see Calvert Dodge, *A World without Prisons* (Lexington, Mass.: Lexington Books, D. C. Heath, 1979), p. 71.

4. See Saint Thomas Aquinas, *Summa Theologiae* (London: Blackfriars, 1974), Part I–II, Q. 87, art. 6. The earlier English version by the Fathers of the English Dominican Province (London: Burnes Oates & Washbourne, 1935) translates *poena satisfactoria* as "satisfactory punishment," which is indeed a less satisfactory translation, being somewhat ambiguous.

5. See Lawrence Kohlberg, *Essays on Moral Development,* vol. 1: *The Philosophy of Moral Development* (San Francisco: Harper & Row, 1981), Appendix, "The Six Stages of Moral Judgment," pp. 409–412; Lawrence Kohlberg and Clark Power, "Moral Development, Religious Thinking, and the Question of a Seventh Stage," in ibid., 1:311–372.

6. See Chapter 1, note 13.

7. Saint Thomas Aquinas, *Summa Theologica,* Part III, supp., Q. 2, art. 1. It was much disputed among Roman Catholic authorities whether the sacrament of penance obtains absolution for an attrite, but uncontrite, penitent. See *The New Catholic Encyclopedia,* s.v. "Contrition."

8. *The Hasidic Anthology,* ed. Louis L. Newman (New York: Bloch, 1944), sec. 186, item 7 (p. 495); I have corrected an obvious typographical error. The story of Elisha ben Abuya is found in the *Palestinian Talmud,* Hagigah 77b; another version in the *Babylonian Talmud,* Hagigah 15a. The

words "Repent, ye transgressors," quoted by the heavenly voice, are from Jer. 3:22.

9. On *ordo debitus* see T. C. O'Brien, "Guilt and Punishment," sec. 2. This essay is published as Appendix I to Thomas Aquinas, *Summa Theologiae* (London: Blackfriars, 1974), vol. 27. *Ordo debitus* means, literally, "due order," but the English phrase has been watered down almost to insignificance by frequent use. On *tikkun olam*, see Abraham Isaac Kook, *Orot ha-Teshuvah* ["Lights of Penitence"] (Jerusalem: n.p., [1925]), English version under the title *Rabbi Kook's Philosophy of Repentance*, trans. Alter B. Z. Metzger (New York: Yeshiva University Press, 1968), esp. chs. 11–12. Another, more readily available translation is found in *Abraham Isaac Kook* (Ramsey, N.J.: Paulist Press, 1978). Kook's writings assume familiarity with the sometimes baroque concepts of Lurianic Kabbalism; persons unfamiliar with the topic may consult Jacob Immanuel Schochet, *Mystical Concepts in Hassidism*, 2d ed. (Brooklyn, N.Y.: Kehot Publication Society, 1988), ch. 11, or Gershom Scholem, *Major Trends in Jewish Mysticism* (Jerusalem: Schocken, 1941), Lecture 7, secs. 5–10.

10. See Karl Marx, *Economic and Philosophical Manuscripts of 1844*, "Alienated Labor"; many editions, e.g., in *Karl Marx: Selected Writings*, ed. David McLellan (Oxford: Oxford University Press, 1977).

11. G. W. F. Hegel, *Philosophy of Right*, trans. T. M. Knox (Oxford: Clarendon, 1942), Addition to para. 101 (p. 247); emphasis added.

12. See John Cottingham, "Varieties of Retribution," *Philosophical Quarterly* 29 (1979): 238–246.

13. *Deter* also has a wider sense in which it is synonymous with *dissuade* or *prevent*, but these are not what is usually meant when one speaks of the deterrent function of punishment. Prevention is sometimes mentioned as a separate rationale—someone in prison is not deterred, but prevented, from committing further crimes, except perhaps on the inmates and employees of the prison. But this, too, is unpleasant, since it involves a frustration of the prisoner's illegal purposes. So here, too, unpleasantness is involved.

14. See, e.g., Saint Thomas Aquinas, *Summa Theologica*, Part I-II, Q. 6, art. 6, and Q. 87, art. 6.

15. It is interesting to note that (at least in the contemporary United States) more Jews attend the synagogue for this penitential holiday than for any other occasion—a statistic adequately confirmed by even a casual conversation with members of the rabbinate.

16. Common-sense psychology, though not without its pitfalls, is adequate for present purposes. There is, of course, a large psychological literature, of which I mention here only two especially pertinent works: Sigmund Freud, *Civilization and Its Discontents* (1929) in the *Standard Edition of the Complete Psychological Works of Sigmund Freud*, ed. James Strachey, vol. 21 (London: Hogarth, 1961), pp. 59–148, esp. chs. 6–8. Theodor Reik, *Geständniszwang und Strafbedürfnis* (Leipzig: Internationaler Psychoanalytischer Verlag, 1925); translated into English by Norbert Rie and published as Part 2 of *The Compulsion to Confess* (New York: Farrar, Straus and Cudahy,

1959). The original title more clearly states the topic of the whole; it can be translated "The Compulsion to Confess and the Need for Punishment"— i.e., the punishee's need.

17. Unto Tähtinen, *Non-Violent Theories of Punishment: Indian and Western*, Annals of the Finnish Academy of Sciences, Series B, vol. 219 (Helsinki: Suomalainen Tiedeakatemia [Finnish Academy of Sciences], 1982), p. 45.

18. Saint Thomas Aquinas, *Summa Theologica*, Part I-II, Q. 87, art. 6.

19. See, e.g., Saint Anselm, *Cur Deus Homo?* bk. I, chs. 11–12, in *Basic Writings*, trans. S. N. Deane (LaSalle, Ill.: Open Court, 1962). "Penance" here translates Anselm's Latin word *satisfactio*.

20. Thomas Hobbes, *Leviathan*, ed. C. B. Macpherson (Harmondsworth, England: Penguin, 1968), Part 2, ch. 28, p. 161.

21. Ibid.

22. Ibid., Part 3, ch. 38.

23. Ibid., ch. 35, pp. 216–220.

24. Ibid., ch. 38, p. 238.

25. John Rawls, "Two Concepts of Rules," *Philosophical Review* 64 (1955): 10; H. L. A. Hart, "Prolegomenon to the Principles of Punishment," in *Punishment and Responsibility* (Oxford: Clarendon Press, 1968), pp. 4–5.

26. S. I. Benn, "An Approach to the Problems of Punishment," *Philosophy* 33 (1958): 326.

27. Igor Primoratz, *Justifying Legal Punishment* (Atlantic Highlands, N.J.: Humanities, 1989), pp. 1–4.

28. See Chapter 3, notes 20 and 21.

29. Hart, "Prolegomenon," pp. 4–5.

30. Hegel, *Philosophy of Right*, secs. 99–100; Bernard Bosanquet, *Philosophical Theory of the State* (London: Macmillan, 1910), pp. 227–228.

31. Tähtinen, *Non-Violent Theories of Punishment*.

32. Ibid., p. 66.

33. Ibid., pp. 34–39.

34. James F. Doyle, "Justice and Legal Punishment," *Philosophy* 42 (1967): 60, 61.

35. Richard Swinburne, *Responsibility and Atonement* (Oxford: Clarendon Press, 1989), chs. 5–6. Not surprisingly, the conscientious paradigm is here found in a theological setting.

36. A *perfect duty* or *duty of perfect obligation*, as I am using these terms, is one that, if neglected, results in a situation of injustice. An imperfect duty, by contrast, is one whose neglect does not produce injustice. An example of the latter: Suppose I have promised my now deceased friend Hagopian that I will give at least $1,000 a year to charity. Suppose further that by the time he dies, there is no one left in the world so poor as to be in need of charitable assistance to lead a decent life. Well, my duty is clear: I must give to the remaining charitable organizations, which will be those that provide amenities, like the Symphony Guild and the Horticultural Society. I obviously have a duty to give, but an imperfect one. If I kept all my

money for myself, society would want for some pleasant amenities but no injustice would result, neither to poor people (who might be entitled to my consideration) nor to Hagopian (who is now dead).

I will not consider the various other definitions that have been given for this pair of concepts.

37. Saint Anselm, *Cur Deus Homo?* in *Basic Writings*, trans. S. N. Deane (LaSalle, Ill.: Open Court, 1962), bk. 1, chs. 11–12, pp. 201–206.

38. John Rawls, *A Theory of Justice* (Cambridge, Mass.: Harvard University Press, 1971), pp. 115–116.

39. Rawls offers a similar argument to show that the (moral) right to engage in civil disobedience must be limited by the duty to prevent serious social disorder. See ibid., pp. 373–374.

40. Ibid., pp. 8–9, 241.

41. See Cottingham, "Varieties of Retribution," pp. 238–246.

42. See Joel Feinberg, "Justice and Personal Desert," in *Justice*, Nomos, vol. 6, ed. Carl W. Friedrich and John W. Chapman (New York: Atherton Press, 1963), pp. 69–97; reprinted in Feinberg, *Doing and Deserving* (Princeton, N.J.: Princeton University Press, 1970), pp. 57–58, 64. See also John Kleinig, "The Concept of Desert," *American Philosophical Quarterly* 8 (1971): 71–78, esp. 74–75. The second conception of desert is used most notably by John Rawls in "Two Concepts of Rules," *Philosophical Review* 64 (1955): 9–11.

43. Saint Thomas Aquinas, *Summa Theologica*, Part III, supp., Q. 12, art. 3, reply to obj. 4. A similar point is made in a different context by Plato in *Euthyphro*, 14c–15a.

44. See Chapter 1, note 30. An even better illustration: I believe it is *Beyond the Fringe*, the British comedy troupe, who present a skit in which a bully says to his victim, "I'm going to make you say 'uncle.'" Before the bully has a chance to go to work, the victim placidly says, "Uncle." The bully is exquisitely frustrated. He wanted to *make* the victim say "uncle." The retributivist wants the authorities to *make* the criminal suffer. It is not enough if she just happens to suffer, or she chooses to go along with the scheme.

45. I owe this observation to Roderick Firth.

46. See Chapter 6.

47. See Jean Hampton, "The Moral Education Theory of Punishment," *Philosophy and Public Affairs* 18 (1984): 208–238.

48. Randy E. Barnett, "Restitution: A New Paradigm of Criminal Justice," in *Assessing the Criminal*, ed. Randy E. Barnett and John Hagel III (Cambridge, Mass.: Ballinger, 1977), pp. 349–383; a shorter version appeared in *Ethics* 87 (1977): 279–301. Margaret Holmgren, "Punishment as Restitution: The Rights of the Community," *Criminal Justice Ethics* 2 (1983): 36–49.

Chapter 3. It Doesn't Have to Hurt

1. By *disvalue* and its cognates I mean to designate the most general category of things that are painful, unpleasant, not in someone's interest, or bad in any other respect. See further discussion in section 1.

2. E.g., H. L. A. Hart, "Prolegomenon to the Principles of Punishment," in *Punishment and Responsibility* (Oxford: Clarendon Press, 1968), p. 5.

3. E.g., Kurt Baier, "Is Punishment Retributive?" in *Philosophical Perspectives on Punishment*, ed. Gertrude Ezorsky (Albany, N.Y.: State University of New York Press, 1972), p. 18; Tziporah Kasachkoff, "The Criteria of Punishment," *Canadian Journal of Philosophy* 2 (1973): 365–366.

4. Plato, *Gorgias*, 525b–c; Aristotle, *Nicomachean Ethics*, 1104b15–20.

5. Plato, *Gorgias*, 525b–c.

6. Saint Thomas Aquinas, *Summa Theologica*, trans. Fathers of the English Dominican Province (London: Burnes Oates & Washbourne, 1935), Part I–II, Q. 39, art. 5.

7. J. F. Niermeyer and C. van de Kieft, *Mediae Latinitatis Lexicon Minus* (Leiden: Brill, 1976), s.v. "poena."

8. Saint Thomas Aquinas, *Summa Theologica*, Part I, Q. 48, art. 5. For Jewish sources of this doctrine, see Solomon Schechter, "The Doctrine of Divine Retribution," in *Studies in Judaism* (New York: Meridian Books, and Philadelphia: Jewish Publication Society of America, 1958).

9. Thomas Hobbes, *Leviathan* (original ed., London: Andrew Crooke, 1651), ed. C. B. Macpherson (Harmondsworth, England: Penguin, 1968), Part 2, ch. 28, p. 161.

10. Ibid., Part 1, ch. 6, p. 25.

11. John Locke, *An Essay Concerning Human Understanding*, ed. Peter H. Nidditch (Oxford: Clarendon Press, 1975), bk. 2, ch. 28, para. 5.

12. Jeremy Bentham, *An Introduction to the Principles of Morals and Legislation* (London: University of London Press, 1970), p. 49.

13. Immanuel Kant, *Critique of Practical Reason*, trans. L. W. Beck (Chicago: University of Chicago Press, 1949), sec. 8, remark ii; Prussian Academy ed., p. 149.

14. Immanuel Kant, *Lectures on Ethics* (London: Methuen, 1930), p. 55 (section entitled "Reward and Punishment").

15. G. W. F. Hegel, *Philosophy of Right*, trans. T. M. Knox (Oxford: Clarendon Press, 1942), sec. 99.

16. J. Ellis McTaggart, "Hegel's Theory of Punishment," *International Journal of Ethics* 6 (1896): 480.

17. Hastings Rashdall, *The Theory of Good and Evil* (Oxford: Clarendon Press, 1907), 1: 292.

18. W. D. [Sir David] Ross, *The Right and the Good* (Oxford: Clarendon Press, 1930), p. 56.

19. Antony Flew, "'The Justification of Punishment'," in *Philosophy of Punishment*, ed. H. B. Acton (London: Macmillan, and New York: St. Martins, 1969), p. 85.

20. J. D. Mabbott, "Professor Flew on Punishment," in Acton, *Philosophy of Punishment*, p. 118; S. I. Benn and R. S. Peters, *The Principles of Political Thought* (New York: Free Press, 1965), p. 202 (originally issued as *Social Principles and the Democratic State*, 1959); Hart, "Prolegomenon," p. 4; H. J. McCloskey, "The Complexity of the Concepts of Punishment," *Philosophy* 37 (1962): 321; Thomas McPherson, "Punishment: Definition and Justification," *Analysis* 28 (1967): 21; Richard Wasserstrom, "Some Problems with Theories of Punishment," in *Justice and Punishment*, ed. Jerry B. Cederblom and William L. Blizek (Cambridge, Mass.: Ballinger Books, 1977), p. 174; George Fletcher, *Rethinking Criminal Law* (Boston: Little, Brown, 1978), pp. 409–410; Richard Burgh, "Do the Guilty Deserve Punishment?" *Journal of Philosophy* 79 (1982): 193n–194n. Ted Honderich, *Punishment: The Supposed Justifications*, rev. ed. (Harmondsworth, England: Penguin, 1976), pp. 18–19; Igor Primoratz, *Justifying Legal Punishment* (Atlantic Highlands, N.J.: Humanities, 1989), pp. 4–5.

21. Burgh, "Do the Guilty Deserve Punishment?" pp. 193n–194n; Hugo Bedau, "A World without Punishment?" in *Punishment and Human Rights*, ed. Milton Goldinger (Cambridge, Mass.: Schenkman, 1974), p. 144; Kasachkoff, "Criteria of Punishment," pp. 363–364.

22. McTaggart, "Hegel's Theory of Punishment," p. 479.

23. Wasserstrom, "Some Problems," p. 174.

24. Rashdall, *Theory of Good and Evil*, p. 287n.

25. Francis Herbert Bradley, "Some Remarks on Punishment," *International Journal of Ethics* 4 (1894): 284.

26. Rashdall, *Theory of Good and Evil*, p. 287n.

27. Baier, "Is Punishment Retributive?" in Ezorsky, *Philosophical Perspectives on Punishment*, p. 18.

28. A. M. Quinton, "On Punishment," in ibid., p. 6.

29. Joel Feinberg, "The Expressive Function of Punishment," in *Doing and Deserving* (Princeton, N.J.: Princeton University Press, 1970), pp. 95–118, reprinted in Ezorsky, ibid., p. 25.

30. Herbert Fingarette, "Punishment and Suffering," *American Philosophical Association Proceedings and Addresses* 50 (1977): 510.

31. Richard B. Brandt, *Ethical Theory* (Englewood Cliffs, N.J.: Prentice-Hall, 1959), p. 482n. Brandt is here quoting Webster's dictionary.

32. T. L. S. Sprigge, "Punishment and Moral Responsibility," in Goldinger, *Punishment and Human Rights*, p. 74.

33. Brandt, *Ethical Theory*, p. 480.

34. Wasserstrom, "Some Problems," p. 173.

35. Jonathan Bennett, "Towards a Theory of Punishment," *Annual Proceedings of the Center for Philosophical Exchange* 3 (1980): 47.

36. George Schedler, "Can Retributivists Support Legal Punishment?" *The Monist* 63 (1980): 185–198 passim.

37. Claudia Card, "Retributive Penal Liability," in *Studies in Ethical Theory*, American Philosophical Quarterly Monograph Series 7 (1973): 27.

38. Robert Nozick, *Philosophical Explanations* (Cambridge, Mass.: Harvard University Press, 1981), p. 365.

39. Andrew Von Hirsch, *Doing Justice* (New York: Hill and Wang, 1976), p. 89.

40. Alan Wertheimer, "Should Punishment Fit the Crime?" *Social Theory and Practice* 3 (1975): 403–423.

41. [Pseudo-] Dionysius Areopagita, *The Divine Names*, ch. 4, sec. 22; quoted in Saint Thomas Aquinas, *Summa Theologica*, Part I, Q. 48, art. 6.

42. [Pseudo-] Dionysius Areopagita, *The Divine Names*, trans. C. E. Rolt (London: SPCK, 1920), ch. 4, sec. 19.

43. Card, "Retributive Penal Liability," p. 22. The others are noted immediately below.

44. John Rawls, "Two Concepts of Rules," *Philosophical Review* 64 (1955): 10.

45. Bedau, "A World without Punishment?" pp. 145–146.

46. Ibid., pp. 146, 153.

47. Baier, "Is Punishment Retributive?" p. 8; Kasachkoff, "The Criteria of Punishment," pp. 365–366; Richard Wasserstrom, "Retributivism and the Concept of Punishment," paper presented in the American Philosophical Association Symposium on "The New Retributivism," December 27, 1978, at the Eastern Division meetings of the association, Washington, D.C. A summary of Wasserstrom's paper appears in the *Journal of Philosophy* 75 (1978): 620–622.

48. A. R. Manser, "It Serves You Right," *Philosophy* 37 (1962): 293–306. He, in turn, cites Plato, *Laws*, trans. Jowett, p. 862.

49. James F. Doyle, "Justice and Legal Punishment," *Philosophy* 42 (1967): 60.

50. Unto Tähtinen, *Non-Violent Theories of Punishment: Indian and Western*, Annals of the Finnish Academy of Sciences, Series B, vol. 219 (Helsinki: Suomalainen Tiedeakatemia [Finnish Academy of Sciences], 1982), p. 67.

51. See, e.g., Antony Flew, " 'The Justification of Punishment,' " in Acton, *Philosophy of Punishment*, p. 85.

52. See Georg Henrik von Wright, *The Varieties of Goodness* (New York: Humanities Press, 1963), ch. 4, sec. 4. The word *unpleasure* was apparently coined by the translators of Freud as an equivalent of the German *Unlust*; see Gregory Zilboorg, Introduction to Sigmund Freud, *Beyond the Pleasure Principle*, in the *Standard Edition of the Complete Psychological Works of Sigmund Freud*, ed. James Strachey, 18 (London: Hogarth, 1955), p. 9.

53. Calvert Dodge, *A World without Prisons* (Lexington, Mass.: D. C. Heath, Lexington Books, 1979), p. 71.

54. I must note here that some Catholic authorities use the Latin word *satisfactio* for acts of penance, reserving the word *poenitentia* (the cognate of *penance*) for the attitude with which such acts should be done, or the sacrament with which they are connected. *Satisfactio* is sometimes translated by

its cognate, *satisfaction*, sometimes by *atonement* or *expiation*.

55. See Richard Swinburne, *Responsibility and Atonement* (Oxford: Clarendon, 1989), pp. 81–84.

56. Feinberg, "Expressive Function," in Ezorsky, *Philosophical Perspectives on Punishment*, pp. 31–33.

57. " 'Fly' Pays $1.10, a Cent a Floor; City Drops Suit," *New York Times*, May 28, 1977, p. 1, col. 2.

58. Hart, "Prolegomenon," pp. 4–5.

59. Benn and Peters, *Principles of Political Thought*, p. 202.

60. Freud, *Civilization and Its Discontents*, in the *Standard Edition*, 21 (1961): 125.

61. See Lawrence Kohlberg, "Moral Stages and Moralization," in *Essays in Moral Development*, vol. 2: *The Psychology of Moral Development* (San Francisco: Harper & Row, 1984), p. 168; Lawrence Kohlberg and Daniel Candee, "The Relationship of Moral Judgment to Moral Action," in ibid., p. 501.

62. A saying of the Lekhivitzer Rebbe, in *The Hasidic Anthology*, ed. Louis I. Newman (New York: Bloch, 1944), p. 386.

63. A saying of the Ziditzover Rebbe, in ibid., pp. 113–114.

64. Abraham Isaac Kook, *Orot ha-Teshuvah* ["Lights of Penitence"], trans. Alter B. Z. Metzger under the title *Rabbi Kook's Philosophy of Repentance* (New York: Yeshiva University Press, 1968), ch. 5, secs. 1 and 6. Another translation appears in *Abraham Isaac Kook* (Ramsey, N.J.: Paulist Press, 1978).

65. Freud, *New Introductory Lectures in Psycho-Analysis*, in the *Standard Edition*, 22 (1964): 64–65.

66. Joseph Sandler, Alex Holder, and Dale Meers, "The Ego Ideal and the Ideal Self," in the *Psychoanalytic Study of the Child* (hereafter, *PASC*) 18 (New York: International Universities Press, 1963): 146–148. I here follow the opinions of Nunberg, Piers and Singer, Lampl-de Groot, and Hartmann and Loewenstein, as there summarized. See also Heinz Hartmann and R. M. Loewenstein, "Notes on the Superego," in *PASC* 17 (1962): 42–81, esp. pp. 59–63; and Jeanne Lampl-de Groot, "Ego Ideal and Superego," *PASC* 17 (1962): 94–106.

67. Erich Fromm, *Man for Himself* (Greenwich, Conn.: Fawcett, 1947), pp. 145–175. Fromm presents a different interpretation of the ego ideal from the one I suggest here (p. 150), making it appear more authoritarian. Freud's own remarks are sparse enough to allow for either interpretation.

Chapter 4. What Is Punishment?

1. H. L. A. Hart, "Prolegomenon to the Principles of Punishment," in *Punishment and Responsibility* (Oxford: Clarendon Press, 1968), pp. 4–5.

2. This provision allows us to make sense of a judge who says, "I am punishing you, although nothing you have done justifies it."

3. James F. Doyle, "Justice and Legal Punishment," *Philosophy* 42 (1967): 60. The significant differences are two. (1) Doyle's definition refers only to criminal offenses; mine, to other offenses as well. (2) To bring Doyle's definition in line with mine, one would have to add two words at the end, so that punishment is "the satisfaction of all the just claims invoked by the commission of criminal offenses *qua offenses*." To see why, consider the case in which someone who is not a medical doctor treats a gunshot wound. He is perhaps guilty of practicing medicine without a license; if so, he incurs a duty to submit to punishment for this offense. He also incurs a duty to report the gunshot wound to the proper authorities. This additional duty (or claim, looking at it from the authorities' point of view) arises from the criminal act but has nothing to do with the criminality of the act. The person may be acquitted, because it was an emergency, or he may be convicted: Either way, he must report the injury. No one would say that reporting the injury is a punishment.

4. I think this is true, Rawls notwithstanding. (See his "Two Concepts of Rules," *The Philosophical Review* 64 [1955]: 11–12.) Of course, he is right in saying that one could not have a system that explicitly called for punishment of scapegoats—i.e., what Rawls calls a system of *telishment*; but that is not the issue. The problem is that a system that explicitly forbids telishment may nonetheless be liable to abuse by public officials, who carry out telishment under an informal understanding. For example, the public may widely believe that Mulcahy has committed a terrible crime, and they may believe this on good evidence. The police, however, have access to more information than the public at large, and this information strongly suggests that Mulcahy is in fact innocent. Yet punishing her will produce good deterrent effects, since she is of bad character and has committed many crimes in the past. The public will probably never come to suspect that the police have exculpatory evidence, and thus the deterrent effect of the punishment will not be spoiled by public perception that Mulcahy is being framed. In this manner, law enforcement officials may systematically "telish" many innocents, though the rules forbid it.

Something like this actually happens under plea bargaining. A supposed criminal is punished even though exculpatory evidence has been knowingly ignored. Of course, the police do not go out and frame a perfectly innocent victim but, rather, take advantage of a suspect, who may in fact be guilty as charged.

5. As noted before, the definition of (legal) punishment in terms of rights-violation has been suggested (but in a very offhand way) by Rawls, Claudia Card, and Hugo Bedau. (See Chapter 3, notes 43–45.) K. G. Armstrong comes closest to recognizing the present point: "Surely," he says, "our principal objection is to the deliberate infliction of *undeserved* pain, to the *injustice* of it." (K. G. Armstrong, "The Retributivist Hits Back," in *Philosophy of Punishment*, ed. H. B. Acton [London: Macmillan, and New York: St. Martins, 1969], p. 154.) This is true; but we must also object to injustice even if no pain is involved.

6. This example refers to the early 1980s.

7. Doyle's definition we have just seen. Max Grünhut, *Penal Reform* (Oxford: Clarendon Press, 1948), p. 3. Unto Tähtinen, *Non-Violent Theories of Punishment*, Annals of the Finnish Academy of Sciences, Series B, vol. 219 (Helsinki: Suomalainen Tiedeakatemia [Finnish Academy of Sciences], 1982), p. 67.

8. Ted Honderich, *Punishment: The Supposed Justifications*, rev. ed. (Harmondsworth, England: Penguin, 1975), pp. 18–19. Igor Primoratz, *Justifying Legal Punishment* (Atlantic Highlands, N.J.: Humanities, 1989), pp. 4–5.

9. Primoratz, *Justifying Legal Punishment*, p. 5.

10. Rawls, "Two Concepts of Rules," pp. 11–12.

11. Note that similar exceptionalist objections could be raised with regard to other features of a definition of punishment. If we were to say that punishment is an evil, a single *odd* counterexample would not refute us: e.g., if a masochist enjoyed being flogged. For flogging in general is intended as an imposition of an evil, and for most persons it is an evil.

12. I should perhaps note a possible objection. One might object: "People may make whatever life plans they wish, so long as they do not act on them." These would be idle life plans—fantasies or daydreams—and one may of course fantasize or daydream as one likes. But when I talk about life plans, I am referring to plans that the planner actually attempts to carry out.

Chapter 5. The Rectification Theory of Punishment

1. H. L. A. Hart, "Are There Any Natural Rights?" *Philosophical Review* 64 (1955): 178; see also following pages. Hart develops this view at much greater length in "Bentham on Legal Rights," in *Oxford Essays in Jurisprudence*, 2d series (Oxford: Clarendon Press, 1973), pp. 171–201. At the end of the Bentham article Hart qualifies his support of the choice theory, saying that it is "satisfactory only at one level."

Hart is, of course, not the originator of this theory of rights, nor does he claim to be; but he may be called its chief articulator.

I use Hart's theory principally by way of fixing ideas, choosing it over its rivals mainly because it meshes most closely with the present theory of punishment. Certainly, as Hart notes, his view is not beyond criticism; see, e.g., Carl Wellman, *A Theory of Rights* (Totowa, N.J.: Rowman & Allanheld, 1985), ch. 3. By building in an extra cog, we can make the present theory of punishment work with other theories of rights. For any acceptable theory of rights will find room for the notion of *exercising a right*, and for present purposes this notion can substitute for Hart's notion of choice.

2. Although a person cannot dispose of inalienable rights, some say that one can forfeit them. Many believe that the right to life is of this sort. On such a view, I may not commit suicide nor authorize anyone else to kill me; but if I commit murder, I lose my own right to life, and the state may

execute me.

3. Hohfeld, of course, uses the word *liberty* in a different sense, referring to a certain kind of right. When referring to this kind of right, I use the phrase *liberty-right*. See my discussion of these terms in the Introduction.

4. Making such an announcement is irrelevant, except insofar as the announcement is itself an exercise of liberty. E.g., a murderer might say, "I can kill you and fix it up with the cops afterwards," perhaps thereby asserting certain rights. But the operative aspect is that this statement is a threat.

5. The words *to us* show that we are asking, "What normative theory would a conscientious person have to hold in order to be willing to act as the offender did?" This as opposed to a more subjective approach, "What normative theory must the offender hold, given the way she has acted?" This latter question has been investigated by Gresham M. Sykes and David Matza; see "Techniques of Neutralization: A Theory of Delinquency," *American Sociological Review* 22 (1957): 664–665.

6. Joel Feinberg, "The Nature and Value of Rights," *Journal of Value Inquiry* 4 (1970): 251–252. Alan R. White makes a similar distinction in *Rights* (Oxford: Clarendon Press, 1984), p. 117. White uses the term *subjunctive claim* in place of Feinberg's *performative claim,* and *indicative* in place of Feinberg's *propositional.*

7. I am using the word *coordinate* in its everyday sense. The technical usage familiar to game theorists is not at issue here.

8. A *rights-claim,* as the phrase itself suggests, is a kind of claim, namely, a claim of rights. This concept is not to be confused with that of a *claim-right,* which is a kind of right. See my discussion of the latter term in the Introduction.

These two terms are so well coined, so seemingly pedestrian, that those of us who use them regularly may be surprised at the need for this clarificatory note. We tend to forget that they are, after all, technical terms, not part of ordinary language.

9. Donald Davidson, "Mental Events," in *Experience and Theory*, ed. Lawrence Foster and J. W. Swanson (Amherst: University of Massachusetts Press, 1970), p. 97; reprinted in Davidson, *Essays on Actions and Events* (Oxford: Clarendon Press, 1980), p. 222.

10. See Nelson Goodman, *Languages of Art* (Indianapolis: Bobbs-Merrill, 1968), pp. 52–67.

11. Cf. Alan Gewirth, *Reason and Morality* (Chicago: University of Chicago Press, 1978), sec. 2.17.

12. Of course, I do not pretend that anyone can explain this mysterious notion of simplicity; it is enough that we can make such judgments. For some problems in applying the concept of simplicity, see Nelson Goodman, "Seven Strictures on Similarity," in *Problems and Projects* (Indianapolis: Bobbs-Merrill, 1972).

13. See Sveinn A. Thorvaldson, "Does Community Service Affect Offenders' Attitudes?" in *Victims, Offenders, and Alternative Sanctions*, ed. Joe Hudson and Burt Galaway (Lexington, Mass.: D. C. Heath, Lexington Books,

1980), pp. 71–72, and Chapter 6, section 4.

14. See, e.g., Dan B. Dobbs, *Handbook on the Law of Remedies* (St. Paul, Minn.: West Publishing, 1973), p. 144; the discussion there concerns a unique tract of land.

15. Cf. Ronald Dworkin, "What is Equality?" Part 1, *Philosophy and Public Affairs* 10 (1981): sec. 8 (pp. 228–240).

16. In ancient and medieval times, pain was said to be a means for curing a sick soul. See Chapter 1, section 2, and Chapter 3, section 1. Even now this idea is met with, as when "aversion therapy" is used in an attempt to get a criminal to lose the desire to commit her typical crime. Even imprisonment was not always intended as a painful infliction. One of the original arguments in favor of incarceration as a punishment was that solitary confinement would promote meditation and penitence (hence the word *penitentiary*). See, e.g., Michel Foucault, *Discipline and Punish*, trans. Alan Sheridan (New York: Random House, Vintage Books, 1979), pp. 236–239.

17. Alan Gewirth discusses at length the idea that actions, by virtue of their purposiveness, involve a claim of rights. See Gewirth, *Reason and Morality*, Part 2. This book is highly commended to skeptical or curious readers.

18. To be precise, I should claim the baggage only if it is mine, or if I am acting on behalf of its owner.

19. For the concept and details of plans of life I am indebted to Charles Fried, *An Anatomy of Values* (Cambridge, Mass.: Harvard University Press, 1970), esp. pp. 36–39 and 162–166.

20. The term is from Claudia Card, "Retributive Penal Liability," in *Studies in Ethical Theory*, American Philosophical Quarterly Monograph Series 7 (1973): 27.

21. John Stuart Mill, *Collected Works*, ed. J. M. Robinson, vol. 10: *Utilitarianism* (Toronto: University of Toronto Press, and London: Routledge & Kegan Paul, 1969), ch. 5.

22. The terms *agapism* and *agapistic* were coined or popularized by William Frankena; see his *Ethics* (Englewood Cliffs, N.J.: Prentice-Hall, 1963), pp. 42–45, and "Love and Principle in Christian Ethics," in *Faith and Philosophy*, ed. Alvin Plantinga (Grand Rapids, Mich.: Eerdmans, 1964), pp. 203–225. Though shunned to date by the dictionaries, these two terms have gained some currency in writing on ethics. See, e.g., Gene Outka, *Agape: An Ethical Analysis* (New Haven, Conn.: Yale University Press, 1972), pp. 94–104, 135–137. These sources, needless to say, are in the first instance useful for their substantive discussion of agapism.

23. Herbert Morris, "Persons and Punishment," *The Monist* 52 (1968): 475–501; reprinted in *On Guilt and Innocence* (Berkeley and Los Angeles: University of California Press, 1976), p. 34.

24. Jeffrie G. Murphy, "Three Mistakes about Retributivism," *Analysis* 31 (1971): 166–169; see also his essays "Marxism and Retribution," *Philosophy and Public Affairs* 2 (1973): 217–243, and "Kant's Theory of Criminal Punishment," in *Proceedings* of the Third International Kant Congress, ed.

L. W. Beck (Dordrecht: Reidel, 1971), pp. 434–441; all three essays are reprinted in Jeffrie G. Murphy, *Retribution, Justice, and Therapy* (Dordrecht: Reidel, 1979), pp. 77–81, 82–92, and 93–115, respectively. Michael Davis, "How to Make the Punishment Fit the Crime," *Ethics* 93 (1982–83): 742–743.

25. Of course, such a scheme will no doubt prevail. But it plays no particular role in the rectification theory.

26. Morris, "Persons and Punishment," p. 33.

27. This distinction is discussed (using somewhat different terminology) by Robert Nozick in *Anarchy, State, and Utopia* (New York: Basic Books, 1974), pp. 155–160, 218–224. What I am calling *procedural principles* correspond to Nozick's "historical principles" or to Rawls's "pure procedural justice." See John Rawls, *A Theory of Justice* (Cambridge, Mass.: Harvard University Press, 1971), pp. 85–86.

28. Morris, "Persons and Punishment," p. 33 (emphasis added). See also Davis, "How to Make the Punishment Fit the Crime," p. 743.

29. This objection is raised by Richard Wasserstrom, "Some Problems in the Definition and Justification of Punishment," in *Values and Morals*, ed. A. I. Goldman and J. Kim (Dordrecht: Reidel, 1978), pp. 311–312; and by Davis, "How to Make the Punishment Fit the Crime," p. 743. Davis there responds to the objection, but I have amplified it to show that his reply will not suffice.

30. This point is discussed at length by Ronald Dworkin in "What is Equality?" Part I, esp. sec. 7.

31. Justice may also require that the rich should not be too much richer than the poor. But this requirement does not concern *individual* entitlements, which form our present concern.

32. Morris, "Persons and Punishment," p. 34.

33. Murphy, "Three Mistakes," pp. 79–80; Hugo Bedau, "Retribution and the Theory of Punishment," *Journal of Philosophy* 75 (1978): 617.

34. Alan H. Goldman, "The Paradox of Punishment," *Philosophy and Public Affairs* 9 (1979): 44.

35. An excellent discussion of Morris's view of punishment and its further elaboration by Michael Davis is found in Don Scheid, "Davis and the Unfair-Advantage Theory of Punishment: A Critique," *Philosophical Topics* 18 (1990): 143–170. To my regret, Scheid's article appeared too late for me to take into consideration here.

36. J. D. Mabbott, "Punishment," *Mind*, n.s. 48 (1939): 152–167; reprinted in *Philosophy of Punishment*, ed. H. B. Acton (London: Macmillan, and New York: St. Martins, 1969), pp. 48–49.

37. Saint Anselm, *Cur Deus Homo?* in *Basic Writings*, trans. S. N. Deane (LaSalle, Ill.: Open Court, 1962), bk. 1, ch. 15.

38. On the moral education theory, see Jean Hampton, "The Moral Education Theory of Punishment," *Philosophy and Public Affairs* 18 (1984): 208–238.

A similar contrast can be found among religious theories of repentance.

The counterpart of the rectification theory is found most frequently among Catholics (see the quotation from Anselm, above, in this section). The counterpart of the moral education theory is found most frequently among Jewish writers. Consider, for example, the very frequent statement that complete repentance, sufficient to gain God's favor, means completely overcoming one's tendency to repeat the offense. See Moses ben Maimon (Maimonides), *Mishneh Torah*, vol. 1, *Book of Knowledge*, trans. Moses Hyamson (Jerusalem and New York: Feldheim, 1981), Laws of Repentance, ch. 2, sec. 1, p. 82b.

Chapter 6. The Theory: Application and Evaluation

1. I mean to include in these "values" nonteleological values, such as the preservation of rights, the doing of duty, etc., as well as the teleological ones that may come to mind first.

2. Saint Anselm, *Cur Deus Homo*, trans. S. N. Deane (La Salle, Ill.: Open Court, 1962), bk. 1, ch. 21. The example of a glance is Anselm's.

3. See, e.g., Alan Wertheimer, "Victimless Crimes," *Ethics* 87 (1977): 311–312. Margaret Holmgren, "Punishment as Restitution: The Rights of the Community," *Criminal Justice Ethics* 2 (1983): 36–49.

4. See Saint Anselm, who considers God to be the victim of every sin. This is discussed below, section 6.

5. Michael Davis, "How to Make the Punishment Fit the Crime," *Ethics* 93 (1983): 744n.

6. The point is not just that the recantation was insincere, but that it was immediately undone by a contrary statement. The legend would be pointless if it ended with Galileo's thinking to himself, "*Eppur si muove.*" He has to say it out loud.

7. On community service, see generally the following anthologies: *Considering the Victim*, ed. Joe Hudson and Burt Galaway (Springfield, Ill.: C. C. Thomas, 1975); *Victims, Offenders, and Alternative Sanctions*, ed. Joe Hudson and Burt Galaway (Lexington, Mass.: D. C. Heath, Lexington Books, 1980); and *Offender Restitution in Theory and Action*, ed. Burt Galaway and Joe Hudson (Lexington, Mass.: D. C. Heath, Lexington Books, 1977). Also useful is Stephen Schafer, *Compensation and Restitution to Victims of Crime* (Montclair, N.J.: Paterson Smith, 1970), which describes programs in a large number of countries.

8. Sveinn A. Thorvaldson, "Does Community Service Affect Offenders' Attitudes?" in Hudson and Galaway, *Victims, Offenders, and Alternative Sanctions*, pp. 71–72.

9. Roman Tomasic and Ian Dobinson, *The Failure of Imprisonment: An Australian Perspective* (Sydney: Law Foundation of New South Wales, George Allen & Unwin, 1979), p. 127.

10. Alan T. Harland, "Restitution Statutes and Cases: Some Substantive and Procedural Constraints," in Galaway and Hudson, *Victims, Offenders, and Alternative Sanctions*, p. 153.

11. Howard Feinman, "Legal Issues in the Operations of Restitution Programs in a Juvenile Court," in ibid., p. 144. In spite of the title of the article, Feinman is referring in this quotation to adult as well as juvenile offenders. See also Patrick D. McAnany, "Restitution as Idea and Practice: The Retributive Process," in Hudson and Galaway, *Offender Restitution*, p. 15.

12. See Feinman, "Legal Issues," pp. 145–146.

13. See, e.g., Sveinn A. Thorvaldson, "Toward the Definition of the Reparative Aim," in Hudson and Galaway, *Victims, Offenders, and Alternative Sanctions*, pp. 26–27; Gerald F. Waldron, "Problems with Operating Restitution Programs," ibid., pp. 33–34; John T. Gandy and Burt Galaway, "Restitution as a Sanction for Offenders: A Public's View," ibid., p. 89; Robert Kigin and Steven Novack, "A Rural Restitution Program for Juvenile Offenders and Victims," ibid., p. 131; Thorvaldson, "Does Community Service Affect Offenders' Attitudes?" ibid., pp. 71–72; Robert Keldgord, "Community Restitution Comes to Arizona," in Hudson and Galaway, *Offender Restitution*, pp. 161–166; Alan T. Harland, "Theoretical and Programmatic Concerns in Restitution: An Integration," ibid., pp. 195–196.

14. Randy E. Barnett, "Restitution: A New Paradigm of Criminal Justice," in *Assessing the Criminal: Restitution, Retribution, and the Legal Process*, ed. Randy E. Barnett and John Hagel III (Cambridge, Mass.: Ballinger, 1977), p. 363. This article originally appeared in a shorter form in *Ethics* 87 (1977): 279–301.

15. For the first of these see, e.g., Alan Wertheimer, "Victimless Crimes," *Ethics* 87 (1977): 311–312; for the second, Paul W. Keve, "The Therapeutic Uses of Restitution," in Hudson and Galaway, *Offender Restitution*, p. 60.

16. See Holmgren, "Punishment as Restitution."

17. See *Dillon v. Legg*, 68 C. 2d 728, 69 Cal. Rptr. 72, 441 P. 2d 912.

18. One might be tempted to say that sitting in a room for months or years would promote deterrence and thus indirectly promote security, an admittedly basic good. But see Chapter 2, section 5, where I argue that willing submission to punishment does not generally promote deterrence. As I note there, the few cases in which willing submission does promote deterrence involve offenses so minor as not to fall under the rectification principle. Such minor offenses do not constitute a claim of excess basic rights, but at most of other, less basic, rights, to which the rectification theory does not apply. Cf. Chapter 5, sections 5 and 7.

19. *Pro:* See Hayim S. Nahmani, *Human Rights in the Old Testament* (Tel Aviv: Joshua Chaichik, 1964). *Contra:* See Alasdair McIntyre, *After Justice* (Notre Dame, Ind.: University of Notre Dame Press, 1981), pp. 65–67; H. L. A. Hart, "Are There Any Natural Rights?" *Philosophical Review* 64 (1955): 176–177, 182.

20. For a discussion of this issue in a legal context, see Jeffrie Murphy, "Mercy and Legal Justice," in Jeffrie Murphy and Jean Hampton, *Forgiveness and Mercy* (Cambridge: Cambridge University Press, 1988); and Jacob Adler, "Murphy and Mercy," *Analysis* 50 (1990): 264–267.

21. Joel Feinberg, "Justice and Personal Desert," in *Justice*, Nomos, vol. 6,

ed. Carl W. Friedrich and John W. Chapman (New York: Atherton Press, 1963), pp. 69–97. See also Chapter 2, note 42, and text thereto (p. 72).

22. Saint Anselm, *Cur Deus Homo?* bk. 1, ch. 15.

23. I here differ from Anselm, who holds that human beings have no rights (bk. 1, ch. 20), and that even the slightest sin merits infinite penance (bk. 1, ch. 21).

24. Elaine Walster, Ellen Berscheid, and G. William Walster, "New Directions in Equity Research," in *Equity Theory: Toward a General Theory of Social Interaction,* ed. Leonard Berkowitz and Elaine Walster, Advances in Experimental Social Psychology, vol. 9 (New York: Academic Press, 1976), p. 6.

25. Ibid., pp. 2–4.

26. See Unto Tähtinen, *Non-Violent Theories of Punishment: Indian and Western,* Annals of the Finnish Academy of Sciences, Series B, vol. 219 (Helsinki: Suomalainen Tiedeakatemia [Finnish Academy of Sciences], 1982), pp. 109–112; Burt Galaway, "Restitution as an Integrative Punishment," in Barnett and Hagel, *Assessing the Criminal.* Pierre Boulle, *The Bridge over the River Kwai* (New York: Vanguard, 1954).

Chapter 7. Punishment and Contract

1. Cesare Beccaria, *Of Crimes and Punishments,* trans. Henry Paolucci (Indianapolis: Bobbs-Merrill, Library of Liberal Arts, 1963), chs. 2, 3, 16; Lawrence Kohlberg and Donald Elfenbein, "The Development of Moral Judgments Concerning Capital Punishment," *American Journal of Orthopsychiatry* 45 (1975): 636–637; James P. Sterba, "Retributive Justice," *Political Theory* 5 (1977): 349–362; idem, *The Demands of Justice* (Notre Dame, Ind.: University of Notre Dame Press, 1980), ch. 3; idem, "Is There a Rationale for Punishment?" *American Journal of Jurisprudence* 29 (1984): 29–43. John Rawls, *A Theory of Justice* (Cambridge, Mass.: Harvard University Press, 1971), pp. 240–241. Sterba's article in *Political Theory* spurred an interesting exchange on this topic. See T. M. Reed, "On Sterba's 'Retributive Justice,'" *Political Theory* 6 (1978): 373–376; James P. Sterba, "Contractual Retributivism Defended," *Political Theory* 7 (1979): 417–418; T. M. Reed, "Contractual Retributivism Unveiled," *Political Theory* 8 (1980): 121–122; James P. Sterba, "Social Contract Theory and Ordinary Justice," *Political Theory* 9 (1981): 111–112.

2. The best representative of this third category is David A. J. Richards, though his view is too complex for easy classification. Richards puts questions of punishment to the parties in the original position of the Rawlsian procedure, but they answer only by interpreting the two principles of justice they have already agreed on, not by selecting new principles. See David A. J. Richards, *A Theory of Reasons for Action* (Oxford: Clarendon Press, 1971), pp. 127–132.

3. Strictly speaking, I should speak of *notional* societies, rather than hypothetical. The difference is explained in note 6.

4. Rawls, *A Theory of Justice;* John Rawls, "Kantian Constructivism in Moral Theory," The Dewey Lectures 1980, *Journal of Philosophy* 77 (1980): 515–572. Aside from these main sources, Rawls has devoted a number of articles to aspects of the view developed in *A Theory of Justice.* A listing through the early 1980s can be found in *John Rawls and His Critics,* ed. David T. Mason and J. H. Wellbank (New York: Garland, 1982).

5. John Locke is probably the most prominent exponent of the view that society is based on an actual contract: Our consent, he says, is tacit but real, being indicated by our voluntarily remaining in the land where we live. Hume's essay "Of the Original Contract" devastatingly criticizes this sort of social contract theory. See David Hume, "Of the Original Contract," in *Social Contract,* ed. Sir Ernest Barker (Oxford: Oxford University Press, 1947). Some critics of Rawls have maintained that Justice as Fairness is not a social contract theory at all; see, e.g., Jean Hampton, "Contracts and Choices: Does Rawls Have a Social Contract Theory?" *Journal of Philosophy* 77 (1980): 315–338.

6. A hypothetical contract is one that actual people might have entered into, particularly one whose existence is inferred from some sort of empirical observation of human behavior. E.g., we might consider what kind of agreement a thousand people would reach if they could overcome the difficulty of conducting negotiations. A notional contract, by contrast, is a thought-experiment: It is completely irrelevant to a notional contract whether real people would have, or might have, entered into such a contract under given conditions.

7. The concept of the well-ordered society is stated most concisely in Rawls's Dewey Lectures, pp. 521–522.

8. Rawls actually says that the parties in the original position represent continuing family lines. See *A Theory of Justice,* pp. 128–129. For present purposes this proviso makes no difference, and I consequently ignore it.

9. Rawls often uses the phrase "conception of the good" as a synonym for the more familiar "plan of life." This usage can be a bit disconcerting to those who have not encountered it before. Its basis is the liberal idea, that the definition of "the good" is simply what each person chooses for himself: There is no general, substantive theory of things that are good for everyone, or absolutely good. Hence, my conception of the good is simply whatever plan of life I choose for myself after due deliberation.

10. Rawls, *A Theory of Justice,* p. 60.

11. Ibid., p. 302.

12. Ibid., pp. 61, 302–303.

13. This difficulty has been noticed and discussed most directly by James Sterba. See *The Demands of Justice,* ch. 3, and "Is There a Rationale for Punishment?" Other discussions of the difficulty raised by the contrast between ideal and nonideal theory: Jeffrie Murphy, "Marxism and Retribution,"

Philosophy and Public Affairs 2 (1973): 217–243, reprinted in *Retribution, Justice and Therapy* (Dordrecht: Reidel, 1979), pp. 82–93; Richard Miller, "Rawls and Marxism," *Philosophy and Public Affairs* 3 (1973–74): 168–191.

14. Students of religious philosophy will be reminded of a parallel problem involving God's creation of the universe: If God is perfect, how can He create evil? Yet if He is imperfect, how can He be God? If God is a simple unity, then how can He create the multiplicity of things in the world? Yet if He is not a simple unity, how can He be God? If He is unchanging, how can He create or take cognizance of the changeable? But if not . . . , etc.

15. The most pressing actual example of this question arises in connection with affirmative action. One frequently heard objection to affirmative-action plans is that they hinder progress toward a society free of invidious racial discrimination. For example, according to many critics, racial preference in college admissions promotes resentment and racism on the part of the majority and lets the minority members think they can have an easy ride into college. However, a plan aimed at diversity in general overcomes this objection: Even in a society completely free of racist sentiments, college officials would still want to seek out a diverse class—though in such a society they would only need to worry about geographical, cultural, and other forms of diversity. Such a plan is mentioned by Justice Powell in his opinion in the *Bakke* case. See *University of California Regents v. Bakke*, 438 U.S. 265 (U.S. Supreme Court, 1977), Opinion of Powell, J., Section IV D (pp. 311ff.) and Appendix (pp. 321ff.).

16. In some cases this obligation is reinforced by the Principle of Fairness; this principle, however, applies not to citizens generally, but only those who have accepted special benefits or positions of power. See Rawls, *A Theory of Justice*, pp. 113–114. Moreover, it merely reinforces, and does not extend, the duties of those to whom it applies. I therefore ignore it here.

17. Ibid., p. 115.

18. The example is *Jacob & Youngs, Inc., v. Kent*, 230 N.Y. 239, 129 N.E. 889, 23 A.L.R. 1429, rearg. denied 230 N.Y. 656, 130 N.E. 933 (Court of Appeals of New York, 1921).

19. Rawls, *A Theory of Justice*, sec. 40.

20. Rawls, Dewey Lectures, p. 525. Regarding the phrase "conception of the good," see note 9.

21. Rawls, *A Theory of Justice*, p. 253.

22. Sterba, "Is There a Rationale for Punishment?"

23. John Rawls, "Reply to Alexander and Musgrave," *Quarterly Journal of Economics* 88 (1974): 636.

24. Rawls, *A Theory of Justice*, p. 145.

25. There are those who would, in various ways, deny what I say here about Hobbes. See essays by A. E. Taylor, "The Ethical Doctrine of Hobbes," in *Hobbes's Leviathan: Interpretation and Criticism*, ed. Bernard H. Baumrin (Belmont, Calif.: Wadsworth, 1969), pp. 35–48; Stuart M. Brown, Jr., "Hobbes: The Taylor Thesis," in ibid., pp. 49–66; Howard Warrend-

er, "Hobbes's Conception of Morality," in ibid., pp. 67–82; and Bernard Gert, "Hobbes and Psychological Egoism," *Journal of the History of Ideas* 28 (1967): 503–520.

26. See Rawls, *A Theory of Justice*, sec. 40.

27. Immanuel Kant, *Groundwork of the Metaphysics of Morals*, trans. H. J. Paton (New York: Harper & Row, 1964), p. 89; Prussian Academy ed., p. 421; emphasis added.

28. Arthur Linton Corbin, *Corbin on Contracts*, one-vol. ed. (St. Paul, Minn.: West Publishing, 1952), sec. 1355.

29. See, e.g., American Law Institute, *Restatement of the Law, Second: Contracts, 2d* (St. Paul, Minn.: American Law Institute Publishers, 1981), sec. 265: "Where, after a contract is made, a party's principal purpose is substantially frustrated without his fault by the occurrence of an event the non-occurrence of which was a basic assumption on which the contract was made, his remaining duties to render performance are discharged, unless the language or the circumstances indicate the contrary."

30. Rawls, *A Theory of Justice*, pp. 240–241; Dewey Lectures, p. 538.

31. Rawls, *A Theory of Justice*, p. 240.

32. See *Corbin on Contracts*, sec. 104.

33. Readers unfamiliar with the term *maximinimize* may ignore it for the time being. A definition will be found in note 49.

34. Rawls, *A Theory of Justice*, pp. 176ff.

35. This is true, for example, of penal bonds. These are bonds by which one person, the obligor, guarantees some performance on the part of another; if the performance does not take place, the obligor must pay a certain sum. "In a penal bond, after a statement that the obligor is 'held and firmly bound in the penal sum of ———— dollars,' appears such words [*sic*] as the following: 'the condition of this obligation is that if John Doe shall duly appear in court [or, if the obligor shall duly prosecute his appeal; . . . ; or, other specified performance] then it shall be void, otherwise to remain in full force and effect.' Words such as these make it appear that the bond creates an immediate indebtedness, subject to be defeated and discharged by a condition subsequent. In its actual effect, however, such is not the case. . . . [I]t does not create an immediately enforceable indebtedness." Moreover, it would appear from the words of the bond that if the performance does not occur, the obligor must pay the named sum; but this is not so. "It is only in cases in which the harm is not capable of being measured and liquidated in money that the penalty of a bond will be enforced. In other cases, the plaintiff's recovery will not exceed the amount of the injury that he proves." *Corbin on Contracts*, sec. 258; the bracketed phrase is Corbin's.

36. Rawls, *A Theory of Justice*, p. 136; John Rawls, "The Basic Structure as a Subject," in *Values and Morals*, ed. A. I. Goldman and J. Kim (Dordrecht: Reidel, 1978), p. 60.

37. In a more complete taxonomy of societies I would include the *Very Fragmented Society*, in which so many people repudiate the contract that it

interferes with the operation of the contract even among those who do not repudiate it. Such an anarchic society is of little relevance to our present concerns.

38. Rawls, Dewey Lectures, p. 526.

39. Rawls, *A Theory of Justice*, p. 546.

40. There is *some* degree of substitutability among the basic liberties. Freedom of speech, for example, may be realized in various ways. One may have access to radio or television or newspapers, or have the opportunity to address people directly. The situation is satisfactory so long as each citizen has a reasonable chance to address fellow citizens and to be addressed by them. The point still holds that freedom of speech is not intersubstitutable with the other basic liberties, nor are they with one another.

41. See Chapter 5, section 5, and Chapter 6, section 2.

42. Rawls, *A Theory of Justice*, p. 61; "The Basic Liberties and Their Priority," in *The Tanner Lectures on Human Values*, vol. 3, ed. Sterling M. McMurrin (Salt Lake City: University of Utah Press, and Cambridge: Cambridge University Press, 1982), p. 12.

43. Rawls, *A Theory of Justice*, p. 241.

44. There is much more—probably infinitely more—to be said on this topic. Especially one might want to ask: What do we mean by a "small surprise"? Which surprises count as large and which small? A small surprise, of course, involves a situation different from, but fairly similar to, the one expected. But here someone will cite Goodman's strictures on similarity. (Nelson Goodman, papers on similarity in his *Problems and Projects* [Indianapolis: Bobbs-Merrill, 1972].) I can only say here that expectation and surprise carry with them their own standard of similarity. To continue further would take us too far afield.

45. Some qualifications are required. The point is that all temporally identifying features of the individual are obliterated by the veil of ignorance.

46. Rawls, *A Theory of Justice*, pp. 240–241.

47. Lawrence Kohlberg and Donald Elfenbein avoid this error by having persons in the original position consider the possibility that they themselves may be subject to punishment. So far they are right. But they are gored by the other horn of the dilemma: If parties in the original position are allowed to consider crime and punishment, their prudential deliberation will undermine the status of their contract. See section 1, and Kohlberg and Elfenbein, "The Development of Moral Judgments Concerning Capital Punishment," pp. 636–637.

48. Rawls, "The Basic Liberties," sec. 8.

49. The word *maximin* is a contraction of *maximum of the minimum*, and a *maximin* principle or procedure is thus one that directs us to *maximize* the *minimum* of something. E.g., if a doctor were to follow a maximin procedure in treating her patients, she would (roughly speaking) devote the most attention to the sickest one—i.e., *maximize* the care given to the person in the *minimum* state of health. To put it more strictly, our doctor would

choose a course of treatment for all her patients that resulted in the healthi-est outcome for whoever turned out to be sickest at the end of the treatment. More generally, a maximin principle or procedure instructs us:

Act so as to maximize the well-being of whoever ends up worst off.

(In its original use, the term *maximin* refers to a procedure to be followed by one person faced with self-regarding choices. This sense of the term can be explained in terms of the apocryphal Murphy's Law: "If anything can go wrong, it will." The maximin procedure can be understood to say, "Behave as if Murphy's Law were true." In other words, the chooser is to pick an alternative on the basis of how much she likes the worst-case scenario that can be projected for each alternative. It is a principle suited for someone who cares to avoid risk at all cost. I am using *maximin* in an extended sense that considers the effects of a choice on a number of people.)

The meaning of *maximinimize* is derived in the obvious way from that of *maximin*.

50. Joel Feinberg, "The Expressive Function of Punishment," *The Monist* 49 (1965): secs. 3–4; reprinted in Joel Feinberg, *Doing and Deserving* (Prince-ton, N.J.: Princeton University Press, 1970), pp. 105–113.

51. Rawls, *A Theory of Justice*, p. 454.

52. As always, I am assuming that the repentant can be separated from the stiff-necked. In reality, of course, this is not so.

Chapter 8. Punishment, Contract, and Fraternity

1. On this term see note 49 to Chapter 7.

2. John Rawls, *A Theory of Justice* (Cambridge, Mass.: Harvard Univer-sity Press, 1971), p. 62.

3. John Stuart Mill, *Considerations on Representative Government* (South Bend, Ind.: Gateway, 1962), ch. 8, pp. 178–187.

4. Rawls, *A Theory of Justice*, pp. 232ff.

5. Ibid., pp. 544–545.

6. Of course, there are marriages of convenience, in which the spouses keep each other at arm's length. And there are, too, business partnerships that do not involve any real working relationship among the partners; an example can be found in the realm of real estate, where partners often join in buying a building for the sole purpose of enjoying tax write-offs. The exis-tence of these arm's-length relationships does not exclude the possibility of creating more intimate relationships by means of contract. Indeed, in the case of marriage especially, we can assume that the relationship is to be an intimate one, unless the opposite is made explicit beforehand.

7. Edmund Burke, *Reflections on the Revolution in France*, excerpted in *The Philosophy of Edmund Burke*, ed. Louis I. Bredvold and Ralph G. Ross (Ann Arbor: University of Michigan Press, 1960), pp. 43–44.

8. Ian Macneil, *The New Social Contract* (New Haven, Conn.: Yale University Press, 1980), passim. My account in this chapter draws heavily on Macneil's account. For a discussion of similar issues, see I. A. Melden, *Rights and Persons* (Berkeley and Los Angeles: University of California Press, 1980). Melden speaks of promises, not contracts, but his remarks apply to the latter if we consider a contract to be an exchange of promises.

9. Macneil, *New Social Contract*, p. 13.

10. Ibid.

11. Ibid., p. 20.

12. Ibid., p. 11; cf. Melden, *Rights and Persons*, p. 43.

13. Ayn Rand and Nathaniel Branden, *The Virtue of Selfishness* (New York: New American Library, 1965).

14. One thinks of a rhetorical question once posed by Ronald Reagan's budget director, David Stockman: "Why should a farmer in North Dakota pay for a subway in New York?" Well, there's one good reason: New Yorkers really need a subway. This reason may not be sufficient to justify diverting the Dakota farmer's resources, but surely it is not a nothing. (The quote from Stockman was heard on the radio; the wording is, if not exact, a very close approximation. The thought, in any case, is classic Stockman: He acknowledges that federal funding of mass transit was something of a bête noire with him. See David Stockman, *The Triumph of Politics* [New York: Avon, 1987], pp. 149–151.)

15. I have in mind as a model the old Newport (R.I.) Jazz and Folk Festivals.

16. Quoted in E. F. Schumacher, *Good Work* (New York: Harper & Row, 1979), p. 72.

17. This example is in essence an actual case, to which I am no longer able to provide a reference.

18. Rawls, *A Theory of Justice*, p. 106.

INDEX